Thera and the Exodus

The Exodus explained in terms
of natural phenomena and
the human response to it

Thera and the Exodus

The Exodus explained in terms
of natural phenomena and
the human response to it

Riaan Booysen

BOOKS

Winchester, UK
Washington, USA

First published by O-Books, 2013
O-Books is an imprint of John Hunt Publishing Ltd., Laurel House, Station Approach,
Alresford, Hants, SO24 9JH, UK
office1@jhpbooks.net
www.johnhuntpublishing.com

For distributor details and how to order please visit the 'Ordering' section on our website.

Text copyright: Riaan Booysen 2012

ISBN: 978 1 78099 449 9

A CIP catalogue record for this book is available from the British Library.

Design: Stuart Davies

Printed and bound by CPI Group (UK) Ltd, Croydon, CR0 4YY

We operate a distinctive and ethical publishing philosophy in all
areas of our business, from our global network of authors to
production and worldwide distribution.

CONTENTS

List of Appendices

List of Tables

List of Figures

Introduction

One of the greatest enigmas of ancient times is the biblical Exodus of the Israelites from Egypt[1]. Not only is the event itself of importance, of even greater significance is the formation and identity of the Israeli nation, a people later also referred to as Jews or Hebrews, from the Hebrew language[2]. It was during the Exodus that God designated the Israelites as his Chosen People, an appellation that has arguably caused them more persecution than anything else. This belief in a single, personal God is widely recognised as in all probability the first truly monotheistic religion, and from Judaism would spring the two most dominant religions of the world, Christianity and Islam. If, as proclaimed by many academics, the Exodus had not occurred, then all three religions and the very existence of the God worshipped by these religions can be brought into question.

To date no academic consensus has been reached on when, if ever, this event took place, and therefore who the role players were. The narrative of the book of *Exodus* in the Bible (henceforth simply referred to as *Exodus* and likewise for other books of the Bible) is suspiciously vague about the identity of, for instance, the king of Egypt at that time and refers to him and his successor only as Pharaoh. The lack of corroborating evidence in ancient Egyptian records that can be dated to a specific ruler further raises suspicion about the likelihood of the Exodus ever having taken place. Despite these doubts, numerous independent accounts written by later historians suggest that the Exodus story must be based on historical events that took place in Egypt. Though there can be little doubt that the biblical and other legends would have become distorted through centuries of oral tradition and copying of manuscripts, something must have given rise to these legends.

The general approach adopted in my research and consequently in this treatise is therefore to assume that every legend is based on an element of truth, unless it can otherwise be shown to have been falsely introduced for political or other purposes. Another basic assumption is that no divine intervention of any kind actually occurred during the Exodus event, specifically ruling out the miracles associated with the Exodus. In other words, every aspect of the Exodus must have had a natural and logical cause or explanation. The purpose of this treatise is to link together the numerous legends about the Exodus in an attempt to reconstruct the actual events of the Exodus, whatever they may be.

The first phase of my research into the Exodus was to collect as many of the early accounts of the Exodus as possible, and to interpret these as nations other than the Egyptians and Israelites could have seen them. The reconstructed Exodus events were then linked to specific historical accounts, occurrences and persons. The next step was to analyse the effects that an eruption of the volcano on the island of Santorini, which was known as Thera in ancient times, may have had on Egypt, specifically in the context of the biblical plagues of Egypt. Since the eruption of the volcano on Thera can potentially be dated through archaeology, it should be possible to pinpoint the time frame of the Exodus. In this treatise I will endeavour to prove that the fate of the Israeli nation was determined by not one but possibly up to three eruptions of Thera. The final eruption and the subsequent sequence of events occurred at a time when Egypt was the most dominant nation in the Middle East, and the chaos that ensued reverberated throughout the civilized world of that era. Numerous legends survived that will all be shown to be linked to the calamity that befell Egypt and nearly caused its total annihilation.

Several new interpretations of names attributed to Joseph, Moses, the Pharaoh of the Exodus and other individuals are explored and presented in this treatise. A cornerstone of this process is the identification of the most likely origin of the aliases associated with these individuals. As the Exodus story revolves around the Israelites in

2

Egypt, it is to be expected that many of the names will be of either Hebrew or Egyptian origin. Since the majority of ancient historians wrote either in Greek or in Latin, one can also expect some of the names to be of either Greek or Latin origin. This could mean that certain names may not be mere *transliterations* of the original Hebrew or Egyptian names of the characters in question, but rather *translations* into Greek or Latin of the actual meaning of the name. For instance, if a pharaoh was known as 'The Fat One' in Egypt and the Near East, the Greeks may have recorded that nickname in Greek words meaning precisely that, the Israelites in Hebrew and the Latin writers in Latin. It is also possible that Egypt's neighbours may have invented other names for a particular pharaoh, based on how they perceived either him or Egypt under his rule. For example, it will be shown that the name of the legendary King Sesostris is a concatenation of the Greek words *Se, sos* and *tris*, meaning 'You and what's Yours the Third'. Sesostris is identified as Tuthmosis the Third, so nicknamed because of the manner in which Tuthmosis I, II and III enslaved and moved entire nations to work in Egypt. To my knowledge the name Sesostris is consistently interpreted in academic circles as a transliteration of Egyptian kings with phonetically similar names, like Seti and Senusret.

Some topics used in constructing a new version of the Exodus events are based on crucial work performed by other researchers, work which by itself may not necessarily be accepted among mainstream Egyptologists. This for instance includes Ahmed Osman's theory that the biblical Joseph was the same person as the Egyptian official Yuya[3], Graham Phillips' argument that the biblical Moses was Crown Prince Tuthmosis, the son of Amenhotep III and grandson of Yuya[4,5], and David Rohl's hypothesis that the biblical kings Saul, David and Solomon were contemporaries of Amenhotep III and his son Akhenaten[6]. The theory presented in this treatise shows these hypotheses are correct and can all be interlinked.

Before proceeding with the theory in detail, the following list gives a brief summary of the key arguments of the treatise:

- As claimed by the ancient historian Manetho[7], the people known as the Hyksos were indeed the ancestors of the Israelites. The Hyksos were a group of foreigners who invaded Egypt from the north and controlled Lower Egypt for nearly 100 years during the so-called Second Intermediate Period[8]. They were eventually expelled by Ahmose, the ruler of Upper Egypt[9].

- Two Exodus events took place; the first when Ahmose overpowered the Hyksos throughout Egypt except in Avaris, the Hyksos capital, from where the inhabitants of the city managed to escape to Canaan. The second Exodus occurred roughly 200 years later when the Hyksos originally taken captive by Ahmose in the other parts of Egypt and possibly later by Tuthmosis III in Canaan, left Egypt under the leadership of Moses.

- The biblical plagues of Egypt can be linked to the after-effects of the eruption of Thera. The most devastating of these was the plague of boils and blisters which decimated the Egyptian population, as well as the enslaved portion of the Hyksos nation.

- The Pharaoh of the Oppression was Amenhotep III, while his son Akhenaten was the Pharaoh of the Exodus whom Moses confronted.

- By interpretation of Manetho's account of the Exodus and an Egyptian hieroglyphic record known as the *El Arish Shrine Text*, the biblical Moses is confirmed to be Crown Prince Tuthmosis, the firstborn son of Amenhotep III.

- In a desperate attempt to bring an end to the plague, Amenhotep III, on the advice of his oracle also called Amenhotep, issued a decree that all firstborn offspring in Egypt should be sacrificed in the fire. Prince Tuthmosis (Moses) was the first in line to be sacrificed, but was saved from the fire in the nick of time. This event was recorded in *Exodus* as the 'burning bush' in which Jehovah, the God of the Israelites, is claimed to have revealed himself to Moses[10].

- The *El Arish Shrine Text* and other ancient historical records confirm that Moses led a violent and successful rebellion against his father. His army consisted of the enslaved Hyksos captives and those Egyptians affected by the plague. Moses was assisted by an army of the Hyksos nation that had escaped Ahmose 200 years earlier to settle in Jerusalem.

- Faced with such strong opposition, Amenhotep III and those Egyptians unaffected by the plague retreated into Ethiopia for between 10 and 13 years. Moses, the slave rebels, the plague-infected Egyptians and the army from Jerusalem ravaged and plundered Egypt during that period.

- When the Egyptian army eventually returned to Egypt, the Hyksos army from Jerusalem retreated to Canaan, while Moses and his mixed nation of Egyptians and Hyksos slaves moved into the Sinai desert. From there they would later invade Canaan under the leadership of Joshua.

- As argued by Rohl, the biblical Saul and David were the Labayu and Dadua of the Amarna period, the period of sun worship in Egypt inaugurated by Akhenaten[11]. This makes Nefertiti, his wife, and Solomon's Queen of Sheba, called the Queen of Egypt and Ethiopia by Josephus, not only contemporaries, but in fact one and the same person. Unlike Rohl, who used the Labayu-Amarna link to move the reign of Amenhotep III later in time to the conventional period of the reigns of Saul, David and Solomon, *ca.* 1000 BCE[12], it is shown that the Amarna period must remain in place while the date of the United Monarchy under David and Solomon should be moved back in time to the Amarna period of *ca.* 1353 BCE.

- Although not directly related to the events of the Exodus, Herodotus' account in which Helen of Troy remained in Egypt for 10 years during the Trojan War, and the association of Agamemnon with Amenhotep III through the latter's famous statues, suggest that Helen of Troy was in fact Nefertiti, who must have been the inspiration for the fable of the Trojan War[13].

For the sake of the reader who may not be familiar with the geographical and political settings of the time frame during which the Exodus will be argued to have occurred, the dominant nations and their territories are shown in Figure 1.1. The border between Egypt and Canaan is not defined as Egypt was in control of Canaan at *ca.* 1350 BCE. The island of Thera is shown encircled north of Crete.

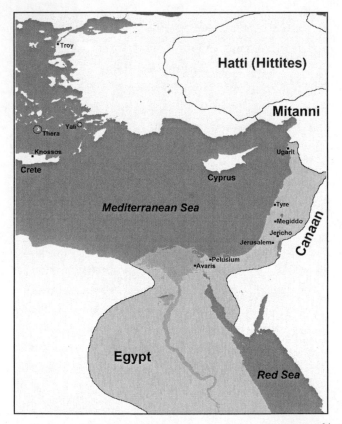

Figure 1.1 Map of the ancient Near East *ca.* 1350 BCE[14]

The Egyptians divided their country into two parts, Lower and Upper Egypt, as shown in Figure 1.2. The land of Nubia, usually translated as Ethiopia in the Works of Josephus[15], was increasingly referred to as Kush by the Egyptians from 1550 BCE onwards, and later became the common name for the region in Egyptian, Assyrian, Persian and Hebrew[16]. The New Kingdom era of Egypt began with the expulsion of the Hyksos from Egypt by Ahmose, the first king of the Eighteenth Dynasty, and lasted until the end of the Twentieth Dynasty[17].

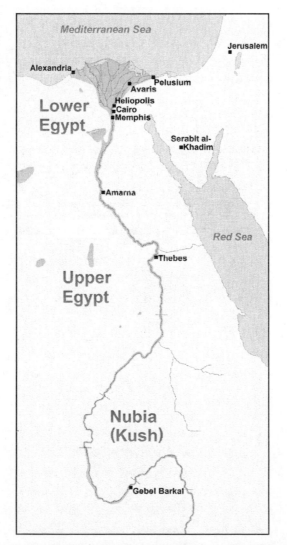

Figure 1.2 The Land of Egypt during the New Kingdom era[18]

The circular archipelago formed by the islands Santorini, Therasia and Aspronisi (see Figure 1.3) is the remnant of a volcanic caldera and is collectively also referred to by the name Santorini. The ancient settlement at Akrotiri was buried during the eruption of the volcano and excavation of the site has revealed remarkably well-preserved artefacts from that era. The modern capital of the island is called Phira, which is a different pronunciation of Thira (Thera), the ancient name of the island.

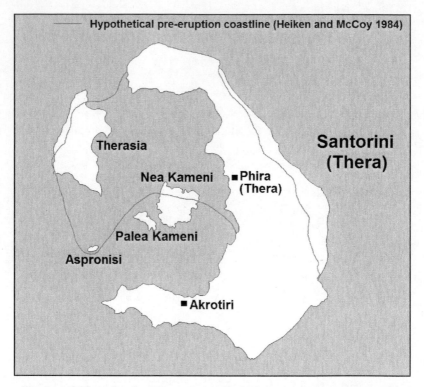

Figure 1.3 The island of Santorini, called Thera in ancient times, with hypothetical pre-eruption coastline[19]

Figure 1.4 shows the pre-eruption coastlines of Thera as proposed in 2007 by McCoy[20] and Friedrich and Sigalas[21], respectively. Their pre-eruption coastlines differ somewhat from the coastline suggested by Heiken and McCoy (see Figure 1.3). The proposed coastlines are based on the assumption that only one major eruption had occurred. As will be shown in this treatise, two such eruptions occurred approximately 200 years apart. The coastline before the first eruption may therefore have enclosed the entire caldera of Santorini.

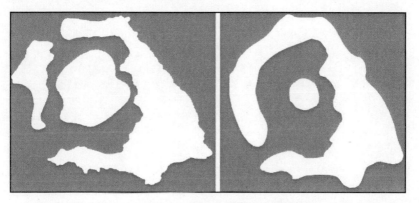

Figure 1.4. Pre-eruption coastlines following McCoy (left) and Friedrich and Sigalas (right)

2

The Exodus as described in religious sources

The Israeli nation traces its origins back to the times of its patriarchs, Abraham, Isaac and Jacob[1]. The latter was given the name Israel after he had wrestled with an angel of God. Jacob, who resided in Canaan, had 12 sons, one of whom was sold by his brothers into slavery in Egypt. This son, Joseph, rose to fame in Egypt and was appointed as the chief administrator of Egypt by the Pharaoh. During a severe famine in Canaan several of his brothers came to Egypt and, following Joseph's death, their descendants began to grow in number in Egypt. Eventually a new king who did not remember Joseph came to power in Egypt. This Pharaoh enslaved the Israelites[2], a state in which they remained until the time of Moses, who would lead them out of Egypt.

Exodus is the best known source of the Exodus story. A closely related account was given by the first century Jewish historian Josephus who wrote an extensive history of the Israelites in his *Antiquities of the Jews*[3]. He also defended the Jewish history against attacks by other historians in his treatise today known as *Against Apion*. For the reader not familiar with the biblical or Josephus' narratives, the key aspects of these accounts are summarised below. These will also serve as background to the arguments presented later in this treatise.

2.1 The biblical narrative

In the well-known account of the Exodus, the Pharaoh instructed his people that all newborn Israeli boys should be cast into the Nile because of his fear of the growing numbers of Israelites in his country. Moses was born to Hebrew parents, Amram and Jochebed[4], and his mother hid him from the Egyptians for three months after his birth. When this was no longer possible, she placed him in a basket made of papyrus, sealed with pitch, and hid the basket in the reeds of the Nile. The Pharaoh's daughter happened to be bathing at that same spot, noticed and retrieved the basket and eventually adopted the Israeli child as her own. The grown Moses one day saw an Egyptian beating an Israeli slave and in a fit of rage killed the Egyptian. When the Pharaoh was informed of this, he sought to kill Moses, who subsequently fled to the land of Midian. Moses remained there until this Pharaoh and those who sought to kill him had died.

The pleas of the enslaved Israelites were heard by God, who appeared to Moses in a burning bush and instructed him to return to Egypt and lead the Israelites to freedom. He was to confront the new Pharaoh and convey God's message that he should release the Israeli slaves, but God warned Moses that the Pharaoh would initially not comply. Moses protested that he was not eloquent and had a speech impediment, and the Lord reluctantly assigned Aaron the Levite to speak on behalf of Moses. God gave Moses a magical staff and the ability to perform miracles with it. Through Moses God inflicted a series of plagues upon the Egyptians. At the time of each plague the Pharaoh initially agreed to let the Israelites go, but 'the Lord hardened Pharaoh's heart' so that he refused to do so when the plague had passed. This continued up to the tenth plague, when God through Moses brought death to all the firstborn males in Egypt, from the firstborn son of the Pharaoh to the firstborn of the animals. There was 'a wailing in Egypt as had never before been heard, for there was not a house in Egypt without someone dead'.

The Pharaoh then instructed the Israelites to take their flocks and herds and depart from Egypt. They left Egypt with silver and gold they 'asked' from the Egyptians, 'thus having spoiled (plundered) Egypt'. God warned the Israelites that the Pharaoh would change his mind once again and instructed them to march toward the Red Sea. The Pharaoh did change his mind and pursued the Israelites with the entire army of Egypt, trapping them at the Red Sea. Moses instructed the sea to part, upon which a strong wind drove the sea back, forming a path of dry land with a wall of water on the left and on the right. The Israelites escaped through the Red Sea along this path, but when the Egyptian army followed, Moses instructed the sea to collapse onto them, leaving no survivors. From there the Israelites wandered through the desert for 40 years, until Joshua led them to conquer Canaan.

In the biblical narrative the following points are of particular interest (specific references are given to facilitate finding the relevant text):

- The Pharaoh warned his people that the Israelites might rise against Egypt, join forces with its enemies and overcome Egypt[5].
- Every newborn male should be killed to prevent the number of Israelites in Egypt from increasing[6].
- The baby Moses, born of Hebrew parents, was placed in a watertight basket and concealed among reeds, where he was found by the Pharaoh's daughter. She could not breastfeed the baby and instructed a slave woman to be brought to her to suckle the child, that woman being Moses' Hebrew mother. Moses was eventually adopted as a son into the royal family[7].
- Moses had to flee Egypt because he killed an Egyptian who had assaulted an Israeli slave[8].
- Moses had a rod or staff with which he performed the miracles which are known as the 'Ten Plagues of Egypt'[9].
- The king's firstborn was killed in the tenth plague[10].
- A 'mixed multitude of no number' (exceedingly many) joined the Israelites on their Exodus from Egypt, the Israeli men alone numbering 600,000[11].
- Having plundered Egypt, the Israelites were armed[12] and laden with treasure[13] when they left the country.
- The entire Egyptian army, including horsemen, chariots and infantry, gathered in Pihahiroth, which was located between

Magdal and the sea near Baal Zephon[14].

- Egypt's entire army vanished (in the sea) when the walls of water collapsed onto it[15].
- The Israelites had been in Egypt for 430 years[16].

2.2 Josephus' account

Josephus recorded a more detailed account of Moses' upbringing in the Egyptian court in his *Antiquities of the Jews*[17]. According to him the Egyptians had grown envious of the prosperity of the Israelites in Egypt, and planned to altogether exterminate the Israelites in their country through hard labour. One of the sacred scribes of the ruling Pharaoh warned him that a child would be born to the Israelites, who would lead them in an uprising against the Egyptians. The king then ordered that all newborn Israeli boys be thrown into the Nile and that those parents who attempted to save their sons be killed. When Moses was born, his mother placed him in a cradle and set the basket afloat in the Nile (not among the reeds as described in *Exodus*), trusting his fate to God. Thermuthis, the Pharaoh's daughter, noticed the cradle floating down the river and sent swimmers to retrieve it. Moses was such a beautiful baby that she fell in love with him and arranged for an Israeli woman (Moses' own mother) to breastfeed him. Thermuthis named him Mouses (Moses) and because of his remarkable beauty she eventually adopted him as her own son. She presented him to her father as the future heir of the Pharaoh's kingdom, to which the Pharaoh apparently did not object. When the sacred scribe learned of this, he attempted to have Moses killed, warning the king that this was the child who would 'trample on your government and tread on your diadem'. Thermusis, however, intervened and Moses was saved.

Moses grew up in the royal court and eventually became the commander of the Egyptian army, which he led on a victorious campaign against Ethiopia. The victory was sealed by Moses taking a daughter of the Ethiopian king as his wife. The Egyptians, however, had developed a hatred for Moses and planned to have him killed. The king also intended to have him killed, not only because of the prediction of his sacred scribe, but also because of his envy of Moses' success in Ethiopia. Moses was alerted and fled to Midian.

Josephus' account of the God's revelation in the burning bush, the plagues of Egypt and the release of the Hebrews more or less matches the biblical account.

Key points from Josephus' account are:

- The name of the Pharaoh's daughter was Thermuthis and she adopted Moses because of his physical beauty[18].
- As an infant Moses was given the Pharaoh's crown, but he trampled on it[19].
- The sacred scribe saw this, 'made a violent attempt to kill him (Moses)' and warned the king that Moses would one day trample on his government[20].
- Apart from Moses there was no other royal heir to the throne[21].
- Moses led a successful military campaign into Ethiopia (Nubia) and was seen by the Israelites as their future general[22].
- Moses had to flee Egypt because the Egyptians suspected him of seditious activity and advised the king that he should be slain. In addition, the king was envious of his success and feared that Moses would rise against him. At the instigation of the sacred scribes he prepared to have Moses killed[23].
- Moses learned of the plans to kill him and fled from Egypt to Midian[24].
- Following the series of plagues brought upon them, culminating in the death of the firstborn, the Egyptians 'honoured the Hebrews with gifts' before their departure[25].
- The Israelites encamped at Baal Zephon on the Red Sea[26].
- The multitude that departed could not be numbered, but those fit for war (the men) totalled 600,000[27].

- The Egyptian army entrapped the Israelites, upon which Moses parted the sea so that the Israelites could pass through it on dry ground[28].
- The entire Egyptian army was drowned when they attempted to follow the Israelites through the sea. The drowning of the army was accompanied by storms of wind, showers of rain, dreadful thunder and lightning, flashes of fire and darkness[29].
- The weapons of the drowned Egyptian army were washed up to the camp of the Israelites by the sea current, with which the Israelites then armed themselves[30].

One would expect that such a significant event in Egyptian history would have been recorded by the Egyptians themselves as well as by historians from other nations. For reasons to be discussed there are practically no extant Egyptian records to confirm the Exodus story. What we have comes largely from Josephus, who repeated accounts by other historians verbatim for the purpose of refuting their 'false' interpretations. Scraps of information also survive in the records of various other ancient historians including Diodorus, Artapanus and Africanus. Key points from these records are listed below.

2.3 Rabbinic accounts outside the Torah

Despite the huge loss of Jewish documents during centuries of persecution[31], numerous traditions about the Exodus survived. The most well-known of these are the five books of the Torah, which also form the first five books of the Old Testament in the Bible. Some rabbinic traditions recorded outside the Bible are summarised in *The Jewish Encyclopedia*[32], from which the following key points are listed:

- The name of the daughter of the Pharaoh who adopted Moses was Bithia. She was afflicted by leprosy, which the baby Moses cured.
- When Moses was three years old, he took the king's crown and placed it on his head, upon which a soothsayer predicted that

Moses would destroy the kingdom of the Pharaoh and liberate the Israelites. One of the king's counsellors advised him to kill Moses.

- Moses' tongue was burned, causing him to stutter.
- Moses did not 'murder' an Egyptian, as he deserved death for forcing an Israelite woman to commit adultery with him.
- Moses was between 18 and 40 years of age when he fled from Egypt to Ethiopia.
- In Ethiopia Moses joined the Ethiopian army, was made its general and was later crowned as King of Ethiopia. He ruled Ethiopia for 40 years.
- From Ethiopia Moses, laden with treasure, went to Midian.
- Other versions say that Moses fled Egypt at the age of 20 and stayed in Midian for 60 years, or that Moses was in the house of Pharaoh for 40 years, fled to Midian and stayed there for another 40 years.
- Moses was initially taken prisoner upon his arrival in Midian by Jethro, the priest of Midian. Jethro's daughter Zipporah kept Moses alive during his imprisonment of 10 years.
- Moses' marvellous rod had been in Pharaoh's possession. Moses was the only one of Zipporah's suitors who was able to pull this rod from the ground, in which it had been planted by Jethro, and she became his wife.
- Moses was nearly killed on the way to Egypt, but was saved by the intervention of Zipporah.
- God caused a flaming bush to appear and spoke to Moses through the voice of his father.
- In the night of the final plague, all firstborn, male and female, were killed. According to the *Legends of the Jews* the Egyptians were forewarned about the impending death of their firstborn and tried to hide their children, to no avail.
- During the Exodus the Israelites thought only of taking the gold and silver of the Egyptians.
- Joseph's coffin was among the royal tombs of the Egyptians.

- When the Israelites saw the Egyptian army vanquished, they wanted to return to Egypt to set up their own kingdom in that country.
- The Israelites made a golden calf to worship, initially with the blessing of Moses:

> For love of the Israelites he [Moses] went so far as to count himself among the sinners, saying to God: 'This calf might be an assistant [to] God and help in ruling the world.'

- Moses officiated as high priest and king of the Israelites.
- Moses was very wealthy, having obtained his riches from the Ethiopians and the booty taken from the Egyptians.
- Moses repeatedly but in vain begged for his life to be spared, then begged the Israelites for forgiveness for injuries he might have done them, and died shortly afterwards.
- Joshua, who addressed the Israelites in a language Moses could not understand, became Moses' successor.

2.4 Accounts in the Koran

The Koranic version of the Exodus more or less follows that of *Exodus*, with a few crucial additions[33-35]. The most significant points are:

- Joseph was given power over the land of Egypt[36].
- The 'chiefs of Pharaoh's people' warned him that Moses would cause disruption in the land and abandon him and the gods of Egypt[37].
- The first plague sent to Egypt was a flood[38].
- The plagues included a violent tornado with showers of stones, a mighty blast, earthquakes and the flood[39].
- During the plagues the great works and buildings of the Egyptians were levelled to the ground[40].
- Moses saw a fire and went to it for guidance[41] (the burning

bush in the Bible).

- The main opponents of Moses were the Pharaoh and Haman, as well as a particularly wealthy individual known as Qarun (Korah), who was 'of the people of Moses' [42].
- The wife of the Pharaoh was called Asiyah (or Asia) and she feared her husband. He had her tortured and killed her because 'she believed in Moses'[43].

The Exodus in the words of the historians

Josephus in particular attempted to refute the historical accounts of Manetho, Cheremon, Lysimachus and Apion in his text popularly known as *Against Apion*[1]. Key points from their accounts follow.

3.1 Manetho

Manetho was an Egyptian historian and priest who lived *ca.* third century BCE[2]. His *Aegyptiaca* (History of Egypt) has been preserved mainly in excerpts and quotations from it by later historians, in this case Josephus. Specific references to the writings of Manetho are given in the following list:

- Men from the east invaded Egypt encountering little resistance and subsequently plundered and ravaged Egypt. They founded and settled in a city called Avaris[3].
- The invading nation was known as the Hyksos or alternatively the shepherd kings or captive shepherds. They 'kept possession of Egypt for 511 years' and they were, as acknowledged by Josephus, the ancestors of the Israelites[4].
- An Egyptian king called Alisphragmuthosis drove the shepherds from all parts of Egypt except their city Avaris. His son Thummosis (Tethmosis, Tefilmosis) attempted to force them from Avaris, but eventually had to allow its 240,000 inhabitants to retreat from Egypt to Syria[5].
- The shepherds went out of Egypt to Judea, where they founded Jerusalem[6].
- The Israelites were affected by the plagues of Egypt as much as the Egyptians[7].
- A king called Amenophis (Amenhotep) was advised by his oracle also named Amenophis, who was the son of Papis, that

he would 'see the gods' if he were to clear the country of the lepers and other impure people. He drove 80,000 of them into the quarries, which resulted in a revolt[8].

- Moses, called Osarsiph by Manetho, was a priest born in Heliopolis. He became leader of a rebellion against king Amenophis and later sent ambassadors to the shepherds in Jerusalem, explaining the situation in Egypt and asking for their assistance in his war against Egypt. He also promised that he would first of all bring them back to their ancient city and country Avaris[9]. Moses had already engaged Amenophis in battle when he sent the invitation to the shepherds in Jerusalem[10].

- The shepherds were delighted at this news and 200,000 men from Jerusalem came to Avaris, already fortified by Osarsiph. Amenophis gathered his army but 'did not join them in battle' and instead fled with his army and a multitude of Egyptians into Ethiopia. There they remained for a 'fatally determined 13 years'[11].

- Under the leadership of Moses, the people of Jerusalem who had invaded Egypt, along with the 'polluted' Egyptians, set cities and villages on fire, destroyed the images of the gods, abused the priests of Egypt and 'got possession of all of Egypt'[12]. Manetho, however, accuses the Egyptians themselves, under guidance of their own priests, of being guiltiest of these atrocities[13].

- Thirteen years later Amenophis returned from Ethiopia with a great army and along with his son Rhampses, who had his own army totalling 300,000 men, engaged in battle with the shepherds and polluted people, beat them, killed a great many of them and pursued them to the bounds of Syria[14].

- Amenophis ruled for 19 years. He was succeeded by Sethosis (also called Sethos and Aegyptus) and his brother Ramesses. Sethosis, who ruled for 59 years, left his brother Armais (also called Hermeus, Danaus, and by inference from the previous statement Ramesses) in charge of Egypt during his absence. Rhampses, the son of Sethos, ruled for 66 years[15] (a detailed discussion of Manetho's king list is presented in Chapter 11).

- Sethosis killed Ramesses and appointed his brother Armais to be his deputy over Egypt, with instructions not to wear the crown and not to use violence against the queen. While on campaign outside Egypt, Armais did all of that, upon which priests informed Sethosis. He returned and recovered his kingdom[16]. Sethosis cast Hermeus (Armais) out of Egypt, and his son Rhampses reigned for 66 years after him[17].
- Amenophis' son was called both Sethos and Ramesses[18], who as a young man had assisted his father in war and fled with him into Ethiopia[19].

3.2 Cheremon

Cheremon (also spelled Chaeremon) of Alexandria (first century CE)[20] wrote a *History of Egypt*, which has been lost but fragments of which were preserved by historians including Josephus. Josephus records the following regarding Cheremon's account:

- Like Manetho, Cheremon named the king in question as Amenophis, and his son Ramesses[21].
- A sacred scribe called Phritiphantes advised Amenophis to 'purge Egypt of the men that had pollutions upon them'. Amenophis then expelled 250,000 men who had pollutions upon them from Egypt[22].
- Moses and Joseph were scribes who made a league of friendship with 380,000 men left by Amenophis at Pelusium, and instigated a revolt against Amenophis[23].
- The polluted people had initially left Egypt but later returned, joining up with the 380,000 men to face Amenophis' army. Amenophis fled to Ethiopia[24].
- Amenophis could not sustain their attack and fled to Ethiopia, leaving his pregnant wife behind. She gave birth in

a cave to a second son called Messene, who when grown up pursued the Jews into Syria with 200,000 men. He then welcomed his father Amenophis out of Ethiopia[25].

- Moses and Joseph were driven away at the same time[26].
- A total of 430,000 men either perished or joined Ramesses[27].

3.3 Lysimachus

Lysimachus was a first century BCE anti-Jewish writer (see Hata[28] for an extensive list of ancient historians who alluded to the Jews in their writings). From his version as recorded by Josephus:

- The people of the Jews were leprous and scabby in the days of Bocchoris, king of Egypt[29].
- Bocchoris was advised by an oracle named Hammon to purge his temples of impure and impious men by expelling them into the desert, but to drown the scabby and leprous people by wrapping them in sheets of lead and casting them into the sea[30].
- The leprous people who survived came together and were addressed by Moses, upon whose advice they plundered and burned the temples of other men (the Egyptians). They reached Judea, where they built a city called Hierosyla, meaning '"Robbers of temples'[31].

3.4 Apion

Apion was a Greco-Egyptian writer who flourished in the first half of the first century CE (died *ca.* 48 CE)[32], but few of his works survived. From Josephus' quotations we learn that:

- Moses was of Heliopolis. He used to 'follow the customs of his forefathers' and he 'offered his prayers in the open air, towards the city walls', but he 'reduced them all to be directed towards sun-rising'[33].
- Moses brought the leprous people, the blind and the lame out

of Egypt[34].

Josephus' counterparts were not the only historians to tell more or less the same story.

3.5 Africanus

Sextus Julius Africanus was a Christian historian who lived round about 170 to 240 CE[35]. His works were written in Greek, but he knew Hebrew and it is possible that this was his first language[36]. The following key points are quoted verbatim from extant fragments of his *Chronographiae*[37] (the translator's remark in brackets):

- Polemon, for example, states ... At the time of Apis, the son of Phoroneus, king of Argos, a portion of the Egyptian army was expelled from Egypt; they settled the part of Syria called Canaan, not far from Arabia (these clearly went with Moses).
- And Apion ... states in his book *Adversus Judaheos* ... when Amosis was king of the Egyptians, the Jews revolted, under leadership of Moses.
- Herodotus has also made mention both of this revolt and of Amosis in his second book and in a certain way of the Jews themselves, numbering them among those who practice circumcision and calling them Assyrians in Canaan.
- Ptolemy of Mendes, who recorded the history of the Egyptians from the beginning, agrees with them all [the historians listed above].

3.6 Artapanus

Artapanus of Alexandria was a historian of Jewish-Egyptian origin who lived sometime between 250 and 100 BCE[38]. Although his *Concerning the Jews* has been lost, excerpts have been preserved in quotations from, among others, Eusebius in his *Praeparatio Evangelica* (Preparation for the Gospel)[39]. Some key points follow:

- The Jews were called Ermiuth, meaning Judeans in the Greek language.
- Abraham came to Egypt under a pharaoh called Pharethothes, but returned to Syria after 20 years. Many of those who came with him remained in Egypt because of the prosperity of the country.
- Joseph, the administrator and master of the whole country of Egypt, married Asenath, a daughter of the priest of Heliopolis.
- The pharaoh who mistreated the Jews was called Palmanothes.
- His daughter Merris was betrothed to a pharaoh called Chenephres. The barren Merris adopted Moses as her own son.
- Chenephres made Moses commander of an Egyptian force which was to invade Ethiopia.
- Moses sent generals to occupy Ethiopia. The battle lasted 10 years, during which the Ethiopians became enamoured with Moses.
- Moses proposed the use of oxen for ploughing in Egypt, upon which Chenephres gave the name Apis to the bull and commanded a temple to be erected in honour of the bull, and where those bulls consecrated by Moses could be buried.
- Chenephres instructed a person by the name of Chanethothes to kill Moses, but Moses killed Chanethothes and managed to escape to Arabia.
- Moses married the daughter of Raguel, the ruler of Arabia, who wanted to restore Moses to the Egyptian throne. Raguel ordered Moses to plunder Egypt.
- Chenephres died and a divine voice instructed Moses 'to march against Egypt, rescue the Jews and lead them into their old country'. Moses 'took courage and determined to lead a hostile force against the Egyptians'.
- When Moses confronted the king, he was arrested and locked away in prison. A divine power opened the doors of the prison

at night, allowing Moses to escape.

- Moses performed miraculous signs for the king (the biblical plagues), including causing the Nile to flood and 'deluge' the whole of Egypt. A reluctant king eventually agreed to let them go. The Jews took with them many drinking vessels, clothing and much other treasure.
- The Egyptian army was destroyed by fire and walls of water collapsing onto them.

3.7 Herodotus

Herodotus was an ancient Greek historian who lived *ca.* 484 to 425 BCE and was the first author to produce a narrative history of the ancient world[40]. He made no direct reference to the Exodus, only to King Sesostris, some of whose exploits will be shown to match the circumstances of the Exodus[41] as listed below.

- Sesostris, the legendary Egyptian conqueror, had left his brother in charge of Egypt during one of his campaigns. Upon his return his brother 'invited him and his sons to a banquet and then piled wood around the house and set it on fire'. Following consultation with his wife, Sesostris laid down two of his six sons to make a bridge over which all the others could escape.
- Sesostris was the only Egyptian king to rule Ethiopia.
- In commemoration of his name, Sesostris erected in front of the temple of Hephaestus two 50 feet high stone statues of himself and his wife, as well as statues of his four sons.
- Sesostris was succeeded by his son Pheros, a king who waged no wars.
- Pheros became blind when a flood of the Nile, 27 feet (or 18 cubits, just over 8 m) high, occurred and he hurled his spear into the onrushing river. An oracle from Buto advised him that he would be healed by washing his eyes with the urine of a woman who had never been unfaithful to her husband. He

eventually found that woman and had all the others burnt in a town called Red Clay.

- Pheros was succeeded by a man whose name in Greek was Proteus, who had a 'well-appointed temple precinct at Memphis, south of the temple of Hephaestus'.
- Alexandrus carried off Helen of Troy from Sparta and was forced to Egypt by a violent storm.
- Proteus took Helen from Alexandrus and spared his life only because he had taken an oath not to kill strangers driven to his coast.
- After the rape of Helen, a Greek army descended upon Troy and was informed that Helen and the wealth stolen by Alexandrus were not there, but in Egypt with Proteus.
- Menelaus went to Egypt, got Helen back and sacrificed two Egyptian children because of adverse weather that prevented him from leaving.
- Menelaus fled with his ships to Libya, a hated and hunted man. From there he departed to an unknown destination.

3.8 Diodorus

Diodorus Siculus was a Greek historian who lived in the first century BCE[42]. From his universal history *Bibliotheca Historica* in 40 books only Books 1 to 5 and 11 to 20 survive. He also recorded a slave revolt matching the one described by Manetho, but placed it in the time of Sesoösis[43], an alternative spelling of Sesostris. From Diodorus we learn the following:

- Sesoösis brought labourers from Babylonia, who under his severe rule revolted against the king.
- These slaves 'seized a strong position on the banks of the river', made war against Egypt and ravaged the neighbouring territory.
- On being granted an amnesty, they established a colony on the spot, which they also named Babylon after their native land.

- A city called Troy once existed on the banks of the Nile.
- Sesoösis' son conducted no major military campaigns.
- This son lost his sight reportedly because he had hurled his spear into the rushing current of the river.
- Having attempted to propitiate a deity for 10 years with no success, an oracle predicted that he would regain his eyesight if he could bathe his face in the urine of a woman who had never been unfaithful to her husband. He burned to death all those women who failed to restore his eyesight in this manner.
- Once he had been healed, he erected two monolithic obelisks, 8 cubits wide and 100 cubits high.

3.9 Justin

Justin (Marcus Junianus Justinus) was a Latin historian who is believed to have lived in the third century CE[44]. In his *Epitoma Historiarum Philippcarum*[45] he states (my note in brackets):

- The Jews originated from Syria.
- Moses was the son of Joseph.
- 'The Egyptians, being troubled with scabies and leprosy and moved by some oracular prediction, expelled him [Moses], with those who had the disease, out of Egypt.'
- Moses became the leader of those affected by the disease and 'carried off by stealth the sacred utensils of the Egyptians, who, endeavouring to recover them by force of arms, were obliged by tempests to return home.'

3.10 Tacitus

Publius Cornelius Tacitus, born *ca.* 56 CE, was a senator and historian of the Roman Empire who concentrated on Roman affairs in his *Histories* and his *Annals*[46], but made a brief reference to the Jewish people and their origins[47,48]:

- The Jews were refugees from the island of Crete who settled in the remotest parts of Libya.
- There was an ancient belief that the Jews had flourished under Isis in Egypt, but that the Egyptians eventually managed to drive them into adjacent countries (Maier's version of Tacitus' account). The standard translation reads 'that in the reign of Isis the surplus population of Egypt was evacuated to neighbouring lands under the leadership of Hierosolymus and Juda'.
- Some reported the Jews to have been of Ethiopian origin, while others considered them to be Assyrians refugees who, lacking their own land, settled in Egypt.
- Many authors known to Tacitus agreed that under King Bocchoris an infectious disease had broken out in Egypt and, to rid him of this evil, he was advised by the oracle of Hammon (Jupiter) to purge Egypt of the infected people.
- The Jews were banished to a desert, where one of the exiles, Moses, advised them not to look for any assistance from either mankind or gods, and so became their 'celestial leader'.

3.11 Strabo

Strabo, a Greek historian (63 BCE to 23 CE)[49], records the following information about Sesostris[50]:

- Sesostris advanced as far as Europe.
- He crossed into Arabia, from where he invaded the whole of Asia.
- Sesostris invaded ('traversed') the whole of Ethiopia.
- He began the construction of a canal that flowed through the Bitter Lakes and ended in the Red Sea and Gulf of Arabia. This canal was constructed before the Trojan War.
- Babylon was a place near Memphis.

3.12 Other writers

Several ancient historians made reference to an Egyptian king Busiris, who sacrificed strangers who entered his country. Key points from some of these accounts are:

- Apollodorus wrote that Busiris was a brother of Proteus and one of the 50 sons of Egyptus (Aegyptus), son of Belus. When Egypt experienced a drought (scarcity) lasting for nine years, Phrasius, a seer from Cyprus, advised Busiris that it would come to an end if he should sacrifice a stranger every year. Busiris obliged, beginning with the sacrifice of Phrasius himself. Hercules was about to be sacrificed in this manner, but broke his bonds and killed Busiris and his son Amphidamas[51].
- Isocrates in his *Busiris* castigates Polycrates for his *Defence of Busiris,* in which Polycrates asserts that Busiris forced the Nile to 'break into branches and surround the land' and sacrificed and ate strangers who visited his country[52].
- St Augustine specifically places Busiris in the period from Israel's Exodus from Egypt to the death of Joshua the son of Nun[53].

4

Interpretation of various accounts of the Exodus

Combining the accounts of the Exodus presented in Chapter 3, the following version of the Exodus can be derived.

4.1 Reading between the lines

The Hebrews or Israelites who had settled in Egypt were known to the Egyptians as the Hyksos and had been present in Egypt for hundreds of years. The Hyksos were Asiatic foreigners who invaded Lower Egypt *ca.* 1700 BCE. The Hyksos eventually ruled Lower as well as Middle Egypt, but in a series of battles they were driven from all parts of Egypt except the city of Avaris. After a long and protracted battle Avaris finally fell. Whether the entrapped Hyksos were allowed to leave Egypt without harassment by the Egyptian army as claimed by Manetho, or whether they simply managed to escape cannot be known for sure. There can be little doubt, however, that a huge portion of the Hyksos population would have been captured in other parts of Egypt and would have remained there as slaves.

When a natural disaster caused the outbreak of a deadly plague in Egypt during the reign of a pharaoh called Amenhotep, the king was advised by his sacred scribe to purge the country of all infected slaves and Egyptians. This led to a revolt instigated by a priest from Heliopolis, who would become known as Moses among the Israelites. Moses, supposedly born from Hebrew parents, was in fact the heir to Amenhotep's throne and had earlier accompanied his father on a military campaign into Ethiopia. He was informed of a plot instigated by Amenhotep's sacred scribe to have him killed, and fled to Midian. He later returned to Egypt to incite a rebellion against Amenhotep. Moses commanded his own army of infected slaves and Egyptians and ordered them to fortify Avaris in preparation for war with

Amenhotep. He also sent a request for assistance to the Hyksos who managed to escape from Avaris to Jerusalem 200 years earlier. He promised to lead them to victory against Amenhotep and his army, and return them to their ancient city Avaris.

Those in Jerusalem reacted swiftly and joined Moses' army of slaves and Egyptians. Faced by these foreigners and an army of slaves and Egyptians led by his son, Amenhotep retreated into Nubia with his entire army and the majority of Egyptians who had not yet been affected by the plague. The foreigners together with Moses' army plundered and wreaked havoc in Egypt for nearly 13 years, after which Amenhotep and his army returned to Egypt. The Hyksos of Jerusalem returned to Canaan and those under the leadership of Moses also left Egypt, initially for Sinai. Although most of the ancient historians interpreted the latter action as Moses (the king's son) having joined Amenhotep's army to pursue the Hyksos to the borders of Syria, this was not the case. Moses and his army merely left Egypt at the same time as or soon after the Hyksos of Jerusalem returned to Canaan.

In this brief summary of the Exodus events one must also consider the most controversial aspect of the Exodus, the miracles performed by Moses. The biblical account of the plagues unleashed upon the Egyptians by Moses and the hardening of the heart of the Pharaoh must be understood to be legend most likely based on actual events. Against this backdrop, a natural explanation must be found for the plagues supposedly brought upon the Egyptians by Moses. It will be argued in Chapter 15 that the biblical plagues of Egypt, excluding the tenth, can be directly linked to an eruption of the Thera volcano.

Of the 10 plagues, the most significant was the death of the firstborn of Egypt. Despite conflicting reports, it is clear that the firstborn males, females and animals were killed. In biblical history, the defining moment in Moses' life was when he supposedly came face to face with the Hebrew God, who appeared to him in the fire of a burning bush. This burning bush will be shown to represent the fires lit to burn the firstborn of Egypt, the ultimate sacrifice any nation could make to appease the gods. As the firstborn of Amenhotep, Moses would have been the first to be sacrificed by burning. He was, however, almost literally snatched from the fire and it was this near-death experience that forever changed his concept of God and his relationship with the Israelites.

Herodotus' narrative about the Egyptian King Sesostris and his brother who ruled Egypt in his absence (Section 3.7), repeated in part by Diodorus (Section 3.8), cannot be linked directly to the Exodus. Manetho, however, makes this Sesostris a Nineteenth Dynasty king of Egypt, which will be shown to be an error (Chapter 6). Diodorus mentions a slave revolt against Sesostris (here called Sesoösis), which resulted in a war with the Egyptians and the ravaging of the neighbouring territories. This slave revolt links Sesostris to Manetho's slave revolt against Amenhotep. The brother in question could only have been Ay, argued by some scholars to have been a brother-in-law of Amenhotep III[1].

Sesostris was also known as Aegyptus (Section 3.1), to whom Busiris (Section 3.12), the legendary tyrant of Egypt, can be linked. Busiris was infamous for having sacrificed all strangers who visited Egypt as will be discussed. Busiris can be linked to the Exodus and therefore to Amenhotep.

It is important to note that Manetho recorded two exoduses of the Hebrews from Egypt[2], the first when Avaris was besieged and its inhabitants managed to escape to Canaan, where they founded Jerusalem, and the second when Moses and his nation of Hebrews and Egyptians left Egypt for the Sinai desert. It will be shown that various elements of these two distinct events were combined into the single biblical Exodus of the Israelites from Egypt.

4.2 What evidence to seek

Given the various accounts of the Exodus as recorded by ancient historians, one now has to look for evidence that might support their claims. There are a number of very specific aspects of the Exodus narratives that have to be investigated in search of corroborating evidence. These are listed below, with no particular reference to relative importance or timeline.

Can a foreign people living in Egypt for hundreds of years be identified?
A key aspect of the Jewish accounts of the Exodus is their claim that the Hebrews had been present in Egypt for hundreds of years. If a corresponding period in Egyptian history can be identified, the Hebrews as a nation may thereby be identified as well. Manetho unequivocally identifies the Hebrews as the Hyksos who occupied Egypt for an extended period of time. Can these claims be supported?

In Egyptian history, was there ever an equivalent of the biblical Joseph?
Joseph is closely associated with the time frame of the Exodus. If a matching official of the Egyptian royal court can be identified, the time frame of the Exodus can be determined, not to mention the accuracy of the Hebrew accounts of their early history.

Can the name of the pharaoh and his sacred scribe be identified?
Only one source, Manetho, gives the name of the Pharaoh of the Exodus in a form we can recognise. That name is Amenophis (Amenhotep), and although there were a number of Amenhoteps who ruled Egypt, this particular Amenhotep had a sacred scribe by the same name. The only Egyptian king who matches this description is Amenhotep III, who had a famous scribe called Amenhotep, the son of Hapu. Several other names of both the king and his scribe are listed by other historians. Can these be linked to Amenhotep III?

Was there ever an heir to the Egyptian throne who mysteriously disappeared?
From sources outside the Torah it is clear that Moses was far more than simply the adopted son of the Pharaoh. He was, in fact, the heir

to the Egyptian throne. If there is any truth in this aspect of the Exodus story, it should be possible to identify a specific individual at a time of great upheaval in Egypt. Can such an individual be identified?

Is there a pharaoh who twice invaded Ethiopia?
According to Josephus and rabbinic records, Moses was the commanding officer of an Egyptian force that invaded Ethiopia. It was only after this invasion that Moses had to flee Egypt. Manetho records that Amenhotep was confronted by Moses, his army and a foreign army from Jerusalem, and subsequently retreated into Ethiopia with his entire army. Can evidence of such a retreat into Ethiopia be found?

Was there ever such a period of extreme chaos and upheaval in Egypt?
The biblical plagues of Egypt describe a period of extreme chaos and upheaval in Egypt. Whoever may be identified as the biblical Moses and Pharaoh of the Exodus must have lived in a period charac-terised by chaos. Can such a period be identified?

Do any Egyptian records of the Exodus or aspects of it exist?
Apart from the annals of later historians like Manetho, one would expect there to be ample Egyptian records of the Exodus dating to that specific period, or shortly afterwards, in the form of hiero-glyphic inscriptions on either papyrus or stone. If these are not to be found, there should at the very least be an acceptable explanation as to why such records may have been destroyed.

Are there any foreign records of the Exodus or aspects of it to be found?
Egypt was a major power, if not the main power, in the ancient Near East for hundreds of years. It is almost inconceivable that other nations would not have recorded the catastrophic events that befell the leading nation of that era. Can any such references be found?

Did Egypt ever suffer a plague that may be linked to the biblical plague of boils and blisters?

From Manetho's records it is evident that the problem Amenhotep faced was that of the so-called 'polluted' people, matching the biblical description of the Egyptians who had been struck with boils and blisters on their skin. It was in order to rid Egypt of this disease that Amenhotep attempted to expel the infected slaves and Egyptians from his country. Can such period in Egyptian history be identified?

Is there any archaeological evidence to be found supporting any aspect of the Exodus?

Archaeological evidence in support of the Exodus would mainly be focused on natural disasters that may have struck Egypt. In particular, this treatise argues along with others (see Chapter 15) that the plagues of Egypt had been caused by an eruption of Thera's volcano. The archaeological evidence of the Thera eruption would at least have to match the time frame of the Exodus. Ideally, one would hope to find archaeological evidence in Egypt of the after-effects of this volcanic eruption.

Is there any evidence to be found of a mass influx of people into Canaan?

If the Exodus ever occurred, there should not only be evidence of Joshua's conquests, but also of a mass settlement of people in Canaan.

In the chapters that follow an attempt will be made to answer the above questions and present sufficient circumstantial and other evidence to confirm that the Exodus of the Israelites from Egypt was a historical event that can be linked to recorded Egyptian history. Chapters 5 to 15 deal with evidence from the narratives of the Exodus, while Chapters 16 to 19 focus on the eruption of Thera, the plagues of Egypt and archaeological evidence pertaining to various eruptions of Thera.

5

From the arrival of the Israelites in Egypt to Joseph

Of all the historical accounts of the Exodus, Manetho's is probably the most trustworthy. He was a third century BCE Egyptian priest who, without a doubt, had access to records not available to all and sundry. This would have included the texts in the library of Alexandria, probably the greatest library of the ancient world. This library flourished from the third century BCE to its successive destruction first by the Romans during their conquest of Egypt in 47 BCE, then during the sacking of the city by Caracalla in the third century, followed by mobs incited by Theodosius in 391 CE and finally during the Arab conquest of 641 CE[1].The historical accounts which survived in Hebrew tradition would have been slanted to favour the Hebrews, as suggested by the introduction of the miracles of Moses. Other accounts may be regarded as second-hand and therefore potentially as less accurate.

5.1 The Hyksos and the Hebrew sojourn in Egypt

According to Hebrew tradition, their nation originated from the patriarchs Abraham, Isaac and Jacob. Abraham came from the city of Ur in Chaldea, located in ancient Sumer[2]. Jacob was renamed Israel by God and had 12 sons who became the heads of the 12 tribes of Israel. One of these sons was Joseph, to whom he had given a coat of many colours[3]. Joseph was the envy of his brothers and they conspired to sell him as a slave to the Egyptians. There Joseph ultimately rose to such prominence that he became the adminis-trator of Egypt. Joseph brought his entire family to Egypt during a drought and there they grew in number until they became a concern to the Pharaoh, who subjected them into slavery. Jewish tradition holds that the Israelites had spent altogether between 400[4] and 430[5] years in Egypt before the Exodus occurred. Manetho claims that the Hyksos (the Hebrews) had held possession of Egypt for 511 years[6]. According to various rabbinic sources either the total duration of the Hebrew sojourn in Egypt, or only their period of bondage, was 210 years[7-10]. Two specific references read:

> From the day when our forefathers came down to Egypt until the day when Moses was born, a period of a hundred and thirty years elapsed, Israel having spent in Egypt two hundred and ten years.[11],

> Why was our Father Abraham punished and his children doomed to Egyptian servitude for two hundred and ten years?[12]

However, most of the rabbinic sources seem to imply that it was the period of bondage that was 210 years. Therefore the 430 years of *Exodus* implies that the Israelites had been present in Egypt more than 200 years before the beginning of the period of bondage.

Although it is possible that the Hebrews had been present in Egypt for that long merely as a minority group of traders, this is unlikely as Manetho makes it clear that they had in fact dominated Egypt for at least a couple of centuries. Josephus also claims that the Hebrews 'had had dominion over Egypt' before they departed from that country[13]. There are only two periods in early Egyptian history during which foreigners dominated Egypt, the periods appropriately having being named the First and Second Intermediate Periods. The First Intermediate Period spanned about 125 years, generally assumed to be *ca.* 2181-2055 BCE, while the Second Intermediate Period lasted roughly 100 years, from 1650-1550 BCE, the period of the Hyksos domination of Egypt[14]. Later periods of foreign occupation in Egypt are too late in history for any of these periods to be associated with the Israelite Exodus.

Both the First and Second Intermediate Periods are too short to match the Hebrew duration of 430 years, not to mention Manetho's 511 years of rule. However, following Manetho's claim that the

Hebrews and the Hyksos invaders were one and the same people (strictly speaking it was Josephus who associated the Hyksos with the Hebrews, perhaps assuming that was what Manetho had implied), there is ample evidence to be found suggesting that the Hyksos had been present in Egypt long before they managed to overpower and take possession of Lower Egypt. In other words, the Hyksos had systematically been expanding their influence in Egypt long before they initiated the Second Intermediate Period by formally taking control of Lower Egypt.

Some scholars date the beginning of the Second Intermediate Period back in time to about 1720 BCE[15] or even further. A text dating to Sobekhotep III (around 1745 BCE) contains a list of Hyksos servants in the king's household, indicating their presence in Egypt[16]. There is in fact evidence of Canaanite settlements at Avaris from as early as 1800 BCE[17]. It is possible that the entry of Hyksos into Egypt was at first slow and limited to workers seeking employment there or traders selling goods. A wall painting found in the tomb of the vizier Khnumhotep under Senusret II (ca. 1880-1874 BCE) in Beni Hasan shows Semitic traders entering Egypt to sell eye paint[18] (see Figure 5.1). The most striking aspect of this wall painting is the multi-coloured robes worn by the traders, matching

Figure 5.1 Wall painting in the tomb of Khnumhotep in Beni Hasan, showing a group of Semitic traders entering Egypt wearing multi-coloured robes *ca.* 1880-1874 BCE[19]

the description of Joseph's multi-coloured coat. The biblical story about Joseph's coat is therefore more than likely based on a vague memory that Joseph came from the people who wore such coats.

Assuming them to be the Semitic traders depicted in the Ben Hasan wall painting, the first influx of Hyksos traders into Egypt seems to have occurred around 1880 BCE, if not earlier. In this treatise I postulate that Ahmose not only expelled the Hyksos from Egypt, but also enslaved of a large part of their population during his initial advance to their capital. This would have occurred sometime during his reign (1550-1525 BCE[20]), and the year 1540 BCE will be assumed for argument's sake. If the mass settling of the Hyksos traders began around 1750 BCE, their time in Egypt as free men becomes 210 years. Following Manetho, their exodus from Egypt took place possibly within the reign of Amenhotep III (1390-1352 BCE), but more likely during the reign of his successor, his son Akhenaten (1352-1336 BCE). Assuming that they left Egypt *ca.* 1340 BCE, the duration of their enslavement would then be 200 years (closely matching the 210 years of the rabbinic sources) and the total length of their sojourn in Egypt becomes 410 years. This duration is close to the biblical duration of 430 years.

The exact duration of the Hebrew sojourn in Egypt depends very much on the date that the ancient historians assigned to the arrival of the Hyksos in Egypt. If this was assumed to be around 1880 BCE, and with the Exodus dated to 1340 BCE, the Hyksos would have been in Egypt for 540 years, matching Manetho's 511 years. He seems to have confused the duration of the *rule* of the Hyksos with their accumulated presence in Egypt, first as rulers and then as slaves.

Whichever duration is accepted, it is clear the Hebrews did not originate from the biblical patriarchs Abraham, Isaac and Jacob, and the question of the origin of the Hyksos must be answered instead. The antiquity of the Jewish people is discussed in Chapter 20.

Following the biblical narratives, the first Hebrew of note to appear in Egypt is Joseph, the son of Jacob[21]. Is it possible to identify an Egyptian official that would match the biblical Joseph?

5.2 Joseph, son of Jacob

Joseph was sold into slavery by his brothers. He was eventually bought by Potiphar, a eunuch (modern translations seem to prefer 'officer') of the Pharaoh and captain of his soldiers. Joseph was an attractive young man and was soon noticed by the mistress of his house. She attempted to seduce him, but when he would not comply, she accused him of attempted rape. Having been thrown into prison, Joseph interpreted a dream of the Pharaoh that none of the Egyptian interpreters could. In this dream the Pharaoh was warned that seven years of abundance lay ahead, but that this would be followed by seven years of famine. The Pharaoh was so impressed with Joseph's ability that he promoted Joseph to the highest civilian office in his empire. In *Genesis* we read (my comment in brackets):

> So Pharaoh said to Joseph, 'I hereby put you in charge of the whole of the land of Egypt.' The Pharaoh took his signet ring from his finger and put it on Joseph's finger. He dressed him in robes of fine linen and put a gold chain around his neck. He had him ride in a chariot as his second-in-command, and men shouted before him, 'Make way!' Thus he put him in charge of the whole land of Egypt. Then Pharaoh said to Joseph, 'I am Pharaoh, but without your word no one will lift hand or foot in all Egypt.'[22]

Joseph told his brothers:

> He [God] made me father to the Pharaoh, lord of his entire household, and ruler of all Egypt.[23]

Genesis also tells us that Pharaoh gave Asenath, the daughter of Potiphar, to Joseph as his wife, and renamed Joseph Zaph(e)nath-Paaneah[24]. Under Joseph's supervision Egypt began stowing provisions for the famine that was to come. By the time the seven years of scarcity arose and 'famine prevailed in the whole world', an abundance of grain had been stored in every city in Egypt. The famine eventually drove Jacob's sons to Egypt, where they were welcomed by Joseph and the Pharaoh, who confirmed to Joseph's brothers that 'the best of the land of Egypt'[25] (also translated 'all the riches of Egypt'[26]) would be theirs. Joseph sent his father 10 donkeys loaded with the best things of Egypt[27], and requested his brothers to bring his father to him. Jacob and his entire family, who were all shepherds by occupation, then entered Egypt. Joseph instructed them to tell the Pharaoh their occupation as this would allow them to settle in a specific part of Egypt as 'all shepherds are detestable to the Egyptians'[28]. Joseph 'bought all the land in Egypt for Pharaoh. The Egyptians, one and all, sold their fields, because the famine was too severe for them.'[29] The land he bought, however, excluded the land belonging to the priests because they received support from the Pharaoh. When Joseph died at the age of 110 years, his body was embalmed and laid in a coffin in Egypt[30]. After Joseph's death a pharaoh arose who did not know about Joseph, and began oppressing the Hebrews as they had grown too numerous[31].

From the discussion above and the biblical texts regarding Joseph, the following points are important:

- Potiphar was a eunuch in service of the king of Egypt.
- Joseph had in one way or another become involved with the mistress of his house.
- This event caused great upset in the royal house, but Joseph was excused and later appointed as the administrator of Egypt.
- A severe famine and a time of scarcity lasting seven years had struck Egypt and its neighbouring countries, forcing his brothers to come to Egypt to buy food.
- Joseph, made an extremely wealthy man by the Pharaoh, sent messengers (his brothers) to his father in Canaan, inviting him to come to Egypt, with a promise that all the great riches of Egypt would be theirs.

- Joseph's family members, who numbered 70 when they came to Egypt, were the progenitors of the Hebrew nation and were known as shepherds. They moved with all their possessions from Canaan to Egypt and settled in an area of Egypt called Gessen (Goshen), east of the Nile Delta[32], that is, in Lower Egypt. They had to settle there because the Egyptians loathed all shepherds.
- On his death Joseph's body was embalmed and buried in a coffin in Egypt.

5.3 Yuya, the biblical Joseph

From the preceding description of Joseph, the Egyptologist Ahmed Osman concluded that there was indeed an Egyptian official of note that matched the biblical Joseph[33]. His name was Yuya, a powerful courtier who may have served under Tuthmosis IV, the father of Amenhotep III, and became the key adviser of Amehotep III. Yuya was married to a woman called Tuyu and their daughter Tiye became the Great Royal Wife of Amenhotep III. Osman bases his conclusion on the following similarities between Yuya and Joseph:

- Yuya was an official who was put in charge of all of Egypt, as was Joseph.
- Judging from his mummy (see Figure 5.2), Yuya appears to be of Semitic descent, and his name, of which many variants exist, likewise appears to be of foreign origin.
- Yuya was mummified and buried in the Valley of Kings even though he was not of royal descent. Osman points out that although Moses supposedly took the 'bones' of Joseph with him and his departing Israelites, the scribe who edited the Exodus narrative had no idea what a mummy looked like. This suggests that the removal of the bones of Joseph was a later insertion by a scribe[34].
- The biblical Joseph is linked to the interpretation of a dream of his pharaoh. Tuthmosis IV is renowned for his *Dream Stele,*

which narrates a dream Tuthmosis had while resting between the paws of the Sphinx. In this dream the Sphinx promised him the Egyptian throne should Tuthmosis clear away the sand from his body. Tuthmosis did so and subsequently became king of Egypt. Tuthmosis' dream is therefore most probably the origin of the legend of Joseph interpreting the dream of a pharaoh, a highly unlikely actual event[35].

- Yuya was the only high ranking Egyptian official who was demonstrably honoured by the title 'Father to the Pharaoh'[36,37], a title also held by Joseph.

- One of Yuya's numerous titles was Bearer of the Ring of the King of Lower Egypt. Joseph received the ring of the Pharaoh.

- Yuya had a gold necklace that had fallen inside his coffin and came to rest under his head when the thread was cut by robbers. Joseph received a chain of gold from his king.

- Yuya also bore the titles Master of the Horse and Deputy Charioteer of His Majesty, while Joseph drove the second chariot of the Pharaoh. Incidentally, the Hyksos brought the horse and chariot to Egypt for use in war[38], implying that Joseph lived sometime after the arrival of the Hyksos in Egypt.

- Two other titles of Yuya, Overseer of the Cattle of Amun, and Overseer of the Cattle of Min, match the instruction given by Joseph's Pharaoh that he should find able men to look after his cattle[39].

- Yuya most likely served two pharaohs, Tuthmosis IV and his son Amenhotep III. In the Talmud it is recorded that before that Pharaoh, who was the friend of Joseph, died, he commanded his son, who was to succeed him, to obey Joseph in all things and left instructions to that effect in writing[40]. Yuya is known to have been alive at least until the eleventh year of Amenhotep's reign[41].

- Yuya is described as the person 'whom the king has made his double'[42], echoing the words of the king to Joseph, 'only in the throne will I be greater than thou.'[43]

- Yuya's beard is similar to those of ancient Hebrews, while according to Herodotus, the Egyptians shaved off their beards and were only allowed to let it grow during times of mourning[44]. That Yuya's beard does resemble the beards of the captive Hyksos is suggested by the so-called Megiddo Ivory (see Section 13.2).

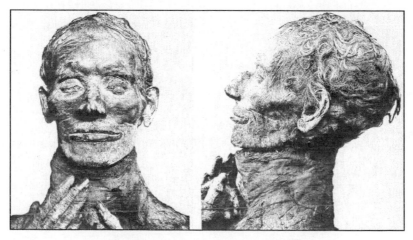

Figure 5.2 The mummy of Yuya[45]

5.4 Criticism of Osman's Hypothesis

It is necessary to mention some points of criticism of Osman's theory as summarised above. One formal refutation of his hypothesis was presented by Sweeney[46]. Included in the principal objections are the following:

- Joseph's title 'Father to Pharaoh' does not necessarily identify him with Yuya, who bore the title 'God's Father', since other high officials of the Eighteenth Dynasty also held that title.
- If Yuya and Joseph were indeed one and the same person, Hebrew scribes must surely have recorded that Joseph's daughter became queen of Egypt. Tiye, Yuya's daughter, married Amenhotep III and became queen of Egypt.

Although Hebrew sources name Joseph's sons, no reference is made to a daughter.

- Hebrew sources record that the remains (bones) of Joseph were moved to Canaan. Yuya's remains (mummy) were found in the Valley of the Kings.
- Joseph came into Egypt as a slave, while Yuya appears to have originated from a place in Egypt called Akhim.
- According to Egyptian foreign policy for that period it was not appropriate for a foreigner to be appointed to such a high ranking office.
- Joseph served the God of Israel, while Yuya was devoted to the gods of Egypt.

Although these objections are valid, they do not necessarily disqualify Osman's hypothesis, for the following reasons:

- Whereas it is true that other officials may also have borne the title Father of the God, Yuya was the only person who actually was a father of a pharaoh, albeit the father-in-law. The title may therefore very well identify Yuya with Joseph – it most certainly does not disqualify this possibility.
- Osman is fully aware that Hebrew sources make no mention of a daughter of Joseph, let alone one who became a queen of Egypt. His explanation for this omission is rather unsatisfactory, asserting that female descendants were only mentioned if they were relevant to the story[47]. This may be true in the sense that Yuya's daughter, Tiye, only rose to prominence after her father had already done so. Yuya certainly never became monarch of Egypt and neither did his wife, but upon her marriage Tiye did. One certainly would have expected Hebrew sources to mention such a glorious achievement. That she may actually have been mentioned in early Hebrew sources is suggested by the claim in the apocryphal *Joseph and Asenath*[48], that Joseph and Asenath

became king and queen of Egypt and ruled for 48 years. Whoever wrote *Joseph and Asenath* must therefore have come across records indicating that a female in the immediate family of Joseph had risen to the level of queen of Egypt, and adapted his version of events accordingly.

Amenhotep III is generally accepted to have ruled for about 38 years, but as postulated in this treatise, he continued his rule for some years after that during his retreat into Ethiopia. He would therefore have co-reigned with Akhenaten for a couple of years, so an effective reign of 48 years cannot be ruled out altogether. Tiye was Amenhotep's wife for almost that entire period, which must be the origin of the legend that Joseph's queen ruled for 48 years.

There is a high likelihood that early Hebrew scribes had deliberately removed many details of the events of the Exodus they found to be too controversial or contradictory to the legend. The biblical narratives about exactly which pharaoh was involved in the Exodus are suspiciously vague, probably deliberately so. It is possible that the scribes omitted any mention of Joseph's daughter as queen of Egypt for a particular reason, which may be as simple as that they would then have been required to list her offspring as well. A royal ancestral line of mixed blood (Hebrew and Egyptian) originating from Joseph's daughter may have been seen as an embarrassment or perhaps even a disgrace. Such difficulties could be bypassed altogether by simply omitting any reference to a daughter of Joseph.

- As argued by Osman[49], the departing Hebrews must have encountered difficulty in locating the grave of Yuya, which the Egyptians had taken great care to conceal. According to Osman 'later editors did not like the idea that the Patriarch was still buried in the land of the oppressors when the Exodus had become the cornerstone in the new religion of the Jews.' By contrast, as pointed out by Osman, the remains of the greatest ever leader of Israel, Moses himself, were buried in an unknown grave[50].

- If the Israelites were indeed the captured Hyksos rulers of Egypt, the idea of the Hebrew nation being fathered by Abraham, Isaac and Jacob becomes untenable (see Chapter 20). It is highly likely that Joseph was born into slavery as a member of the enslaved Hyksos people and originally worked as a slave in a high ranking Egyptian household, possibly from Akhim. The story of Joseph being sold off into slavery by his brothers and their eventual entry into Egypt in search of food can be explained simply by recognising that his 'brothers' would have belonged to the Hyksos who managed to escape from Ahmose about 200 years earlier.

- As the Hyksos were former rulers of Egypt, the Egyptians would no doubt have recognised their value. It is therefore not unlikely that a highly skilled Hyksos slave may have risen to a high ranking position in the Egyptian royal court.

- As far as his religion is concerned, Joseph as Yuya would have been intelligent enough to realise that if he wanted to excel in Egypt, he would have to embrace the religion of the Egyptians. Whether he actually believed in any god no one will ever know.

Not one of the objections raised against Osman's hypothesis can by itself dismiss it and all of them can be addressed. His critics, however, seem to conveniently ignore the crucial points of correlation argued by Osman. Based on Osman's arguments one must therefore conclude that Yuya and Joseph were indeed one and the same person.

5.5 Moses, the grandson of Joseph

There appears to have existed in ancient times a recurring belief that Moses was directly related to Joseph. Justin claims that Moses was the son of Joseph[51], while Cheremon makes both of them scribes who were in fact contemporaries[52]. According to Manetho Moses (Osarsiph) was a priest from Heliopolis[53], which suggests that Cheremon mistakenly recorded both of them as having been scribes instead of priests. Among the many titles of Yuya was 'Prophet (priest) of the God Min [54, 55], confirming Cheremon's statement in this regard. An indignant Josephus claims that at least four generations had passed between Joseph and Moses[56], and this appears to be the modern conviction. Although such a close family relationship between Joseph and Moses may seem unlikely, it is probable that it is based on the truth.

Amenhotep III married Yuya's daughter Tiye and their firstborn son was Crown Prince Tuthmosis. As Yuya became an old man he would have witnessed his grandson growing up. If prince Tuthmosis was the biblical Moses and Yuya was the biblical Joseph, Moses would not have been the son but the grandson of Joseph. Moses and Joseph would have been contemporaries for a number of years, as recorded by Cheremon.

One of the main reasons for such a close link between Moses and Joseph not being accepted by scholars must certainly be the impossibility of Jacob's family of 70 growing to 600,000 men (excluding women and children) within one or two generations. This is, however, easily explained by fact that the Hebrews were indeed the Hyksos invaders of Egypt as claimed by Manetho.

5.6 Names linked to Joseph

If Joseph is to be linked to Yuya, it should also be possible to link names and persons associated with Joseph to those associated with Yuya. The first step will be to compare the names of the two individuals, Yuya and Joseph. Osman lists numerous variants of the name Yuya, these being Yaa, Ya, Yiya, Yayi, Yu, Yuyu, Yaya, Yiay, Yia and Yuy, and concludes that the first syllable of the two names are phonetically similar, and that the variety in the spelling of Yuya's name indicates that it was a foreign name, which scribes found difficult to record in hieroglyphs. It should be noted that the

Hebrew spelling of Joseph is either *Yhowceph*[57] or *Yowceph*[58] (to add or augment), which can be interpreted as '(let him / he will) add'. This name could, however, have originated from the words *'aciyph* [59] (to gather crops) or *'oceph*[60] (a collection of fruit or gathering). Joseph was famous for storing (gathering) corn for the famine.

If Yuya was indeed a foreigner with a foreign name, and he is to be equated with Joseph, then the name Yuya must be of Hebrew origin. The Hebrew word *Yâhh*[61] is a contracted form of the name of God, *Jᵉhôvâh*[62]. When used in conjunction with other words, it is usually expressed as *Yôw* to denote Jehovah, for example *Yôwkebed*[63], which means 'Jehovah gloried'. Other words corresponding to the syllables used to form Yuya's name are *yâ'*[64] (a shovel), *yâ'âh*[65] (to be suitable, appertain) and *yâ'âh*[66] (to brush aside or sweep away). It is unlikely that Yuya's name could be interpreted God-God, so a better combination would be either *Yôw-yâ'* or *Yâhh-yâ'*, both meaning 'God's shovel'. Joseph was renowned for the success of his corn crops, and Artapanus wrote of him:

And whereas the Egyptians previously occupied the land in an irregular way, because the country was not divided, and the weaker were unjustly treated by the stronger, he was the first to divide the land, and mark it out with boundaries, and much that lay waste he rendered fit for tillage, and allotted certain of the arable lands to the priests.[67]

In its crudest interpretation tillage means spadework, and it is therefore very likely that Joseph earned himself the nickname 'God's shovel', the man who organised Egypt's agriculture.

The second step will be to compare the names and background of the wives of Yuya and Joseph. Yuya was married to Tuyu (also spelled Tjuyu, Thuyu), a lady probably of royal descent who was involved in various religious cults and bore the titles Singer of Hathor, Singer of Amun and Chief of the Entertainers of both Amun and Min[68].

The biblical name for the wife of Joseph was Asenath, the daughter of Potiphar, a priest of Heliopolis, while some rabbinic sources record her name as Zelekha[69]. In the story of *Joseph and Asenath*[70] she was the beautiful virgin daughter of a priest of Heliopolis called Pentephres. She rejected all suitors until the arrival of Joseph, who eventually married her. The Pharaoh's own son, who was forbidden by his father to pursue Asenath, planned to kill Joseph but was slain:

> And Pharaoh mourned for his eldest son, and he was worn out with grief. And Pharaoh died at the age of one hundred and nine; and he left his crown to Joseph. And Joseph was king of Egypt for forty-eight years. And after this Joseph gave the crown to Pharaoh's grandson; and Joseph was like a father to him in Egypt.[71]

This is an obvious embellishment of the legend of Joseph, as an Egyptian king would never have left his throne to a stranger and there is no record of a stranger becoming king of Egypt under similar circumstances. Nevertheless, this particular legend repeats some aspects of Manetho's account (quoted by Josephus in *Against Apion*), that the king's son was killed (Sethosis having killed Ramesses[72], Crown Prince Tuthmosis who disappeared, see Chapter 8), and that the crown was handed over to a pharaoh's grandson.

The crown was handed over to Akhenaten, the son of Amenhotep III and Tiye and therefore a grandson of Yuya (Joseph), but also a grandson of Tuthmosis IV. As stated before, it also confirms that a female member of Joseph's family became queen of Egypt.

Returning to the names Asenath and Zelekha, both appear to be of Hebrew origin, and both appear to be associated with Moses and the Hebrews. There are several Hebrew words that can be used to form the name Asenath, for example *'â'* [73] (a tree or wood, timber), *seneh* [74] (a bramble, bush) and either *'êth* [75] (against, among, in) or *'êth* [76] (a hoe, digging implement, plowshare, pronounced *ayth*). Combining the first three words would render 'Among the wood of the bramble bush', which may allude to Moses' burning bush episode. As argued in this treatise, the burning bush Moses observed was in fact a pyre built for the sacrifice of the firstborn of Egypt, and he most likely found himself facing a pyre constructed of the branches of a bramble bush before he was freed. According to Artapanus, Moses was locked away in prison by the Pharaoh he was supposed to confront, but escaped through divine intervention[77].

The word *'êth* meaning 'a hoe', however, suggests that the name Asenath can somehow be related to Yuya meaning 'God's shovel'. This is indeed possible, from the words *'âsâh*[78] (to make) and *nâ'âh*[79] (a home, pasture). The combination *'âsâh-nâ'âh-'êth* renders '(He who) made pastures (with) a hoe'. Asenath would then be directly linked to Joseph as Yuya, the man who prepared grazing for the king's cattle and flocks of sheep. This interpretation is confirmed by the rabbinic name of the wife of Joseph, Zelekha. This name is a straight-forward combination of the words *zeh*[80] (a sheep) and *lêkâh*[81] (to walk, a journey). Freely interpreted, Zelekha would mean 'Where the sheep graze'. It could of course also be interpreted as 'The journey of the shepherds', a reference to the Hebrew (Hyksos, shepherds) sojourn in Egypt, but this is less likely.

Having with reasonable certainty established that the name Yuya is of Hebrew origin, it is possible that the name of his wife, Tjuyu or Thuyu, may also be of Hebrew origin, despite the fact that she appeared to be of Egyptian origin from the appearance of her mummy. In other words, the Egyptians adopted the Hebrew names of this famous couple. If so, of several possibilities the most likely origin of her name would be 'God's Bulls', from *tôw'*[82] (a wild ox, wild bull) and *Yâhh*[83] (God). This curious name may be related to Yuya being the overseer of the cattle of the king, but more likely it may have been a nickname that she later earned when her son-in-law Amenhotep III embarked on his fabled wild bull hunt (see Section 7.3).

5.7 Other nicknames of Joseph

In *Genesis* we read that the Pharaoh bestowed upon Joseph the names Zaphnath Paaneah, which are claimed to be Egyptian words[84]. If so, the names may be transliterations of equivalent Egyptian names, or they may be Hebrew translations of the Egyptian names. Yet another possibility could be that the Hebrew scribes deliberately attempted to obscure the Hebrew meaning of the names by insisting that they were of Egyptian origin. Whatever be the case, the names have a Hebrew sound to them and can indeed be translated from Hebrew. The words *zâ'aph*[85](anger, indignation, wrath) and *nâtha'* [86] (to tear out, break), *pâ'âh*[87] (to blow away, scatter into corners) and *nâ'âh*[88] (to be at home, to be beautiful) or *nâ'âh*[89] (a home, a pasture, pleasant place) can be combined to yield either 'The wrath of a broken and shattered beauty', or 'The wrath of a broken and scattered home'. Both interpretations are reminiscent of a curious episode in the life of Joseph, his encounter with the wife of Potiphar, his master[90].

Joseph, a man of extraordinary beauty, was coveted by Potiphar's wife, who attempted to seduce him. Joseph refused her advances, upon which the scorned woman accused him of attempted rape. He was thrown into prison, interpreted the dream of the Pharaoh, was forgiven and was finally promoted to the position of administrator of Egypt. This curious legend may actually have some elements of truth in it, as suggested by the Hebrew interpretation of the name Potiphar.

Although the office of Potiphar is usually translated as 'officer', the original text of *Genesis* and several rabbinic references clearly state that he was a eunuch:

Potiphar is identical with Poti-phera. He was called Potiphar because he fattened bullocks (me-fattem parim) for idolatrous sacrifice; Poti-phera, because he uncovered himself (po'er) in honour of idols. Again, it denotes that when the bullock (par) came there, he was enlightened (potinom). A Eunuch of Pharaoh.

This intimates that he was castrated, thus teaching that he [Potiphar] purchased him for the purpose of sodomy, whereupon the Holy One, blessed be He, emasculated him[91],

And Joseph was brought down to Egypt. R. Eleazar said: Read not 'was brought down' but 'brought down', because he brought Pharaoh's astrologers down from their eminence. And Potiphar, an officer of Pharaoh's bought him, Rab said: He bought him for himself; but Gabriel came and castrated him, and then Gabriel came and mutilated him [pera], for originally his name is written Potiphar but afterwards Potiphera.[92]

The role of a eunuch in service of the royal court would have been that of a slave tending to either the queen or to her princesses. One cannot imagine that the pharaoh would have employed as his senior officers only Egyptians who had been castrated. None would have volunteered for the job! It is furthermore highly unlikely that a eunuch would have been married. From the rabbinic references listed it is clear that the rabbis were also of the opinion that the name was of Hebrew origin. The name Potiphar then appears to be a concatenation of the Hebrew words *pothâh*[93] (from a root meaning to open: a hole, hinge, the female pudenda) or *Pûwthîy*[94] (a named derived from the word for a hinge), and *Par'ôh*[95] (Pharaoh). The name can then be interpreted as 'The Pharaoh's X', where X could represent any crude expression for the female genitalia. In other words, the name Potiphar is not to be associated with a male individual, but either a daughter or even the wife of the Pharaoh. It is extremely improbable that the wife of a king would have dared to look at other men, as she along with her paramour would probably have been executed on the spot if found out. However, fathers have a soft spot for their daughters and it is therefore more likely that it was one of his daughters who had become involved with Joseph. If this daughter of the Pharaoh had indeed been as licentious as portrayed in the biblical narrative, she could very well have earned herself the nickname Potiphar among the commoners, a name meaning something like 'Pharaoh's little whore'.

From the Hebrew interpretation of Zaphnath Paaneah it would seem then that this episode must have caused quite a disturbance in the house of the Pharaoh, who afterwards teasingly gave Joseph the nickname 'Wrath of a woman scorned'. For all we know Joseph may have had a full-blown affair with the lady, but at some point decided to move on or refused to become her permanent lover. It was possibly this very episode that brought Joseph in contact with the Pharaoh, following which a relationship of mutual trust and respect began to develop.

Joseph had also received the nickname Peteseph[96]. Following the same procedure as above, the name could have originated from a combination of the words $pâthâh$[97] (delude, entice, deceive, flatter, allure), $p^ethîy$[98] (silly or seducible, foolish, simple), p^ethay[99] (open, width, breadth), $petha'$[100] (quickly, unexpectedly, suddenly), $sa'aph$[101] (to divide up, disbranch) and $se'êph$[102] (divided in mind, a skeptic, thoughts). One interpretation would be 'Divider of the breadth (of Egypt)', a possible reference to Artapanus' statement that Joseph was the first to divide Egypt into demarcated areas. Egypt had always been divided into the Two Lands, Upper and Lower Egypt, and this particular name may have been used to indicate that Egypt was divided into smaller areas, perhaps areas dedicated to specific crops or cattle. Given Joseph's attempted seduction by a high ranking woman, a better translation may be 'Seducer of the mind' or 'The sceptic seduced'. Whichever interpretation may be preferred, both appear to be of Hebrew origin.

As a matter of interest, from *Joseph and Asenath* we have the name of Joseph's father-in-law as Pentephres. Like Joseph's name Peteseph, this name is most likely also of Hebrew origin, meaning something like 'Unless it is hoof branded', from $pên$[103] (lest), t^ephar[104] (a fingernail, hoof) and $'êsh$[105] (fire). The most likely explanation would be that he granted anyone who found cattle on his property the right to claim it as his own, unless it had been hoof-branded by someone else. To have been known by this decree, he must have been in a position of power, in other words he must have been a public figure.

5.8 The seven years of famine

From the biblical description of the seven years of famine it is clear that this calamity was no normal drought affecting crops, but a natural disaster of major proportions. It is probably more than coincidence that the disaster accords with the biblical plagues of Egypt (Chapter 15), which affected animals and crops. It is recorded that Busiris, the Egyptian tyrant, experienced a drought or period of scarcity for nine years[106]. Immanuel Velikovsky lists several letters of the king of Sumur (Samaria) to either Amenhotep III or Akhenaten, in which he bewails his lack of food, for which his people had to sell their children in exchange for food. This is illustrated by the following extracts from the letters:

#74 Our sons and daughters have come to an end, together with ourselves, because they are given in Iarimuta for the saving of our lives. My field is a wife, who is without a husband, deficient in cultivation.

#75 The sons, the daughters, have come to an end, and the wooden implements of the houses, because they are given in Iarimuta for the saving of our lives.

#79 Give me something to feed them [the archers], I have nothing.

#83 ... Give grain for my provision.

#85 There is no grain for our support. What shall I say to my peasants? Their sons, their daughters have come to an end. ... Send grain in ships and preserve the life of his servant and his city. ... May it seem a good thing to the king, that grain be given, produce of the land of Iarimuta.

#86 There is nothing to give for deliverance. ... And from the land of Iarimuta should grain be given for our nourishment.[107]

Velikovsky concludes that Iarimuta was the biblical Ramoth in Gilead[108, 109], a city possibly located close to the Jordan River in Syria. It is strange, however, that a king of Samaria would write to the king of Egypt for the supply of grain from another country. It is more likely that Iarimuta would refer to a place in Egypt. Phonetically the name appears to be of Hebrew or Aramaic origin, which would make sense if this king was the king of Samaria. The name can then be made up of the words *yârê'* [110] (to fear, revere) and *mûwth*[111] (die, dead, the dead), rendering '(Where they) revere the dead'. In ancient times Egypt was known for its belief in the Land of the Dead (the Underworld)[112] and its reverence of the Dead, but it is possible that this title referred to a specific area of Egypt. The Land of the Dead was situated in the west, which is along the west bank of the Nile where the dying sun disappeared[113]. It is probably for that reason that the west bank was reserved for agriculture, while the east bank (in Akhetaten and probably in all other cities of the Nile) was reserved for the urban core[114]. It is therefore very likely that the agricultural region of Egypt was referred to as the Land of the Dead.

Incidentally, although I am convinced that Joseph's 'brothers' were descendants of the Hyksos who escaped to Canaan during the military campaign conduct against them by Ahmose, the king laments having to sell his children to Egypt as slaves in exchange for food. This must certainly have been the origin of the Joseph narrative in which his brothers sold him into slavery in Egypt. For all we know, he may very well have been the son of a high profile family in Samaria who was sold into the Egyptian royal court, where he excelled.

There can be no doubt that a massive food shortage occurred in the Mediterranean region during the Amarna era, although Egypt appears to have suffered less because of its granaries and, of course, the omnipresent Nile. That era is therefore linked to the time of Joseph's fabled famine. The exact time when these years of scarcity occurred is discussed in Chapter 19. A food shortage of this nature may have been caused by a lack of rainfall, but a more likely reason is the ash cloud of the eruption of Thera, which would have poisoned the soil and prevented crops from growing.

The story of the origins of Joseph appears to have been constructed from events associated with the Hyksos in Jerusalem rather than from events surrounding a specific individual. Of key importance is that a pharaoh sent messengers (in the Joseph story they are identified as his brothers) to invite a group of foreigners to come and settle in Egypt, with a promise that the wealth of the country would be theirs. The most common modern translation of this peculiar text appears to be 'because the best of all Egypt will be yours'[115], suggesting that Joseph's family would be allowed to share in the prosperity of Egypt without restriction. There was, however, one and only one event in the history of ancient Egypt where a pharaoh sent messengers to Canaan, inviting them to settle in Egypt and effectively carry off the wealth of Egypt. That happened when Prince Tuthmosis, having escaped being sacrificed by his father, sent messengers to the Hyksos in Jerusalem, requesting them to join him in his rebellion against his father and the Egyptian army. The Hyksos from Jerusalem (Joseph's 'family'), together with Prince Tuthmosis' rebels, plundered Egypt for 13 years (see Chapter 10). This singular event ties Joseph's 'family' directly to the Amarna era and the circumstances that led to the final exodus of the Israelites from Egypt. Joseph (Yuya) was probably still alive when the rebellion took place.

5.9 Joseph and Yuya – a DNA link?

The most powerful modern tool for tracing the ancestry of a person is DNA analysis[116]. The Egyptian authorities have recently allowed DNA extraction and analysis to be performed on several Eighteenth Dynasty mummies[117]. The genetic link between several of the mummies was confirmed, but for some reason the complete DNA profiles of the mummies have as yet not been made public. Egyptologists must be painfully aware of Osman's claims and DNA analysis of the mummy of Yuya should easily confirm or disprove whether he was of Semitic descent. There can be no doubt that political and religious storms will erupt should DNA analysis confirm a link between Yuya and the Jews. Regardless, we as the general public have the right to know.

6

The identity of King Sesostris

Before proceeding with the identification of the leading characters of the Exodus narratives, it is necessary to identify the legendary King Sesostris of Egypt. The reason for this is that certain events attributed to him by Greek and Latin historians can be shown to pertain to events in Egypt during the Exodus.

Our primary sources about Sesostris are Herodotus[1], Diodorus Siculus[2] and Strabo[3], according to whom Sesostris was an Egyptian king who had conquered lands as far as classical Asia and Europe. The conquered nations included Ethiopia, Canaan, Scythia, Thrace and Colchia (areas in Eurasia surrounding the Black Sea), as well as eastern parts of Greece and even parts of India. Sesostris was called Sesoösis by Diodorus and Sesonchosis by the Greek philosopher Dicaearchus (*ca.* 350-285 BCE) in his *Life of Greece*[4].

According to Diodorus neither the Greeks nor the Egyptians themselves could tell exactly who this king was. From the earliest times historians appear to have searched their archives for names of Egyptian kings phonetically similar to Sesostris, as is evident from Manetho's list of Egyptian kings. He places Sesostris in both the Twelfth and Nineteenth Dynasties, as the kings Senwosret I (Senesret I) and Seti I. As the following extract shows, Eusebius actually records Sesostris and Sesonchosis (Sesonchoris) as two separate individuals in Manetho's Twelfth Dynasty king list:

From the Second Book of Manetho, 12th Dynasty: 7 Kings from Diospolis. Sesonchoris the son of Ammenemes, 46 years. Ammanemes, 38 years. He was killed by his own eunuchs. Sesostris, 48 years. Supposedly he was 4 cubits, 3 palms and 2 digits tall. He conquered all of Asia in nine years, as well as Europe as far as Thrace. Everywhere he erected monuments to show his control over the nations; he depicted men's genitals on the columns for brave nations, and women's genitals for cowardly nations. Therefore the Egyptians evaluated him as coming after Osiris. Lamares, 8 years. He built the maze at Arsinoite for his own tomb. His descendants ruled for 42 years. Altogether (these kings) reigned for 245 years.[5]

Manetho refers to the legendary king of Egypt as Sethosis and even Sethos[6] and places him in the Nineteenth Dynasty. This reference to Sethosis is made in the context of Sethosis having placed his brother in charge of Egypt during his absence, and a clash between the two upon his return. Both Herodotus[7] and Diodorus[8] recorded this incident.

At present the accepted academic view appears to be that Sesostris refers to Senwosret of the Twelfth Dynasty and some scholars have gone to great lengths to prove that the military campaigns of Senwosret can be linked to the legendary accomplishments of Sesostris[9].

Of all the Egyptian conquerors the most famous was Tuthmosis III, whose empire was greater than that of any other. In terms of military achievements, Tuthmosis III is therefore by far the most likely candidate to be the legendary King Sesostris. His grandfather, Tuthmosis I, embarked on large scale military operations far from the borders of Egypt, beginning with a military campaign into Nubia. He also engaged Mitanni (modern Syria) and proceeded as far as the River Euphrates[10]. His father, Tuthmosis II, likewise conducted military campaigns, but on a smaller scale. When Tuthmosis II died, he had no son with his principal wife Hatshepsut. He did have a son (Tuthmosis III) with a secondary wife called Iset, but he was still too young to rule. Hatshepsut ascended to the throne and Tuthmosis III only became sole regent of Egypt when she died. He was to become the greatest conqueror in Egyptian history, earning him the epithet 'Napoleon of Egypt' among modern scholars[11]. His empire stretched from Nubia in the south to the banks of the River Euphrates in Syria, with its sphere of influence reaching even further[12]. He even controlled some of the Aegean islands as recorded on the *Gebel Barkal Stela* of Tuthmosis III[13] (see Appendix A), although it is not clear just how far into the Aegaen his control reached.

The name Sesostris and its derivatives are generally accepted to be Greek transliterations of the Egyptian name of the legendary Egyptian king, who must have been a specific individual and not for instance a group of kings with similar names. It is curious, however, that scholars appear not to have considered the possibility that the names may be Greek descriptions of that specific king. This is indeed the case.

The name Sesostris is formed by the Greek words *sē*[14] (thee, thou, you), *sōs*[15] (thine, yours) and *trís*[16] (three times), which can be interpreted as 'You and (what's) yours the third'. This implies that the Tuthmosid family (I, II and III) of conquerors was nicknamed 'You and what's yours' among the Greeks, and that Sesostris was the third member of this family. Although Greeks who lived at the time of Tuthmosis III must certainly have known his real name, it would appear that over time his name was forgotten and he was remembered only through his exploits. As discussed in Section 17.1, the Greeks suffered numerous natural disasters from the earliest times, and every time most of their records about their past were lost.

The strange spelling of Sesoösis suggests that the name was originally pronounced Se-so-osis, in which case the name was most likely formed from *sē* (thee, thou, you), *sōu*[17] (of thee, thine, yours) and *hōsōs*[18] (as many as, whatsoever), rendering 'You and as much as is yours', or 'You and everything that is yours'.

Finally, Sesonchosis has essentially the same meaning if considered to be a concatenation of the words *sē* (thee, thou, you), *sun*[19] (with, together), *chōōs*[20] (a heap, rubbish) and *sōs* (thine, yours). This can be interpreted as 'You with the heap of what's yours'.

The origin of these peculiar nicknames is readily explained.

Tuthmosis appointed several commanders ('overseer of the army') of his forces, two of whom were Djehuty and Tjanuny[21]. In Tjanuny's tomb it was recorded that 'I it is who established the victories which he performed in every foreign country, having made in writing according to what was done', and he was named 'scribe of the army' and 'overseer of the scribes of the army'.

The *Gebel Barkal Stela*, written by one of his commander-scribes, provides a number of links between Tuthmosis III and Sesostris. The scribe boasts that he captured the inhabitants of enemy states, their children and their property as well. He also described the enemy as 'falling in heaps'. These remarks confirm that Tuthmosis had a policy of removing captives with everything they owned, including their children, to Egypt. This he did to establish a workforce of slaves. His military campaigns likewise seem to have been characterised by stacking those killed in heaps, hence the nickname. When Tuthmosis had dealt with you, you and what was yours were found either as slaves in Egypt or on heaps of the dead in your own country.

6.1 Links between Sesostris and Tuthmosis III

Apart from the nicknames, there are several other links between Sesostris and Tuthmosis III:

- According to Herodotus and Diodorus, Sesostris / Sesoösis subjugated Nubia, Asia as far as India and parts of Europe, whatever the ancient definitions of these territories might have been, and he was urged by his daughter to 'acquire empire over whole world'[22,23]. Tuthmosis III was not only the greatest Egyptian conqueror of all time, but both he and his people seemed to have made those very claims. From the *Gebel Barkal Stela* (GBS) we learn that Tuthmosis' 'southern borders reach to the crest of the world, to the ends of this world, and the northern to the ends of Asia, to the supports of heaven', he travelled to and was feared 'to the ends of Asia' and his fame had 'pervaded the crest of the world'.

- Sesostris brought captives to Egypt for forced labour[24,25]. Tuthmosis likewise brought captive people with their belongings to Egypt (GBS).
- Sesoösis was a vigorous builder of monuments[26], as was Tuthmosis III, who had construction sites all along the Nile, in Nubia, Thebes, Middle Egypt, Heliopolis, Memphis and the Nile Delta[27].
- Sesostris erected (boundary) stelae in the conquered territories[28,29], as did Tuthmosis III (GBS).
- Strabo records that Sesostris traversed the whole of Aethiopia (Nubia). Tuthmosis III likewise had penetrated Nubia beyond the Third Cataract (a shallow stretch of water) of the Nile[30]. His grandfather, Tuthmosis I, however, had proceeded even further, to between the Fourth and Fifth Cataracts[31].
- Early in his reign Sesoösis subdued the larger part of Libya[32]. Tuthmosis 'crushed Tjehenu (Libya)' as recorded in the *Poetical Stela of Tuthmosis III* [33], but the initial subjugation of Libya was most likely done by his predecessors. Hatshepsut, his co-regent during his early years, received tribute from Libya[34]. This was most likely the reason why Diodorus places this conquest during his early years, writing that 'though in years (he was) still no more than a youth'[35].
- According to Herodotus and Diodorus, Sesostris used slave labour for the digging of canals in Egypt[36,37]. Strabo records that it was Sesostris who cut the canal which flowed through the Bitter Lakes of Egypt and ended in the Red Sea[38]. Tuthmosis III undertook the clearing of the canal in the fiftieth year of his reign[39] and is therefore linked to the canal.
- As a young man Sesoösis was laboriously trained in the hunting of wild animals[40], while Tuthmosis III was an accomplished hunter, killing 120 elephants (GBS).
- Sesoösis first confirmed the support (goodwill) of his people before implementing his plans[41], while Tutmosis III seems to

have been renowned for his 'excellent plans' (GBS). He evidently made a point of discussing his plans in detail with his generals and possibly other high ranking Egyptian citizens before the plans were executed.

- Sesoösis 'bestowed allotments of the best land in Egypt' on his commanders and they lacked nothing[42]. This was also true of Tuthmosis III, as boasted by one of his commanders about the honours bestowed upon him by his king (GBS). General Djehuty received similar rewards following his victory over Joppa[43], as did Amenemheb, a royal register in the army, for deeds of valour performed during military campaigns and for diverting an attack of an elephant on the king during an elephant hunt[44].

- Herodotus claims that Sesostris 'set out with a fleet of long ships from the Arabian Gulf and subjugated all those living by the Red Sea, until he came to a sea which was too shallow for his vessels. After returning from there back to Egypt, he gathered a great army ... and marched over the mainland, subjugating every nation to which he came'[45]. According to Diodorus, after having conquered Ethiopia, Sesoösis 'sent out a fleet of four hundred ships into the Red Sea, being the first Egyptian to build warships, and not only took possession of the islands in those waters, but also subdued the mainland as far as India, while he himself made his way by land with his army and subdued all Asia'[46].

This incident is similar to an event in Tuthmosis' campaigns. In Year 33 of his reign the Egyptian army sailed to the friendly Lebanese port of Byblos, where its carpenters built a series of flat-pack boats. These were loaded in pieces onto carts and lumbered along behind the army over mountains on the way to the Euphrates, where the boats were assembled. Tuthmosis' army could now cross the river and defeat the Mitannians[47].

It is highly unlikely that an Egyptian king would have sent

his navy on a route up the Gulf of Arabia as shown in Figure 6.1. It is generally accepted that what Herodotus refers to as the Gulf of Arabia was in fact the Red Sea, as is also implied in his own records[48]. However, Diodorus' statement that Tuthmosis' navy 'subdued the coast of the mainland (the Arabian Peninsula?) as far as India' ('India' extending to modern Iraq and Iran?) implies that the Egyptian navy must have sailed up the modern Arabian (Persian) Gulf. Both Strabo[49] and Diodorus[50] mention India and the river Ganges in the same context, so they most likely placed India more or less in its present location, perhaps even extending it into modern Iraq and Iran. The Egyptian empire at its peak was limited to the region as indicated in Figure 1.1, which makes it highly improbable that Sesostris would have sent his navy as far as the 'India' shown in Figure 6.1. Furthermore, there would have been few if any islands in the Red Sea that would have been of significance to the Egyptians. By contrast, the islands of the Aegean would have been as important as any other neighbour of Egypt. Tuthmosis' general 'tied up ... the islands in the middle of the ocean, the inhabitants of the Aegean Sea and the rebellious lands' (GBS). This is also attested to in the following inscription from the *Poetical Stela*:

My serpent-diadem on your head consumes them ... it devours the Aegean islanders with its flame, it severs the heads of the Asiatics ... I came to let you crush the western land, Keftiu (Crete) and Isy (Cyprus) being in awe of you ... I came to let you crush the Aegean islanders, the lands of Metjen (Mitanni) trembling for fear of you.[51]

It therefore seems that Herodotus mistook Tuthmosis' naval campaign up the eastern coast of the Mediterranean Sea for a naval campaign up the Gulf of Arabia (boats carried across land / sea too shallow for boats). There is no archaeological or other evidence to suggest that Tuthmosis' empire ever stretched as far as 'India'.

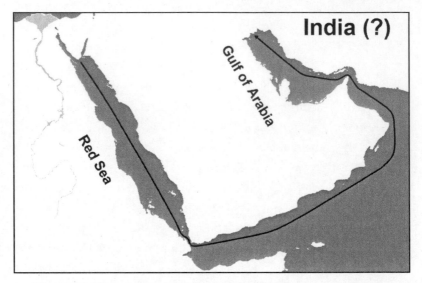

Figure 6.1 The supposed route of the Egyptian navy to 'India'

- Sesostris set up two stone obelisks at the Temple of the Sun[52], while Tuthmosis III had two obelisks at erected at the Temple of the Sun at Karnak[53] (see Figure 6.2).
- Herodotus informs us that Sesostris erected two stone statues, each fifty feet high, of himself and his wife at the temple of Hephaestus (Ptah) in Memphis[54]. Diodorus records the height of the statues as 45 feet high[55]. There is indeed a Temple of Ptah at Memphis, located opposite the Temple of Amun. Memphis was the capital of Egypt before the Middle Kingdom pharaohs gradually moved it to Thebes. At Thebes, now called Luxor, we find the cult Temple of Ptah started by Tuthmosis III, nearby which are the remains of two colossal statues of Tuthmosis III[56]. These probably are the remains of Sesostris' two stone statues as recorded by Herodotus. It is therefore very likely that Herodotus and Diodorus meant 'capital of Egypt' when they (mistakenly) named Memphis as the location of the statues.

Figure 6.2. Tuthmosis III shown opposite two stone obelisks he erected at Karnak

- One of the main objectives of military campaigns was to collect tribute from the conquered nations. Sesoösis was renowned for the tribute he collected[57], as was Tuthmosis III (GBS).

- Although it sounds like nothing more than common sense, Sesoösis appears to have made it public knowledge that only the strongest men would serve in his army[58]. Tuthmosis seems to have done the same, judging from the boast of his general, 'because I am very skilled in strength and victory' (GBS).

- Sesoösis was encouraged by his daughter Athyrtis to conquer the whole world[59]. As is the case with Sesostris, his daughter's name is of Greek origin, a[60] (without) – $th\bar{e}r$ (a wild animal, as game, hunting: see $th\bar{e}ra$[61]) – $tís$[62] (some, certain), rendering 'Without certain wild animals'. This name is similar in meaning to *Thermuthis* ('Wild animal fable', see Section 7.2), the name of the daughter of the Pharaoh of the Exodus[63]. In Sections 7.2 and 7.3 it is argued that Thermuthis was a nickname given to the young wife of Amenhotep III (the son of Tuthmosis IV and also the Pharaoh of the Exodus), who jubilantly reported that her brave husband had just slain a herd of wild bulls in the desert. In reality he had slaughtered, in a fit of rage, a herd of domesticated cattle that regularly used to drift onto his property. *Athyrtis* was thus a mocking nickname the young Tiye, daughter-in-law of Tuthmosis IV (not Tuthmosis III who was Sesostris), had earned herself among the Greeks when the truth finally surfaced. The association of Sesostris with Amenhotep III is discussed below.

- Sesoösis built a wall on Egypt's eastern border, from Pelusium to Heliopolis, to protect it against attacks from Syria and Arabia[64]. This wall was referred to as the 'Walls of the Ruler' by Neferti, a sage in the court of King Snofru (Sneferu), who prophesied that a king called Ameny would rise and expel the Asiatics (a general name by which the Egyptians referred to the peoples of Canaan and further north) who were occupying Egypt at that time, and that this wall would be built to protect Egypt from them in the future[65] (see Section 17.1 for a further discussion of the Prophecy of Neferti):

There will be built the Wall of the Ruler ... and the Asiatics will not be permitted to come down into Egypt that they might beg for water in the customary manner, in order to let their beasts drink. And justice will come into its place, while wrongdoing is driven out.

The Prophecy of Neferti appears to have been written to justify Amenemhat I's ascension to the throne[66,67], as Ameny is generally assumed to have been a shortened form of this pharaoh's name. The wall is referred to as the 'Wall of the Prince' in the *Tale of Sinuhe*, probably written shortly after the end of the reign of Senesret I[68], the son of Amenemhat I. The Wall of the Prince was most likely constructed by the latter, but if Amenemhat had not been able to complete the construction of the wall, his son would certainly have done so. It would appear that even the early historians such as Diodorus equated Sesostris with Senesret I purely on the basis of the phonetic similarity of the names, hence the association of Sesoösis with the 'Wall of the Ruler'. However, Sesostris as Tuthmosis III more than likely only reinforced the walls created by his predecessors, if he had worked on the walls at all. Returning to the Second Intermediate Period, it is possible that the Hyksos, the Asiatics who had invaded Egypt, could have demolished this wall during their occupation of Egypt. If so, the pharaohs of the Eighteenth Dynasty would no doubt have rebuilt the wall, in which case Tuthmosis III may well have been involved. On the other hand, it is possible if not likely that the construction of this wall was mistakenly attributed to the legendary Sesostris, simply because he was the most famous of Egyptian kings.

• Sesoösis ruled for 33 years, and supposedly took his own life after having become blind ('his eyesight failed him')[69]. The reign of Tuthmosis III can be divided into two parts, first as co-regent with Hatshepsut, followed by the period in which he ruled as sole sovereign of Egypt. His reign is usually given as 1479-1425 BCE, a period of approximately 54 years, but this includes the years of co-regency. Hatshepsut ruled for about 22 years and 6 months[70]. Tuthmosis III therefore ruled as sole monarch of Egypt for approximately 32 years, which matches Sesostris' 33 years. Sethos (Sethosis) ruled for 59 years according to Manetho[71], which more or less matches Tuthmosis' total reign of 54 years.

6.2 Legends about Amenhotep III mistakenly attributed to Sesostris

With the evidence presented above, there can be little doubt that Sesostris and Tuthmosis III were one and the same person. It will be shown next that some of the events that occurred in the life of Amenhotep III were mistakenly attributed to Sesostris. In contrast to the reign of Tuthmosis III, which was characterised by military conquest, Amenhotep III enjoyed unprecedented prosperity and relative peace during his reign. Historians have dubbed him 'Amenhotep the Magnificent', the king who preferred to call himself 'The Dazzling Sun Disk' and during whose reign Egypt was wealthier and more powerful than ever before[72]. For this reason it is certainly possible that he could have been mistaken for the legendary Sesostris, as is evident from further analyses of ancient descriptions of Sesostris:

- Both Herodotus and Diodorus mention a curious episode in which Sesostris, during his absence from Egypt, leaves his brother in charge of the country. Upon his return this brother invites him to a banquet and attempts to burn Sesostris and his family to death. The king escapes, although two of his sons die in the fire, and he avenges himself on his brother[73,74]. Manetho likewise mentions Sesostris (Sethosis) who had a brother (Armias) whom he had left in charge of Egypt during his absence[75]. Armais usurped the throne, but Sethosis returned to recover his kingdom and cast Armais (Hermeus) out of Egypt[76].

There are no records whatsoever of the beloved Tuthmosis III having left a brother in charge of Egypt, who furthermore attempted to usurp his throne during his absence and then to kill him at a banquet, and was subsequently expelled from Egypt. The circumstances, however, perfectly match those of Amenhotep III, who must have left his brother-in-law Ay (Armais) in charge of Egypt during the Amarna interlude. As argued throughout this treatise, Amenhotep III had to retreat into Nubia when he had to face an army commanded by his own son, along with an army from Jerusalem. Ay had served every pharaoh from Amenhotep III to Tutankhamun, upon whose death he usurped the throne (Tutankhamun had apparently selected his general Horemheb to succeed him)[77]. Ay's mummy has never been found[78], which accords with him having been expelled from Egypt.

- Apollonius of Rhodes does not agree with what Dicaearchus had to say about Sesostris (Sesonchosis):

> Dicaearchus in the first book of his Life of Greece (calls him) Sesonchosis and says that he established laws that no one should abandon his father's trade. For he assumed that this was the origin of greed. (Dicaearchus) says that he was the first man to discover the mounting of horses. Others (say) that **Oros (Horus) did these things**, not Sesonchosis. [Ed. Note: one of the scholia reads 'Sesostris'] ... In the first book Dicaearchus says that after **Oros (Horus), the son of Isis and Osiris, Sesonchosis became king**. From Sesonchosis to the kingship of Nilus was 2,500 years, (from the kingship of Nilus to the destruction of Ilium was 7 years), from the capture of Ilium to the first Olympiad was 436 years, altogether 2,943 years.[79]

In Section 7.1 and Chapter 11 it is shown that the King Orus listed by Manetho in his list of Eighteenth Dynasty kings can be identified as Amenhotep III. Apollonius' account shows that Sesonchosis was mentioned in the same context as Orus, suggesting that they were the same person.

- In ancient times some have associated the statues erected by Sesostris with those erected by Memnon[80]. Probably the most famous of all the statues erected by Amenhotep III are his so-called Colossi of Memnon, two massive stone statues erected at Thebes. The reason the Greeks referred to these statues by a name associated with the Trojan War is discussed in Section 13.6. It will be argued that the Greeks knew Amenhotep III by the name of Memnon. The statues of Sesostris are therefore directly linked to the statues of Amenhotep III.

- Herodotus makes the curious remark that Sesostris was the only Egyptian king who also ruled Ethiopia[81]. This is odd since several Egyptian kings had control of Ethiopia during their reigns. The most likely reason for this remark is to be found in Manetho's claim that Amenhotep had fled to Ethiopia with his army and a large section of the Egyptian population. Amenhotep would therefore have been the only Egyptian king who actually lived in Ethiopia for many years, hence Herodotus' seemingly out-of-context remark.

- Sesoösis 'built a ship of cedar wood, which was two hundred and eighty cubits long and plated on the exterior with gold and on the interior with silver. This ship he presented as a votive offering to the god who is held in special reverence in Thebes'[82]. Amenhotep III had a sacred lake constructed at Thebes, as well as an accompanying royal bark for him and his wife Tiye to sail in. The bark was named 'The Aton Gleams' in honour of the sun god Aten[83], and one can imagine that boat to have been plated with gold and silver to create the illusion of a glittering sun. It is easily understood that the construction of the fabled boat would have been attributed to Sesostris, whom some assumed to be Amenhotep.

- The two most outstanding pharaohs of ancient Egypt were Tuthmosis III, the conqueror, and Amenhotep III, the pharaoh who ruled when Egypt's dominion over her neighbours was at its peak. Both were the third king who had the same name in their respective families (Tuthmosis I, II and III, Amenhotep I, II and III). This may also have contributed to both kings being associated with the legendary King Sesostris.

- Sesostris, who took his own life because he had become blind, matches the Amenhotep III's aliases Pheros (see Section 7.1) and Shu (see Section 8.4), who both became blind. Diodorus' statement that he took his own life is most likely based on the fact that Amenhotep III had 'vanished' from Egypt, having retreated with his army into Ethiopia.

There are three reasons in particular for distinguishing which parts of the Sesostris legend actually pertain to Amenhotep III. These are:

- Two of Amenhotep's sons were burnt to death, while the others escaped. These deaths will be linked to the tenth plague of Egypt, the death of the firstborn. Two of Amenhotep's firstborn sons, presumably a child by Tiye and a child by a secondary wife, would have been targeted for sacrifice through fire. Of these two (if 'two' does not imply 'many') Prince Tuthmosis narrowly escaped death, initially unbeknown to the general population.

- The successors of Sesostris, Pheros and Proteus, and therefore also Helen of Troy, can be linked to Amenhotep III and the Amarna period (see Sections 7.1 and 13.6).

- The actions of the brother of the king suggest what the ultimate fate of Nefertiti was (see Section 13.5).

Amenhotep III and his scribe Amenhotep, Son of Hapu

Manetho unequivocally names the Pharaoh of the Exodus as Amenophis who had a sacred scribe called Amenophis, son of Papis[1]. From this perspective alone, there is only one pharaoh who would match this description, namely Amenhotep III who had a famous royal scribe known as Amenhotep called Huy, the son of Hapu[2]. The name Papis is most likely simply a corruption of the phonetically similar Hapu.

In order to further establish Amenhotep III as one of the pharaohs of the Exodus (the Pharaoh of the Oppression), one needs to interpret the names given to this pharaoh by various ancient historians, as well as the names of individuals associated with the Exodus. The latter include the name of the wife of this pharaoh, as well as the names given to his sacred scribe.

It must be kept in mind at all times that the names given to individuals by historians depend on two critical factors, these being that the name can be a transliteration of a name in a foreign language, for instance a Greek transliteration of an Egyptian or a Hebrew name, and secondly that the name can be a translation in the language of the historian of a nickname given to the specific individual. All therefore depended on which sources the historian had consulted, and how he had interpreted those sources. The four languages to be considered are firstly Egyptian and Hebrew as the languages of the peoples of the Exodus, and secondly Greek and Latin as the most common languages of ancient historians.

7.1 Names associated with Amenhotep III, Pharaoh of the Oppression

Orus

The first name to be considered is that of Orus, the name by which Manetho identifies Amenhotep III in his king list (see Chapter 11). Egyptian kings were often referred to by the name of an Egyptian god, so it is certainly possible that the king could have been known as Horus, which in oral tradition or through differences in the pronunciation of Horus in other languages became Orus.

A second possibility is that the name was of Hebrew origin, as derived from the words *'ôwr*[3] (light, shine, fire), *'ûwr*[4] (flame, fire) or *'ôwr*[5] (skin, hide) and *'ûwsh*[6] (assemble yourselves). The most likely interpretation would be 'Assemble yourselves (for) the fire', agreeing with the sacrifice of the firstborn offspring through fire as argued in this treatise (see Section 15.10 for a discussion of the tenth plague).

It is also possible that the name could be of Greek origin, either *ōrōs*[7] (a mountain) or *ōrussō*[8] (to dig), but neither would make any sense in terms of the Exodus.

Should it be of Latin origin, the name Orus can be linked to *aurum* (gold) or *aureus* (golden)[9], which would be an apt description of this fabulously wealthy king. It could also be derived from the word *auris* (the ear, to listen)[10], suggesting the nickname '(He who) listened (to the advice of the oracle)'.

It is obvious that it will be difficult to select with certainty a specific interpretation of this name of the king, although the Egyptian or Hebrew interpretations would seem to be the most likely candidates.

Bocchoris

This is the name given to the Pharaoh by Lysimachus and also Tacitus (see Sections 3.3 and 3.10, respectively). As I have no knowledge of the Egyptian language and despite an extensive search I could not find any Egyptian gods with phonetically similar names,

I had to assume that this name was not of Egyptian origin.

The Hebrew words *bûwqâh*[11] (emptiness) and *rîysh*[12] (poverty) would render a name phonetically similar to Bocchoris, but it would be meaningless in the context of a pharaoh of Egypt, specifically Amenhotep III, who was anything but poor.

An interesting possibility is presented by combining the Greek words *bōē*[13] (a halloo, a call) and *chōris*[14] (separately, apart). This would at first glance suggest 'Called apart', which would rather seem to refer to Moses, speaking for his god, who instructed the Hebrews to separate themselves from other peoples. Alternatively, it could mean 'Separated (by) hallooing', which creates the impression of cattle being cordoned off by the shouts of their herders. This interpretation actually stems from the possible Latin interpretation of Bocchoris.

The Latin word *boo* means 'to low' or 'to bellow like an ox'[15], and the word *chorus* simply means 'choir'[16]. Boochorus, which over time became Bocchorus, would then mean 'The choir of bellowing (oxen)'. Not only does the name Orus apply to Amenhotep III according to Manetho's chronology, but it will be shown below that this was more than likely a nickname Amenhotep III earned himself following his so-called magnificent wild bull hunt, during which he slaughtered 96 of these animals (Section 7.3).

It should be noted that according to Eusebius, Manetho placed Bocchoris in Egypt's Twenty-fourth Dynasty:

The Twenty-fourth Dynasty: Bochchoris of Sais, 6 (or 44) years. In his reign, a lamb spoke.

...

The Twenty-fifth Dynasty consisted of three Ethiopian kings. Sabacon, who, taking Bochchoris captive, burned him alive, and reigned for 8 (or 12) years. Sebichos, his son, for 14 (or 12) years. Tarcus (Taracus, Saracus) for 18 (or 20) years. Total: 40 (or 44) years.[17]

The lamb which spoke must certainly refer to an oracle or adviser, and Bocchoris being burnt alive matches the sacrifice of the firstborn of Egypt by Amenhotep III as argued in this treatise. Sabacon sacrificing Bocchoris likewise matches Hercules who, when about to be sacrificed by Busiris, managed to free himself and kill him. The generally accepted name of Manetho's King Bocchoris is Bakenranef[18] and it would seem that Manetho associated the name Bocchoris with this minor king based on the vague phonetic similarity between the two names. Manetho most likely was familiar with the legends surrounding Bocchoris, but did not know where to place them in his chronology.

That Manetho incorrectly placed Bocchoris in the Twenty-fourth Dynasty is confirmed by Herodotus, who also places Abacon (Abacos) in the Late Period of Egypt (*ca.* 747-332 BCE), but clearly associates some legends about Amenhotep III with him. According to Herodotus:

> ... **He was succeeded on the throne, they said, by a blind man**, a native of Anysis, whose own name also was Anysis. Under him Egypt was invaded by a vast army of Ethiopians, led by Sabacos, their king. **The blind Anysis fled away to the marsh-country, and the Ethiopian was lord of the land for fifty years**, during which his mode of rule was the following: When an Egyptian was guilty of an offence, his plan was not to punish him with death: instead of so doing, he sentenced him, according to the nature of his crime, to raise the ground to a greater or a less extent in the neighbourhood of the city to which he belonged. **Thus the cities came to be even more elevated than they were before. As early as the time of Sesostris, they had been raised by those who dug the canals in his reign**; this second elevation of the soil under the Ethiopian king gave them a very lofty position.
>
> ...

The Ethiopian finally quitted Egypt, the priests said, by a hasty flight under the following circumstances. **He saw in his sleep a vision: a man stood by his side, and counselled him to gather together all the priests of Egypt and cut every one of them asunder.** On this, according to the account which he himself gave, it came into his mind that the gods intended hereby to lead him to commit an act of sacrilege, which would be sure to draw down upon him some punishment either at the hands of gods or men. So he resolved not to do the deed suggested to him, but rather to retire from Egypt, as the time during which it was fated that he should hold the country had now (he thought) expired. For before he left Ethiopia he had been told by the oracles which are venerated there, that he was to reign fifty years over Egypt. The years were now fled, and the dream had come to trouble him; he therefore of his own accord withdrew from the land.

As soon as Sabacos was gone, **the blind king left the marshes, and resumed the government.** He had lived in the marsh-region the whole time, **having formed for himself an island there by a mixture of earth and ashes.** While he remained, the natives had orders to bring him food unbeknown to the Ethiopian, and latterly, at his request, each man had brought him, with the food, a certain quantity of ashes. Before Amyrtaeus, no one was able to discover the site of this island, which continued unknown to the kings of Egypt who preceded him on the throne for the space of seven hundred years and more. The name which it bears is Elbo. It is about ten furlongs across in each direction.

The next king, I was told, was a priest of Hephaestus, called Sethos. This monarch despised and neglected the warrior class of the Egyptians, as though he did not need their services. Among other indignities which he offered them, he took from them the lands which they had possessed under all the previous kings, consisting of twelve acres of choice land for each warrior. Afterwards, therefore, **when Sanacharib, king of the Arabians**

and Assyrians, marched his vast army into Egypt, the warriors one and all refused to come to his aid. On this the monarch, greatly distressed, entered into the inner sanctuary, and, before the image of the god, bewailed the fate which impended over him. As he wept he fell asleep, and dreamed that the god came and stood at his side, bidding him be of good cheer, and go boldly forth to meet the Arabian host, which would do him no hurt, as he himself would send those who should help him.

Sethos, then, relying on the dream, collected such of the Egyptians as were willing to follow him, who were none of them warriors, but traders, artisans and market people; and with these marched to Pelusium, which commands the entrance into Egypt, and there pitched his camp. As the two armies lay here opposite one another, there came in the night a multitude of field-mice, which devoured all the quivers and bowstrings of the enemy, and ate the thongs by which they managed their shields. Next morning they commenced their flight, and great multitudes fell, as they had no arms with which to defend themselves. There stands to this day in the temple of Hephaestus, a stone statue of Sethos with a mouse in his hand, and an inscription to this effect 'Look on me, and learn to reverence the gods.'[19]

There are several aspects of Herodotus' Sabacos and Sethos that suggest they refer to Amenhotep III as king of Ethiopia and king of Egypt, in other words, the legends involving Amenhotep III who was both king of Egypt and Ethiopia were mistakenly attributed to two different individuals of the Twenty-fourth and Twenty-fifth Dynasties:

- The Egyptian king who became blind was known in other legends as Pheros (see 'Pheros and Proteus' below). This king fled and was replaced by a king of Ethiopia, who ruled Egypt for 50 years. His construction programmes exceeded those of Sesostris. It was Amenhotep III who fled Egypt for Ethiopia with his entire army and his temples and other constructions are as magnificent as those of his grandfather Tuthmosis III, the real Sesostris. Pheros was reportedly a king who waged no wars, matching Herodotus' description above of Sethos who supposedly despised his own army.

- The one 'who stood by his side' in a dream, urging him to kill all the priests of Egypt, must certainly be linked to Amenhotep's scribe and oracle of the same name, who advised him to sacrifice the firstborn offspring of Egypt. When this failed to bring an end to the plague, the Egyptians revolted against the priesthood of Amun, to whom Amenhotep, the son of Hapu, belonged. Faced by this revolt, Amenhotep III fled Egypt, as did Sabacos.

- The 38-year reign of Amenhotep III in Egypt, and Sabacos' reign of 50 years suggest that Amenhotep III remained alive in Ethiopia for at least another 12 years.

- The blind king who lived on an island and was supported by Ethiopians matches the king of Ethiopia who was obliged to give Amenhotep III and his army refuge and sustenance in his country.

- Arguably the clearest indication of an incorrect association of the legends surrounding Amenhotep III with Sabacon is that he was supposedly succeeded by Sethos. There is no king of that name in Egypt's Late Period. Manetho, however, equates Sethos (Sethosis) with Aegyptus[20], who was Amenhotep III. The story of Herodotus' Sethos who had no regard for his army, which refused to march against an invading army from the north, matches Manetho's account in which Amenophis chose not to confront the invading force from Jerusalem and fled to Ethiopia[21]. The fact that the invading army was opposed only by civilians may suggest that the army was not present, having departed to Ethiopia, and the victory over the invading army is no doubt a garbled version of the exploits of Amenophis who later returned from Ethiopia to pursue the invaders 'to the bounds of Syria'. However, a more likely interpretation is that the army of civilians was in fact the rebel army of Prince Tuthmosis.

It must be kept in mind that according to Tacitus[22], most ancient writers agreed on the fact that it was during Bocchoris' reign that a disease causing horrible disfigurement of the body broke out in Egypt. On the advice of his oracle Hammon, Bocchoris expelled the Jewish race from Egypt. Moses was an exile from Egypt who took charge of this expelled nation, which would later take possession of a country (Canaan) from which they expelled the inhabitants and founded a city and a temple (Jerusalem). The identity of Bocchoris as Amenhotep III is therefore clearly established.

Busiris

Busiris was a legendary Egyptian king infamous for sacrificing strangers who dared visit his country (see Section 3.12). He is linked to the Exodus by St Augustine who places him in the same timeframe as the Exodus[23]; by Apollodorus who considers him to be one of the 50 sons of Egyptus (Sesostris, according to Manetho) and records that the slaughter of strangers to Egypt was instigated by his oracle Phrasius[24]; by Isocrates who records that Busiris forced the Nile to break its banks and flood the land[25] (the Koranic flood which was the first plague of Egypt, see Sections 15.12 and 17.1) and by Diodorus who claims that Busiris was seized with a desire to seize the beautiful maidens of the Atlantides[26]. As discussed above, some exploits of Amenhotep III have mistakenly been associated with Sesostris, and it will be shown that the slaughter of strangers can likewise be linked to the sacrifice of the firstborn as advised by Amenhotep's scribe of the same name. The flood will be linked to the tsunami that followed the eruption of Thera and it will be argued that Amenhotep III must have been notorious for his demand for beautiful women.

The etymology of the name Busiris is relatively straightforward.

It must certainly be a combination of the Greek words *bōus*[27] (pronounced 'booce', an ox, as grazing, a cow) and *iris*[28] (a rainbow, from a symbol of the female messenger of the pagan deities). The meaning is 'Iris and the oxen' or 'The ox messenger of the gods', a mocking nickname earned by the young Tiye for her ecstatic report about her husband's successful wild bull hunt. She evidently did not know the difference between wild bulls and domesticated cattle (see Section 7.3). The Latin version of the name is similar, from *bos* (an ox) and *Iris*, the female messenger of the gods[29].

Palmanothes and Chenephres

Atrapanus, a Jewish historian, names the two pharaohs of the Exodus as Palmanothes and Chenephres, and he in fact makes them contemporaries (see Section 3.6). Not only do the names have a Hebrew ring to them, but it is also likely that the names were recorded in the Hebrew language and probably have a Hebrew meaning. This is indeed the case. Palmanothes is best interpreted as '(He) who performed the miracle of the fire' from *pâlâ'*[30] (to be great, wonderful, do wonderful acts), *mân*[31] (who, what), *'ôwth*[32] (sign, omen, miracle) and *'êsh*[33] (fire). Another interpretation would be '(He) who made the allotment for the fire', from *pâ'al*[34] (to do, make), *m^enâth*[35] (an allotment, portion) and *'êsh*. Strangely, and possibly one of the reasons why the name survived in oral tradition, both of these interpretations link this pharaoh to Amenhotep III who, on the advice of his trusted scribe of the same name, had issued a decree that the firstborn of Egypt should be sacrificed in the fire to appease the gods and so bring an end to the plague in Egypt. When it did not work, he was quickly labelled as such so as not to forget this most infamous of his deeds. This interpretation is confirmed by the meaning of the other name of this pharaoh, Chenephres. This name is also a sarcastic reference to this king and can be interpreted as 'The grace of the ashes of the fire', from *chên*[36] (grace, favour), *'êpher*[37] (ashes) and *'êsh*.

That the names Palmanothes and Chenephres actually refer to

the same pharaoh is confirmed by Artapanus' peculiar tale about Chenephres, namely that it was Moses who pointed out the use of oxen for ploughing to the Pharaoh. For this reason, Chenephres:

> ...having given the name Apis to a bull, commanded the troops to found a temple for him, and bade them bring and bury there the animals which had been consecrated by Moses, because he wished to bury the inventions of Moses in oblivion.[38]

The burial of the first Apis bull was performed at a cemetery in Saqqara during the reign of Amenhotep III[39]. Artapanus' record therefore not only links both names to Amenhotep III, but also confirms that Moses, by whom the Apis bull was consecrated, was indeed Prince Tuthmosis, who as high priest of Ptah assisted his father during the burial ceremony.

Pheros (Pheron) and Proteus

Herodotus informs us that Sesostris was succeeded by his son Pheros, who threw his spear at the raging Nile and was struck blind as a result. He was succeeded by his son Proteus, who had sworn never to sacrifice a stranger to his country. It was shown in Chapter 6 that Sesostris was Tuthmosis III, which places him shortly before the Amarna period. As some events in the life of Amenhotep III were mistakenly associated with Sesostris, Pheros and his son Proteus are therefore also linked to the Amarna period. The name Pheros appears to be of Greek origin, probably derived from one if not both of the words $ph\bar{e}r\bar{o}$[40] (to bear, carry) and $ph\bar{o}r\bar{o}s$[41] (a load, tax, tribute paid by a subjugated nation). The latter interpretation could refer to this key aspect of the reigns of both Tuthmosis III and Amenhotep III (their taxation of other nations). However, it may also refer to the burden Amenhotep had to bear, either the devastating plagues Egypt suffered following the eruption of Thera, but more likely the terrible decision he had to make, to call for the sacrifice of the firstborn. When that failed to bring relief to Egypt, Amenhotep would have had a terrible psychological burden to bear.

As discussed in Section 17.1, the raging river into which Pheros had hurled his spear must represent the tsunami caused by the eruption of Thera. The name Proteus can be translated as 'Before the gods', from *prō*[42] (in front of, prior, before) and *thēŏs*[43] (god). This interpretation is too vague to associate it with any particular pharaoh, who, as the son of Amenhotep III, must have been either Prince Tuthmosis or Akhenaten. See Section 13.6 for a link between Proteus, Helen of Troy and Nefertiti, the wife of Akhenaten.

A plurality of names

For the sake of clarity, the names associated with Tuthmosis III and Amenhotep III are shown in diagrammatic form in Figure 7.1. In ancient times two Egyptian pharaohs stood out in terms of their domination over the ancient Near East, Tuthmosis III (the Napoleon of Egypt) and Amenhotep III (Egypt's 'Golden' Pharaoh). This explains why both of them had become associated with the

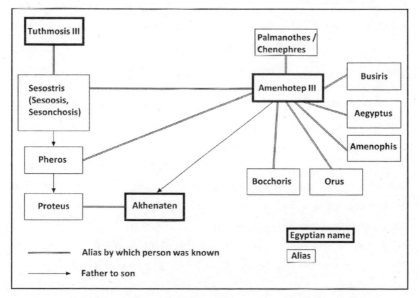

Figure 7.1. Diagram of names associated with Tuthmosis III and Amenhotep III

legendary King Sesostris, and since Amenhotep came after Tuthmosis, probably also why Pheros (Amenhotep III) was regarded by Herodotus as the son of Sesostris (Tuthmosis III). That Amenhotep was remembered by so many nicknames must certainly stem from the natural disaster that struck Egypt when the volcano on Thera erupted. The ensuing chaos, the sacrifice of the firstborn in Egypt and the flight of this magnificent king with his entire army to another country would certainly have sparked numerous legends in the ancient world. The loss of the library of Alexandria is simply incalculable as its vast collection of ancient records would no doubt have told us in much greater detail what had happened during that fateful era.

7.2 Names associated with the wife of the Pharaoh

The Exodus narrative mentions neither the name of the Egyptian princess who supposedly adopted Moses, nor the name of the wife of the Pharaoh of the Exodus. Josephus, writing in Greek, calls Moses' Egyptian mother Thermuthis[44], while Artapanus gives her name as Merris[45]. She is not mentioned by name in the Koran[46], but in Arab tradition she is known as Asiyah[47].

Thermuthis

The name Thermuthis is formed by the Greek words *thēr*[48] (wild animal, hunting) and *muthōs*[49] (a tale, fable, myth), and can be interpreted as 'The wild animal fable' and her nickname must have been something like Princess 'Wild animal myth'. This nickname was earned for her report on her young husband's legendary hunting trip during which he killed 96 'wild bulls' (see Section 7.3), and matches the interpretation given in Section 7.1 of Busiris as 'The ox messenger of the gods'. It also matches the interpretation of the name of Athyrtis as 'Without certain wild animals' as discussed in Section 6.1.

Merris

Artapanus' names of the Pharaoh have been shown to be of Hebrew origin and the name Merris is no exception. There are in fact two possible interpretations, namely 'Cattle husband', from $m^e r \hat{\imath} y'^{50}$ (fat cattle) and $'\hat{\imath} y s h^{51}$ (man, husband), or 'Rebellion husband', from $m^e r \hat{\imath} y^{52}$ (rebellion) and $'\hat{\imath} y s h$. Although the latter would link this pharaoh to the rebellion described by Manetho and others, the more likely interpretation is the former, as it matches the meaning of Thermuthis. The name Thermuthis is in turn linked to the name Athyrtis, the daughter of Sesoösis.

If Moses was indeed the same person as Prince Tuthmosis, his mother would have been Tiye, the daughter of Yuya and Tuyu. Furthermore, if Yuya and Joseph were one and the same person, it is possible that Joseph would have given their daughter a Hebrew name. This is suggested by Hebrew names like $T\hat{\imath}yts\hat{\imath}y^{53}$, $T\hat{\imath}yrey\hat{a}'$ [54] and $T\hat{\imath}yr\hat{a}s^{55}$, or in other words, Tiye may have been a shortened version of a longer Hebrew name that began with $T\hat{\imath}y$. Whether or not her name was of Hebrew origin, as Yuya's daughter Tiye would have been half Israelite, which may be the origin of the biblical legend which claims that Moses was raised by his Israelite mother while in the house of the Pharaoh (see Section 2.1).

Having established that Sesostris, named Egypt by Manetho, was indeed Amenhotep III, one must consider the meaning of the name of Egypt's mother as given by Apollodorus, who wrote in Greek. According to Apollodorus:

> But Belus remained in Egypt, reigned over the country, and married Anchinoe, daughter of Nile, by whom he had twin sons, Egyptus and Danaus...[56]

Belus is a legendary king whose name appears to refer to a spear, from the Greek $b\bar{e}l\bar{o}s^{57}$ (a spear or arrow). It may be linked to Herodotus' Pheros, who threw a spear into the raging Nile and was struck by blindness[58] (as discussed earlier this episode is actually a reference to Amenhotep III). The mother (actually, his mother-in-law) of Amenhotep III was Tuyu, and if Manetho's Egypt indeed refers to Amenhotep III, Tuyu and Anchinoe must be one and the same person. The name Anchinoe is most likely of Greek origin, in which case it would be formed by the words an[59] (whosoever), $ch\bar{e}\bar{o}$[60] (to pour) and $n\bar{o}\bar{e}\bar{o}$[61] (to comprehend, understand), yielding 'Whoever understands how to pour'. Tuyu was married to Yuya, who was argued to be the biblical Joseph in Section 5.3. In *Genesis* there is a curious legend about Joseph and two of his fellow inmates. It tells of his interpretation of the dreams of the king's butler and baker while they were in prison with him[62]. It was the duty of the butler to press grapes (make wine) and pour the wine into the king's cup, and Joseph assured him that the king would soon restore him to his place as the royal butler. By contrast, the baker would be executed. The most likely interpretation or origin of this nonsensical legend would be that Joseph was looking for workers who 'knew how to pour', in other words how to become a butler in the royal palace, or perhaps people who knew how to cultivate vineyards and make wine. The name Anchinoe may have been a nickname given to Tuyu as 'She who knew (best) how to pour'. She or her family may in fact have owned vineyards themselves, hence the nickname. The pouring of wine for one's husband appears to have been an expression of devotion during the Amarna era (see Nefertiti offering wine to Akhenaten, Figure 13.6).

Asiyah

Finally, Moses' adoptive mother is named as Asiyah in Arab tradition. It will be argued that Asiyah was the Arabic name for Nefertiti, who was closely linked to Prince Tuthmosis (Moses) and his brother Akhenaten (she became his wife). The names of Moses' Hebrew parents were Amram and Jochebed[63]. The name Amram seems to be derived from the Hebrew word *'am*[64] (people, nation) and *râ'am*[65] (to rise, lifted up), meaning 'The elevated nation'. This is unlikely to have been a name given to an individual. It is possible that the Hebrew letter *b* could have been mistaken for the Hebrew letter *m*, in which case the name would originally have been Abram, implying that he was given the generic name of the father of the Hebrew nation. Even more so is the name Jochebed, which is usually translated 'God is great', from $Y^ehôvâh$[66] (Lord, God, Jehovah) and $kâbêd$[67] (great, multitude, numerous, grievous, heavy). Given the actual meaning of $kâbêd$, the translation should read 'God is numerous', which is rather nonsensical. A better translation would be obtained using the words $châbâ'$[68] (to secrete, hide, do secretly) and $'êd$ [69] (a witness, prince), then meaning 'God hid the witness' or 'God hid the prince'. Both of these interpretations would apply to Moses. He was a prince in the house of the Pharaoh, and his downfall supposedly came when he witnessed an Egyptian striking a Hebrew slave and then killed the Egyptian. Consequently Moses had to flee Egypt and hide, so Jochebed appears to be a generic name describing either the hiding of the baby Moses in the reeds of the Nile, or Moses who had to hide in fear of the Egyptians. In other words, her name was invented in later legend. The real reason why Moses had to hide was that he was about to be sacrificed in the fire, but managed to escape this horrendous death.

Arab tradition offers a vital clue in the process of identifying the Egyptian princess who came to be associated with Moses. Asiyah was remembered as having been of Israelite and not Egyptian descent[70]. In Chapter 13 evidence will be presented to show that Nefertiti was the daughter or granddaughter of an Israelite called Sheba, whose daughter Bathsheba was married to Uriah, a Hittite, before the biblical King David murdered Uriah and took Bathsheba as wife. Nefertiti would have been either a young daughter of Sheba or a daughter of Bathsheba by Uriah.

7.3 Amenhotep's Magnificent Wild Bull Hunt

As alluded to several times in previous sections, the names Busiris, Bocchoris, Thermuthis, Athyrtis and Merris can all be linked to an episode involving cattle or bulls. Amenhotep was an avid hunter, even as a teenager. Already married to Tiye, in Year 2 of his reign the young Amenhotep one day received news about wild bulls in the desert, which he ordered to be confined and then proceeded to hunt and kill:

> A wonder that befell His Majesty. One came to His Majesty saying, 'There are wild bulls on the desert of the region of Shetep'. His Majesty sailed downstream in the royal bark Kha-em-maat at the time of evening, making good time, arriving in peace at the region of Shetep at the time of morning. His Majesty appeared in his chariot with his whole army [backing] him. One instructed the officers and private soldiers in their entirety and the children of the nursery to keep a watch over these wild bulls. Then His Majesty commanded to be caused that one surround these wild bulls with an enclosure with a ditch, and His Majesty proceeded against all these wild bulls. The number thereof: 170 wild bulls. The number His Majesty took in hunting on this day: 56 wild bulls. His Majesty waited four days, to give rest to his horses. His Majesty appeared in the chariot. The number of bulls he took in hunting: 40 wild bulls. Total of wild bulls: 96.[71]

Although this report seems to describe a perfectly normal hunting trip, the nicknames given to both Amenhotep and Tiye suggest that it was not quite as wonderful as portrayed by the scribe. It would rather appear that the 'wild bulls' he killed were domesticated cattle found abandoned in the hills or having drifted onto his property. This is confirmed by the king instructing children to keep an eye on the 'wild bulls'. The king had the animals driven into an enclosure where he managed to slaughter 96 of them, probably in a fit of rage. He must then have sent his proud young wife home, who announced to all and sundry, 'Ooh ooh, my husband killed 96 wild bulls while hunting in the desert!'

When the truth finally surfaced, it was to the great amusement of the people of Egypt, not to mention its neighbours, hence the string of nicknames. Tiye was obviously not a farm girl and must have mistaken domesticated cattle for wild animals. His scribes would of course never have put their king in a bad light.

That Amenhotep III had indeed been associated with the slaughter of tamed animals is suggested by Apollodorus, who named the son of Busiris as Amphidamas[72]. The latter name can be translated as 'Surrounded by the tamed', from *amphi*[73] (around) and *damazō*[74] (to tame, tame). A variant of the son's name is Iphidamas[75], which should probably be interpreted as (He of the) tamed horses', from *hippōs*[76] (a horse) and *damazō*, an interpretation which most likely derived from tamed bulls. It would appear that the name Amphidamas was mistakenly associated with Amenhotep's son instead of with himself.

7.4 Names of and references to the sacred scribe

Common to virtually all Exodus narratives excluding that of *Exodus* is the role played by the scribe or oracle of the pharaoh. These references are summarised below (see Chapter 3 for references):

- Manetho names the sacred scribe as Amenhotep the son of Papis (Hapu), the clearest and unequivocal identification of the sacred scribe of Amenhotep III.
- Cheremon calls the sacred scribe Phritiphantes. Although the name once again has a Hebrew sound to it, I could not find any meaningful combination of Hebrew words that would be phonetically similar to this name. It may, however, be of Greek origin, as a combination of the words *prēthō*[77] (to blow a flame, to fire or burn) and *pantē*[78] (wholly) or *pantōs*[79] (entirely, at all events), rendering 'Burn all'. This may suggest that this scribe advised Amenhotep to burn all of those who had become infected by the plague, or to burn as sacrifice all the firstborn sons, daughters and animals of the Egyptians.

An entirely different explanation is, however, to be found in Greek mythology, which recorded that one of the sons of Aegyptus was called Phantes[80]. Aegyptus was synonymous with Sesostris, who was often equated with Amenhotep III (see Section 6.2). Phantes would then become the son of Amenhotep III and the name Phritiphantes would mean 'Burn Phantes'. This would have been his instruction to Amenhotep, to burn his firstborn son Prince Tuthmosis.

- Both Lysimachus and Tacitus name Hammon as Bocchoris' oracle. This name is possibly a corruption of the name of the Egyptian god Amon or Amun, of whom Amenhotep the son of Hapu would have been the high priest. It is, however, also possible that the name could be related to the Hebrew word *'âman* (pronounced *[h]aw-man*, to trust or believe)[81], a fitting description of an oracle who was 'trusted' by Amenhotep when he issued his infamous decree of the sacrifice of the firstborn.

- The Koran names the adversaries of Moses as Pharaoh and Haman, without offering any information about the latter. Haman must certainly be related to the Hammon of Bocchoris.

- Justin does not mention a name and only states that Moses was expelled from Egypt 'by some oracular prediction'.

- Both Herodotus and Diodorus state that an oracle (from Buto) advised Pheros how he could be cured of his blindness which had lasted 10 years, matching the advice of Amenhotep the son of Hapu to his king.

- Josephus claims that the sacred scribe had made a violent attempt to kill the infant Moses, matching the priest's advice to Amenhotep that he should kill his son.

- Artapanus does not mention an oracle, but rather the name of the person who was supposed to kill Moses, Chanethothes. This name is readily translated from Hebrew and means '(He who had to) pitch a tent after the miracle of the fire', from *chânâh*[82] (to pitch a tent), *'êth*[83] (after, now), *'ôwth*[84] (a sign, miracle) and *'êsh*[85] (fire). This name suggests that he had been expelled when the sacrifice of the firstborn failed to cure Egypt of the plague that was devastating its population.

As can be expected, the sacrifice of the firstborn failed to appease the gods and the Egyptians continued to die in large numbers. The high priest evidently did not escape the wrath of the Egyptians, but exactly how he met his end is not clear. In year four of his reign Akhenaten sent the high priest of Amun on a quarrying mission (literally 'to fetch basalt for the image of the Lord')[86], while Josephus records that the beloved scribe of Amenophis had killed himself in despair[87]. Phrasius, who suggested the sacrifice of strangers to Busiris, reportedly was the first to be sacrificed. In order to survive, the high priest would have had to pitch a tent in the wilderness, where he may simply have died or even killed himself.

- When Egypt had been suffering a severe drought, famine or scarcity for nine years, Busiris was advised by Phrasius, a learned seer from Cyprus, to sacrifice a stranger to Zeus each year and so avert this punishment by the gods. Busiris is the Latin spelling of the Greek Bousiris, so the name of his oracle is also likely to be of Latin origin. This appears to be the case. *Phrasis* means 'diction' or 'edict' in Latin[88] and the most notorious edict in the history of Egypt would have been the instruction by the king to have all firstborn sacrificed in the fire. Alternatively his name may have been derived from the Greek words *phrassō*[89] (to block up, silence, fence in) or *phraussō*[90] (to snort, make a tumult, rage). The latter would make better sense, as the failed sacrifice of the firstborn children of Egypt was one of the causes of the rebellion.

In conclusion, there can be no question about the involvement of a sacred scribe in the Exodus affair, and his nicknames link him to Amenhotep as well to the sacrifice of the firstborn of Egypt. One can imagine how this scribe would have felt when it transpired that the ultimate sacrifice the Egyptians could bring had no effect whatsoever on their plight. Having once been the most powerful person in Egypt next to the Pharaoh, he suddenly found himself hated by everyone and expelled to live and work among the slaves.

He could very well have taken his own life in the end. The failure of the sacrifice to bring an end to the plague is probably the single most important reason why the Egyptian people turned their back on their traditional gods, specifically Amun. Why they had turned to the sun god Aten instead is hard to tell. It was perhaps a return to the oldest of their gods, the sun god Ra, but in the form of the sun-disc, the Aten (see Chapter 9).

7.5 Amenhotep III in Ethiopia

Of crucial importance in establishing whether Amenhotep III would match the extra-biblical narratives of the Exodus is to determine whether he had conducted any military campaigns into Ethiopia. From rabbinic accounts and those of Josephus and Manetho (see Sections 2.2, 2.3 and 3.1) it would appear that there must have been two campaigns into Ethiopia. The first appears to have been led by Moses, probably with his father at his side. The second would have been the retreat into Ethiopia of Amenhotep and the Egyptian army when they were faced with the combined forces of the slave rebels and the shepherds from Jerusalem. However, Amenhotep III ascended the throne when he was still a child, probably aged between 10 and 12[91], and his first campaign into Ethiopia took place in Year 5 of his reign[92]. If born by that time at all, Moses as Prince Tuthmosis would then have been no more than an infant or toddler, hardly capable of joining his father on a military campaign.

From Egyptian records we know that Amenhotep III had in fact conducted only two military campaigns during his entire reign and both were into Ethiopia[93]. The first, which occurred in of Year 5 of his reign, was led by Amenhotep himself, apparently in order to quell an uprising. The second took place after Year 30 and was led by the viceroy of Kush. This viceroy, whose name was Merymose, was also known as The King's Son of Kush[94], suggesting that he may have been a true son of the king, possibly by a lesser wife, who was put in charge of Ethiopia (Kush).

Josephus claims that Moses was a general who had led a military campaign against the Ethiopians (see Section 2.2), but this is unlikely. As firstborn son of Amenhotep III, Moses (Prince Tuthmosis) would as an adult by default have become the commander of the Egyptian army. It is more likely that with Moses having been general of the Egyptian army for an extended period of time, legend mistakenly attributed the invasion of Ethiopia (Amenhotep's retreat) to him. Amenhotep III and the Egyptian army must have retreated into Ethiopia only when Moses had returned from exile to lead the uprising against his father. Although the second campaign was led by Merymose, it is also possible that his exploits were mistakenly attributed to Prince Tuthmosis, also called Thutmose, because of the phonetic similarity of their names and both of them being sons of Amenhotep III.

The circumstances of the latter invasion are rather obscure, to the extent that some scholars doubt whether there was a second campaign at all. The relatively small number of captives taken has inclined David O'Connor to suspect that only a specific elite group was targeted and effectively taken as hostages[95]. This would make sense if Amenhotep had indeed 'invaded' Ethiopia with the intent of remaining there for a prolonged period of time. Having taken hostage some of the family members of the local leaders would have ensured that they would not contemplate any attempt to drive the Egyptians back to their native country. This prolonged stay in Egypt would also explain Herodotus' strange remark that Sesostris was the only king who had been known as the king who ruled both Egypt and Ethiopia[96].

Against the backdrop of an unprecedented natural disaster having occurred in Egypt, the Ethiopians in all probability saw this as an opportunity to free themselves from Egyptian rule. Their uprising was, however, quickly suppressed by Amenhotep through Merymose, and Amenhotep would have been free to move unhindered into Ethiopia some years later when he was confronted by the rebels. The absence of any Egyptian records of this retreat is readily understood, as such a humiliating event would hardly have been recorded by scribes who were loyal to their king.

Many Egyptian kings had held dominion over Ethiopia during their reigns. Ethiopia, then known as Nubia, only gained independence from Egypt during the upheaval of the First Intermediate Period of Egypt[97]. Future kings such as Senwosret I (1965-1920 BCE[98]) had full control over Lower Nubia up to the Second Cataract of the Nile[99]. Tuthmosis I, the grandfather of Tuthmosis III (the real Sesostris), likewise subjected Nubia to his rule. As discussed, though, some aspects of the Sesostris legend have mistakenly been attributed to Amenhotep III and his prolonged stay in Nubia is another example. Amenhotep III would have been the only Egyptian pharaoh ever to have physically translocated to Nubia. His 10 to 13-year stay in Nubia no doubt earned him Herodus' appellation, that he was the only king who ruled Egypt and Ethiopia.

Amenhotep's prolonged stay in Ethiopia is attested to by scarabs of him found in that country[100], rock carvings at Soleb depicting him as weak and sickly (effectively proving that he was in Ethiopia at the time) and numerous of his monuments being scattered all over the country[101]. The rock carvings at Soleb also show Akhenaten, then still named Amenhotep IV, making an offering to his still-living father, Nebmaatre (a throne name of Amenhotep III), Lord of Nubia[102]. This would imply that Amenhotep III had indeed moved to Ethiopia, leaving his son in charge of Egypt. Soon afterwards Akhenaten would have lost control of Egypt to his brother, Prince Tuthmosis. Amenhotep III may have died in Ethiopia, as his mummy was estimated to have been that of a 50-year-old man. If he became king at the age of 10 or 12 and ruled for 38 years, he would have been around 50 when he died, in other words soon after entering Ethiopia. This is, however, unlikely, as the numerous temples and monuments erected by him suggest that he must have lived in Ethiopia for a number of years, possibly the entire 10 to 13 years as recorded by Manetho. If so, he would have been in his early sixties when he died.

Irrespective of where he died, one must ask why the Ethiopians had all of a sudden become obsessed with Amenhotep as attested to by all the monuments erected in his honour and his title 'Lord of Nubia'. The only logical explanation is that one of the mightiest kings of ancient Egypt had moved to Ethiopia, exactly as claimed by Manetho.

7.6 Make love, not war

Due to the military successes of his predecessors, Amenhotep III could enjoy a life of peace and prosperity. In many respects the Egyptian empire was at its zenith with all its enemies subdued and, apart from the two minor military operations into Ethiopia, Amenhotep had no wars to fight and no new enemies to conquer. This aspect of his reign must have been well known among Egypt's neighbours and he must have been known as the pharaoh who fought no wars (Herodotus' Pheros).

In order to establish another link between Amenhotep and Busiris, it is instructive to look into Amenhotep's life of luxury before disaster struck Egypt. Diodorus records a peculiar story about Busiris:

> And since these Atlantides excelled in beauty and chastity, Busiris the king of the Egyptians, the account says, was seized with the desire to get the maidens into his power; and conse-quently he dispatched pirates by sea with orders to seize the girls and deliver them into his hands.[103]

This passage suggests that Busiris must have had a particular taste for young women, if he had to go to such lengths to have them captured. Can the same be said of Amenhotep III? Despite being married to Tiye, Amenhotep sent numerous requests to his foreign subjects for young women to be sent to him. For example:

> To Milkilu, the ruler of Gazru: Thus the king … Send extremely beautiful female cupbearers in whom there is no defect…[104],

and the reproach of Kadasman-Enlil I, the king of Babylon, when he dared ask Amenhotep for an Egyptian princess as wife, but was refused:

> You are a king, you do as you please ... [Someone's] grown daughters, beautiful women, must be available...[105].

These examples clearly demonstrate what Amenhotep expected from the kings of conquered nations. There were numerous foreign princesses in his harem, including Gilukhepa, the daughter of the Mittanian king Shuttarna II, who was presented to Amenhotep along with 317 handmaidens. Shuttarna was succeeded by Tushratta who likewise sent his daughter Tadukhepa to Amenhotep, along with 270 women. Some of the women in his harem had names which seem to match their specific sexual skills, including an 'excessive sexual zeal' lady (Tawosret) and a woman who appears to have indulged in sadomasochism (Sati, 'Miss Whiplash')[106]. It would seem that the sexual endeavours of the mightiest man in the world at that time enjoyed as much attention in his own country and in international circles as it would today.

Given his multiple partners, it is to be expected that Amenhotep III would have fathered many children. This aspect of his life was indeed preserved in legend, namely as the 50 sons of Aegyptus[107], who, as stated earlier, can be equated to Sesostris and therefore to Amenhotep III. It would appear that the number 50 simply implies 'many'.

8

Prince Tuthmosis, the prince who disappeared

Of all the ancient biblical characters, Moses is arguably the most important to identify. Failure to do so may be judged by some as evidence that the Exodus never happened. A positive identification will place the emergence of the Israelites as a people in a specific timeframe under verifiable circumstances.

Given Manetho's now verified claim that the Pharaoh of the Exodus (the Oppression) was Amenhotep III, one must look for a suitable candidate for the biblical Moses. This line of investigation of my research into the Exodus events was prompted by Graham Phillips' identification of Moses as Crown Prince Tuthmosis, the firstborn son of Amenhotep III[1]. Phillips argues that an eruption of Thera caused the biblical plagues of Egypt and that Amenhotep III responded to the ensuing plague in Egypt by erecting hundreds of statues to Sekhmet, the goddess of destruction, evidently in order to appease her. He initially identified Prince Tuthmosis as the only known historical figure who would fit the profile of Moses having been raised as a royal prince, but vanishing under mysterious circumstances (Moses' flight from Egypt). Phillips later revised his theory[2], suggesting that the biblical Moses may have been inspired by two historical persons, a Hebrew priest called Kamose who inspired the Israelites with a new religion, and Prince Tuthmosis who led them out of slavery. It will be shown, however, that there was only one Moses, and that he was indeed Tuthmosis as originally argued by Phillips.

8.1 The birth of Moses

The biblical version of the birth of Moses is highly suspect. It goes without saying that the greatest figure in Israelite history would have had to be of Hebrew and not Egyptian descent. For Prince Tuthmosis, their former oppressor, to be accepted as the new leader of the Israelites, a suitably adapted version of his birth would have been made up, either at the time of the Exodus or by later scribes. If Yuya was indeed the biblical Joseph, Tuthmosis would have been of partial Hebrew descent, but his all-important paternal line of descent would have been Egyptian. There can be little doubt that the narrative in *Exodus* of Moses' birth to a Hebrew woman and his concealment in a waterproofed basket among the reeds of the Nile[3] was based on the following much older legend about the birth of the Babylonian king Sargon (2270-2215 BCE):

> Sargon, the mighty king, king of Agade, am I. My mother was lowly, my father I knew not. And the brother of my father dwells in the mountain. My city is Azuripanu, which lies on the bank of the Euphrates. My lowly mother conceived me, in secret she brought me forth. She set me in a basket of rushes, with bitumen she closed my door. She cast me into the river, which rose not over me. The river bore me up, unto Akki, the irrigator, it carried me. Akki, the irrigator, with ... lifted me out. Akki, the irrigator, as his own son ... reared me, Akki, the irrigator, as his gardener appointed me. While I was a gardener, the goddess Ishtar loved me, And for ... four years I ruled the kingdom. The black-headed peoples I ruled, I governed.[4]

8.2 Crown Prince Tuthmosis, son of Amenhotep III

In the preceding discussions several other direct or indirect references have been made to Prince Tuthmosis being the biblical Moses. These are summarised below:

- The claims by Justin that Moses was the son of Joseph, and by Cheremon that they were contemporaries, combined with the assumption that Yuya and Joseph were one and the same person (see Chapter 3), leave only Prince Tuthmosis as a possible candidate for Moses.

- The name Moses is very likely an abbreviated version of either (Tuth)mosis or (Thut)mose, the name of the firstborn son of Amenhotep III.

- According to the Koran, Moses was not simply one of the many sons of the Pharaoh, but the one who used to ride in the carriage of the Pharaoh and dress like the Pharaoh, so that he was called 'the son of Pharaoh' by the people[5]. In other words, he was the most cherished of all the sons, the firstborn son of the Pharaoh.

- Moses' so-called stutter or speech impediment must be interpreted as him not being able to speak Hebrew. He would have been raised as a true Egyptian who would have had no need to master the language of the slaves. His only means of communicating with the freed Israelites was through his priests, specifically Aaron[6]. When Joshua took over the leadership from Moses, Moses begged for his life to be spared. Joshua then 'delivered a speech of which Moses understood nothing'[7], or in other words, Joshua spoke to the Israelites in Hebrew, which Moses did not understand. After this speech Moses died, which one may interpret as Joshua publically usurping the leadership and ordering the ousted Moses to be killed.

- The strongest link between Moses and Tuthmosis may very well be the fact that both of them are associated with the first burial of the Apis bull (see Section 7.1).

- According to Manetho, after having fled to Ethiopia:

> Amenophis returned back from Ethiopia with a great army, as did his son Rhampses with another army also, and that both of them joined battle with the shepherds and the polluted people, and beat them, and killed a great many of them, and pursued them to the bounds of Syria.[8]

and (my comment in brackets):

> Amenophis' son had three hundred thousand men with him, and met them [the shepherds from Jerusalem] at Pelusium....[9]

Cheremon essentially records the same information:

> ...that Amenophis could not sustain their attacks, but fled into Ethiopia, and left his wife with child behind him, who lay concealed in certain caverns, and there brought forth a son, whose name was Messene, and who, when he was grown up to man's estate, pursued the Jews into Syria, being about two hundred thousand, and then received his father Amenophis out of Ethiopia.[10]

One can safely assume that under normal circumstances Egypt would have had only one army, which would have been commanded by the Pharaoh and later by his son. It is clear that Manetho slightly misinterpreted the actual events, namely that it was this very son of Amenhotep who commanded the armies of the shepherds and polluted people (the king's son was the priest Osarsiph whom Manetho names as the leader of those armies). Only the Egyptian army 'pursued' them, while the shepherds from Jerusalem merely retreated to Canaan. Moses' army of slaves and exiled Egyptians invaded Canaan years later. The mysterious son called Messene must be either Rhampses, elsewhere called Ramesses (see Section 3.1), or Akhenaten himself (see Chapter 10), although he did not partake in any action against the shepherds and the 'polluted people'. The reference to his mother hiding in certain caverns or caves can only be a distortion of the fact that this son had gone into hiding, as did Moses.

- According to Manetho, Osarsiph sent a delegation to the shepherds in Jerusalem, asking them for assistance against Amenhotep[11]. In the *El Arish Shrine Text* (see Section 8.4) it is stated that the person who sent those messengers was Geb, the son of King Shu, who is readily identifiable as Amenhotep III.

- Prince Thutmose served as the high priest of Ptah (in ancient Memphis)[12,13], while Manetho's Osarsiph, likewise, was a priest[14], albeit from Heliopolis. Geb of the *El Arish Shrine Text* 'went not to Heliopolis', thereby also linking Geb as Tuthmosis to Heliopolis.

8.3 Moses who was called Osarsiph

According to Manetho, Moses was originally called Osarsiph. The Egyptian name of Moses was Tuthmosis, leading one to suspect that the name Osarsiph might have been a Hebrew name for Moses. Constructed as *Os-ar-siph*, it would mean 'Assemble yourselves to destroy the enemy', from *'ûwsh*[15] (hasten, assemble yourselves), *'âr*[16] (a foe, enemy) and *sûwph*[17] (snatch away, terminate). This was exactly the instruction Moses gave to the slaves who revolted against Amenhotep and they subsequently got themselves together in Avaris.

Moses had also been given the Egyptian name Tisithen[18]. If true, one should look for a phonetically similar Egyptian word, or view the name as the Hebrew equivalent of an Egyptian name with the same meaning. Pursuing the latter route, as with Joseph's name Peteseph (see Section 5.7), a probable interpretation of the name is 'Did he not hasten (cause) the tumult?', from *tûws*[19] (pounce, haste), *shêth*[20] (a tumult) and *'îyn*[21] (is it not?). The tumult this appellation may refer to would be either the Egyptians bewailing the death of their firstborn offspring, or the rebellion instigated by Moses.

8.4 Corroboration by the text of the El Arish Shrine

The Exodus events as captured in the annals of several ancient historians and discussed above may appear to have no matching first-hand Egyptian accounts as corroboration, in other words there appear to be no original papyri or inscriptions that would support their records. This is, however, not the case. During the 1860s a traveller noticed a black granite shrine (naos) inscribed with hiero-glyphs in the Egyptian town El Arish. The shrine was being used as a cattle trough by local inhabitants. The first translation of the text was made by F.L. Griffith in 1890, in English, followed by a French translation by George Goyon in 1936[22]. Griffith's English translation is given in Appendix B.

Immanuel Velikovsky studied these translations and came to the conclusion that the text describes various aspects of the biblical Exodus event. Most notably, he observed that the biblical plague of darkness was mentioned in the *El Arish Shrine Text*, as well as the supposed drowning of the Pharaoh in the sea. He based this conclusion on the passage that describes King Shu jumping into a whirlpool. In his opinion this meant that he had drowned. Velikovsky's work, which encompassed much more than just his interpretation of the *El Arish Shrine Text*, sparked a flurry of academic debates and publications, including 10 special issues of the Pensée magazine[23], and the Kronos Journal (1975-1988), evidently founded in order to deal with Velikovsky's work[24].

In this section I will show that the *El Arish Shrine Text* can be associated with the Exodus in the context described by Manetho and others, although not necessarily as interpreted by Velikovsky. It will be shown that King Shu of this text refers to Amenhotep III, his son Geb to Prince Tuthmosis and Queen Tefnut to Nefertiti. The text also refers to what must be Moses' staff and the Ark of the Covenant, and offers an explanation for Moses' 'horns'.

The key arguments can be summarised as follows, with text in Appendix B quoted directly when required for clarity:

- The text begins with King Shu and his court relocating from Memphis to a place called At Nebes (Yat Nebes). Amenhotep

III is known have broken from tradition by moving his court from Memphis to Thebes[25]. Khaftet-hir-Nebes, the goddess of western Thebes, was associated with Tuthmosis III who named Khaftet-hir-Nebes as the 'favourite place of my father from the beginning'[26]. The Egyptian word *At* means 'father'[27], while *Ha-t*, if not merely a mispronunciation of *At*, means 'tomb' or 'grave'[28]. *At Nebes* would then simply mean 'Father's Nebes'. Tuthmosis III lost his father at a very young age and he must have called this place 'Dad's Nebes', an endearing name which was preserved in the Egyptian society of that period for decades. Tuthmosis III grew up to become arguably the greatest pharaoh in Egyptian history and tales and legends about him would have abounded. Goyon[29] interpreted *Yat* as 'hill' (he appears to have used the word a[30] (hill, top) which would render the translation 'Hill of Nebes'. What significance this name might have had is not clear.

- The palace of Shu faced east, implying that it was built on the west bank of the 'canal', the Nile. The palace of Amenhotep III was constructed on the site known as Malqata[31] on the west bank of the Nile, facing east.

- King Shu dug a sacred lake measuring 190 cubits by 110 cubits at At Nebes. In Year 11 of his reign, Amenhotep ordered an artificial lake measuring 3,700 by 700 cubits to be dug at Thebes for his wife Tiy, where they sailed on their imperial barge named 'The Aton Gleams' or alternatively 'The Dazzling Sun Disc'[32]. The difference in size may be attributed to confusion by the author of the shrine text as to which sacred lake was being referred to. There are at least two sacred lakes in the Karnak temple complex on the east side of the Nile[33], namely the sacred lake in the precinct of Amun-Ra ('in at Nebes is a pool ...' ?) and another in the precinct of Mut ('Another pool is mentioned...' ?). The former lake is rectangular and approximately 136m by 86m in size, with a length to width ratio of about 1.6. An Egyptian cubit is equal to about 0.523m[34], so King Shu's lake was about 99m by 58m. The length to width ratio is 1.7, which is approximately the same as that of the Amun-Ra sacred lake. This size is much smaller than the lake of Amenhotep III and Tiye, but the construction for Amenhotep's pleasure of an enormous lake (1.94 km by 0.37 km) must have prompted the author to refer to the event.

- Egypt was invaded by the 'children of Apep' and the 'evil-doers' from the 'red country'. King Shu fortified Hat Nebes and the surrounding areas, but the next time we hear of him, he and his attendants had 'departed to heaven' following an evil that fell on his land and a great disturbance in the palace. This account must be read in conjunction with his son Seb (Geb) 'having sent messengers to summon to him the foreigners and Asiatics from their land'. As related by Manetho, Moses (Osarsiph) sent messengers to the 'shepherds' in Jerusalem to join him in a struggle against Amenhotep. The mention of two distinct groups correlates with Manetho's two groups, the Hyksos slaves and the people from Jerusalem. The 'children of Apep' must refer to the Hyksos, who had a king called Apepi[35]. Manetho records that a large number of the Hyksos were trapped by Ahmose at Avaris[36] and were allowed to escape to Canaan where they founded Jerusalem. This group of the Hyksos would therefore have been 'children of Apep'. The red land refers to the deserts of Egypt and appears to be the place into which the plague-infected Hyksos slaves were driven by Amenophis[37], from where they were called into rebellion by Osarsiph. Amenhotep intended to confront the combined forces of Osarsiph and the shepherds from Jerusalem, but decided against it and retreated into Nubia with his own (the Egyptian) army. To the Egyptians remaining in Egypt this king and his court would seem to have vanished overnight ('departed to heaven'), matching the biblical account that the Pharaoh and his entire army were killed, supposedly by the walls of water of the parted sea having collapsed onto them.

- Before he 'departed to heaven', Shu had become sick and 'confusion seized his eyes'. This is reminiscent of Herodotus' account of Pheros, the son of Sesostris[38], in which Pheros is described as a king who had fought no wars (see Section 3.7) and who became blind after having hurled his spear into the raging Nile. In both accounts, Shu and Pheros having become blind should probably be interpreted figuratively rather than literally. Perhaps 'lost his mind' would be a better translation. The incident must certainly refer to the unsuccessful sacrifice of the firstborn offspring of Egypt. As discussed in Section 7.1, the name Pheros may be interpreted as 'He who had to bear', an apt description of Amenhotep III.

- The 'nine days of violence and tempest' in which no man could see the face of another corresponds to the three days of darkness (the ninth plague) in Egypt. No natural cataclysm other than a volcanic eruption can block out the sun to the extent described in *Exodus* and the *El Arish Shrine Text*.

- Seb (Geb), who effectively took charge of Egypt following his father Shu's disappearance 'went not to Heliopolis'. According to Manetho, Moses (Osarsiph) was a priest from Heliopolis who conducted a successful campaign against Amenhotep (III), who then fled to Nubia (disappeared from Egypt). The statement 'went not to Heliopolis' should probably have been translated 'did not return to Heliopolis'.

- Tefnut, who was enthroned in Memphis, must be Nefertiti, who ruled as Smenkhkare following the death of Akhenaten (see Section 13.3). Seb met her and 'seized her by force' in a place called Pekharti, which Velikovsky argues to be the biblical Pihahiroth[39], the place where the Egyptian chariot division was encamped before its destruction by the collapsing walls of water[40]. If true, this prominent place provides another link between the *El Arish Shrine Text* and the Exodus. According to Manetho it was not Seb but Armais (Ay) who 'used violence to the queen'[41]. The Koran confirms that she was killed by the Pharaoh[42] (see Section 2.4), a position and title Prince Tuthmosis (Seb) never held.

- Seb was briefed by his servants (priests) about the ancient history of Egypt, going back as far as the time of the god Ra and the conflicts of a king called Tum (Toum). This name most likely corresponds to Manetho's Timaus[43], also named Tutimaeus and Timaios[44], during whose reign the Hyksos invaded Egypt. This pharaoh must have been one of the minor kings of the Fourteenth Dynasty. This links the *El Arish Shrine Text* to the era of the Hyksos in Egypt.

- Seb desired to put the uraeus on his head, 'stretched forth his hand' and 'the snake came forth'. One of the miracles Moses performed before the Pharaoh was to cast his staff onto the ground, upon which it turned into a snake[45]. He then 'put forth his hand' and took hold of the snake by its tail, whereupon it returned to its former shape. Whatever the background of these tales might have been, something must have happened to cause the public to remember an incident involving Seb (Moses) reaching for a serpent. This incident must be interpreted as Seb reaching for the throne of Egypt, which was symbolized by the uraeus[46]. The uraeus, as shown on the crown of Amenhotep III in Figure 8.1, was a symbol of divine authority in ancient Egypt. It was also the symbol of the goddess Wadjet[47], whose cult was based in Per-Wadjet, called Buto by the Greeks[48]. Herodotus mentions that Buto was the place of the Egyptian oracle[49] and it was this very oracle who advised Pheros what he should do to be healed[50].

- When Seb reached for the snake, it 'breathed its vapour upon him', causing him to burn (with venom) while all of those around him died. This passage can be linked to the sacrifice of the firstborn, by fire, as discussed in Section 17.3. It is actually stating that when Seb was about to ascend to the throne, the throne (his father) attempted to burn him (the biblical

Figure 8.1. The snake symbol of the uraeus symbolising kingship on the crown of Amenhotep III.[51]

Pharaoh who wanted to kill Moses). All other firstborn offspring died in the fire, but Moses (Seb) managed to escape.

- The *El Arish Shrine Text* mentions a mysterious box of hard stone or metal which healed Seb. This can be linked to the equally mysterious Ark of the Covenant, which was covered with gold and had supernatural powers[52,53]. Years passed before this box was taken back to At Nebes and thrown in the great lake of the Per Aart (meaning 'House of the Serpent')[54,55], matching the years that passed between Moses' escape from Egypt and his eventual return to confront the Pharaoh.

- Seb fought with evil-doers in a pool (a great lake) called the Place of the Whirlpool. These evil-doers could not defeat Seb, but he nevertheless had to jump into this pool, evidently to gain divine powers, before he could defeat them. Griffith was not sure of his interpretation of the name of this place and it was translated differently as *Yat Desoui*, 'the hill of the two knives', by Goyon. The 'knives' may refer to the two obelisks mentioned by Herodotus and it must be noted that obelisks may have been moved to other locations without record of their original site. Shu had by then 'departed into heaven' with his attendants.

If At Nebes was indeed Thebes, one should look for a pool that may have been known by that name in ancient times. The Mut temple complex is surrounded by a sacred lake called Isheru[56], a name which seems to be referred to in the *El Arish Shrine Text* as Usheru. Here it is associated with Apep, the evil Serpent. This lake may very well have been known as the Serpent Lake in ancient times (the lake of Per Aart).

According to Manetho (see Section 3.1), Osarsiph led a combined force of 'polluted' Hyksos slaves and Egyptians and the shepherds from Jerusalem against Amenhotep, while Africanus unequivocally states that a portion of the Egyptian army was expelled from Egypt and settled in Canaan (see Section 3.5). Both Manetho and Cheremon refer to the son of Amenhotep remaining in Egypt with his own army before welcoming his father from Ethiopia[57]. This matches Shu who fought the 'evil-doers', who did not prevail against him (Seb?) but were smitten when Seb reappeared with a headdress with horns. Seb eventually gained control of Egypt ('he smote the evildoers ... Now the majesty of Seb appeared in the seat of the crocodile gods'), matching Manetho's account in which Osarsiph and his rebels ravaged Egypt for 13 years.

Incidentally, that Moses was commanding a rebel army and not merely a pious group of liberated slaves is confirmed by Josephus' illogical explanation for why the Israelites were in possession of the arms of the Egyptian army, namely that those weapons had been washed to their camp by the sea current[58]. Seb (Moses) was therefore involved in a full-scale war within the borders of Egypt.

When the Egyptian army eventually returned from Ethiopia, the Hyksos and that part of the Egyptian army under the control of Prince Tuthmosis left the country. This action was interpreted by later Egyptian historians as the Egyptian army pursuing the Jews into Syria. They must have rejected the notion that a part of their famous army could have turned against their own king, in defence of the enemy. The son who welcomed back his father could not have been Akhenaten, as he had already been killed by that time (see Chapter 9).

- The *El Arish Shrine Text* specifically mentions the Asiatics carrying the sceptre of Seb, which they called Degai. This matches Moses' fabled rod or staff, which features as an instrument of magic throughout the Exodus narrative. Shu's staff is also mentioned. The name Degai does not appear to be of Egyptian origin, so it could be of Asiatic (Hebrew) origin. A possible interpretation may be derived from the Hebrew words *dâgâh*[59] (fish) or *dîyg*[60] (to fish, fish) and *'îy*[61] (a ruin, a heap), meaning 'Heap of fish'. Since this name is associated with the staff of Geb (Tuthmosis, Moses), it may refer to the 'miracle' supposedly performed by Moses, the turning into blood of the river Nile and all sources of water in Egypt (see Sections 15.1 and 17.2). The Egyptians would no doubt have scooped up the dead fish in the rivers and lakes poisoned by the ash from Thera in an attempt to purify the water. One can imagine heaps of decaying fish along the length of the Nile and in the flooded areas giving rise to an awful stench[62]. It would appear that the rumour of Moses' magical staff had spread not only among the Hebrews, but also among the Egyptians.

- In the Exodus narrative Moses ascends Mount Sinai, remains there for 40 days and eventually returns with two tablets containing the Ten Commandments[63,64]. Curiously, biblical legend records that his face was 'horned' when he returned[65]. The 'Horns of Moses' has remained a topic of speculation ever since scholars began to question the Bible and modern translations prefer to use the word 'shine' instead of 'horned', from the Hebrew word *qâran*[66,] which in the figurative sense means to shoot out rays or to shine. In reality neither interpretation would be physically possible. The most plausible origin of this obscure text is to be found in the *El Arish Shrine Text*, in which it is stated that Seb's head became that of a hawk with the horns of a bull upon it. The Egyptian god Horus was usually shown with a hawk's head and the cow goddess Hathor wearing a headdress of two horns embracing the sun, as shown in Figure 8.2.

Figure 8.2. The hawk-headed Horus[67] and Hathor with a horned headdress[68]

It is therefore clear that *the El Arish Shrine Text* should not be interpreted literally, but rather that it meant Seb had attained divine blessing or powers. For reasons to be discussed next, the horns of Hathor can be linked to Moses.

Although the location of Mount Sinai is generally accepted to be near Saint Catherine City in the Sinai Peninsula of Egypt[69], other locations have also been suggested. The most likely of all locations is the archaeological site of Serabit el-Khadim, famous for its turquoise mines, but more significantly for the Hathor Temple Complex on top of the mountain[70]. According to the biblical narrative Moses went up Mount Sinai and remained there for 40 days and nights, evidently without food and water[71]. No human being can survive that long without food and water and, if there is any truth in this legend, Moses must have received sustenance from this temple.

Returning to the link between Moses and the horns of a bull, there can be no doubt that Moses did not meet with God atop Mount Sinai, but with priests who were loyal to him. When he eventually returned from the mountain, he would have been wearing a crown of Hathor on his head, which in legend became the 'horns' on his head.

- Finally, one should ask why the author would have referred to the characters in the *El Arish Shrine Text* by the names of ancient gods. From specific events such as the move of the palace from Memphis to Thebes (At Nebes), the construction there of an artificial lake, the invasion by the children of Apep, the Asiatics carrying around the staff of Geb, Geb sending messengers to foreigners, summoning them to him, and the nine days of utter darkness, etc., there can be no doubt that this narrative relates to actual events and people. Why then these use the names of gods instead of official throne names?

In ancient Egyptian mythology the gods Shu and Tefnut were born to the sun god Re and they in turn had twins called Geb and Nut[72]. During the latter part of the reign of Amenhotep III, but more specifically during the reign of his son Amenhotep IV (Akhenaten), the Aten became the sole god of Egypt (see Chapter 9). In a hymn to the god Ra[73] (see Appendix C), two of Amenhotep III's 'directors of the works of Amun' praise Ra and also the Disc (Aten) of the Day. The Aten was seen as the 'throne' or 'place' of the sun god Re during the New Kingdom, but later became a direct manifestation of Re[74]. It is therefore very likely that the new sun god was initially called Re by the common people instead of by his relatively unknown name, the Aten.

Without exception the rulers of the Eighteenth Dynasty termed themselves offspring of the gods[75] and as son of Re, Amenhotep III would have been known as Shu and his son as Geb. Due to the chaos and confusion that characterised the Amarna period, it would seem that Tefnut was mistakenly remembered as having been the wife of Shu, instead of being his daughter (strictly speaking, Tefnut as Nefertiti was his daughter-in-law). There can be no doubt that the deeds attributed to Shu and Geb in the *El Arish Shrine Text* were recorded after the Amarna period. This shrine, also called the Phakussa (Faqus) shrine, is in fact dated to the Ptolemaic Period[76], which ran from 332-30 BCE[77].

Probably the clearest indication that Shu was linked to the Amarna era comes from Akhenaten's *Great Hymn to the Aten* (see Appendix D), of which the opening stanza reads:

> Praise of Re Har-akhti, rejoicing on the Horizon, **in his name as Shu who is in the Aton-disc**, living forever and ever; the living great Aton ... (and praise of) the King of Upper and Lower Egypt, who lives on truth, the Lord of the Two Lands: Nefer-kheperu-Re Wa-en-Re; the Son of Re, who lives on truth, the Lord of Diadems: Akh-en-Aton ...[78]

Re-Harakthi is an alias of Re and simply means 'Re [is] Horus of the Horizon'[79]. Akhenaten therefore viewed Shu and Re as the same god instead of Shu as the son of Re. An Aten cult in Heliopolis in fact taught that Re was 'Shu in his Aten'[80]. In the hymn Akhenaten calls himself the son of Re and thus also the son of Shu. With Shu of the *El Arish Shrine Text* identified as Amenhotep III, Akhenaten would indeed have been a son of Shu (that is, besides the king's firstborn son, Geb). A whip-stock knob of blue faience, inscribed with the names of Akhenaten and Nefertiti and decorated with representations of the royal couple as Shu and Tefnut, confirms that Nefertiti was equated with Tefnut[81]. Shu therefore appears to have been identified with both Amenhotep III and his son Akhenaten, possibly due to their co-regency of several years when Amenhotep III was stationed in Ethiopia.

All in all there can be little doubt the *El Arish Shrine Text* was based on the same events recorded by Manetho as pertaining to the Exodus of the Israelites from Egypt. As a final note on the traitorous actions of Prince Tuthmosis, Akhenaten was described as the 'real son' of the king[82], which suggests that another son was not. The son who was deemed not to be a true son of Amenhotep III could only have been Prince Tuthmosis.

Akhenaten and his religious revolution

Akhenaten is widely known as the heretic pharaoh of Egypt who abandoned the traditional religious beliefs of his country in favour of the worship of the Aten, the sun disc[1,2]. Scholars view him as possibly the first monotheist due to the nature of his relationship with his god, the Aten. Following his reign, he was dubbed a 'the criminal' and 'the enemy' by the Egyptians and every attempt was later made to eliminate him and the Amarna era as a whole from Egyptian history[3].

Akhenaten was born to Amenhotep III and queen Tiye and was initially known as Amenhotep IV. He ruled as king from *ca.* 1353 – 1336 BCE[4] and changed his name to Akhenaten, meaning 'Effective for the Aten', before the fifth year of his reign[5]. Akhenaten decided to move the capital of Egypt from Thebes to a new city dedicated to the Aten, which he would call Akhet-Aten (usually spelled Akhetaten), meaning 'The Horizon of the Aten'. He selected the site for this city at what is today known as el-Amarna or simply Amarna, and paid his first formal visit to the construction site towards the end of Year 5 of his reign[6]. The royal family and the Egyptian court moved to Akhetaten three years later when construction was completed.

The Aten was not a new god in the Egypt but had been recognised as a god from the Middle Kingdom onwards[7] and began to rise to prominence during the reign of Tuthmosis IV (Menkheperure), the father of Amenhotep III. This is attested to by an inscription on a scarab that recorded the princes of Mitanni, known as Naharin to the ancient Egyptians[8], bringing gifts to the pharaoh:

The princes of Naharin bearing their gifts behold Men-kheperu-

Re as he comes forth from (?) his palace, they hear his voice like (that of) **the son of Nut**, his bow in his hand like the son of **the successor of Shu**. If he arouses himself to fight, **with Aten before him**, he destroys the mountains, trampling down the foreign lands, treading unto Naharin and unto Karoy, in order to bring the inhabitants of foreign lands like **subjects to the rule of** (?) **Aten for ever.**[9]

The Aten's ascent accelerated during the reign of his son, Amenhotep III, and wholesale conversion to the new religion was introduced by Akhenaten[10]. It is widely accepted that Akhenaten later began to shut down temples all over Egypt, specifically those belonging to Amun (see Section 10.2 for a different interpretation). Akhenaten had effectively declared that there was no god but the Aten, and that Akhenaten was his prophet[11].

Note should be taken that the gods Shu, Geb and Nut had already begun to feature alongside the Aten in the time of Tuthmosis IV. In the *El Arish Shrine Text* the names of the gods Shu and Geb were used as aliases for Amenhotep III and his son Prince Tuthmosis (see Section 8.4). It would appear that Tuthmosis IV had more or less associated himself with the sun god Re, and specifically in his form as the Aten.

9.1 Akhenaten and Moses

Numerous scholars have noticed the similarities between the monotheism of Akhenaten and of Moses. One of the first to do so was Sigmund Freud, who in his book *Moses and Monotheism* argued that Moses was a distinguished Egyptian who may have been a prince, priest or high official[12]. The link between Atenism and Moses was taken one step further by Osman, who argued that Moses was none other than Akhenaten himself[13]. It has already been shown that Moses was Crown Prince Tuthmosis, the firstborn son of Amenhotep III, but the role of his brother Akhenaten has to be investigated.

According to *Exodus*, Moses repeatedly confronted the Pharaoh, who following each plague would initially agree to let the Israelites leave Egypt, but then changed his mind. At first glance one could argue that Moses returned to Egypt to confront his father, Amenhotep III, to convince him that all those evils had befallen Egypt because they had enslaved the Hebrews. *Exodus* and the account of the Exodus by Josephus both state that Moses only returned to Egypt when all of those who had sought his death, including the Pharaoh in whose household he grew up, had died[14,15]. That pharaoh would have been Amenhotep III, and the Pharaoh whom Moses confronted would have been Akhenaten.

The biblical narrative of a powerful king being confronted by his adopted son does not make sense if one takes into account that no miracles had actually been performed by either Moses or the priests of the Pharaoh. The adopted son would have had no authority to confront his all-powerful father. On the other hand, if Prince Tuthmosis returned to confront his younger and weaker brother about the fate of Egypt, one can imagine the authority with which he would have approached Akhenaten. There cannot be any doubt that the Egyptians must have searched their souls for reasons why the gods were punishing them so severely. Assuming that Yuya was of Hebrew origin, both Prince Tuthmosis and Akhenaten would have been affiliated with the Hebrew slaves and they may have argued that the enslavement of the Hebrews had caused Isis' anger at Amenophis (for the destruction of her temples)[16]. Moses (as Prince Tuthmosis) appears to have become convinced that this was the greatest sin of the Egyptians, and most likely went to see his brother (and possibly his father) about this issue. However, in the end he had to resort to an outright uprising against his father, sending messengers to Jerusalem to ask for their assistance.

9.2 The cause of Egypt's rejection of Amun

Akhenaten is invariably credited for the religious revolution Egypt experienced during the Amarna period, but a question that remains unanswered is why this revolution had taken place at all. Graham

Phillips, for instance, remarked that the reason why Akhenaten opted to establish Atenism as the state religion of Egypt 'is something of an enigma'[17]. Before the Amarna revolution the dominant god in Egypt was Amun, to whom the victory over the Hyksos was attributed. As Amun-Re he held absolute supremacy over Egypt and was considered to be the ruler of Egypt through the pharaoh[18]. For the entire Egyptian nation to so readily have turned away from Amun to follow Akhenaten and his sun god, the Aten, something drastic must have happened.

A possible reason for the rejection of Amun may have been that the Egyptians could not understand why their god was punishing them so severely with the plagues, but this is unlikely. It is human nature to humble oneself before one's god and accept his punishment, rather than to reject that god. The only reason why an entire nation would have reacted so spontaneously would have been that Amun through his priests had revealed himself to be a fake. When the Egyptians had made the ultimate sacrifice, the sacrifice of their firstborn to a god, they certainly expected the plague to disappear, possibly even overnight. The sacrifice could not and, of course, did not change anything and the plague continued to devastate the Egyptian population. The Amun priesthood was banished and Egypt followed Akhenaten in his dedication the sun god, the Aten.

The historian Apion associated this revolution with none other than Moses himself, who had directed his prayers and, as a priest, also the prayers of the nation, towards the sun (the Aten). Josephus records that Apion wrote:

I have heard of the ancient men of Egypt, that Moses was of Heliopolis, and that he thought himself obliged to follow the customs of his forefathers, and offered his prayers in the open air, towards the city walls; but that he reduced them all to be directed towards sun-rising, which was agreeable to the situation of Heliopolis.[19]

It then comes as no surprise that many of the Egyptian beliefs of that time had spilled over into the religion Moses would impose on the Hebrews.

9.3 Egyptian beliefs, the Aten and Jehovah

It has long been recognised that numerous biblical narratives have counterparts in other religions and languages. To begin with, the laws given by Moses to the Israelites bear a marked resemblance to those of Hammurabi, a Babylonian king who dates to *ca.* 1848-1806 BCE or 1728-1686 BCE[20], several centuries before the Hebrew Exodus from Egypt. On the famous Code of Hammurabi stele[21], the upper part of which is shown in Figure 9.1, King Hammurabi, with his right hand reverently upraised, salutes the sun god Shamash. Shamash, seated on his throne at the summit of E-sagila, presents to Hammurabi the stylus with which to inscribe the legal code.

Figure 9.1. Hammurabi receives his Code of Laws from the sun god Shamash[22]

Similarities between Hammurabi's Code of Laws and those introduced by Moses, for example, include 'If a son struck his father, they shall cut off his hand'[23], compared to Moses' law 'Whoever strikes his father or his mother shall be put to death.'[24] Similarly, Hammurabi's code 'If a [man] has stolen the young son of another [man], he shall be put to death'[25] conveys the same principle as Moses' law 'Whoever steals a man and sells him, and anyone found in possession of him, shall be put to death.'[26]

Given the background of the origins of Moses, it is to be expected that many of his concepts of right and wrong would have been based on Egyptian beliefs. In the Egyptian *Book of the Dead*, which predates Menes, the first historical king of Egypt[27], we find the so-called *Negative Confessions* (NC), three versions of which will be quoted from, namely from the *Papyrus of Ani* (NCA), the *Papyrus of Nu* (NCU) and the *Papyrus of Nebseni* (NCE)[28]. These have much in common with the Mosaic Ten Commandments[29,30] as shown below with my comments in brackets:

The Ten Commandments and the Negative Confessions

1. I am the Lord, your God, who brought you out of Egypt out of the land of slavery (the mandatory introduction). **You shall have no other gods before me** (reject all your Egyptian gods).

2. You shall not make for yourself an idol in the form of anything ... You shall not bow down to them or worship them ... (like the Egyptians do).

3. You shall not misuse the name of the Lord your God ... (NCA #10: I have not uttered curses; NCA #37: I have not cursed God; NCE #42: I have not scorned the god of my town).

4. Remember the Sabbath day by keeping it holy. ... On it you shall do no work ... (it may very well be that the Hebrews travelled non-stop for six days before they were allowed to rest; much to Josephus' chagrin, Apion offered the following explanation for the origin of the name Sabbath, the seventh day[31]: 'when the Jews had travelled a six days' journey, they had buboes in their groins; and that on this account it was that they rested on the seventh day, as having got safely to that country which is now called Judea; that then they preserved the language of the Egyptians, and called that day the Sabbath, for that malady of buboes on their groin was named Sabbatosis by the Egyptians.')

5. Honour your father and your mother ... NCU #7: I have not opposed my family and kinsfolk).

6. You shall not murder. (NCU #10-11: I have not committed murder; NCA #4: Have not slain men and women).

7. You shall not commit adultery. (NCA #11: I have not committed adultery; NCA #20: I have not debauched the wife of any man).

8. You shall not steal. (NCA #2: I have not committed robbery with violence; NCA #3: I have not stolen; NCA #5,6,7: I have not stolen grain, offerings or the property of God).

9. You shall not give false testimony against your neighbour. (NCU #8: I have not acted fraudulently; NCA #8: I have not uttered lies; NCE #9: I have not told lies).

10. You shall not covet your neighbour's house ... wife ... (NCA #3: I have not stolen; NCU #13: I have not filched land from my neighbour's estate).

Other negative confessions likewise appear to reflect biblical principles, including the following:

I have not committed sin (NCA #1), I have not lain with men (NCA #11, 'Do not lie with a man as one lies with a woman; that is detestable.' in *Leviticus*[32]), have not grieved uselessly (NCA #13), have not slandered (NCA #18), have not been angry without just cause (NCA #19), have not polluted myself – I have not masturbated (NCA #22, NCU #12, possibly implied in *Job*[33], 'I have made covenant with my eyes not to look lustfully at a girl ... if my heart has been led by my eyes, or if my hands have been defiled'), I have not acted (judged) with undue haste (NCA #30),

I am not a man of violence (NCA #28), have not acted with arrogance (NCA #38), have never stopped the flow of water (NCA #35).

These moral laws were probably characteristic of most societies and countries of that time. The crucial aspect, however, is that the Ten Commandments and many of Moses' other laws were not unique to him or to the Hebrews, and may have been adopted from Egyptian beliefs.

Psalm 104 and the Great Hymn to the Aten
Beginning with Breasted in 1909[34] and Weigall in 1910[35], numerous scholars have referred to the similarities between the *Great Hymn to the Aten* (see Appendix D) and *Psalm 104* in the Bible, potentially providing further evidence that Egyptian beliefs had influenced Hebrew scriptures. *Psalm 104*, most likely a garbled recollection of the *Great Hymn to the Aten*, is listed below[36], followed by the corresponding texts in the *Great Hymn to the Aten* in brackets:

1. Praise the Lord, O my soul. O Lord my God, you are very great; you are clothed with splendour and majesty ('Praise of Re Har-akhti ... Thou appearest beautifully on the horizon of heaven').

2. He wraps himself in light as with a garment; he stretches out the heavens like a tent ('Thou art ... glistening, and high over every land'),

3. and lays the beams of his upper chambers on their waters. He makes the clouds his chariot and rides on the wings of the wind ('Thy rays encompass the lands ... thy rays are on earth').

4. He makes winds his messengers, flames of fire his servants.

5. He set the earth on its foundations; it can never be moved ('Thou didst create the world according to thy desire'?).

6. You covered it with the deep as with a garment; the waters

stood above the mountains ('For thou has set a Nile in heaven, that it may descend for them and make waves upon the mountains').

7. But at your rebuke the waters fled, at the sound of your thunder they took to flight;

8. they flowed over the mountains, they went down into the valleys, to the place you assigned for them ('... and make waves upon the mountains').

9. You set a boundary they cannot cross; never again will they cover the earth.

10. He makes springs pour water into ravines; it flows between the mountains.

11. They give water to all the beasts of the field; the wild donkeys quench their thirst ('The Nile in heaven, it is ... for the beasts of every desert ...').

12. The birds of the air nest by the waters; they sing among the branches ('The birds which fly from their nests, their wings are (stretched out) in praise to thy ka.').

13. He waters the mountains from his upper chambers; the earth is satisfied by the fruit of his work ('All beasts are content with their pasturage').

14. He makes grass grow for the cattle, and plants for man to cultivate – bringing forth food from the earth ('Trees and plants are flourishing').

15. wine that gladdens the heart of man, oil to make his face shine, and bread that sustains his heart.

16. The trees of the Lord are well watered, the cedars of Lebanon that he planted ('Trees ... are flourishing').

17. There the birds make their nests; the stork has its home in the pine trees ('The birds which fly from their nests...').

18. The high mountains belong to the wild goats; the crags are a refuge for the coneys.

19. The moon marks off the seasons, and the sun knows when to go down ('Thou makest the seasons...').

20. You bring darkness, it becomes night, and all the beasts of the forest prowl ('When thou settest in the western horizon, the land is in darkness').

21. The lions roar for their prey, and seek their food from God ('Every lion is come forth from his den').

22. The sun rises, and they steal away; they return and lie down in their dens ('At daybreak, when thou arisest on the horizon ... Thou drivest away the darkness').

23. Then man goes out to his work, to his labour until evening ('wake and standing upon (their) feet ... All the world, they do their work').

24. How many are your works, O Lord! In wisdom you made them all; the earth is full of your creatures ('How manifold it is, what thou hast made! ... Thou didst create the world according to thy desire, ... All men, cattle, and wild beasts, whatever is on earth').

25. There is the sea, vast and spacious, teeming with creatures beyond number – living things both large and small ('Like the great green sea').

26. There the ships go to and fro, and the leviathan, which you formed to frolic there ('The ships are sailing north and south as well').

27. These all look to you to give them their food at the proper time ('Thou suppliest their necessities: everyone has his food, and his time of life is reckoned').

28. When you give it to them, they gather it up; when you open your hand they are satisfied with good things.

29. When you hide your face, they are terrified; when you take away their breath, they die and return to the dust ('When thou hast risen they live, When thou settest they die').

30. When you send your Spirit, they are created, and you renew the face of the earth ('(But) when (thou) risest (again), [Everything is] made to flourish for the king' ?).

31. May the glory of the Lord endure forever; may the Lord

rejoice in his works.

32. he who looks at the earth, and it trembles, who touches the mountains, and they smoke ('In order to see all that thou dost make').

33. I will sing to the Lord all my life; I will sing praise to my God as long as I live.

34. May my meditation be pleasing to him, as I rejoice in the Lord.

35. But may sinners vanish from the earth and the wicked be no more. Praise the Lord, O my soul. Praise the Lord.

The similarities between Atenism and the Hebrew religion do not end here:

- A possible link between Atenism and the Hebrew religion is suggested by the discovery of the tomb of an Atenist priest called Aper-El, also spelled Aperia, who appears to have been of Semitic rather than Egyptian descent[37,38]. The second part of his name appears to be the Hebrew word *'êl* [39] (God), but the origin of the first part is not clear. The word Aper (spelled *'pr* without the vowels) has been argued[40] to be a variant writing of the Hebrew word *'ebed* spelled *'bd*[41] (servant), but this is clearly an ambiguous interpretation. The nearest Hebrew equivalent to Aper appears to be the word *'āphêr*[42] (a turban, ashes), but this is pronounced *af-ayr* and not *ap-ayr*. We can however find Egyptian words with similar pronunci- ation, namely *āper*[43] (to be equipped, to be provided with, to be furnished of a house) and *āper*[44] (mantle, garment). The most likely interpretation of Aper-El is therefore 'Provided for (by) El', where El must indeed be of Hebrew origin as there appears to be no equivalent in the Egyptian language. An association of Aper-El with Yahweh is also suggested by the alternative spelling Aper-Ia, or Aper-Yah (see Section 5.6 for a discussion of the names of Yuya). As the second most powerful man in Egypt, Yuya seems to have appointed other high ranking officials from the enslaved Hebrew community, such as Aper-El.

The names of several Levite priests are recognised by scholars to possibly be of Egyptian origin[45]. These include Merari, the youngest son of Levi, compared to a high priest of the Aten called Mery-re (II). The name of Phinehas, the son of Eleazar, chief of the Levites, likewise appears to have been derived from the Egyptian *p3-nhsy*, meaning 'Nubian' or 'a person with a dark skin'. There is also Hur, a companion of Moses and Aaron, whose name most likely was derived from the Egyptian *hr*, 'Hor(us)'.

- Moses forbade the making of idols (the Third Commandment), while Akhenaten similarly forbade the making of graven images of the Aten[46].

- The Egyptian creator god Khepera 'came into being by pronouncing his own name, and when he wanted a place where on to stand, he first conceived the similitude of that standing place in his mind, and when he had given it a name, and uttered that name, the standing place at once came into being'[47]. This matches the biblical god Jehovah who brought the world into being by speaking[48]. From Khepera were born Shu and Tefnut and from their union Keb (Geb) and Nut. Khepera, also known as Khepri, was therefore an alias of Ra (Re), the original sun god of Egypt.

- In Egyptian mythology Isis poisoned Ra and offered him a cure in exchange for his secret name[49], matching the 'hidden and mysterious' name of Jehovah[50].

- The sacred name of the God of the Israelites is Jehovah[51] (*Y^ehôvâh*) or Jahweh, from the so-called Tetragrammaton, the four Hebrew letters YHWH (vowels were omitted in written Hebrew). Although its meaning is a topic of much debate, it appears to have been derived from the word *hâyâh*[52], which means 'to exist' or 'to be', rendering 'The self-existent'. The most common use is, however, simply Lord, which is also the meaning of the word *'Ādônây*[53] (the Lord, my Lord). *'Ādônây* is the emphatic form of *'âdôn*[54] (sovereign, controller, lord, master). As early as 1927 Alexandre Moret suggested that the name Aten could be linked to Adonai, Lord of the Syrians and Adonis of Byblos[55]. In 1937 Sigmund Freud also suggested such a link between this Hebrew title of God and the Egypt god Aten[56], a hypothesis later expanded by Osman[57]. His argument was that the Egyptian 't' would be pronounced as 'd' in Hebrew, so that the Aton (Aten) became the Adon in Hebrew. If Moret, Freud and Osman are on the right track, one may expect that the name Jehovah (Jahweh) or at least in is abbreviated from YHWH, may likewise be linked to an Egyptian deity.

Taking a closer look at the composition of the name YHWH, several possibilities other than the traditional interpretation arise. It has already been shown that Hebrew word *yâ'* means 'a shovel' [58], but this would not make much sense as part of the name of a god. The word *yâ'âh*[59], however, means to brush aside or sweep away, which may apply to 'god' in the following manner. Several Hebrew words can be used as the second part of the name (Je)hova, namely *hâvâh*[60] (to breathe, to be, to exist), *hâvvâh*[61] (desire, ruin, calamity) and *hôvâh*[62] (ruin, mischief). Although the number of consonants would differ, *Yâ'âh- hôvâh* would then mean 'Ruined and swept aside', a name reminiscent of the Great Flood of the Bible (see Chapter 20). It should be noted that the phonetically similar Egyptian syllables *heh*[63] (breath) and *ha*[64] (fall down, destroyed) have meanings similar to its Hebrew counterparts, while the Egyptian words *ia*[65] and *ua*[66] respectively mean 'to wash' and 'something which happened a long time ago'. Assuming that the latter is pronounced as 'ya', *Ua-ha* would then mean 'The ruin that happened a long time ago'. In Chapter 20 it is argued that the first inhabitants of Egypt were the original Hebrews, who lived in Egypt alongside the Egyptians. The ancient Hebrew and Egyptian languages may, therefore, have had similar roots.

- Jehovah revealed himself to Moses as 'I am who I am'[67], while a Karnak Talatat inscription revealed that the Aten was addressed as 'Thou art what thou art, radiant and high over every land'[68].

The influence of Egyptian religious beliefs on the formation of the Hebrew religion is, therefore, undeniable. It would seem that many of the fundamental principles and laws we find in the Mosaic texts were in fact derived from much earlier Egyptian concepts, as is to be expected given the identity of Moses as Prince Tuthmosis of Amenhotep III.

10

'Those fatally determined 13 years'

If Manetho's version of the events leading up to the Exodus is correct, there should be evidence of a period in Egypt's history during which its king fled Egypt, leaving it to be plundered by rebels. Manetho labelled that period 'those fatally determined 13 years'[1].

10.1 Manetho's 13 years of anarchy

It is not known when Amenhotep III ordered the erection of more than 700 statues to Sekhmet, the goddess of destruction[2], the date of which would give an indication of when the Thera volcano had erupted. We do know, however, that Amenhotep's famous scribe of the same name was still alive during Year 31 of Amenhotep's reign, having just been granted permission by the king to have a mortuary temple constructed for himself [3]. No mention is made of any circumstances that might suggest a natural disaster of some kind had struck Egypt by that time. However, if the Thera eruption had already occurred, and Egypt was already suffering its consequences, it may be that Amenhotep the scribe hastily requested permission to construct his mortuary temple in case he too should succumb to the plague. As discussed in Section 7.5, the second campaign of Amenhotep III into Ethiopia in Year 30 may have been necessitated by the Ethiopians trying to capitalise on the upheaval in Egypt.

According to Manetho, King Amenophis decided not to engage the combined armies of Moses and the shepherds from Jerusalem and marched into Ethiopia with his whole army and a multitude of Egyptians. There he would remain for what Manetho described as 'those fatally determined 13 years'. The rebels subsequently set cities and villages on fire, destroyed the effigies of the Egyptian gods, forced the priestly caretakers of the holy animals to slaughter and roast them and ejected the priests naked out of Egypt. These deeds seem to suggest a singular motive – revenge for 200 years of enslavement. Manetho's earlier record of the savagery of the Hyksos when they first occupied Egypt, when they burned down Egyptian cities, demolished the temples of the Egyptian gods, slew the inhabitants and sold their children into slavery[4], may in fact be an incorrectly placed reference to the acts of barbarity perpetrated by rebels following Amenhotep's departure from Egypt.

With Amenhotep III having been identified as King Amenophis who fled to Ethiopia, one needs to look for evidence that might suggest his absence from Egypt for more or less 13 years. This is not an easy task, as Horemheb attempted to erase all evidence relating to the Amarna period[5]. What little may have survived this act of cleansing would most likely have ended up in the library of Alexandria, which was tragically destroyed through various acts of aggression.

10.2 Akhenaten's reign

The reign of Amenhotep III is generally assumed to have begun *ca.* 1391 BCE and ended around 1352 BCE[6], when the kingship passed on to his son Akhenaten. Amenhotep's highest attested regnal year is Year 38[7] and he had reached an age of greater than 50 years[8]. At his accession he could have been of any age between two and 12 years old[9]. The absence of any evidence of his reign beyond Year 38 may be attributed to his departure to Ethiopia during a time of chaos in Egypt, so his reign could have ended anywhere between about 1350 BCE and 1340 BCE. In other words, Amenhotep III could have been alive significantly later than 1352 BCE, well into the reign of Akhenaten. There appears to be no specific record of the circumstances or time his death.

In a letter from King Tushratta to Akhenaten, he laments the passing away of Amenhotep III (Nimmuwareya):

When I heard that my brother Nimmuwareya (Nimmureya) had

gone to his fate, on that day I sat down and wept. On that day I took no food, I took no water. When they told me that Naphureya, eldest son of Nimmuwareya and Teye (Tiye) his principle wife, is king in his place, I said, 'Nimmuwareya my brother is not dead! Naphureya his eldest son is in his place, and nothing whatsoever will ever be changed from the way it was before.'[10]

Under normal circumstances it would be correct to assume that Akhenaten inherited the throne following the death of his father. However, if Amenhotep had retreated into Ethiopia as claimed by Manetho and as suggested by the Exodus narratives and the *El Arish Shrine Text*, Amenhotep would have remained the true king of Egypt for that time, while Akhenaten would have been serving as his deputy in Egypt. Only upon the death of Amenhotep would that news have been released to the public, evidently while Akhenaten was on the throne.

Returning to the biblical version of the Exodus, Moses fled Egypt to Midian where he remained for several years before returning to Egypt to confront the ruling pharaoh. The subject of his confrontation with this pharaoh (Akhenaten) is not clear, as contrary to biblical legend the fabled plagues of Egypt had occurred many years before. Only the plague of boils and blisters must have been showing no signs of abating. As stated to earlier, only Moses as Prince Tuthmosis would have had the authority to confront his younger brother about the Hebrews in Egypt. If Manetho is to be believed, the Hyksos rebels were already in control of large areas of Egypt, so Moses could hardly have been seeking Akhenaten's permission to let the Hebrews go. The discussions would more likely have been focused on the future, perhaps whether Moses (Tuthmosis) should reclaim the throne that originally was his, but certainly what the army of rebel slaves and Egyptians should do once the army of the shepherds from Jerusalem had returned to their homeland. At that time the Egyptian army would still have been stationed in Ethiopia, but there would have been no doubt in Moses' mind that it would eventually return to Egypt. Moses' rebel army by itself would probably not have been able to withstand the full might of the Egyptian army, and he, the rebel slaves and the 'mixed multitude' of Egyptians would not have been welcome in Canaan.

The most likely sequence of events can be constructed as follows. The eruption of Thera must have occurred during the late twenties or early thirties of the reign of Amenhotep III. When the erection of hundreds of statues to appease Sekhmet failed to bring an end to a deadly plague in his country, Amenhotep III resorted to the sacrifice of the firstborn offspring in a desperate attempt to end the plague. First to be sacrificed would have been his son Prince Tuthmosis, who was informed about this plan of the pharaoh and his sacred scribe, and managed to escape the fires of sacrifice. After a couple of years in exile, Tuthmosis organised the slaves and Egyptians infected by the plague into an army stationed at Avaris. Amenhotep III, now hugely unpopular with most of the Egyptian population because of the sacrifice of their children, appointed Akhenaten as the deputy king of Egypt and prepared to engage the rebel army. Tuthmosis soon had to call on the shepherds in Jerusalem for assistance and, when they obliged, Amenhotep was faced with the daunting task of engaging two armies at the same time, one of which was led by his own son. He evidently chose to retreat into Ethiopia, not only because of the threat of these two armies, but also to escape the scourge of the plague. His departure must have taken place either when Akhenaten ascended to the throne, or possibly even some years into Akhenaten's official reign.

It is possible that Akhenaten decided to build Akhetaten only after his father had departed to Ethiopia. Construction of the city was already under way in Year 5 of Akhenaten's reign. The family, together with what remained of the Egyptian court, moved there in Year 8. Akhenaten's highest attested regnal year was Year 17[11], which implies that he must have died shortly afterwards. If his father had departed to Egypt around Year 4, the remaining 13 years would match Manetho's 'fatally determined 13 years'. This timeline would assume that the Egyptian army returned to Egypt around the end of Akhenaten's reign.

Akhenaten was succeeded by a king named Smenkhkare who ruled for a further two years before Tutankhamun became king of Egypt[12]. The identity of Smenkhkare is a topic of much debate, being identified either as a male, or as a female who could have been either Nefertiti, the wife of Akhenaten, or Ankhesenamun, the wife of Tutankhamun[13]. In Section 13.3 evidence will be presented that Smenkhkare and Nefertiti were one and the same person, and that it was Ay who had 'used violence to the queen' (presumably raped and killed her)[14]. When Sesothis (Sesostris, Amenhotep III, see Section 6.2) received this news, he returned to regain his kingdom from his brother. This suggests that the Egyptian army returned shortly after the death of Smenkhkare (Nefertiti), around 1336 BCE. One can only speculate whether Amenhotep III was alive at that time or if he had died some years before.

There can be no doubt that the ransacking of Egypt had begun either shortly before or early on in the reign of Akhenaten. That something had long been going wrong elsewhere in Egypt by Year 5 of his reign is confirmed by a verbatim recording of the king's speech on a boundary stele of Akhetaten, which he abruptly interrupted to say:

As for the ... in Akhetaten:
-it was worse than those things I heard in regnal year 4;
-it was worse than [those things] I heard in regnal year 3;
-it was worse than those things I heard [in regnal year 2;
-it was] worse than [those things I heard in regnal year 1];
-it was worse [than] those things [Nebmaat]re [Amenophis III] heard;
-[it was worse than those things which ... heard];
-it was worse [than] those things which Menkheperre [Tuthmosis III] heard;

-[and it was] worse [than] those things heard by any kings who had ever assumed the white crown![15]

At the end of his reign and that of Smenkhkare, Egypt lay in ruin as attested to by the so-called *Restoration Stele of Tutankhamun*:

> ... the temples and the cities of the gods and goddesses, starting from Elephantine as far as the Delta marshes ... were fallen into decay and their shrines were fallen into ruin, having become mere mounds overgrown with grass. Their sanctuaries were like something which had not yet come into being and their buildings were a footpath [i.e. public] – for the land was in rack and ruin. When an army was sent to Djahy [Palestine] to broaden the boundaries of Egypt, it was unsuccessful; ... After some time passed over this, his majesty [Tutankhamun] appeared upon the throne of his father and he ruled over the shores of Horus [i.e. Egypt]. ... His majesty took counsel with his heart, investigating every excellent deed, seeking benefactions from his father Amun and fashioning his noble image out of genuine electrum. ... and his majesty made monuments for the gods ... building their shrines anew as monuments of eternity ... [16]

Georges Legrain, who pioneered the excavations at Karnak, summarised the fury of those responsible for the destruction:

> At that time, the images of Amon were everywhere forbidden or destroyed by the King's command. Few monuments, tombs, statues, statuettes, or even small objects escaped mutilation. At Thebes, wherever the fanatics found the name of Amon they destroyed it. Gradually, as success increased their ardour, not only the name of the great Theban god went, but also those of Ptah and Hathor; and all the gods would have had the same fate if Amenophis had stayed at Thebes. They climbed to the tops of obelisks, they went down into the depths of tombs, to destroy the

names and images of the gods. There were in the temples groups in which the Ancestral Kings were represented by the side of Amon, their arms entwined in his with filial respect. The icono-clasts vented their rage on the divine figure and obliterated every trace of it, while they respected that of the sovereign.[17]

Whether archaeologists have ever found explicit orders of Akhenaten for the destruction of everything associated with Amun or whether he is just assumed to have issued such orders is not clear. As stated earlier, the failed sacrifice of Egypt's firstborn on the orders of the priests of Amun would without doubt have provoked acts of aggression against this god. Even if Akhenaten had issued such orders, he would not have ruined the entire country. Those acts of destruction can then only be attributed to Manetho's marauding rebels and Asiatics. The extent of their control of Egypt is clear from the *Restoration Stele* description – the land from the Nile Delta to Elephantine encompasses all of Egypt (see Section 13.6 for the siege of Akhetaten). The cities of an entire country cannot be laid waste overnight, suggesting that the ravaging of Egypt lasted several years, exactly as claimed by Manetho. The army that was sent on an unsuccessful campaign into Canaan may refer to one sent by Tutankhamun himself, but more likely confirms the misconception by Manetho and Cheremon, that Moses' army had pursued the Hebrews into Syria. The Hyksos founders of Jerusalem were in fact his allies.

Further corroboration of Manetho's version of events is presented by the following two steles of Akhenaten, both describing a war in Nubia (quoted verbatim from the original translations):

Behun Stele: [Regnal year 1]2 (?). third (?) month of Inundation, day 20 (of) HEKA-[ATEN] ..., (and of) the King of Upper and Lower Egypt, who lives on Maat, Lord of [the Two Lands]. WAENRE [sic], [the Son of Re who lives on Maat, Lord of Crowns, AKHENATEN, long in his lifetime] ..., having appeared on [the throne of] his father, the Aten ... [Now his Person. l.p.h., was in Akhet-Aten when one came to tell his Person that] the enemies of the foreign country Ikayta [were plotting rebellion and had (even) invaded the land of] the Nilotic Nubians, while taking all sustenance away from them [as they roamed the desert in order to escape from him (?)].

Thereupon his Person charged the King's Son [of Kush and overseer of the southern countries with assembling an army in order to defeat the] enemies of the foreign country of Ikayta, males [as well as females. These enemies were found on the eastern side of] the river, to the north of the cistern(s) of the mining region ... upon the highland, and the fugitive was smitten ..., [while the] cry of victory was in their heart(s) – 'a [fierce] lion slaying [myriads throughout] the land (?) [in] valor and victory!'

List [of the plunder which his Person carried off from the country] Ikayta: Living Nilotic Nubians: 82 [+ x]; [Young warriors]: ...; [Nilotic Nubian women]: ...; Their children: 12; Total of living 'head(s)': 145; Those who were impaled: [...]; [Slain]: [...]; [Hands]: [...]; Total: 225; Total sum: 361 [sic]

The King's Son of Kush, the overseer of the [southern] countries [Thutmose, said]: '... [Fear of you is in the]ir [hearts]. There are no rebels in your time, for they have achieved nonexistence! The chiefs [of ... have fallen] to your might. Your battle cries are like a fiery flame (following) after every foreign country. [...], (and) every foreign country is united with one wish, (namely) that they might despoil their land(s) daily [...] in order that breath may be sent to their nose(s) by your Ka. (O) [Lord of] the Two Lands, WAENRE, may your Ka act in order to reach [all your enemies].

Amada Stele: '... Now his Person [l.p.h., was in Akhet-Aten when one came to tell his Person that] enemies of the foreign country Ikayta were plotting [rebellion and had (even) invaded the lands of the Nilotic Nubians] while taking all sustenance away from them [as they] roamed (?) the desert (?) in order to [fill their bellies (?)].[18]

The following key observations are made from these crucial texts:

* Among other names, ancient Ethiopia was known to the
Egyptians as 'the land of the Nehsyuw' ('Nehsyw' or
'Nehesi')[19]. The country Ikayta appears to be equated to
Nubia (the land of the Nehesi) by a late Ramesside papyrus in
which a specific group of Egyptian mercenaries is referred to
as 'the bow-carrying Nehesi from Ikayta'[20]. However, the
stele translations quoted above relate that the foreigners from
Ikayta attacked Nubians and unless one group of Nubians
(those from Ikayta) attacked another group of Nubians (the
Nilotic ones), the enemies from Ikayta could not have been
Nubians themselves. Would the king of Egypt really have
sent his army to intervene in tribal fighting in a neighbouring
country? Probably not, unless the rebellion posed a direct
threat to Egypt. The 'bow-carrying Nehesi' may instead refer
to bowmen from Nubia who had been trained in the country
of Ikayta, not unlike the French Foreign Legion, the military
wing of the French Army comprising mostly foreign
nationals[21].

* The mention of a rebellion by foreigners from Ikayta must
certainly refer to the slave rebellion Amenhotep III had to
face, the foreigners being Manetho's Hyksos from Jerusalem
who joined the Egyptian uprising at the invitation of Moses.
The name Ikayta appears to mean 'the vile Hittites'[22], derived
from the words *Ia*[23] (unwashed, impure) and *Kheta*[24] (Kheta,
a district and town of the Hittites). The principal weapon of
the Hittite chariot contingent was the bow and arrow[25],
which means that these archers had to be able to shoot
accurately from a rapidly moving platform. To have been
trained in archery by the Hittites may have been regarded as
a great distinction in ancient times, hence 'the bow-carrying

Nehesi from (trained in) Ikayta'. If Ikayta referred to the country of the Hittites, it may have been a generalisation for the Caucasian races from the north, which would have included the Canaanites. That King Saul had diplomatic links with the Hittites is suggested by the presence of Uriah the Hittite in his court (see Section 13.2). The Egyptian king Merikare (*ca.* 2100 BCE) referred to Canaanite nomads who continued to harass Egypt with guerrilla warfare tactics as 'the miserable Asiatic'[26], echoing the interpretation of Ikayta as 'the vile Hittites'.

- If indeed they were foreigners from the north, the implication would be that these foreigners must have been in charge of Egypt to be able to launch an attack on Nubia (from the north). This matches the Hyksos from Jerusalem having joined the rebels in Egypt against Amenhotep III. It would seem that based on their success in Egypt, they intended pursuing Amenhotep all the way into Nubia to where he had retreated, but were met by the Egyptian army which repelled their invasion.

- Akhenaten's scribe must have attributed the defeat of the foreigners in Nubia to the viceroy of Kush, who had been stationed there. The army 'assembled' by him would have been the Egyptian army which, under the leadership of Amenhotep III, had retreated into Nubia years before.

- Before being defeated in Nubia, the foreigners still had the 'cry of victory in their hearts', likening themselves to a fierce lion slaying multitudes in the conquered land. This matches the victorious marauders from Jerusalem, who must have been known to the Egyptians as those who branded themselves 'lions' after Labayu (see Section 12.3).

Proof of the slave rebellion in Egypt is presented by the so-called *Admonitions of Ipuwer*, a manuscript written between 1350-1100 BCE[27] (see Appendix E). This text describes an Egypt overrun by foreigners and ruled by slaves. According to John Wilson, the original translator of the document, Ipuwer describes how he arrived at the palace to report to the pharaoh about what was happening in Egypt, ending with a denunciation of the king who was evidently avoiding his responsibilities. The following important points from this text should be noted:

- Egypt had been invaded by foreigners and barbarians ('Foreigners have become people everywhere ... Barbarians from outside have come to Egypt ... Behold, it (the Delta marshland) is in the hands of those who did not know it, ... foreigners are (now) skilled in the work of the Delta'), with few Egyptians still being around. Egyptians regarded only themselves as real people[28]. These foreigners were Asiatics as claimed by Manetho.

- Slaves had become the masters, the rich became the poor and the poor became the rich, in other words, Egypt had suffered a slave rebellion as described by Manetho ('it has come to a point where (men) rebel against the uraeus').

- Egyptian society was being destroyed. This included the destruction of buildings and, by implication, towns.

- The children of the nobles were being killed or were abandoned on the streets. This aggression against children, or at least against their parents, again suggests a slave rebellion.

- Egypt was effectively without a king ('it has come to a point where the land is despoiled of the kingship by a few irresponsible men'). The king having been 'taken away by poor men' must certainly be a reference to Amenhotep III who had disappeared.

- The king being addressed by Ipuwer did not suffer this fate. His palace had been spared, although Ipuwer warned the king that his residence too may fall to the rebels ('The residence (may) be razed within an hour'). He openly accused the king, or at least his men, of doing nothing to remedy the situation, and in fact sarcastically addressed the king at the beginning of his report, 'The heart of the king must indeed be glad when the truth comes to him!'. This description matches Akhenaten who was effectively isolated from what was happening in Egypt while his father was exiled in Ethiopia.

- Although some Egyptologists have argued that these events must refer to the earlier invasion of Egypt by the Hyksos, this theory is disqualified by Ipuwer mentioning that the military classes had become barbarians themselves who began to destroy Egypt and 'showed the Asiatics the state of the land'. This description is a perfect match for Manetho's account in which those Egyptians who had been infected by the plague along with the Hyksos slaves, joined the rebellion and summoned the Asiatics from Jerusalem to join in the fight against Amenhotep III. It was therefore widely known that this section of the military, those still loyal to Prince Tuthmosis, had sent messengers to Jerusalem, inviting them to invade Egypt as it had been weakened by the plague. As related earlier, Africanus clearly states that a part of the Egyptian army had joined Moses.

- The final part of the text, which regrettably has been lost, describes an old man near death, who had a young son. One can imagine that the old sage was about to use an analogy between an old king and his son to inspire Akhenaten to do something that would make his elderly father proud, that father being Amenhotep in Ethiopia.

- One can also speculate that it was this sage who at one time brought Akhenaten the terrible news of what was going on in Egypt, causing the king to lament 'it was worse than those things I heard ...' in the speech recorded on a boundary stele.

- Some researchers have suggested that the Ipuwer papyrus is based on the biblical plagues of Egypt, specifically the Nile turning into blood and the Egyptian crops having been destroyed ('grain has perished on every side'). This must certainly be the case, although the events referred to in the Ipuwer papyrus appear to span many years, from the onset of the plagues to the slave rebellion in Egypt.

As a final note on the destruction wrought upon Egypt by the slaves, expelled Egyptians and the Hyksos from Jerusalem, Josephus records that the Hyksos invaded Egypt encountering practically no resistance and that when they had subdued the Egyptian leaders, they **afterwards** burned down the cities, demolished the temples of the gods and brutalized the Egyptians[29]. At first glance it would appear that these acts of barbarity occurred directly after the Hyksos had seized control of Egypt, or Lower Egypt at least. It is, however, perfectly possible that the **'afterwards'** used here refers to the acts of barbarism committed by Moses' freed slaves, for understandable reasons. If so, this statement would implicitly acknowledge that the freed slaves were indeed Hyksos captured when their rule was overthrown by Ahmose, and those captured by Tuthmosis III during his military campaigns. There can, however, be no doubt that the Egyptians hated the foreigners in their land, as suggested by the threats made by Ahmose's predecessor and brother Kamose to the Hyksos. Recorded on the *Kamose Stele*, he threatened 'I shall drag your women to the ships' holds' [30], in other words hand them over to sailors as sex slaves. That this was indeed what had happened is attested to by the so-called *Carnavaron Tablet I*, which describes one particular victory over the Hyksos ruler as follows:

When day broke, I was on him as if it were a falcon. When the time of breakfast had come, I attacked him. I broke down his walls, I killed his people, **and I made his wife come down to the river bank**. My soldiers were as lions are, with their spoil, having serfs (slaves), cattle, milk, fat and honey, dividing up their property, their hearts gay.[31]

In another text concerning the siege and subsequent fall of Avaris, the commander of a crew who was known as Ahmose the son of Eben boasted about his spoils as victor, which included one male slave and five female slaves[32]. Although few Hyksos may have been found in Avaris (see Chapter 18 for the escape of the Hyksos from their capitol), one can only guess the number of Hyksos taken as slaves over the rest of Egypt. It could very well have been in the hundreds of thousands. Most of the adult men would have been killed, while the women and children would have been taken as slaves. Given these circumstances, one can begin to understand why the freed slaves would have exacted such barbaric revenge.

10.3 Queen Tiye who was left behind

Cheremon records that when Amenhotep retreated into Ethiopia, he left behind his wife who was with child. She gave birth to this child in a cave where she was hiding and named him Messene. This son grew up, pursued the Jews into Syria and welcomed his father back from Ethiopia[33].

Amenhotep's wife Tiye outlived him by possibly up to 12 years[34], which could mean precisely that, or that she chose to remain in Egypt with her son Akhenaten while Amenhotep led his army into Ethiopia. The son who supposedly pursued the Jews into Syria was Prince Tuthmosis, but he was certainly not the one to welcome back his father. If Amenhotep had indeed returned to Egypt and did not die in Ethiopia, Akhenaten would have been the son who welcomed him back. It is certainly possible, if not more likely, that Amenhotep had died in Ethiopia and that his mummy was brought back to Egypt when the Egyptian army returned.

The name Messene has no equivalent in Greek, the nearest being *misōs*[35] (hatred). Several interpretations from the Egyptian language are, however, possible. The Egyptian words *mesi* (*mes* when used in conjunction with other words) and *mess* both have several meanings, but the most common appears to be 'to bear' or 'to give birth' [36]. The word *en* means 'of' (belonging to, as for example in Ba-en-Shu, meaning the Soul-of-Shu)[37] and the name or object *mess* is associated with ('of') must then be described by the letter *e* (mess-en-e). There appears to be no meaningful interpretation of *e* in the Egyptian language, but *u* means either 'serpent' or 'serpent-god'[38]. Messene would then be *Mess-en-u*, or 'Born of the serpent'. If the name Messene referred to Tuthmosis and Yuya had indeed been of Hebrew descent, Tuthmosis would have been the grandson of a Hebrew, a descendant of the evil serpent-god Apep (*El Arish Shrine Text*, 'the children of the dragon Apep'). Alternatively, with Egypt's heir to the throne having joined its most hated enemy, the Egyptians may very well have dubbed Prince Tuthmosis 'Son of Satan'. It should be noted that the word *mess* also means 'bull-calf'[39], which may link the name Messene to Prince Tuthmosis. From the burial ceremony of the first Apis bull, Africanus' statement about Moses advocating the usefulness of bulls and Aaron constructing an image of God in the form of a golden calf[40], one can conclude that Moses (Tuthmosis) was closely connected to or possibly even the patron of the bull cult in Egypt.

If Messene referred to Akhenaten instead, he may very well also have earned himself the nickname 'Son of Satan'. A more likely association with Akhenaten may, however, be derived from the Egyptian word *Mesen*, which was the name of an ape-headed fire-god[41]. Akhenaten's eventual rejection by the Egyptian people is evident from descriptions and caricatures of a king who had become despised. He was, for instance, referred to as the king who had called himself the 'Darling Son of Aten', only to become the 'Vanquished One of Akhetaten'[42]. A number of figurines depicting Akhenaten and his family as monkeys were found at Akhetaten[43], and it has even been suggested that the name Kiya, a wife of Akhenaten, was a variant spelling of an ancient Egyptian word for monkey[44]. Messene (Mesen) would then mean 'the monkey'. Cheremon's statement that Messene was born in a cave may simply have been a distorted oral tradition which degraded Akhenaten, namely that he was a monkey born in a cave.

Having presented several possible interpretations of the name

Messene in the Greek and Egyptian languages, one must also consider the possibility that the name was of Hebrew origin, Josephus' native language. It may have been formed by the words *massâ'* [45] (a missile, spear or arrow) and *'ayin* [46] (to be nothing or not exist), rendering 'spear-less'. Although it was Amenhotep III who was known not to have fought any wars and was remembered as having thrown his spear at the Nile, Akhenaten also did not fight any major wars. Another possibility is the word *mish'ênâh* or *mish'eneth* [47] (support, a walking stick, staff). A number of 'walking sticks' were found in Tutankhamun's tomb, but some doubt whether these sticks or staffs were used for walking support [48]. However, in a scene of a royal couple identified by Nicholas Reeves as Akhenaten and Nefertiti (see Figure 10.1, confirmation of this identification is presented in Section 13.1), the king is shown as leaning on a stick. Akhenaten may, therefore, have been known as the 'walking stick' king. I have to state clearly that I have no background of any kind in the linguistics of the Hebrew, Greek or Egyptian languages. How accurate the above interpretations are will have to be assessed by experts in these respective fields.

Just why the Egyptians would have turned against Akhenaten and his Aten can only be conjectured, but pressure from the Amun priesthood must certainly have played a role. If he had been the one who seemingly agreed to let the Hebrew slaves go free (see Section 9.1), perhaps duped by his brother Tuthmosis into publically admitting that the plagues were brought upon Egypt by the God of the Hebrews, one can imagine how he would have been ridiculed by his people.

10.4 Moses' years of exile in Midian

The Bible gives little information about the age of Moses when he received his divine calling. According to rabbinic literature [49], Moses fled Egypt aged 18, 20 or 40. Some sources claim that he first fled to Ethiopia, where he became king after nine years, ruling for another 40 years before departing to Midian. Josephus records that following his success in Ethiopia, Moses returned to Egypt. He was informed of a plot to assassinate him and fled to Midian. Two haggadic accounts[50] agree with Josephus that Moses did not flee to Ethiopia, but to Midian. One relates that Moses fled the Pharaoh's house aged 27 and remained in Midian for 60 years before returning to liberate the Hebrews at the age of 80. The other records that Moses was 40 years old when he fled to Midian, where he remained for another 40 years before returning to Egypt. In biblical legend Moses

Figure 10.1 Akhenaten leaning on a walking stick in an Amarna royal couple scene[51]

supposedly died when he was 120 years of age[52].

Any high age of Moses at his return from exile would not match the Exodus chronology as presented in Sections 10.1 and 10.2. According to this chronology, Moses would have escaped the sacrifice of the firstborn shortly after Year 31 of Amenhotep's reign and would have returned within 8 to 10 years to lead the rebellion against his father. Amenhotep had married Tiye by Year 2 of his reign[53] and Prince Tuthmosis would have been born shortly afterwards. By Year 31 of Amenhotep's reign, Tuthmosis would have been approximately 28 years of age and if he returned to Egypt during the first year or two of Akhenaten's reign, he would have been 9 to 10 years older at that time. That would make him approximately 40 years of age when he returned to Egypt, possibly the origin of the period of 40 years associated with Moses in one way or another. Biblical legend relates that the Hebrews spent 40 years in the desert following their departure from Egypt, which would make Moses at least 80 years of age at the end of their sojourn in the desert. There is simply no means by which the accuracy of any of these legends can be established. The only common thread appears to be that Moses was no longer a young man when he returned to Egypt from Midian, and that he was a much older man when he died.

If Moses as Prince Tuthmosis was around 30 years of age when the Thera volcano erupted, one would expect to find numerous Egyptian texts referring to the prince. As it is, relatively few references to this prince have survived. Among these are a schist statuette on which he is identified as the *sm*-priest of Ptah in Memphis, a sarcophagus of his pet cat and seven vases bearing his name and titles[54], as well as a depiction of him in the shrine of Apis I at Saqqara[55]. The lack of more evidence of his existence can certainly be attributed to Horemheb and subsequent pharaohs who would have attempted to erase all references to a man who must have been considered a traitor to his nation.

10.5 Ay, the brother who was expelled from Egypt

As discussed in Section 6.2, the only Egyptian king who may have left his brother in charge of Egypt during his absence was Amenhotep III. Although Akhenaten was the formal king of Egypt, it would seem that Amenhotep III instructed Ay to keep an eye over the naive young king, making him Amenhotep's unofficial deputy in charge of Egypt. Called Sesostris by Herodotus and Sethosis by Josephus (Manetho), Amenhotep later returned from Ethiopia to reclaim his throne and cast his brother out of Egypt. As argued in Section 10.1, Amenhotep, or at least the Egyptian army, must have returned to Egypt following a period of about 13 years after the first couple of years into the reign of Akenaten. If this happened shortly after the death of Nefertiti (Smenkhkare) at the hands of Ay, the fact that Ay remained in the royal house for several more years contradicts the legend about the immediate eviction of Sesostris' brother. Following Smenkhkare, Tutankhamun ruled for nine more years before Ay eventually declared himself king of Egypt. Ay ruled for four years and then either died or disappeared from Egypt around 1323 BCE (see Chapter 11). Going back 13 years from this date takes us to 1336 BCE, which marks the end of the reign of Akhenaten. If the Egyptian army had returned from Ethiopia shortly after the death of Nefertiti in 1336 BCE, Amenhotep III would have departed to Ethiopia in 1349 BCE, three years into the reign of Akhenaten.

Ay's mummy has never been found, suggesting that he may have fled Egypt, possibly giving rise to the legend that he was expelled from that country. It should be noted that there may have been some confusion among ancient historians as to who was left in charge of Egypt while Amenhotep was in Ethiopia. The king officially in charge was Akhenaten, but Ay was ever present and the post-Amarna rulers of Egypt attempted to wipe out all traces of Akhenaten's name. It is therefore possible that Ay was mistakenly assumed to have been the man left in charge of Egypt.

11

Manetho's New Kingdom king list

At this point it is appropriate to look at the chronology of the Eighteenth (the New Kingdom era) and early Nineteenth Dynasties, in order to link the names reported by ancient historians to actual rulers of Egypt. The chronologies accepted by the majority of scholars were drawn up from various Egyptian king lists as well as king lists provided by historians such as Manetho. Although the process of establishing an accurate chronology is fraught with problems, Egyptologists seem to have reached agreement on the New Kingdom king list[1] shown in Table 11.1 (see also Shaw, *The Oxford History of Ancient Egypt*[2]). The exact dates of reign are often disputed, mostly because of uncertainty regarding overlapping reigns, but the differences usually amount to only a couple of years.

Eighteenth Dynasty (the New Kingdom)			
Ruler	Date (BCE)	Reign (Years)	Notes
Ahmose	1550-1525	25	Expelled the Hyksos
Amenhotep I	1525-1504	21	
Tuthmosis I	1504-1492	12	Also known as Thutmose
Tuthmosis II	1492-1479	13	
Tuthmosis III	1479-1425	54	Sole ruler 1458-1425 (33 years)
Hatshepsut	1473-1458	15	Half-sister of Tuthmosis II Co-ruled with Tuthmosis III for 21 years
Amenhotep II	1427-1400	27	
Tuthmosis IV	1400-1390	10	
Amenhotep III	1390-1352	38	
Amenhotep IV	1352-1336	16	Akhenaten, first of the Amarna kings
Nefernefruaten	1338-1336	2	Smenkhkare
Tutankhamun	1336-1327	9	
Ay	1327-1323	4	Last of the Amarna kings
Horemheb	1323-1295	28	
Nineteenth Dynasty			
Ramesses I	1295-1294	1	
Seti I	1294-1279	15	
Ramesses II	1279-1213	66	
Merenptah	1213-1203	10	

Table 11.1. The conventional Egyptian king list

Manetho's king list[3], which was among other sources used to draw up the Egyptian chronology listed in Table 11.1, is shown in Table 11.2 (see Appendix F for other copies of Manetho's Eighteenth

Dynasty king list)

Name	Reign (years)	Notes
Alisphragmuthosis		Subdued the Hyksos, who retreated to Avaris
Thummosis	25	Besieged Avaris, Hyksos left and founded Jerusalem; also called Tethmosis[4] and Tefilmosis[5]
Chebron	13	Son of Tethmosis
Amenophis	21	Amenhotep I
Amesses	22	Sister of Amenophis, must be Hatshepsut, half-sister of Tuthmosis II
Mephres	13	
Mephramuthosis	26	Also known as Misphragmuthosis
Tethmosis	10	Thumosis IV, father of Amenhotep III
Amenophis	31	
Orus	36	Amenhotep III (see Section 7.1). Reigned for 38 years; also known as Bocchoris[6], the Pharaoh of the Exodus; linked to Amenophis[7] ('Amenophis …as had Orus…')
Acenchres	12	Daughter of Orus (Nefertiti co-reigned with Akhenaten)
Rathotis	9	Brother of the female Acenchres
Acencheres	12	Akhenaten, 'those fatally determined 13 years'?
Acencheres	12	Again Acencheres = Smenkhkare?
Armais	4	Also called Danaus[8], Hermeus[9] and possibly Ramesses[10]

Ramesses	1	Ramesses I
Armesses Miammoun	66	Horemheb? May have been as old as Ay (Armais)
Amenophis	19	Seti I?
Sethosis	59	'...and Ramesses'. His brother was called Armais; he was also known as Egyptus (Aegyptus)[11]; had a 59-year-reign[12]; he killed Ramesses and appointed brother as deputy over Egypt[13]; cast his brother Hermeus (Armais) out of Egypt[14]; also known as Sesostris[15]; confused with Amenhotep III (see Section 6.2)
Rhampses	66	Son of Sethos[16] - must be Ramesses II

Table 11.2. Manetho's king list

A careful study of the numbers of years of reign reveals that Manetho's chronology is in general fairly accurate, but that it occasionally appears to be mixed up with respect to the generally accepted chronology. Rearranging Manetho's list, we obtain a better chronological order for his kings as shown in Table 11.3.

Ruler	Reign	Years	Manetho	Years
Ahmose	1550-1525	25	Thummosis/	
			Tethmosis	25
Amenhotep I	1525-1504	21	Amenophis	21
Tuthmosis I	1504-1492	12	Chebron	13
Tuthmosis II	1492-1479	13	Mephres	13
Hatshepsut	1479-1458	21	Amesses (N1)	22
Tuthmosis III	1458-1425	33	Mephramuthosis	26
Amenhotep II	1427-1400	27	Amenophis	31
Tuthmosis IV	1400-1390	10	Tethmosis	10
Amenhotep III	1390-1352	38	Orus	36
Akhenaten	1352-1336	16	Acencheres	12
Smenkhkare	1338-1336	2	Acenchres	
			(Nefertiti, N2)	2*
Tutankhamun	1336-1327	9	Rathotis (N3)	9
Ay	1327-1323	4	Armais	4
Horemheb	1323-1295	28	Armesses	
			Miammoun (N4)	28*
Ramesses I	1295-1294	1	Ramesses	1
Seti I	1294-1279	15	Amenophis/	
			Sethosis (N5)	19
Ramesses II	1279-1213	66	Rhampses	66

Table 11.3. Manetho's king list rearranged to match the conventional chronology.

Years marked by '*' indicate changes made to Manetho's length of reign, and notes about rulers are denoted by 'N'.

Notes to Table 11.3

1. Even though the rule of Tuthmosis III is generally assumed to have started in 1479 BCE, Hatshepsut ruled Egypt while Tuthmosis was young and he only became sole ruler after her

death in 1458 BCE.

2. Manetho lists one female ruler by the name of Acenchres and two male rulers with identical names, Acencheres. All three ruled for more or less 12 years. There can be little doubt that the female ruler must have been Nefertiti, who is believed by many scholars to have been Akhenaten's co-regent (see Chapter 13). Assuming that she co-ruled or was perceived as co-ruler with Akhenaten for 10 years and a further two years after his death, the number of years of Acenchres was reduced to two. She disappeared from the Amarna scene in year 12 of Akhenaten's reign and must then have assumed the title of Smenkhkare, probably upon the death of Akhenaten. Most of the records of the Amarna era were destroyed by Horemheb and it seems that Manetho only knew that there were two rulers of that name and elsewhere learned of a female ruler of more or less the same name. He therefore seems to have listed all three instead of only two, not realising that the female ruler was one of the first two. Nefertiti was the daughter-in-law of Amenhotep III and therefore the 'daughter' of Orus.

3. Tutankhamun is speculated by some to have been fathered by Amenhotep III[17]. Nefertiti was the daughter-in-law of Amenhotep III, implying that Rathotis would then indeed have been her brother, albeit her brother-in-law.

4. Manetho's list omits a Horemheb equivalent and jumps directly to a Ramesses who ruled for one year. This matches the reign of Ramesses I, but the remainder of the list contains some obvious duplications. Armesses Miammoun is supposed to have ruled for 66 years, but the only ruler who reigned for such an extended period of time was Ramesses II. He was preceded by Seti I, who ruled for 15 years, but Manetho associates Sethosis with Amenhotep III (as Aegyptus), the greatest of all Egyptian rulers. It is possible that Horemheb may have been in the service of the Amarna royals for decades, and that he may have been as old as Ay

himself. He rose to prominence under Tutankhamun and continued to serve under Ay[18], which may in part account for the extended reign of 66 years attributed to him. In Table 11.3 Armesses Miammoun is therefore associated with Horemheb and the number of years of his reign was changed accordingly.

5. The duration of the reign of Manetho's Amenophis corresponds more or less with that of Seti I and the fact that this Amenophis is succeeded by Sethosis and then Ramesses II suggests that Manetho somehow became confused by Amehotep III having been known as Sethosis (Sesostris), and the phonetic similarity between the names Sethosis and Seti.

The reason why Tuthmosis III was known as Mephramuthosis (Misphragmuthosis, see Appendix F) is potentially to be found in the translation of his name. Misphragmuthosis can be interpreted as 'The fence that saves us from being slain by the hated', from *miseō*[19] (hate, the hated), *phragmōs*[20] (a fence, barrier), *thuō*[21] (to sacrifice, immolate, kill) and *sōs*[22] (to save, deliver, protect). The more familiar word *sōs* (thine, yours) as used in the name Sesostris is not meaningful in this context. In Mephra(g)muthosis 'the hated' appears to have been replaced by the word *mē*[23] (me), but this does not make much sense. If derived from the word *ēmeō*[24] (to vomit), it may be interpreted as 'the vomit' instead of 'the hated', a reference to a detested enemy of Egypt. The name Alisphragmuthosis has a similar meaning in which 'the hated' is identified as 'the vagrants' or 'the vagabonds', from *alazōn* / *alē*[25] (a wanderer about the country, a vagabond, an imposter, a boaster). This is a clear reference to the hated Hyksos, who slowly began infiltrating Egypt as traders and nomads before they eventually invaded Lower Egypt. The fence that is referred to is without question the 'Walls of the Ruler', for which Sesostris (Tuthmosis III) was credited as having built (see Chapter 6). That the name Alisphragmuthosis was also associated with Kamose is perhaps best explained by an undertaking either Kamose or his brother Ahmose may have made, that once the Hyksos had been expelled from Egypt, they would build such a fortified fence to protect Egypt from future invasions from the north.

The key rulers in Manetho's king list are the Amarna rulers beginning with Amenhotep III, Akhenaten, Smenkhkare and Tutankhamun. The opinions of researchers on whom the Manetho rulers should be identified with differ greatly, in public literature at least. For example, Orus and Acencheres have been identified with Horemheb and Akhenaten[26], Acencheres and Rathotis with Akhenaten and Tutankhamun[27], Acencheres with Akhenaten[28], Rathotis and the two Acenchereses with Akhenaten, Smenkhkare and Tutankhamun[29] and more recently Orus, Acencheres, Rathotis, two Acenchereses and Armais respectively with Amenhotep III, Akhenaten, Smenhkare, Tutankhamun, Ay and Horemheb[30].

A detailed exposition of Manetho's chronology is given by Gary Greenberg in his book *Manetho – A Study in Egyptian Chronology*[31]. His interpretation of Manetho's Eighteenth Dynasty king list agrees with the revised chronology of Table 11.3 for Ahmose (Thethmosis), Amenhotep I (Amenophis), Tuthmosis I (Chebron), Hatshepsut (Amesses), Tuthmosis III (Mephres and Mephramuthosis), Amenhotep II (Amenophis), Tuthmosis IV (Tethmosis), Amenhotep III (Orus), Tutankhamun (Rathotis) and Ay (Armais). However, he associates Manetho's 'fictitious' king Amenophis with both Akhenaten and Smenkhkare, while Manetho clearly states that this Amenophis had a scribe called Amenophis, which could only refer to Amenhotep III. Greenberg overcomes the problem of the female ruler Acencheres, who was the daughter of Orus, by associating her with Tuthmosis II and indirectly Hatshepsut. He justifies this identification by arguing that Amenhotep III had no daughters on the throne and that 'Hatshepsut tried to create the appearance that she served as coregent with Tuthmosis II'[32]. The remaining two rulers called Acencheres are both linked to Horemheb.

The identities of Acencheres, Rathotis and Armais are possibly confirmed by the interpretation of their names. Acencheres most likely is derived from the Egyptian words *Aakh*[33] (radiance, brilliance, shine), en^{34} (of) and *kheres*[35] (destroy), meaning 'The radiance of the destroyer', or by implication 'The destroyer who belongs to the Aten'. The person who attempted to destroy the all-powerful Amun was Akhenaten, who was devoted to the sun god Aten. If he was perceived to have allowed the rebellious slaves to plunder Egypt, he would indeed have been the destroyer of Egypt in the eyes of the population. A Hebrew interpretation is also possible, from *'ach*[36] (brother), *'îyn*[37] (is it not?) and *cheresh*[38] (magical craft, silence), meaning 'Is it not the brother of magic?' This may link Akhenaten to the magic supposedly performed by the Pharaoh's magicians in response to Moses' miracles[39]. Alternatively, it may derived from *'ach, chên*[40] (beauty, grace, favour) and *cheresh*, resulting in 'Magic by his brother's grace'. This may refer to Akhenaten who was allowed to live an idyllic life as monarch in the isolated Akhetaten, by the grace of his brother Prince Tuthmosis, who had seized control of Egypt.

Tutankhamun's original name was Tutankhaten[41], meaning 'Living image of Aten', from *Tut*[42] (image, likeness), *aankh*[43] (life, live) and *Aten*, the name of Akhenaten's god, but he later changed this to Tutankhamun in favour of the god Amun. He was also known as Ra-neb-Kheperu[44], probably meaning 'Ra's lord of change' or 'Ra's lord of transformation', from *Ra* (name of the deity), *neb*[45] (lord, master) and *kheperu*[46] (shape, image, change, transformation). It was Tutankhamun who effectively brought an end to the worship of the Aten and reinstated Amun as the principal deity of Egypt. Incidentally, he was still very young when he changed his name from Tutankhaten to Tutankhamun and moved the seat of government from Akhetaten to Memphis[47]. His young age suggests that this decision was forced upon him by either Horemheb or Ay, or by both.

The name Rathotis appears to be a combination of the words *Ra* (name of the deity), *thut*[48] (image, form) and either *is*[49] (tomb) or *us*[50] (come to an end, destroy, do away with something). Loosely translated it would mean 'The image of Ra destroyed', with the 'Image of Ra' most likely referring to the Aten itself. The official name of the

Aten was 'The living Ra-Horus of the horizon who rejoices in his identity of light which is in the Aten'[51]. This suggests that the Aten was the physical manifestation or image of Ra. Rathotis would then mean 'The Aten destroyed', matching Tutankhamun's restoration of Amun. I could find no meaningful Hebrew or Greek interpretations of the name Rathotis.

Manetho's Armais was also known as Danaus and Hermeus. Danaus is probably of Greek origin as there appear to be no matching words in the Egyptian language. The name seems to be a form of *daneizo*[52], which means 'to loan or borrow'. *Strong's Expanded Dictionary of Biblical Words, Greek* lists *danos*[53] as referring to a gift, but it can also refer to 'money lent, a loan or debt'[54]. This interpretation must be correct as he was appointed as deputy over Egypt by his brother, and everything Armais (Λy) was and owned was by the grace of his brother-in-law Amenhotep III.

The names Armais and Hermeus are most likely of Egyptian origin (the language used by Manetho) and several Egyptian words can be used to construct them. The first syllable represents the Egyptian word *Er*, of which the old form was *Ar*, meaning 'at, near, upon, with, every' and 'against'[55]. There appear to be no Egyptian words equivalent to *mais* or *meus*, but several combinations of the form *ma-is* or *me-us* are possible. The words *ma* or *mai* can mean either 'youth or young' [56] or 'the seed of men' [57]. The name ends with either *is* or *us*, the latter meaning 'to come to an end' or 'to be destroyed'. The most probable interpretation is *Ar-mai-us*, meaning 'Upon the youth's demise'. Tutankhamun was only nine years old when he became king of Egypt and he ruled for nine years. He was therefore only 18 or 19 years old when he died, and scholars have long speculated that he was murdered by Ay who then usurped his throne[58]. Ay would certainly not have been given the nickname Armais had he not somehow been involved in the death of the young king.

It should be noted that both the Abydos King List[59], which ends with Seti I, and the king list of the Saqqara Tablet[60], which ends with

Ramesses II, totally omit the Amarna kings Akhenaten, Smenkhkare, Tutankhamun and Ay and list Horemheb as the successor of Amenhotep III. With the Amarna era and its upheaval still fresh in their minds, it would seem that the Nineteenth Dynasty pharaohs continued with Horemheb's suppression of all evidence relating to that dreadful period. It is probably for this reason that Manetho, who would have had access to numerous and possibly conflicting ancient sources stored in the library of Alexandria, became somewhat confused about the succession of kings following Amenhotep III.

Of particular interest is that Theophilus, the Christian Bishop of Antioch, places Moses and the Exodus during the reign of Tethmosis (Ahmose, see Table 11.2) who preceded Chebron[61], as did Africanus, using the name Amos instead of Tethmosis[62], while **Eusebius places the Exodus during rule of the first Acencheres[63], who can be identified as Akhenaten.**

That fact that two distinct Exoduses occurred is discussed in Chapters 18 and 19. The first Exodus did not involve Moses, but the escape of a part of the Hyksos nation to Canaan, the rest being captured as slaves. The second Exodus matches the hypothesis presented in this treatise, that Moses was Prince Tuthmosis who confronted or at least interacted with Akhenaten before the departure of the Hebrews from Egypt.

Incidentally, the mother of Seti I, who ruled for 14 years, was called Tia and his wife was called Tuy (sometimes spelled Tuya)[64]. By coincidence Amenhotep III had a mother (in-law) called Tjuya and was married to queen called Tiye. The reign of 14 years is close to the 13 years Manetho claimed Amenhotep III to have spent in Ethiopia, initially leading me to suspect that Amenhotep III had adopted (or became known by) the name Seti while in Ethiopia. If so it would have extend his reign from 38 years to 52 years, approaching Sethos' reign of 59 years. Furthermore, it is known that Seti I had conducted a campaign in Ethiopia during the first decade of his reign, as had Amenhotep. The latter had erected his famous Colossi of Memnon, while the great temple erected by Seti I was called the *Memnonium* by the Greeks[65].

Despite these similarities between Amenhotep III (mistakenly remembered as Sesostris in some accounts) and Seti I, there appears to be more than adequate proof that they were two distinct individuals. These similarities may, however, have confused Manetho and other ancient historians. For example, Seti I had conducted military campaigns into Canaan and Syria[66], possibly influencing Manetho's claim that Amenhotep had pursued the Hebrews into Syria after his return to Egypt.

The next step in establishing the time frame of the Exodus is to determine whether there was ever a period in the history of the Hebrew people, apart from the Exodus itself, that may be linked to Manetho's account. Given the Amarna setting, one would be looking for any evidence that may link the history of the Hebrews to that era. Could any of the Amarna correspondence letters provide a link to the Hyksos in Jerusalem? According to Manetho the invaders from Jerusalem plundered Egypt, matching the rationalised biblical confession, 'so they (the Hebrews) plundered the Egyptians'[67]. Is there any Hebrew record of an influx of wealth into Canaan? The answer is an emphatic 'Yes'.

12

Saul, David and Solomon – Amarna contemporaries

To determine if there is any truth in Manetho's claim that the shepherds in Jerusalem participated in the plundering of Egypt, one needs to look for a period in the history of the Hebrews during which such a campaign into Egypt may have occurred. Was there ever a time that Israel would have been powerful enough and Egypt weak enough for the Hebrews to have dared to launch such an attack? Israel was most powerful during its so-called Golden Age[1], which began with King Saul, who was dethroned by David. According to biblical tradition David's son Solomon became the wisest, most powerful and supposedly the internationally most recognised king of the Hebrews. If ever a Hebrew king would have been able to stand up to Egypt, it would have been Solomon.

By the same token, it would not have been possible for a foreign army to invade Egypt at a time when it was dominating the Middle East. One then needs to identify a period during which Egypt was weakened to such an extent that a foreign army could invade its territory and wreak havoc across the entire land. Unless the invasion of Egypt by foreigners was in fact the original invasion of Egypt by the Hyksos, the only other period during which such an invasion might have occurred would be the Amarna period. Manetho clearly distinguishes between two separate invasions, the first when the Hyksos took Lower Egypt without encountering significant resistance, and the second when the Exodus occurred during the reign of Amenhotep III. The question then remains whether the Golden Age of Israel can be linked to the Amarna era.

12.1 From Saul to Shishak

The story of Saul and David is related only in the Bible[2], and no other well-dated archaeological evidence pertaining to them has been found in Israel, Egypt or Mesopotamia[3]. As background, having long been ruled by their judges and prophets, the people of Israel prayed to God for a king, upon which God selected Saul as the first king of Israel. Later, however, Saul failed to follow the instructions of the prophet Samuel so he declared that God had come to regret appointing Saul as king of Israel, and that Saul's kingship would be overthrown. Samuel then anointed a young shepherd called David, whereupon the spirit of God departed from Saul and was received by David. David initially served as harpist to King Saul, but was also a skilled soldier and was appointed by Saul to defeat Goliath, the giant of the Philistines. David succeeded and became the commander of Saul's army. Saul's son Jonathan and David became close friends and later brothers-in-law when David married Saul's daughter Michal. Saul, however, became increasingly jealous of David's success and planned to have him killed. Michal helped him escape and was given as wife to Palti while David was in hiding. When David later became king of Judah, he would demand to have her back as his wife. Jonathan 'became one in spirit with David and loved him as himself'[4], and helped David escape from Saul. At one stage David gathered together a group of 400 outlaws with which he attacked the Philistines. On two occasions Saul attempted to kill David, but failed. David twice did not kill Saul when he had the opportunity to do so[5], which forced a reluctant Saul to call a truce with David.

David formed an alliance with the Philistines, who then attacked Saul's army at Gilboa. Saul was defeated by the Philistines, having fallen on his sword to avoid the humiliation of capture. A soldier who claimed to have killed Saul was summarily executed by David for killing a king anointed by God. Saul's son Jonathan and his brothers were also killed at Gilboa, causing David to weep for the loss of his friend, uttering the famous words, 'How the mighty have fallen'[6].

Scholars have long recognised that David was anything but the

God-fearing man the biblical scribes portrayed him to be. For a masterful treatise on the character of David read Gary Greenberg's *The Sins of King David* [7]. Of particular interest is David's systematic elimination of the entire family of Saul[8], for a variety of reasons, as well as the murder of high profile officials and leaders for their beautiful young wives. The latter included the murder of Uriah, the Hittite, for his beautiful wife Bathsheba[9] as discussed in Section 13.2.

12.2 Chronology of the Kingdom of Israel

As alluded to earlier, one of the biggest problems in the construction of the chronology of ancient history is the lack of events that can be dated absolutely, in other words to a specific date in the past. This problem is severely compounded when little if any evidence can be found to confirm the existence of specific individuals, as is the case for Israel's kings Saul, David and Solomon. Whereas numerous records and monuments of ancient Egyptian kings and dynasties have survived, the lack of corroborating evidence from Israel has prompted some scholars to state that the first kings of Israel never existed[10].

In constructing a chronology of ancient Israel one first of all has to assume that the major phases of the history of Israel as recorded in the Bible were based on real events. The next step is to identify those events that should be datable, and finally, to attempt to date those events. In this treatise it is assumed that most of the biblical accounts are based on actual events, despite have been embellished by later editors of the biblical texts. Following Finkelstein and Mazar[11], the datable events or eras of Israelite history should be:

- The era of the patriarchs Abraham, Isaac and Jacob. To my knowledge, and as implied by Finkelstein and Mazar, no evidence of the existence of any of these individuals has ever been found.
- The Exodus, the topic of this treatise. This event is one of the

anchors of Israel's history and its scope is so large that it must have been recorded in the historical annals of other nations, specifically those of the Egyptians.

- Joshua's conquest of Canaan when the Israelites who were freed by Moses entered the country. Here one would largely have to rely on corroborating evidence from Israel itself, either through archaeology or documentary evidence outside the Bible.

- The history of Israel as it developed following the Exodus and the return of the Israelites to Canaan, specifically the raid of Jerusalem by a pharaoh called Shishak.

At the end of this treatise it is argued that the patriarch Abraham was not an individual, but rather a reference to a mysterious people dating back several thousands of years before the Amarna period (the time of the Exodus). It is not the purpose of this treatise to discuss the details of evidence or the lack thereof regarding Joshua's conquest, but it suffices to mention that in Finkelstein's opinion the biblical narratives relating to Joshua cannot be accepted as straightforward historical accounts. In other words, there appears to be no hard evidence that would link Joshua's conquests, if these happened at all, to a specific period in time. That brings us to the last potential time marker of Solomon's era, the attack on Jerusalem by Shishak.

According to the Bible, Solomon began construction of the Temple in Jerusalem 480 years after the Exodus[12]. If this is true, fixing either the Exodus or Solomon's reign to a specific date would also fix the other event in time. Solomon was succeeded by his son Rehoboam, during whose reign the Temple was raided by an Egyptian pharaoh called Shishak[13]. One would expect this sacking of Jerusalem by an Egyptian pharaoh to have been recorded in the annals of the military campaigns of that pharaoh. If a matching record can be found, it may help us to place David and Solomon in a specific time window. The circumstances would, however, still have to match those of Solomon's reign as several Egyptian pharaohs have held sway over Canaan.

The period of the reign of Israel's first kings is generally accepted to be *ca.* 1050-1010 BCE for Saul, 1010-970 BCE for David and 970-930 BCE for Solomon[14]. How this dating was derived lies beyond the scope of this treatise, but it may be linked to the identification of Shishak as Sheshonk I (also spelled Sheshonq I), who ruled Egypt from *ca.* 945-924 BCE[15]. Sheshonk is known to have conducted a military campaign into Canaan, destroying about 150 towns and villages in the process[16]. The link between Shishak and Sheshonk is obviously first made by the phonetic similarity of the names, which appears to be confirmed by Sheshonk's known campaign into Canaan. Although leading scholars such as Finkelstein seem to have accepted the identification of Shishak as Sheshonk without any hesitation[17], this may not be the case.

The name Shishak[18] (*Shûwshaq*) appears to be derived from the Hebrew words *shishshâh*[19] (six, sixth), *shâshâh*[20] (to divide into sixths) or *shâsâh*[21] (to plunder, rob, destroyer), and *'âch*[22] (brother, brotherly). If formed by the last two words, Shishak would mean 'The brother who plundered'. This would be an apt description of the brother whom Sesostris had placed in charge of Egypt, but in the end had abused his power over the queen and the harem of the king. In other words, Shishak would be Ay, who witnessed the rebelling Hyksos slaves and the Hyksos (shepherds) who came from Jerusalem to destroy Egypt, and could not wait to retaliate when the Egyptian army had at long last returned to Egypt.

The biblical description of the Shishak's raid on Jerusalem creates the impression that it was a focussed attack to rob Jerusalem of its wealth. That a successful military campaign against the Asiatics in Syria and by implication Canaan had been conducted is confirmed by a claim to this effect by Horemheb, commander of the boy king Tutankhamun's army[23]. The man who for all intents and purposes was ruling Egypt during Tutankhamun's reign was Ay, and he would have taken particular pleasure in retrieving as much as possible of the gold and other riches that had been plundered from Egypt.

12.3 Identification of Saul and David in the Amarna Letters

In his controversial book *A Test of Time*[24] David Rohl attempts to rewrite the chronology of Ancient Egypt. This includes the Amarna era which he, along with co-workers in the field, manage to link to the United Israelite Kingdom under David and Solomon. Rohl derives his new chronology by reconsidering the four key anchor points or pillars used by orthodox Egyptologists to construct the chronology that is currently accepted by most scholars in the field. The first of these is the sacking of Thebes by Ashurbanipal in 664 BCE, which heralded the beginning of the Late Period of Egyptian history. The second is the identification of Shoshenq I as the biblical king Shishak of Egypt. The link between Shishak and Sheshonk I was made by Edwin Thiele[25] whose work was used to date the event to *ca*. 925 BCE. Egyptologists subsequently used that date to determine an absolute date for the rule of Sheshonk I. The third is the heliacal rising of Sothis (the Egyptian name for the Dog Star) in 1517 BCE for Year 9 of Amenhotep as recorded by the *Papyrus Ebers*. The fourth pillar is the lunar date recorded in the *Papyrus Leiden I 350*, which may be linked to the fifty-second year of the reign of Ramesses II. Of these four time anchors Rohl accepts only the first. Specifically, he identifies the biblical Shishak as Ramesses II, who was recorded to have raided Jerusalem.

Rohl argues that during the Amarna era Egypt had become powerless, at least in terms of military campaigns and control of its vassal states, and that this created an opportunity for those states to free themselves from Egyptian rule. He concludes that Saul, David and therefore Solomon must have been contemporaries of the Amarna kings based mainly on the following observations and arguments[26]:

- The country north of Jerusalem was dominated by a king

called Labayu in the so-called *Amarna Letters*[27], an archive of correspondence on clay tablets found at Amarna, the modern name for Akhenaten's city Akhetaten. Labayu's name can be interpreted as 'Great Lion of N', where N represents a deity. The correlation between the lives of Labayu and the biblical Saul suggests that they must have been one and the same person. Furthermore, Saul appears to have been guarded by the *lᵉbâ'îym*[28-30] which means 'great lions', confirming a possible link to Labayu.

- At least 12 cities and towns of the Amarna era are also mentioned in the Bible in the books of *I Samuel* and *II Samuel*, wherein the history of Saul and David is described.
- Labayu's scribe wrote the first part of one of the letters to the pharaoh in Akkadian, but then switched over to almost pure Canaanite, a dialect of Hebrew.
- Labayu and his Habiru mercenary forces can be linked to Saul and his Hebrew mercenaries.
- Labayu had lost a city with its sacred site to his enemies, but managed to recover the city from the enemy. This matches Saul retaking Gibeah (Geba), a sacred place to the Israelites, from the Philistines.
- In a letter to the Egyptian pharaoh Labayu wrote, 'Moreover, the king wrote for my son. I did not know that my son was consorting with the Habiru.'[31] This matches Saul's tirade against his son Jonathan for having joined David's forces:

> Son of a rebellious slut! Do I not know that you side with the son of Jesse [David] to your own shame and your mother's dishonour?[32]

- Saul and his sons were killed on mountains of Gilboa; Labayu was killed in similar fashion, upon which his surviving sons, identified by Rohl as Ishbaal and David, his son-in-law, request an ally to wage war against the people of Gina for having killed their father. The town of Gina is close to the southern slopes of Gilboa, confirming the location of the death of Saul and Labayu.

- Labayu's surviving son was called Mutbaal, which is Akkadian for 'Man-of-Baal'. Saul's surviving son was called Ishbaal, which is Hebrew for 'Man-of-Baal'.
- Mutbaal was apparently accused of hiding a man called Ayab, whom Rohl identifies as Joab, commander of the Habiru forces under David.
- Following death of Labayu and his son, the 'land of the king has deserted to the Habiru', matching David who had become the new king of Israel. Shuwardata of Gath, who informed the pharaoh of these events, and Akish, the biblical king of Gath, are argued to be the same person as both names appear to mean 'The sun has given'.
- Addadanu, the ruler of Gezer, informed the pharaoh that he was preparing for war and requested his assistance:

> There being war against me from the mountains, I built a house (i.e. a fortress) – its name is Manhatu – to make preparations before the arrival of the archers of the king, my lord...[33]

Rohl identifies Manhatu as the biblical Manahath in the valley of Rephaim, which the Philistines had invaded and where they had deployed their forces.

- An Amarna pharaoh, most likely Amenhotep III, instructed Addadanu of Gezer to 'guard the place of the king where you are'[34], which he evidently did as David did not take Gezer.
- Another vassal of Egypt complained that he was at war with Tianna, identified by Rohl as Zion (in Hebrew *Tsiyon*), which was Jerusalem, the City of David.
- In his letter to the pharaoh, king Mutbaal (Ishbaal) protested:

I swear Ayab is not in Pella. In fact, he has [been in the] field (i.e. on campaign) for two months. Just ask Benenima. Just ask Dadua. Just ask Yishuya.[35]

Benenima can be identified as Baanah, who would later assassinate Ishbaal in his own royal apartments, while Dadua is the biblical King David and Yishuya is Jesse (in Hebrew *Yishay*), David's father.

- Rohl identifies the Amarna king Aziru as the biblical Hadadezer and the Amarna ruler Lupakku as the biblical Shopak.

Apart from Rohl's arguments, the following other scraps of evidence point to the same conclusion, that Saul and David were contemporaries of the Amarna kings:

- The singular form of one of the Hebrew words for 'lion' is *lᵉbîyâ*, which is phonetically almost identical to the name Labayu given that vowels were omitted in early Hebrew.
- As one might expect, Egypt was not the only country in the Levant to suffer from the plague. When he became king, David conducted a census in Israel, which caused the Lord to 'send in anger a plague upon all of Israel', killing 70,000 men[36]. Assuming that this number is correct and that an equal number of women and children would have been affected, the number of people killed by the plague may have been more than 200,000. In ancient times this must surely have represented a significant portion of the population and even the city of Jerusalem was in danger of being destroyed by the plague. It would appear that Canaan was affected by the plague almost as much as was Egypt.
- The biblical King Solomon was renowned not only for his wisdom, but also for his wealth. Although the legend of Solomon has certainly been embellished in written and oral

tradition, the claim that he was honoured by all the kings of the world and received tribute from, among others, the kings of Arabia suggests an element of truth. No kingdom of Israel appears to have been honoured by its neighbours as claimed by the scribes of Jewish tradition, so one must ask from where his enormous wealth would have originated. The answer is simple – it was the wealth plundered from Egypt during the reign of Akhenaten. This wealth had been accumulated by Amenhotep III, who was the king honoured by all nations.

- Solomon built a place called Millo, meaning 'filling', as part of his extensive renovations of Jerusalem. A likely site of Millo was discovered by Kathleen Kenyon[37]. However, pottery found at the terrace fill can be dated back to the reign of Amehotep III and the Amarna era instead of to the orthodox Solomonic era. This dilemma caused Kenyon to reinterpret the Bible, claiming that Solomon had merely rebuilt the Millo, instead of being its original architect.

- Solomon had received a daughter of a pharaoh as wife, for whom he built a palace. Rohl argues that the only Egyptian architectural remains ever found in Jerusalem date back to Late Bronze Age *ca.* 1400-1200 BCE, which accords with Solomon having been a contemporary of the Amarna kings. The reason why an Egyptian pharaoh would have given a daughter to a king of Jerusalem is discussed in Chapter 13, which focuses on Nefertiti.

- Solomon was visited by the fabled Queen of Sheba. In Chapter 13 she is proven to be none other than Nefertiti, the wife of Akhenaten.

- One of Solomon's enemies, Adad the Edomite, fled to Egypt during the reign of David. There he found favour with the king of Egypt, who gave the sister of his wife Taphnes to Adad as wife[38]. The name of this queen of Egypt can be interpreted as '(She of the) fugitive children', from the Hebrew words *taph*[39] (a family, little ones, children) and *nîys*[40] (fugitive). As related below, this description could apply to the wife of Amenhotep III (Aegyptus), who wanted his 50 sons to marry the 50 daughters of Danaus[41]. Danaus escaped to Argos with all his daughters, but the 50 sons of Aegyptus followed and insisted on being married to the daughters of Danaus. Danaus could not refuse permission for the marriages to proceed, but commanded each of his daughters to kill their husband on their wedding night. Only one of the 50 sons was spared (for the origin of this legend, see the discussion on the tenth plague in Section 17.3). The above interpretation of the name Taphnes suggests that the 50 daughters of Danaus were in fact the daughters of the pharaoh. The 50 sons and 50 daughters (the number 50 meaning 'many') may therefore all have belonged to Amenhotep III, and it would seem that they fled from Egypt either before or after the death of Tiye. It is quite possible that they fled to avoid the curse of the sacrifice of the firstborn as soon as they got wind of what was awaiting them.

Based on these observations, there can be little doubt that Saul, David and Solomon were contemporaries of the Amarna kings. Rohl's revised chronology, however, appears to have been rejected by the vast majority of modern scholars. The likely reason for this seems to be the fact that Rohl moved the Eighteenth Dynasty from its orthodox beginning *ca.* 1570 BCE by almost 400 years to 1194 BCE, rather than that they dispute his link between the Amarna and biblical kings.

The reasons why Rohl chose to move the dating of the Amarna era instead of the rather tenuous orthodox dating for the Israelite kingdom are discussed in the next section. His revised chronology would appear to be dubious, as vast amounts of datable evidence and records exist in Egypt and Egypt's interaction with the neighbouring states it controlled is well documented from both sides. By contrast, there is hardly any evidence to be found that would unequivocally prove the existence of the Israelite kings Saul, David and Solomon. In other words, Rohl should have moved the tenuous dates of the Israelite kings to the firmly established dating of the Amarna era and not the other way around.

12.4 Rohl's new Amarna Chronology

As justification for his revised chronology, Rohl uses mainly three arguments:

- Some Egyptologists have identified Ramesses II as the Pharaoh of the Oppression since this pharaoh had forced the enslaved Israelites to build a city called Ramesses[42], and Ramesses II had moved his capital from Thebes to a new city called Pi-Ramesses[43]. This city was, however, built on or near the site of the much older city of Avaris[44] and it is very likely that later scribes of the biblical texts merely referred to the city by its most recent name.

    Ramesses II was recorded to have raided Shalem, an ancient name for the city of Jerusalem[45]. Rohl uses this, along with other arguments, to conclude that the biblical Shishak could be identified as Ramesses II. The fact that Ramesses II had raided Jerusalem does not, however, constitute conclusive proof that he was Shishak. Many pharaohs before him had dominated Canaan and Jerusalem, as one of its largest cities, would have been 'raided' by the invading Egyptian army on several occasions. The possibility of a raid during the later stages of the Amarna era cannot be ruled out because of the deliberate attempt by Horemheb and others to erase that part of Egypt's history from their annals.

- A key argument of Rohl is based on a letter of Abimilku to an Amarna king[46], assumed by some to be Akhenaten, but certainly not ruling out Amenhotep III, reporting that half of the palace of the king of Ugarit was destroyed by fire, and so half of it had thus disappeared. The king of Ugarit has been identified as Nikmaddu II and in the remains of his palace was found a blackened clay tablet with the inscription translated as:

> The day of the new moon of Hiyyaru was put to shame (as) the sun (goddess) set, with Rashap as her gatekeeper.[47]

Rohl interprets the day being put to shame when the sun set as a total eclipse of the sun, at sunset. Astronomical retrocalculation reveals that the only near-sunset total eclipse of the sun between 1400 and 1000 BCE, as observed from Ugarit, occurred on 9 May 1012 BCE[48], thus fixing the event in time.

At first glance Rohl's reasoning seems to be sound, but one has to wonder just how much of an impact an eclipse of the sun would have had just before sunset. Day does not turn into night during a solar eclipse and this eclipse of the sun may simply have been experienced as an early sunset.

A much more likely interpretation of the daylight being shamed at sunset would be the sun setting in darkness which had appeared on the western horizon ('sunset'), the darkness being the ash cloud of Thera's eruption. This event may have been visible for months on end, supposedly heralded by an astronomer-priest on the reverse side of the Nikmaddu clay tablet. In the *Tempest Stele of Ahmose I* mention is made of darkness in the western region (horizon), which in Chapter 16 is argued to be the ash cloud of an eruption of Thera.

- The period of reign of the Babylonian king Ammisaduga can be dated, at least in theory, from his so-called *Venus Tablets*, on which observations of the planet Venus during his reign were recorded[49]. Due to uncertainties in the interpretation of the text, the orthodox dating of these observations ranges from 1702 to 1582 BCE. Further research by the astronomer Wayne Mitchell re-dated Ammisaduga's rule to 1419 BCE. Ammisaduga was preceded by the more famous King

Hammurabi by about 150 years. Hammurabi was recorded to have attacked the palace of King Zimrilim in the city of Mari in north-east Syria, and among the remains of the palace was found a list of gifts received by the king. One of these gifts was a gold cup which he received from Yantin-Ammu, the king of Byblos. A relief of Yantin found at the site of Byblos contained a cartouche of a pharaoh whose name ended with the word *hotep*, the first part having been lost. Rohl then identifies this pharaoh as Neferhotep I of the Thirteenth Dynasty (1795-1650 BCE). In orthodox chronology Yantinammu is made a contemporary of Sehetepibre (Amenemhat I)[50], who ruled from 1985-1955 BCE[51]. Amenemhat was preceded by Mentuhotep IV, who would certainly qualify as Rohl's king whose name ended with *hotep*.

I quoted this example to demonstrate just how difficult it can be to determine a precise date or period for a specific ruler. Much depends on the interpretation of the ancient texts and cross-links to rulers of other nations.

As should by now be clear, Rohl's motivation for moving the Amarna era to a substantially different period in time is dubious. His linking of the Amarna era Labayu to Saul and Dadua to David, however, appears to be perfectly sound, which means that the era of Saul, David and Solomon must be moved back in time to the Amarna period.

As a final note on the chronology of Israel's United Monarchy, the Bible claims that Solomon began constructing the Temple 480 years after the Israelites had left Egypt. If true, this would exclude the possibility of Solomon being an Amarna contemporary as the Exodus occurred during the reign of Akhenaten. The period of 480 years is, however, close to the duration of the Israeli sojourn in Egypt (430 years according to the Bible and 511 years according to Manetho), which suggests that the biblical scribes had become confused about when exactly the Exodus had occurred. It should also be kept in mind that as stated before, there were two Exoduses of the Israelites from Egypt, the first when the Hyksos entrapped by Ahmose in Avaris managed to escape, and the second about 200 years later when those captured by Ahmose were led from Egypt by Moses.

Nefertiti, the Queen of Sheba and Helen of Troy

As if the discovery of Akhenaten's city Akhetaten (Amarna) were not enough, the discovery of a bust of Nefertiti, his wife, caused a sensation. Currently residing in the Egyptian Museum in Berlin, Nefertiti's bust has become one of the most recognisable symbols of ancient Egypt, and also an icon of female beauty (see Figure 13.1). Her origins are not known, although the fact that she had a wet nurse called Tiy, who may have been Tiye, the later wife of Ay, led

Figure 13.1. Bust of Nefertiti[1]

some scholars to believe that she must have been of Egyptian origin[2]. It has been speculated that Nefertiti may have been the daughter of Tiye and Ay, but Tiye was never identified as the queen's mother. Nefertiti had a sister called Mutnodjmet (also read as Mutbenret), but practically nothing is known about their parentage. Nefertiti's name means 'The Beautiful One Is Come' or 'A Beautiful Woman Has Come', which suggests to other scholars that she must have been of foreign descent. It will be shown next that she was of Hebrew descent.

13.1 Solomon's Queen of Sheba

The biblical account of Solomon's enigmatic Queen of Sheba is brief and reveals only scant details of her origins[3]. She had heard of Solomon's famed wisdom and came from her country to try him with questions and talk to him about 'all that she had on her mind'. Impressed with his wisdom, she showered him with gifts including gold and spices. He reciprocated by giving her more than she had given him, upon which she and her servants returned to her country. In Christian tradition she was remembered as the Queen of the South[4].

Josephus' Queen of Egypt and Ethiopia
In his *Antiquities* Josephus gives a valuable account of this queen, parts of which are worth quoting here:

> I suppose also that Herodotus of Halicarnassus, when he said there were three hundred and thirty kings of Egypt after Menes, who built Memphis, did therefore not tell us their names, because they were in common called Pharaohs; for when after their death there was a queen reigned, **he calls her by her name Nicaule**, as thereby declaring, that while the kings were of the male line, and so admitted of the same nature, while a woman did not admit the same, he did therefore set down that her name, which she could not naturally have. As for myself, I have discovered from our

own books, that after Pharaoh, the father-in-law of Solomon, no other king of Egypt did any longer use that name; **and that it was after that time when the forenamed queen of Egypt and Ethiopia came to Solomon** ...

There was then a woman queen of Egypt and Ethiopia; she was inquisitive into philosophy, and one that on other accounts also was to be admired. When this queen heard of the virtue and wisdom of Solomon, she had a great mind to see him; ...

Accordingly she came to Jerusalem with great splendor and rich furnishings; for she brought with her camels laden with gold, with several sorts of sweet spices, and with precious stones. ...

Now when the queen had thus demonstrated in words how deeply the king had affected her, her disposition was known by certain presents, for she gave him twenty talents of gold, and an immense quantity of spices and precious stones. ... Solomon also repaid her with many good things, and mainly by bestowing upon her what she chose of her own inclination, for there was nothing that she desired which he denied her; ... So when this queen of Ethiopia had obtained what we have already given an account of, and had again communicated to the king what she brought with her, she returned to her own kingdom.[5]

The Queen of Sheba in the Koran

In Koranic legend a hoopoe returned from a land called Sheba (Saba) to inform Solomon:

I found a woman ruling over them, and she hath been given (abundance) of all things, and hers is a mighty throne. I found her and her people worshipping the sun instead of Allah.[6]

In Arabic tradition this queen is known as Bilqis[7]. Solomon then sent a letter to her in which he demanded her to come to him in submission, like a person who is surrendering. She responded by sending messengers (translated 'ambassadors' by Ali, one of the English translators of the Koran, see Section 2.4 for reference), to Solomon. He invited her to visit him, and following several demonstrations of his wisdom, she accepted Solomon's faith.

In Jewish legend

As in the Koran, Jewish tradition relates that a hoopoe informed Solomon about the fabulously wealthy land of Sheba and its queen[8]. Solomon sent her a letter, commanding her to appear before him. She loaded her ships with gifts for Solomon, which included slave boys and girls, and in a letter accompanying the gifts she promised to visit him within three years, even though the journey from her country to Jerusalem usually took seven years to complete. As in the other legends, she confronted Solomon with riddles, which he promptly solved.

In Ethiopian legend

The story of Solomon and an Ethiopian queen called Makeda is related to us in an Ethiopian text called the *Kebra Nagast*, the first English translation of which was made by Sir E. A. Wallis Budge in 1932. He named his translation *The Queen of Sheba and Her Only Son Menyelek*[9]. According to Ethiopian legend Makeda was a very beautiful, bright and intelligent woman who ruled a land where the sun was worshipped, along with the stars and the moon. The story is much the same as that of Arabic tradition, except that instead of a hoopoe, it was a trader in service of Makeda who had come to Jerusalem and witnessed Solomon's grandeur. On his return to Ethiopia he informed Makeda about his experience, who at length decided to visit Solomon and took with her a caravan of more than 800 camels, mules and asses. Suitably impressed by Solomon, she eventually succumbed to his charms and became his wife. She later returned to Ethiopia, where her child called Menyelek was born nine months later. As a young man in his early twenties, Menyelek visited Solomon so that he might declare Menyelek king of Ethiopia. This

Solomon did, and sent the firstborn sons of the elders of Israel to accompany him back to Ethiopia, in order to establish a Jewish colony and kingdom in that country. To comfort those who had been chosen to settle in Ethiopia, a deceitful priest allowed them to smuggle the Ark of the Covenant out of the temple to take with them, replacing the original item with a replica.

With these legends and traditions about the Queen of Sheba in mind, it is now possible to reconstruct the most likely sequence of events relating to this enigmatic woman.

13.2 Nefertiti, daughter of Bathsheba

Before we can take a closer look at the origins of the Queen of Sheba, it is necessary to first revisit Solomon's origins as recorded in the Bible[10]. The Bible relates the story of King David walking on the roof of his palace one day, from where he saw a beautiful woman bathing herself. She was Bathsheba, the wife of Uriah the Hittite, who was a member of David's elite group of soldiers. David sent messengers to fetch her, she came and he slept with her. He arranged for Uriah to be murdered and subsequently took Bathsheba as his wife. Seven days after their first son was born, he was 'struck' by the Lord (the child became sick and died) as punishment for David's sin. David comforted his distraught wife, slept with her again and so was born Solomon, the future heir to his empire. For Uriah's house to have been so close to the palace that David could notice the beauty of the naked Bathsheba suggests that Uriah may have been more than just a soldier in his army. He may very well have been a high ranking Hittite official in Saul's court, seized by David, hence the reference to his country of origin.

The name Bathsheba is usually interpreted as 'Daughter of an oath'[11] from the words $bath$[12] (daughter) and $sheba'$[13] (seven, seven times, an infinite number) supposedly in the sense of $shâba'$ [14] (to 'seven' oneself, meaning to swear or to take an oath). The name should, however, first and foremost be read as 'Daughter of Sheba', the latter being a common male Hebrew name. According to the Bible, Bathsheba was the daughter of a man called Ammiel[15] (possibly also Eliam[16]), both names essentially meaning 'People of God' from *'am*[17] (people, nation) and *'êl*[18] (God). Like Uriah, Eliam was one of David's 30 most trusted warriors, but there is no evidence to suggest that he was Bathsheba's father. The 'oath' link between the words *sheba'* and *shâba'* appears to be rather tenuous. If Sheba should instead be interpreted as 'a multitude' or even 'the people' (from 'an infinite number'), it would certainly agree with the name Ammiel which also refers to a large group of people, the People of God. One can therefore argue with reasonable certainty that Bathsheba was the daughter of a man called Ammiel, who was also known as Sheba. Is it possible to identify a man called Sheba in David's reign? The answer is 'yes', and he was not just any man.

One of David's fiercest opponents was a man indeed called Sheba[19]. He publically declared that Israel 'had no part in David, no part in Jesse's son', and 'all the men of Israel' deserted David to follow Sheba. David mercilessly pursued Sheba until he was cornered in a city. Fearing annihilation by David's general Joab, the inhabitants of the city decapitated Sheba and threw his head from the city wall to Joab. As leader of 'all the men of Israel' Sheba could certainly also have been known as Ammiel.

Although there is no direct evidence linking this Sheba to Bathsheba's father, it is very likely that they could have been the same person. This link is supported by the description of Solomon's famous visiting queen as the 'Queen of Sheba', which is almost invariably interpreted as referring to a queen who came from a country called Sheba. No country by that name is known to have existed, although some scholars have attempted to link it to ancient Saba, a region in modern Yemen[20]. Josephus, however, made it clear that the Queen of Sheba was actually the queen of Egypt and Ethiopia, which accords with the New Testament records in which she is called the Queen of the South. From Canaan one has to travel south to reach Egypt. Furthermore, the fact that she and her people expressly worshipped the sun links her to Egypt and the Amarna era.

A much more logical interpretation of her name would simply be 'Sheba's queen', where Sheba would be a person and not a country. If Solomon's Queen of Sheba was in fact a queen of Egypt, she would probably have been known in her country as Sheba's queen, even more so if the father of this queen was the Sheba who dared oppose David.

To understand the circumstances of how an Israelite woman may have become a queen of Egypt, it is necessary to take a closer look at the exploits of David specifically regarding the beautiful women who became his wives or concubines. Invariably the scribes of David's history attempted to justify the seizure of these women in various ways, except of course in the case of Bathsheba. Among these women were:

- Bathsheba, whose husband Uriah was murdered by David. The biblical narrative attempts to portray her as a willing adulteress, but that is highly unlikely given David's true nature.
- The wives of Saul, who were given to David by God,

> I (Jehovah) delivered you from the hand of Saul. I gave your master's house to you, and your master's wives into your arms.[21]

There can be little doubt that David had orchestrated the deaths of Saul and all his sons, including Jonathan, and he naturally took possession of everything and everyone in their households.

- Saul's daughter Michal, whom Saul supposedly had betrothed to David before he became a threat to Saul[22]. She was simply taken from her husband Paltiel, who followed her weeping but was forced to return. In rabbinic tradition Michal was of 'entrancing beauty'[23], and she was just one of the pretty women he took for himself. Reading between the lines of the rationalisation that she secretly loved David, her barrenness, which followed after she had criticised and despised David for publically dancing in the nude[24], suggests that he simply had her locked away, as he did to the 10 concubines of Saul (see below). The extent to which later scribes attempted to clean David's tarnished reputation is illustrated by a comment in the Talmud, that Palti never consummated his marriage with Michal, David's un-divorced wife, but as a token of self-restraint kept a sword between them while in bed[25]. The name Palti[26], who is also referred to as Paltiel, is generally interpreted as 'Delivered (by God)', from *pâlat*[27] (escape, deliver). A different interpretation would be that Palti, perceiving what David was planning, managed to escape to safety with his beautiful wife Michal. David later made a point of catching up with 'the one that got away' and took his wife by force. For all we know David may have taunted Palti that he would one day take his wife from him, causing the young couple to flee. If she had any male children by Palti, they would have been killed.

- Abigail, the beautiful wife of the wealthy Nabal, who according to the scribes was a rude and evil man. The Lord 'struck Nabal and he died'. Abigail then became David's wife[28].

- David's attitude towards women is further demonstrated by the fate of 10 of his concubines he left at the palace when he had to flee from his son Absalom[29]. In order to humiliate his father, Absalom raped all 10 in full public view[30]. When David eventually returned, he kept them in confinement for the rest of their lives[31], irrespective of the fact that they were victims and not willing participants. David's actions regarding these women suggest that he may have had an ulterior motive for leaving them to the mercy of Absalom and his men. He possibly left them behind knowing that Absalom would first indulge in the rape of these beautiful women before continuing his pursuit of his father, allowing David more time to escape.

It would appear that David had come into contact with numerous beautiful young women while still professing loyalty to Saul. They would have been the daughters and the wives of the high ranking officials in Saul's court. Once David became king, he had the power to take possession of any woman he desired, which in present day context would make him a serial rapist. No doubt many readers will disagree with this interpretation, but they would be well advised to read Greenberg's *The Sins of King David* referred to earlier, in the introduction of which he states:

...The same studies will also show, contrary to the biblical image and popular belief, that Saul was not a manic-depressive paranoid, imagining false schemes by David to steal his throne, but a popular and well-balanced king who accurately understood what David was about and who took responsible actions to curtail David's treasonous and disloyal behaviour to Israel. ... This examination will show that David was a corrupt and ambitious mercenary who committed treason against Israel by working with its enemies to seize the throne from King Saul; an ambitious and ruthless politician who initiated, sanctioned, or condoned murder and assassination as a way to eliminate political rivals, royal or otherwise ... a cruel and unjust tyrant who used foreign mercenaries to centralize power under his control and who oppressed the people of Israel with high taxes and forced labour; a military imperialist who waged wars of conquest with his neighbours and exposed the peaceful Israelites to military counter-attacks that left many dead, wounded, or widowed.[32]

One should therefore read the biblical glorification of David with utmost suspicion. My own opinion about David is that he probably did not believe in any god at all, and that everything attributed to him in this regard was introduced by later scribes. History was indeed written by the victors, in this case by David, his henchmen and later Hebrew scribes.

This brings us to Bathsheba and David. As she had already been married to Uriah, the chances are good that she already would have had children by him. David may have spared her daughters, but would never have tolerated any sons of Uriah. The episode of God punishing David through the death of his first son by Bathsheba must be understood to mean that Bathsheba was already pregnant when David seized her, and that the infant was killed shortly after birth. If her father was indeed the Sheba who had opposed David, one can imagine the hatred she must have harboured towards the man who murdered her father, her husband and her son and took her as his lifelong sex slave.

It can be argued that Bathsheba must have had a daughter who ended up becoming a queen of Egypt, for three primary reasons. These are:

- The Queen of Sheba refers to the daughter of a man called Sheba who became queen of Egypt. It is of course also possible that Sheba had another, younger daughter besides Bathsheba, who was sent as a gift to Amenhotep III or perhaps even Prince Tuthmosis himself. This queen could not have been anyone but Nefertiti. If the claim that Nefertiti had a wet nurse named Tiy is true, and there is no reason to suspect otherwise, Nefertiti and her sister Mutbenret must have been smuggled out to Egypt as babies or little girls. Kings would probably never been interested in receiving foreign babies to take care of, in which case there remains only one feasible recipient of the children, namely Yuya, the biblical Joseph. It is then almost certain that the young Tiye, daughter of Yuya and Tuyu, took care of these young children.

- When her husband Akhenaten died, or was killed, Nefertiti wrote to a Hittite king asking for one of his sons as her husband, promising that he would become the king of Egypt (see Section 13.4 for a discussion on this controversial identification). This strongly suggests that she was of Hittite origin, namely that she was a daughter of Uriah the Hittite.

- If Nefertiti was indeed a daughter of Bathsheba, Solomon would have been her half-brother. This would have offered greater motivation for her to visit her country of birth, rather than going there simply to experience the wisdom of Solomon, invariably stated as the purpose of her visit. For all we know Bathsheba may still have been alive at the time, and Nefertiti used the opportunity to meet her aged mother for the first time.

Following this reasoning and assuming that Nefertiti was Solomon's Queen of Sheba, one might hope to find some extra-biblical evidence of a visit by an Egyptian queen to Canaan. Such a link is indeed to be found.

Of the many ivory carvings found during the excavation of Megiddo, the most famous must certainly be the one depicting a Canaanite king seated on a cherubim throne (see Figure 13.2). The ivory carvings were found in a layer dated to the Late Bronze Age

Figure 13.2. The Megiddo Ivory depicting a Canaanite king on a cherubim throne visited by an Egyptian queen[33,34]

(*ca.* 1350 - 1150 BCE)[35]. Due to the conventional dating of the era of Solomon's kingdom to *ca.* 970 BCE, this scene has not received consideration as the Queen of Sheba visiting Solomon, although Rohl did remark that the ivory is dated to the Solomonic era (of his revised chronology), and that the flat-topped crown worn by the queen is similar to those worn by the royal ladies of the Amarna court[36]. He, however, stopped short of identifying her as Nefertiti, the queen renowned for wearing that particular type of crown. The royal chariots on the Megiddo ivory are pulled by a side-by-side pair of horses. Although most likely common practice throughout the ancient world, this is particularly true of the Amarna era (see Figure 13.3).

There is significantly more to be deduced from the scene on the Megiddo Ivory. Regarding the king, the throne appears to be a carbon copy of the throne of Ahiram, king of the Phoenician city Byblos (see Figure 13.4). Two alabaster fragments found in Ahiram's tomb bore the cartouche of Ramesses II, which prompted its discoverer Pierre Montet to date the tomb to the thirteenth century BCE, while vases found in the tomb suggested a eighth or even seventh century dating[37]. Solomon was known to have had a close ally in King Hiram I of the Phoenician city Tyre[38], and he had a throne made of ivory, which had two armrests and two lions standing beside the armrests[39]. The description of Solomon's throne therefore closely matches the throne of Ahiram and that on the Megiddo Ivory, except for the cherubim that may mistakenly have been remembered as lions in oral tradition. One can therefore conclude that the presence of a Phoenician-styled throne on the Megiddo Ivory and Solomon's close links to the Phoenician cities Byblos and Tyre, along with the biblical description of Solomon's throne, all suggest that the king on the Megiddo Ivory represents Solomon.

It should be stressed that the scene on the ivory carving must certainly represent a major historical event rather than an everyday court scene, namely the visit of a queen accompanied by musicians,

Figure 13.3. Pairs of horses in a royal procession from the Amarna period[40]

gifts (as symbolised by the lotus flowers), captive slaves and an armed escort as suggested by the chariot. Jewish tradition concerning the Queen of Sheba relates that she brought slaves to Solomon, albeit children and not men. A misidentification of the

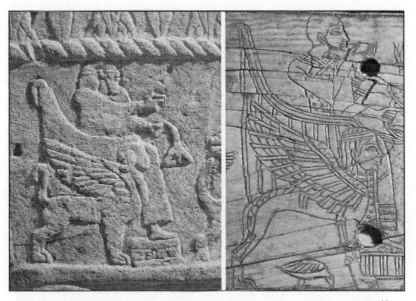

Figure 13.4. King Ahiram of Byblos on his cherubim throne (left)[41], compared to the Megiddo Ivory throne (right)

slaves and their purpose could easily have occurred during years of oral tradition and lost historical records. The captive kings are shown with distinctive beards, as are most of the other men including the king.

The queen and the lyrist, who has long, flowing hair, obviously are not bearded. The Egyptian origins of the queen in the carving can be deduced from the lotus flowers above her arm and elsewhere on the carving, as well as the winged sun disc above the horse, both symbols of ancient Egypt. The lyrist is of special interest (see Figure 13.5). A scene from the Amarna tomb of Ay is described as follows:

We have already noticed that each great house, whether royal or private, seemed to possess a band of female musicians. As the women shown here are all busily engaged in the practice of music and dancing, and the walls both of the hall and the closets are hung with musical instruments of all kinds, we must conclude that this was a prominent part of the duties or recreations of the women of the house. The instruments include the lyre, the lute, the triangular harp, and the standing harp and lyre. **It will be noticed that the women in the upper room of both houses have a peculiar mode of wearing the hair, by dividing it into one or more tresses curling at the ends.** Nor is this mere négligé, for the women in the rooms below wear the hair in an ordinary Egyptian mode. **This lock or tress is quite un-Egyptian, but is familiar to us in men (and women) of Hittite race** and known also in Syrian women.[42]

The hair of the lyrist in the Megiddo Ivory matches the description of the hair of Hittite women, and provides a further link to the Amarna era.

It is interesting to note that Nefertiti appears to have spoiled her husband by offering him wine and fruit as shown in Figure 13.6. The so-called *Unfinished Stele* on the left is housed in the Altes Museum in Berlin and shows Nefertiti pouring wine for Akhenaten, while the

Figure 13.5 Megiddo Ivory female Hittite lyrist with hair divided into tresses

relief on the right is generally assumed to depict Smenkhkare[43] being offered what appears to be fruit or lotus flowers by Meryetaten. This customary gesture of devotion by Nefertiti is evidently duplicated on the Megiddo Ivory scene in which the queen appears to have offered the king wine and lotus flowers, which he is drinking and holding in his hand (see Figure 13.7). Reeves identifies the royal couple in Figures 10.1 and 13.6 as Akhenaten and Nefertiti through the characteristic cap-crown she wore during her later years[44] (see Figure 13.8, the hole in the head of the Berlin statue indicating that the matching pair of uraei was lost). That the king in question is Akhenaten is confirmed by the fragmentary stela of Akhenaten shown in Figure 13.9, in which his names are written on the cartouches before his face[45]. Not only does the curled wig with the single uraeus and scarf on the back of the neck match, but also the pleated linen robe with waistbands he is regularly depicted as wearing.

Figure 13.6. Nefertiti pouring wine into Akhenaten's cup[46] and offering him fruit and lotus flowers

Figure 13.7. Megiddo Ivory queen offering the Canaanite king wine and lotus flowers

Figure 13.8. Head of the Nefertiti standing-striding statue (left)[47], compared to the head of the queen in the royal couple scene (right)

Figure 13.9 Akhenaten in distinctive attire, cropped image from a fragmentary stela of Akhenaten[48]

In a scene of a royal couple found on the back of a golden throne discovered in Tutankhamun's tomb[49], the king is shown dressed in the same garments as Akhenaten's (see Figure 13.10).

Figure 13.10. Royal couple scene engraved on the back of Tutankhamun's golden throne[50]

Reeves asserts that the throne had been altered in antiquity, noticing that the pleated ribbons (scarf) at the back of the queen's neck are not joined to her wig, and he also suspects that the names had been altered[51]. It has in fact been suggested that the chair had originally depicted someone else, but had been repossessed and altered by Tutankhamun[52]. The relaxed posture of the king and the rays of the Aten in which he basks in Figure 13.10 match those of Akhenaten in Figure 13.9. The original couple portrayed in the scene can, therefore, be none other than Akhenaten and Nefertiti. Tutankhamun must have engraved his name over Akhenaten's to claim the magnificent throne for himself.

Figure 13.11 shows Akhenaten and his family worshipping the Aten, but of particular interest are the pleated linen robes both adults are wearing. It is the same as shown in Figures 10.1, 13.9 and 13.10. In Figure 13.11 Nefetiti wears a plumed crown, as does the queen in Figure 13.10.

The Nubian wig of the queen in Figure 13.10 is nearly identical to a Nubian wig worn by Nefertiti (see Figure 13.12, *Talatat: Portrait of Nefertiti*. Egypt, Karnak, New Kingdom, Dynasty 18, reign of

Figure 13.11. Akhenaten and family worshipping the Aten[53]

Amenhotep IV, 1353-1337 BC. Painted sandstone, 22.0 x 22.7 cm. The Cleveland Museum of Art. Purchase from the J. H. Wade Fund 1959.188), and the royal regalia draped over the shoulders of the couple in Figures 10.1 and 13.10 match those worn by Akhenaten and Nefertiti (see Figure 13.13). Although other kings and queens of Egypt may have worn similar clothing at times, the selection of garments shown in the images presented here appears to be unique to Akhenaten and Nefertiti. Akhenaten cherished his queen like probably no other pharaoh before or after him, as is evident from the affectionate scenes shown in Figures 10.1, 13.10 and 13.13.

The identification of the couples in Figures 10.1 and 13.10 is of great importance since it precludes the identification of the king in Figure 10.1 as the male king called Smenkhkare, as discussed in Section 13.3.

Figure 13.12 Portrait of Nefertiti wearing a Nubian wig

Figure 13.13. Limestone statuette of Akhenaten and Nefertiti
dressed in royal regalia and linen robes[54]

Returning to the Megiddo Ivory, it should be noted that in ancient
Egyptian society from the beginning of the Dynastic Period, shaving
had become fashionable and facial hair received low status[55]. It is
furthermore known that Akhenaten had employed Asiatics in his
bodyguard[56], and if Nefertiti was of Asiatic descent, she may
likewise have surrounded herself with Asiatic servants and
bodyguards. As the visit probably took place while Akhenaten was
still alive, he may very well have sent his own bodyguards, specifically its Asiatic members, to escort his beloved wife on her journey
to Jerusalem.

More importantly, though, are the captives who are shown wearing crowns and beards similar to Yuya's beard. According to Manetho, the Hyksos were known as the shepherd kings, some of whom escaped to Jerusalem while the rest, by implication, were taken captive by Ahmose. Osarsiph sent ambassadors to the shepherd kings in Jerusalem, while the *El Arish Shrine Text* relates that it was Geb, earlier identified as Prince Tuthmosis, the son of Amenhotep III, who sent messengers to the Asiatics summoning them for assistance. As described in the previous section, the Queen of Sheba sent ambassadors to Solomon before she eventually visited him. Given the background outlined so far in this treatise, **there can be little doubt that Solomon receiving ambassadors from a queen of Egypt and Osarsiph's dispatching of ambassadors to Jerusalem must refer to the same event**.

One may ask why Nefertiti would have been the one to visit Jerusalem. If an envoy from Egypt had simply appeared on the doorstep of the king requesting assistance in a rebellion against the government of Egypt, he would no doubt have been laughed off. The person who was to convey the request would have had to be trustworthy and able to explain the circumstances of the request in detail. There would not have been a person more ideal to do this than Nefertiti. As the half-sister of Solomon, the true nature of her visit may initially have been kept secret, only to be revealed once they could speak face-to-face. She alone would have been able to reassure Solomon that there was no danger or trap. That she explained the circumstances that had developed in Egypt to Solomon is suggested by the presence of the captured kings on the Megiddo Ivory.

Corroboration of this argument can be found in the death of Asiyah, in Muslim tradition the wife of the Pharaoh of the Exodus. According to notes of commentators as recorded by George Sale in his translation of the Koran, she was the daughter of Mozâhem and suffered a cruel death at the hands of Pharaoh. The commentators claimed that:

....because she believed in Moses, her husband cruelly tormented her, fastening her hands and feet to four stakes, and laying a large millstone on her breast, her face, at the same time, being exposed to the scorching beams of the sun ... at length God received her soul. ... but no more than four of the other sex had attained perfection; ... Asia the wife of Pharaoh, Mary the daughter of Imrân (i.e. the mother of Jesus), Khadijah the daughter of Khowailed (the prophet's first wife), and Fâtema, the daughter of Mohammed.[57]

With Moses identified as Prince Tuthmosis, the only wife of a pharaoh renowned for her beauty at that time would have been Nefertiti. That she 'believed in Moses' not only links her to Tuthmosis, but also suggests that she participated in his revolution. If biblical tradition is to be believed, Tuthmosis regularly confronted or interacted with his brother Akhenaten, not with the miracles of the plagues, but more likely to find a way out of the mess that Egypt had become. He would therefore also have interacted with Nefertiti and he was most likely the one who suggested her visit to the shepherds in Jerusalem, who were then ruled by King Solomon. That visit must have taken place early in Akhenaten's reign, as Amenhotep III must have withdrawn to Ethiopia soon afterwards. The most likely reason for her violent death is discussed in Section 13.5.

13.3 Nefertiti and Smenkhkare

In conventional Egyptian chronology Akhenaten was succeeded by a mysterious king called Smenkhkare who ruled for only two years before the young Tutankhamun became the official regent of Egypt. The identity of this king is hotly debated, primarily because of two sets of pharaonic cartouches[58], one belonged to a king named Smenkhkare who ruled from 1338-1336 BCE[59] and the other to a king named Neferneferuaten. Although initially identified as a male, some scholars, in particular Reeves, maintain that Smenkhare must have been a name assumed by Nefertiti following the death of her husband. The arguments pertaining to this debate will not be repeated here. However, additional arguments to be considered in support for the identification of Smenkhkare as Nefertiti are given below:

- Manetho relates that the female king Acenchres, the daughter of Orus, ruled for 12 years. Orus has earlier been identified as Amenhotep III, which means that his daughter who had become queen could only have been Nefertiti, his daughter-in-law. Nefertiti is believed by some historians to have co-ruled with her husband towards the end of his reign[60], which makes her the only queen following Amenhotep III who could have ruled for more than a decade. Her rule as sole regent of Egypt following the death of her husband appears to have been relatively brief, probably only the two years associated with Smenkhkare.

- The Koran specifically states that the Queen of Sheba ruled a country where her people worshipped the sun. This description would apply to Egypt during the Amarna era and would therefore make Nefertiti the queen in question. Tutankhamun restored Amun as the principal deity of Egypt and brought an end to Atenism. The Koranic record could therefore hardly refer to a later widow of an Egyptian king, by whose time sun-worship had been rejected in Egypt.

- The name Smenkhkare is constructed from the Egyptian words S-menkh[61] (to beautify, endow), ka[62] (image, genius, person, character, vital strength) and Re, the name of an Egyptian god. The 'beautified image of Re' may arguably refer to Nefertiti, who was renowned for her beauty.

- In the so-called Zannanza affair, discussed in Section 13.4, a recently widowed Egyptian queen wrote to the king of the Hittites, asking him for a son to become her husband and king of Egypt. The only female queen of Egypt who could ever have found herself in circumstances that would allow such a request was Nefertiti. In other words, Nefertiti continued to rule after the death of her husband and must therefore be the elusive Smenkhkare.

13.4 The Zannanza Affair

At more or less the same time as the Egyptian Empire reached its zenith under the New Kingdom, the Hittite Empire in Anatolia (modern-day Turkey) became the dominant power in the north (see Figure 1.1). There was no love lost between Egypt and any of its northern neighbours and Egypt and the Hittites in fact feared one another when, to his great surprise, Suppiluliuma I, the king of the Hittites, received a letter from an Amarna queen with a strange request. From the Hittite annals[63] we first learn of the arrival of a messenger following the death of the Egyptian king:

> [The Egyptians] were afraid. And since, in addition, their lord Nibhururiya had died, therefore the queen of Egypt, who was Dakhamunzu, sent a messenger to [Suppiluliuma].

In this letter, later recorded by his son Mursilis II, she asks for one of his sons as husband:

> My husband died. A son I have not. But to you, they say, the sons are many. If you were to give me a son of yours, he would become my husband. Never shall I pick out a servant of mine and make him my husband! I am afraid!

Suppiluliuma was perplexed and suspicious and decided to send a messenger to Egypt:

> Go and bring you the true word back to me. Maybe they deceive me. Maybe in fact they do have a son of their lord.

The messenger returned with the response from the Egyptian queen:

Why did you say 'they deceive me' in that way? Had I a son, would I have written about my own and my country's shame to a foreign land? You did not believe me and you have said as much to me! He who was my husband has died. A son I have not! Never shall I take a servant of mine and make him my husband! I have written to no other country; only to you have I written! They say your sons are many: so give me one of your sons! To me he will be husband, but in Egypt he will be king!

Suppiluliuma eventually sent his son Zannanza to Egypt. Word of his departure to Egypt must have been leaked to Egyptian commanders who were not happy with the prospective arrangement and he was assassinated along the way. The Hittites accused the Egyptians of the murder:

They spoke thus: 'The people of Egypt killed Zannanza' and brought word: 'Zannanza died'. And when [Suppiluliuma] heard of the slaying of Zannanza, he began to lament for Zannanza and to the gods he spoke thus: 'Oh gods! I did no evil, yet the people of Egypt did this to me, and they also attacked the frontier of my country'.

Suppiluliuma retaliated by attacking and taking possession of Amqu, formerly under Egyptian control. Some of the captured Egyptian soldiers were taken back to Hattusa, the Hittite capital[64], with dire consequences for the Hittites. Unbeknown to them, the Egyptian soldiers were infected by the deadly Egyptian plague, which soon spread and devastate the Hittite population as it did in Egypt (see Section 15.6 for a discussion of the sixth plague of the Exodus).

The name Dahamunzu (also spelled Dakhamunzu) is not easily recognisable in terms of the known names of the Egyptian queens of that time. An interpretation advocated by some scholars, however, is 'the king's wife *par excellence*'[65]. This would apply more to Nefertiti than to the other candidate proposed by some researchers, Tutankhamun's young wife Ankhesenamun. The name of the deceased pharaoh Nibhururiya is also spelled Niphururiya[66]. He has been identified as either Akhenaten (Neferkheperure) or Tutankhamun (Nebkheperure), based on the similarity of their throne names to the name recorded in the Hittite annals. Reeves presents a strong case that the king and queen were Akhenaten and his wife Nefertiti, who had six daughters but no sons. Identification of the queen would of course immediately identify her deceased husband and vice versa.

Without repeating the lengthy discussions on the topic, the following additional arguments are presented which identify Nefertiti, who had six daughters but no sons, as the Hittite Dahamunzu:

- It is almost inconceivable that an Egyptian queen would ask for a son of the enemy to become the king of Egypt, and expect to get away with it! Throughout history good relationships between states were often sealed by exchanging royal daughters for wives, but it must be remembered that specifically in ancient times women were generally seen as bargaining chips for the enjoyment of the kings. So what would have possessed this queen to make such a request? Reeves hazards a guess:

  The explanation for her treason remains unclear – perhaps her ultimate, if naive, aim was to prop up Egypt's economy with funds from abroad.[67]

  This is hardly a convincing argument. This queen would never have been in a position to make such a request unless the circumstances she found herself in would allow it. For

Nefertiti such circumstances did exist. Egypt had been overrun by rebellious Egyptians and the freed Hyksos slaves, as well as the army from Jerusalem. With the remains of the Egyptian army and the Egyptian elite still in Ethiopia, it would make sense that she thought it possible to appoint a foreigner as her husband and king of Egypt.

- An even more curious aspect of her request is why she chose to write to a Hittite king at all. She may have reasoned that with the Hittites being the only empire strong enough to rival that of Egypt before the slave rebellion, they would have ensured that the new king remained in control of Egypt. She probably foresaw that Egypt would be flooded with Hittite troops to ensure that the Egyptians in Ethiopia could not return. There is, however, another possibility, namely that as the daughter of Uriah and Bathsheba, she would have been of partial Hittite descent. Her disloyalty to Egypt and her remark that she would not marry a servant of hers may suggest that she was not of Egyptian but foreign descent, although her remark may be related to the circumstances she found herself in. As discussed in Chapter 10, Akhetaten effectively became isolated during the 13 years of rampage in Egypt. With the rest of the Egyptian upper class in Ethiopia there would not have been anyone senior to her to select as husband. As queen of Egypt she may, however, have regarded all Egyptians as her servants.

- Nefertiti's success with her visit to Jerusalem and its king (she managed to convince him to invade Egypt at the request of Prince Tuthmosis) could have bolstered her confidence sufficiently to attempt a similar feat with the Hittite king. At the time she wrote the letter the army from Jerusalem may already have withdrawn to Canaan, which would have left a power vacuum in Egypt. She must have realised that the Egyptian army would soon return, but would have preferred the Hittites to take control of Egypt.

- According to Josephus, Herodotus referred to the Queen of Egypt and Ethiopia as Nicaule[68]. Unless recorded by this name in other copies of his work, this is not quite true as Herodotus' name for her is Nitocris. The text Josephus must have been referring to reads:

> Next, they read me from a papyrus, the names of three hundred and thirty monarchs, who (they said) were his successors upon the throne. In this number of generations there were eighteen Ethiopian kings, and one queen who was a native; all the rest were kings and Egyptians. The queen bore the same name as the Babylonian princess, namely, Nitocris.[69]

Just why Josephus identified Nicaule with this Nitocris is not clear as the only additional information regarding her refers to a banquet she arranged to avenge the death of her husband (see Section 13.5). The name Nitocris is usually associated with the Sixth Dynasty queen Nitiqret, from Manetho's Sixth Dynasty king list[70] and the *Turin Canon*[71]. According to Manetho she was braver than all the men of her time, the most beautiful of all the women, fair-skinned with red cheeks, and she supposedly constructed the third pyramid. Manetho's record may be based on the Turin King list, which lists a Sixth Dynasty queen called Neterikare or Nitiqret. It is, of course, possible that Josephus had access to other records which linked Nicaule to a Nitocris who ruled during the Solomonic era, in which case she could not be Nitiqret of the Sixth Dynasty . Nitocris most certainly did not build the third pyramid, presumably one of the famous three pyramids of Giza, as claimed by Manetho.

Nevertheless, the Queen of Sheba appears to have been known by the name of Nicaule. This name can be translated as '(She who) beckoned the revenge', from the Greek *nēuō*[72] (to nod, signal, beckon) and *chōlaō*[73] (to be bilious, enraged, bitter anger) or *chōlē*[74] (gall, bile). This translation would imply that it was she who had invited the shepherds in Jerusalem to join Moses' fight against his father. The shepherds complied and exacted bitter revenge for the terrible fate they had suffered under Ahmose and during the enslavement of their people by the Egyptians. The name could also mean that she had brought upon herself the bitter anger of the Egyptian people for convincing the shepherds to invade Egypt. It should be noted that according to a rather obscure source, the so-called *Yikhus Letter*[75], Nicaule (of Egypt) was a wife of Solomon. Bilqis of Arabia and Makeda as the Queen of Sheba are also listed as wives of Solomon. If this document can be authenticated, it will support Josephus' link between Nicaule and Solomon. She would not have been a wife of Solomon, but his half-sister, possibly having been confused with the Egyptian princess given as wife to Solomon[76] (see Section 13.7).

As Herodotus wrote in Greek, one may expect that the name Nitocris, like Nicaule, should also be of Greek origin. A Greek interpretation is, however, not obvious, possibly being a garbled combination of the words *nēuō* and *tarachōs*[77] (a disturbance, tumult), echoing Nefertiti who beckoned the shepherds of Jerusalem to enter and plunder Egypt. Her named could also be a distorted form of *nēotērikōs*[78] (juvenile, youthful), although this interpretation would make not particular sense with respect to Nefertiti. An entirely different interpretation could be 'The approval which was condemned', from *nēuō*, *tō*[79] (which, who) and *krisis*[80] (a tribunal, a passing of judgment upon a person, condemnation). This may suggest that the truth about Nefertiti's role as messenger to the shepherds in Jerusalem eventually surfaced, and that she was tried and probably executed. A more likely reason for her execution is discussed in Section 13.5.

A less probable interpretation is 'Gold from the south', from *nōtōs*[81] (the south, the south wind) and *chrusōs*[82] (gold, golden article). This may refer to Egypt as 'the southern land' or perhaps to the queen who obtained her gold from the south, the mysterious land of Punt[83]. Various New Kingdom pharaohs traded with the land of Punt, including Amenhotep III[84]. Solomon supposedly obtained his gold from the equally mysterious land called Ophir[85], which several researchers have suggested must be the same as the land of Punt[86]. Peters supports his claim that this land was located in Southern Africa between the Zambezi and Sabi rivers by referring to the image of the queen of Punt as depicted in the mortuary temple of Hatshepsut (see Figure 13.14). In his opinion her build is typical of the Hottentot tribes of South Africa. Whereas Solomon may in fact have traded with the land of Ophir, it is more likely that the source of his riches was the gold plundered from Egypt. Although Egypt had its own quarries in the Eastern Desert (the stretch of land between the Nile and the Red Sea), much of its gold was imported from African countries including Nubia[87] and also the land of Punt.

Figure 13.14. The Queen of Punt from Hatshepshut's mortuary temple[88]

13.5 The treacherous banquet

Of Nitocris, Herodotus writes the following:

> They say that she succeeded her brother, he had been king of
> Egypt, and was put to death by his subjects, who then placed her
> upon the throne. Bent on avenging his death, she devised a
> cunning scheme by which she destroyed a vast number of
> Egyptians. She constructed a spacious underground chamber,
> and, on pretence of inaugurating it, contrived the following:
> Inviting to a banquet those of the Egyptians whom she knew to
> have had the chief share in the murder of her brother, she
> suddenly, as they were feasting, let the river in upon them, by
> means of a secret duct of large size. This, and this only, did they
> tell me of her, except that, when she had done as I have said, she
> threw herself into an apartment full of ashes, that she might
> escape the vengeance whereto she would otherwise have been
> exposed.[89]

Furthermore, Herodotus records that Sesostris was also part of a
treacherous banquet, set up by his brother:

> This Sesostris, the priests went on to say, upon his return home,
> accompanied by vast multitudes of the people whose countries he
> had subdued, was received by his brother, whom he had made
> viceroy of Egypt on his departure, at Daphnae near Pelusium,
> and invited by him to a banquet, which he attended, together
> with his sons. Then his brother piled a quantity of wood all round
> the building, and having so done set it all alight. Sesostris,
> discovering what had happened, took counsel instantly with his
> wife, who had accompanied him to the feast, and was advised by
> her to lay two of their six sons upon the fire, and so make a bridge
> across the flames, whereby the rest might effect their escape.
> Sesostris did as she recommended, and thus while two of his sons
> were burnt to death, he himself and his other children were
> saved. The king then returned to his own land and took

vengeance upon his brother, ...[90]

As discussed earlier, the only king who might have left his brother in charge of Egypt without being permitted to wear the crown is Amenhotep III, sometimes referred to as Sesostris, his brother being Ay. If Nicaule and Nitocris were indeed one and the same person, the retaliatory banquet must certainly apply to Nefertiti, Josephus' Queen of Sheba. Both narratives involve a treacherous banquet during which some people were killed in a flooded chamber or burning house. The burning of the sons of Sesostris must refer to the sacrifice of the firstborn sons, one of whom would have been Prince Tuthmosis and the other most likely a son by another wife. The second son may collectively refer to all the sons of Amenhotep III who were burned on the pyres. Sesostris returning from another country would be Amenhotep III returning from Ethiopia as discussed earlier. Herodotus' account that Nitocris avenged the death of her brother and not her husband must be a misunderstanding of the fact that Nefertiti was the daughter-in-law of Amenhotep III, and not his daughter. As discussed in Chapter 11, Manetho refers to the female ruler Acenchres as the daughter of Orus, which would make the Acencheres who ruled Egypt her brother. He was in reality her husband and they co-ruled for several years. The incident above in which the wife of Sesostris advises him to burn two of his sons suggests that Amenhotep agreed to have Prince Tuthmosis and his other firstborn sons sacrificed only after long consultation with his wife or wives, who in the end persuaded him to follow the advice of the priests.

Having shown that Nitocris and Nefertiti must have been the same person, Herodotus' account of her banquet clearly states that she not only outlived her husband, who evidently was murdered, but also that she was appointed ruler of Egypt by the people. That would require Nefertiti and Smenkhkare to be one and the same person. If she had indeed exacted revenge on the murderers of her husband, she would very likely have feared for her life, matching

Dakhamunzu's desperate plea that she needed a husband and was afraid, and Asiyah's prayer to god for deliverance from the Pharaoh[91]. If Ay had been involved in the plot to kill Akhenaten, he may narrowly have escaped Nefertiti's act of revenge as suggested by Herodotus' account. One can imagine how he would then have used violence against the queen as recorded by Manetho (see Section 10.2).

The story of a similar treacherous banquet as related by Homer in his *Odyssey* is discussed in the next section.

13.6 Helen of Troy in Egypt

Helen of Troy is reputed to be one of the most beautiful women in history. The following legend about her was recorded by Homer in his *Iliad* and *Odyssey*, with minor details added by later writers. Already married to Menelaus, the king of Sparta (a powerful city-state in Greece), she either eloped with or was abducted by Paris, the son of Priam, the king of Troy, situated in present-day Turkey (see Figure 1). An expedition to retrieve her from Troy was launched by Agamemnon, the brother of Menelaus. However, his fleet was scattered by a storm and it only came together nearly a decade later. More than a thousand ships set off to besiege Troy. The siege lasted nine years and by the tenth year the army was close to deserting. Memnon, the king of Ethiopia and either the uncle or the step brother of Priam, had come to the aid of Troy with his army. The Greeks finally got the better of the Trojans by pretending to acknowledge defeat and departing, leaving behind on the beach a hollow wooden horse concealing soldiers. The horse was dragged into the city and, with the city asleep, the soldiers slipped out and opened the gates to the Greek army. Slaughter and mayhem followed and the city of Troy was sacked. Menelaus intended to kill Helen, but was overcome by her beauty and took her back to Greece.

Numerous books have been written on the topic of the Trojan War[92] and the interested reader should readily be able find detailed treatises on the topic. What is of interest here is the assertion by some of the ancient writers, in particular Herodotus, that Helen was in

Egypt during the 10-year siege of Troy[93]. Tyrian priests belonging to the temple of the Stranger Aphrodite located in the precinct of Proteus related to him that while sailing off with the captured Helen, a violent wind drove Paris, called Alexander or Alexandrus by the Tyrians, to the shores of Egypt. Servants who escaped from Paris spread word of his abduction of Helen, which soon reached the ears of Proteus. Proteus ordered Paris to be brought before him and spared his life only because he, Proteus, had taken a vow never to kill strangers driven to his shores. Paris was instructed to leave without Helen and the wealth Paris had taken from Menelaus. She stayed with Proteus during the 10-year siege of Troy and her true location was only discovered by the Greeks when Troy had fallen.

Proteus was the son of Pheros, who was the son of Sesostris. As discussed in Section 7.1, Pheros can be identified with Amenhotep III, who was sometimes mistakenly referred to as Sesostris (see Figure 7.1). Pheros' son Proteus is then to be equated with Amenhotep III's successor, his son Akhenaten. It is unlikely that Proteus could have been Prince Tuthmosis as suggested by the circumstances surrounding Nefertiti and Helen of Troy. This is supported in the hypothesis on the Trojan War which follows. Proteus is incidentally also mentioned in Homer's *Odyssey*, in an episode where strangers visited the house of Menelaus[94]. Menelaus invited them for supper and later told them that he was detained in Egypt by the gods, who were not satisfied with his sacrifices. When he eventually departed from Egypt, his fleet was saved by Idothea, the daughter of the Egyptian Proteus, the Old Man of the Sea. Proteus instructed Menelaus that he would not be able to return home unless he had offered sacrifices to Jove in Egypt. Menelaus is therefore also linked to sacrifice in Egypt, a recurring theme in this treatise. Homer's version of this event is similar to that of Herodotus recounted in Section 3.7.

It is postulated that even though animosity may have existed between Greece and Troy, the supposed abduction of Helen and subsequent siege and fall of Troy never happened. Instead, that legend grew from the experiences of a small group of Greeks who either survived the eruption of Thera or were visiting Egypt when the eruption occurred. With their native country destroyed, they had no choice but seek refuge in Egypt. There they experienced the Amarna revolution first hand, including the looting of Egypt by Tuthmosis' rebels. During this 10-year period el Amarna was effectively besieged, in the sense that Tuthmosis allowed his brother Akhenaten and his wife Nefertiti to remain untouched by the rebels. When the Greek visitors eventually departed to what was left of Greece, they related their strange encounter in Egypt to other survivors. Over time that curious story which unfolded in Egypt became the legend of the Trojan War, and Nefertiti became Helen of Troy. The following arguments are used to support this hypothesis.

Ignoring for the moment the supposed cause of the Trojan War, arguably the most important of the protagonists is Agamemnon, the commander of the Greek fleet and soldiers. Apart from the Trojans themselves, Agamemnon was opposed by Memnon, king of the Ethiopians. Two massive statues of Amenhotep III were curiously referred to as the Colossi of Memnon by the Greeks (see Figure

Figure 13.15. Statues of Amenhotep III called the Colossi of Memnon by the Greeks[95]

13.15). This suggests that Amenhotep III and Memnon were one and the same person.

Memnon, an Ethiopian, reportedly led a large army to Troy in order to assist King Priam. Looking at the map in Figure 13.16 one must ask how an army of Ethiopians could have been allowed to travel through Egypt, Canaan and Syria, all the way to Troy. Some ancient historians maintained that Memnon came from Susa in modern Iran[96], but this route is equally unlikely. Both routes are in excess of 2,000 kilometres and Memnon's army would have required permission to pass through several countries. A possible reason for this strange association is to be found in the meaning of the names Memnon, Aga-Memnon and Menelaus. Memnon appears to be a corruption of the Greek word *mnēmēiōn*[97] (a memorial or a

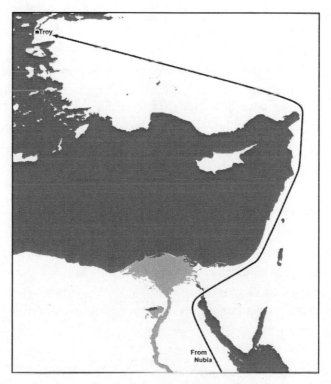

Figure 13.16. The route Memnon's army would have had to follow to reach Troy

monument), and Aga-memnon most likely is a combination of the words *agō*[98] (to lead) and *mnēmēiōn*, rendering 'The monument for the leader (the king)'. Amenhotep III, in his mistaken identity as Sesostris, was known as the king of Egypt and Ethiopia, matching Amenhotep III, the king of Egypt who had retreated into Ethiopia for more than a decade. Agamemnon, Memnon and Amenhotep III must therefore have been one and the same person, but because of the traditional rivalry between Egypt and Ethiopia, in Greek tradition Agamemnon and Memnon erroneously became opposing forces.

The name Menelaus seems to be a combination of the words *mnēmē*[99] (memory) and *laōs*[100] (a people, the people), rendering '(In) the memory of the people'. As Menelaus was the brother of Agamemnon, his character is most likely based on Ay, the brother-in-law of Amenhotep III. Ay was present in Amarna along with Akhenaten and Nefertiti, and like any other normal man would have coveted the beautiful young woman. Menelaus as Ay therefore became the husband of Helen, who was stolen away by Paris as Akhenaten, the son of Priam. Can the meaning of the names Priam and Paris tell us more about the origins of the Trojan myth?

The name Priam seems to be a contraction of the Greek words *preō*[101] (to fire, to burn, to become inflamed with fever) and *iama*[102] (a cure, healing), yielding *preōiama*, which can be interpreted as '(Seeking?) a cure for the fever'. Paris can be viewed as a contraction of the words *para*[103] (near, on account of) and *iōs*[104] (venom, poison, rust), rendering 'On account of the poison'. Priam would therefore be a fitting description of Amenhotep III who desperately sought ways to end the plague, and Paris would describe Akhenaten who only became king on account of the plague and its repercussions.

Several other points provide links between the Amarna era and the Trojan War:

- As recorded by Strabo and Diodorus, a village called Troy once existed on the banks of the Nile[105, 106, 107]. Menelaus had sailed to Egypt with a large number of Trojan captives, who revolted against him and seized a place from where they conducted war against him. Menelaus eventually granted them freedom and safety, whereupon they founded the city. According to Strabo the village of Troy still existed between 25-20 BCE and was located not far from the pyramids (presumably of Giza), at the foot of a rocky mountain that was called 'Trojan' and near the site from which the building blocks of the pyramids were quarried. That the name must have existed during the Amarna era is confirmed by an inscription from the reign of Amenhotep III[108]. Here the quarry is named as Troja.

The Troy on the banks of the Nile appears to have been prominent during the rule of Amenhotep III, which agrees with Nefertiti being Helen of (Egypt's) Troy. The besieged city, however, must have been Akhetaten (Amarna), where the rebels under the leadership of Prince Tuthmosis allowed Akhenaten and Nefertiti to live.

- Homer's *The Illiad* begins with the god Apollo inflicting a deadly plague on Agamemnon's army, which destroyed his men. This is exactly what happened to Amenhotep III when a deadly plague caused by the Thera fallout began decimating the Egyptian population.

- Priam reportedly had 50 sons and some say he had 50 daughters as well[109]. This links Priam to Aegyptus, who also had 50 sons. As discussed in Section 12.3, the 50 daughters of Danaus more than likely referred to the 50 daughters of Taphnes, the queen of the Egyptian king, and therefore the 50 daughters of Amenhotep III.

- The smoking gun linking the legend of Troy to the Amarna events must certainly be the sudden disappearance of the entire army of a country. In *Exodus* it is claimed that the entire Egyptian army vanished when Moses' walls of water collapsed onto it, while Josephus claims that 'there was not one man left to be a messenger of this calamity to the rest of the Egyptians'[110]. Manetho related that the entire Egyptian army fled to Egypt along with their king, Amenhotep (III). In the *El Arish Shrine Text* it was recorded that King Shu jumped into a whirlpool (the two walls of water of the Exodus?), from which he later emerged to destroy the Asiatics, matching Amenhotep's return to Egypt from Ethiopia.

Much the same was recorded by Quintus Smymaeus about the army of Memnon:

But no long time thereafter came to them Memnon the warrior-king, and brought with him a countless host of swarthy Aethiops. ... Then groaned Dawn, and palled herself in clouds, **and earth was darkened**. At their mother's hest all the light Breathings of the Dawn took hands, and slid down one long stream of sighing wind to Priam's plain, and floated round the dead, and softly, swiftly caught they up, and bare through silver mists the Dawn-queen's son, with hearts sore aching for their brother's fall, while moaned around them all the air. As on they passed, fell many blood-gouts from those pierced limbs down to the earth, and these were made a sign to generations yet to be. The Gods gathered them up from many lands, and made thereof a far-resounding river, named of all that dwell beneath long Ida's flanks Paphlagoneion. As its waters flow 'twixt fertile acres, **once a year they turn to blood, when comes the woeful day whereon died Memnon. Thence a sick and choking reek steams**: thou wouldst say that from a wound unhealed corrupting humours breathed an evil stench. Ay, so the Gods ordained: but now flew on bearing Dawn's mighty son the rushing winds skimming earth's face and palled about with night.

Nor were his Aethiopian comrades left to wander of their King forlorn: a God suddenly winged those eager

souls with speed such as should soon be theirs forever, changed to flying fowl, the children of the air. Wailing their King in the winds' track they sped ... so they left far behind that stricken field of blood, and fast they followed after those swift winds. With multitudinous moaning, veiled in mist unearthly, **Trojans over all the plain and Danaans marvelled, seeing that great host vanishing with their King.** All hearts stood still in dumb amazement.[111]

How many such huge and famed armies have simply vanished from sight? Probably only one, and all the myths regarding such a disappearance must in one way or another be connected to that particular event. It should be noted that Smymaeus' account links Memnon to phenomena corresponding to some of the plagues of Egypt, namely the darkness over the earth and the river of blood. In other words, Memnon's era is fixed to the time of the Exodus.

- According to a Trojan legend Agamemnon set out with his fleet, but not knowing where Troy was, ravaged Mysia instead. When he departed from there, his fleet was scattered by a severe storm, regrouping only eight years later[112]. This may refer to the eruption of Thera, which would have destroyed all fleets in the Mediterranean Sea.

- When the fleet gathered a second time, a lack of wind prevented it from sailing and the oracle Calchas informed Agamemnon that wind would not return unless he sacrificed the fairest of his daughters to the goddess Artemis[113]. One daughter in particular is mentioned in Trojan mythology, Iphiginia (Iphianassa in Homer)[114]. Her name can be considered as a combination of $ēpi$[115] (over, upon) and $gēnēa$[116] (age, generation, a nation), yielding '(Brought) upon the people' (of Egypt), hinting at something (a curse, an edict) that was enforced upon the nation, the sacrifice of the firstborn. Amenhotep III had many concubines and he would have had firstborn sons and daughters by probably all of them. The meaning of the name *Iphi-anassa* is more difficult to decipher, but appears to be based on *ēpi* combined with the word *anaseiō*[117] (to excite, move, stir up). This word is derived from the Greek *ana*[118] (apiece, every man) and *xēnizō*[119] (to be a host, entertain, to receive as guest). One gets the impression that this may be related to the legend of Busiris who sacrificed strangers who visited his country, translated as 'his guests' by St Augustine[120]. This would then also be related to Amenhotep's instruction that the firstborn of every household be sacrificed. Menelaus likewise had to sacrifice two Egyptian children before he was allowed to leave Egypt, providing another link to between the Trojan protagonists and Egypt[121].

The name of the oracle (Calchas) can be translated from the words *kaleō*[122] (to call, a divine call) and *cháos*[123] (chaos) which would mean 'The chaos of the divine call', or freely interpreted something like 'He-whose-divine-call-led-to-chaos'. The word *chalkōs*[124] (copper, brass, money) is an alternative, but the consonants κ ('k') and χ ('kh') are interchanged and 'brass man' would have no specific association with an oracle. Either way, an oracle called on Agamemnon to sacrifice one of his offspring, as did the oracle of Amenhotep III.

- In Homer's *Odyssey* Proteus narrates to Menelaus how his brother Agamemnon was killed by his wife Clytemnestra and her lover Aegisthus:

> Your brother [Agamemnon] and his ships escaped, for Juno protected him, but when he was just about to reach the high promontory of Malea, he was caught by a heavy gale which carried him out to sea again sorely against his will, and drove him to the foreland where Thyestes used to dwell, but where Aegisthus was then living. By and by, however, it seemed as though he was to return safely after all, for the gods backed the wind into its old quarter and they reached

home; whereon Agamemnon kissed his native soil, and shed tears of joy at finding himself in his own country. Now there was a watchman whom Aegisthus kept always on the watch, and to whom he had promised two talents of gold. This man had been looking out for a whole year to make sure that Agamemnon did not give him the slip and prepare war; when, therefore, this man saw Agamemnon go by, he went and told Aegisthus who at once began to lay a plot for him. **He picked twenty of his bravest warriors and placed them in ambuscade on one side the cloister, while on the opposite side he prepared a banquet. Then he sent his chariots and horsemen to Agamemnon, and invited him to the feast, but he meant foul play. He got him there, all unsuspicious of the doom that was awaiting him, and killed him when the banquet was over** as though he were butchering an ox in the shambles; not one of Agamemnon's followers was left alive, nor yet one of Aegisthus', but they were all killed there in the cloisters.[125]

Unless murdering kings at banquets was common practice in the ancient world, this incident must certainly refer to Herodotus' infamous banquet as discussed in Section 13.5. The name Aegisthus is suspiciously similar to the alias Aegyptus of Josephus' Sesostris and it is highly likely that Homer either misread his sources or intentionally changed the name while writing his famous work. The roles, however, seem to be swapped, as Herodotus' Sesostris (Amenhotep III) survived, while Agamemnon (Amenhotep III) was killed at the banquet set up by Aegisthus. Furthermore Agamemnon's return to his native country matches Amenhotep's return to Egypt from Ethiopia.

The name Clytemnestra appears to be derived from the words *kleiō*[126] (to close, shut, shut up), *tē*[127] (and, both, also) and *mnēsteuō*[128] (to betroth, indirectly to be asked to marry), probably meaning 'Betrothed and (then) shut away'. This would describe Nefertiti, who was not the wife but the beautiful daughter-in-law of Amenhotep III. For all we know she may initially have been betrothed to him, but became the wife of his son Akhenaten when he (Amenhotep III) departed to Ethiopia. Being shut up would refer to Amarna having been besieged when the rest of Egypt belonged to the rebels. Nefertiti's involvement in the banquet (as Nitocris) then mirrors that of Clytemnestra.

- The unoccupied archaeological site known as Hisarlik in north-western Turkey has widely been recognised as the site of ancient Troy[129]. At least nine distinct layers of ruins have been identified through excavation of the site, the first dating back to *ca.* 3000 BCE, with the ninth dated to the first century BCE. Most scholars appear to agree that layer Troy VIh, which is the layer pertaining to the Fourteenth Century BCE, was destroyed by an earthquake. The most likely cause of an earthquake in that timeframe would have been an eruption of Thera, in which case the fall of Troy would not have been due to a Greek invasion, but to a natural catastrophe.

- The earliest dating of the fall of Troy by ancient historians appears to be the year 1334 BCE[130]. The fall of Troy is associated with the recovery of Helen, and 1334 BCE dates to the beginning of the reign of Tutankhamun (see Table 11.1), who succeeded Smenkhkare (Nefertiti). Therefore the year 1334 BCE more or less marks the fall of Akhenaten's Amarna kingdom, which would be the fall of 'Troy'.

- According to Apollodorus, Agamemnon was in command of the whole army with Achilles, only 15 years old at the time, having been appointed as his admiral[131]. If there were to be any truth in Achilles' young age, probably the only circumstances in which a king would appoint a boy as a commander of his forces would be when that boy was his son. If Agamemnon was Amenhotep III as argued, that son would have been Prince Tuthmosis. Can he be linked to Achilles? It would appear so.

In Apollonius Rhodius' *The Argonautica* he relates the following tale about Achilles, the son of king Peleus and the sea nymph Thetis:

For she (Thetis) ever encompassed the child's mortal flesh in the night with the flame of fire; and day by day she anointed with ambrosia his tender frame, so that he might become immortal and that she might keep off from his body loathsome old age. **But Peleus leapt up from his bed and saw his dear son gasping in the flame; and at the sight he uttered a terrible cry, fool that he was;** and she heard it, and catching up the child threw him screaming to the ground, and herself like a breath of wind passed swiftly from the hall as a dream and leapt into the sea, exceeding wroth, and thereafter returned not again.[132]

Keeping in mind that no gods actually featured in the real-life versions of these events and that their names had probably become muddled with real events over centuries if not millennia of oral tradition, it would appear that Achilles was about to be sacrificed in the fire. This matches Prince Tuthmosis who as the firstborn son of Amenhotep III was destined to be burned, but was rescued at the last moment. The Greek hero Hercules was also to be sacrificed in Egypt by the tyrant Busiris (see Section 3.12). As argued above, Busiris and Amenhotep III were one and the same person. Hercules managed to escape and killed Busiris, suggesting that this episode in his life was, like that of Achilles, linked to Prince Tuthmosis, who eventually rose against his father and effectively expelled him from Egypt.

In the same text the goddess Hera instructs Iris:

Then go to the sea beaches where the bronze anvils of Hephaestus are smitten by sturdy hammers, and tell him to still the blasts of fire until Argo pass by them. Then go to Aeolus too, Aeolus who rules the winds, children of the clear sky; and to him also tell my purpose so that he may make all winds cease under heaven and no breeze may ruffle the sea ... Next she (Iris) came to Hephaestus, and quickly made him cease from the clang of his iron hammers; and the smoke-grimed bellows were stayed from their blast.

Hephaestus was the Greek equivalent of the Roman god Vulcan, the god of among other things fire and volcanoes. These 'blasts of fire' on the beaches of the country must certainly be related to lumps of molten lava that had been ejected from Thera, causing fire wherever it fell (see Section 17.2). It is not possible to tell how long such eruptions may have persisted, but the fallout of molten lava must certainly have occurred during the main eruption and therefore became entrenched in the Trojan War tale.

- An Irob genealogy, recorded in a document which was inserted into the *Kebra Nagast* of Ethiopia, claims that:

David, son of Jesse, was the father of Solomon. Helen, Solomon's sister, married the king of Rome (called Simeon in another text). Helen gave birth to Endreyas, who went to Ethiopia...[133]

It is difficult to judge the extent to which this peculiar legend is based on reality, but the mention of a sister of Solomon who was known as Helen supports the hypothesis presented earlier, that Nefertiti must have been a half-sister of Solomon, her father being Uriah the Hittite. As argued in this treatise, Nefertiti was the Helen of Troy of Greek legend. Nefertiti most certainly did not marry a king of Rome, but she can be linked indirectly to the city.

Josephus went to great lengths to disprove various claims made by Apion, one of which was that the Exodus had occurred the same year Carthage was founded[134]. According to legend Carthage was founded by Dido, who had fled from Tyre after Pygmalion, her brother who was the ruler of city, had murdered her husband[135]. They landed at the site of Carthage where they founded the city. Dido had a brief liaison with Aeneas, one of the survivors of the Trojan War[136]. One particular legend, recorded by Pherecydes, maintains that the seer Phrasius, who advised Busiris to sacrifice strangers visiting his country, was a brother of Pygmalion[137]. As discussed in Sections 7.1 and 7.4, Busiris and Pharius are to be equated with Amenhotep III and his adviser Amenhotep, son of Hapu. Pherecydes' remark therefore links the founding of Carthage to the time of the Exodus, exactly as claimed by Apion.

In Virgil's *Aeneid*, Aeneas and his group became the progenitors of the Roman people, in other words they founded Rome. Through Phrasius, Nefertiti is linked to Dido and Pygmalion, and Dido had an affair with Aeneas who is linked to Rome. Although this is a rather laboured link between Helen (as Nefertiti) and Rome, it is possible that the legend originated from a distant memory that the most beautiful woman of that era had been involved with a person who became a king of Rome. That person may have been one of the royal family members who fled from Amarna to escape the sacrifice of the firstborn, or to escape the wrath of the Egyptian army upon its return to Egypt.

- In some legends Helen was raped (abducted) by Paris rather than willingly accompanying him to Troy[138]. If Nefertiti and Helen of Troy were one and the same person as argued here, the rape of Helen may be linked to the violence Armais used against the queen and Asiyah's death in the desert, as discussed in Sections 10.2 and 13.5.

- Above all, the arguments presented suggest that the legend of the Trojan War was nothing more than a Greek adaptation of the Amarna interlude during the reigns of Akhenaten and Nefertiti. If so, what would be the origin of the legend of the famous Trojan horse? According to Virgil in his *Aeneid*, when Troy could not be taken after more than nine years of siege, the Greeks devised a plan to infiltrate the city. They would pretend to admit defeat and sail away, leaving behind a wooden horse as a gift to the Trojans. Inside the horse they concealed 30 soldiers who, once inside Troy, slipped out and opened the gates to the awaiting Greek army. The Trojan Horse therefore symbolises fatal deceit of some kind, and such a deceitful event did happen in Amarna, namely a treacherous banquet of which we have three versions. In the first Nitocris invited those who had murdered her husband to a banquet in a chamber below the level of the river. She let the water in and they were drowned. Sesostris was invited to a banquet by his brother, who set the place on fire. Aegisthus invited Agamemnon to a banquet in a hall and concealed 20 of his soldiers some distance away opposite the banquet table. Assuming that there was actually only one banquet, of the three versions the latter must have been the most realistic. One can only speculate how the soldiers were hidden. Perhaps inside a hollow statue of a horse, or even a hippopotamus?

An ancient Greek word for a horse is *hippōs*[139], while hippopotamus in ancient Greek literally means 'river horse', from *hippō (s)* and *pōtamōs*[140] (flood, river, stream). Assuming that Virgil, who wrote in Latin, based his narrative on the Trojan War on information gleaned from various Greek sources, it is possible that he misinterpreted the Greek word for a hippopotamus as referring to a horse.

13.7 Solomon's *Song of Songs*

The biblical book called the *Song of Songs* (or the *Song of Solomon* in the Authorised King James Version of the Bible) is attributed to Solomon in the Hebrew title of the work and also in its first verse[141]. It revolves around the relationship between a woman called the Beloved, and a man referred to as the Lover. In biblical tradition Solomon had 700 wives and 300 concubines and, if not a generic description of his lovers, this woman somehow earned greater respect or at least greater recognition than any of the others. Only one other wife of note is mentioned in the Bible, she being the daughter of the King of Egypt. Neither she nor her father is mentioned by name, but she was of such importance to the Egyptian king that he gave her as dowry Gezer, which he had burnt and destroyed its Canaanite inhabitants.

From as early as the Fifth Century it has been speculated that Solomon's *Song of Songs* was dedicated to his Egyptian bride[142], not only because she was the most notable of his wives, but also because Solomon likened her to 'a mare harnessed to one of the chariots of Pharaoh'[143]. This verse implies that she was familiar with the pharaoh of Egypt.

Of particular interest, though, is that she described herself as being dark or black:

Dark am I, yet lovely, ... dark like the tents of Kedar, like the tent curtains of Solomon.[144]

Since the tent curtains were woven from black goat hair[145], she must have been black by birth, not merely deeply tanned by the sun as claimed in the next verse. It must be more than mere coincidence that Solomon is linked to a black or dark bride in a non-Jewish text. As summarised in Section 13.1, the Ethiopian text called the *Kebra Nagast* relates how their queen desired to visit Solomon, showering him with gifts when she arrived. Solomon allowed her to stay in his palace and after several months took her as his bride. When she became pregnant, she returned to her country Ethiopia. To the Ethiopians this queen, called Makeda, was the biblical Queen of Sheba. If this was the woman whom the Israelites referred to as the daughter of the pharaoh of Egypt, how would one explain her being black?

Josephus records that before he had to flee Egypt, Moses led a military campaign against Ethiopia, won their hearts and married Tharbis, the daughter of the Ethiopian king[146]. As discussed in Section 7.5, Moses could not have led Amenhotep's first campaign into Ethiopia and it is more likely that he received his Ethiopian wife as a gift from the king of Ethiopia. When Moses fled to Midian he must have left his Ethiopian wife in Egypt, as he was given a new wife in Midian. She is also referred to in the Bible[147] where Aaron and his sister Miriam began to 'talk against him' because of his Cushite (Ethiopian) wife. This confrontation took place after the Israelites had departed from Egypt and seems to imply that Moses and his Ethiopian wife had been reunited some time after his flight from Egypt. However, this need not have been the case. Aaron and Miriam could merely have reproached him for earlier having married an Ethiopian woman. She is not mentioned again later, so it is likely that she remained in the Egyptian royal household as a daughter-in-law of Amenhotep III. Thus it is also possible, if not probable, that it was this Ethiopian daughter (-in-law) of Amenhotep whom either he or Akhenaten and/or Nefertiti was prepared to give away to Solomon as a wife. It was perhaps just a convenient way to get rid of her.

Another possibility is that when Amenhotep had settled in Ethiopia, he attempted to win the goodwill of his former vassal in Jerusalem by offering him a daughter of his own as bride (Solomon's Egyptian bride), and expected his host, the king of Ethiopia, to do the same (hence Solomon's 'black' wife). Neither would have been the fabled Queen of Sheba, though.

13.8 The history of the Queen of Sheba

A comparatively detailed 'history' of Solomon's Queen of Sheba[148] (see Appendix I), from an Arabic perspective, relates aspects of her life that correspond closely with the image of Nefertiti as the Queen of Sheba presented in this chapter. Although several aspects of the narrative belong to the realm of fantasy, even those events can often be linked to actual events in her life. The following points are of key importance:

- The Queen of Sheba, here called Balkis, was born to a Jinn (a genie) disguised as a woman and a vizier in the service of his king. The mother disappeared and it was left to the vizier to raise her. Given the Amarna setting and Balkis' true identity as Nefertiti, the vizier in question can only be Yuya. As argued earlier, Yuya and Tiye raised an infant of whom the biological mother was not known. Her mother would have been Bathsheba, who feared that her infant daughters would be murdered by David and sent them to Joseph in Egypt for safeguarding. Tiye would then indeed have been Nefertiti's wet nurse.

- The description of the vizier as being of exceptional beauty and having fallen out of favour with the king, a tyrant called Scharabel, only to be reinstated as grand vizier, matches the biblical Joseph in both respects.

- Balkis was also exceptionally beautiful, as was Nefertiti, whose name meant 'The beautiful one has come'.

- She was to be married to the tyrant king, who had assembled himself a large harem and was infamous for demanding beautiful women as his concubines. This matches Amenhotep III who was widely known for his sexual endeavours (see Section 7.6), and also became known as Busiris, the tyrant who sacrificed strangers who visited his country. As speculated earlier, Nefertiti may in fact have been betrothed to Amenhotep III, but was saved from his clutches by the eruption of Thera and its effect on Egypt.

- Balkis arranged a banquet for the purpose of killing the king. Although in reality the tyrant was not killed (he had withdrawn to Ethiopia), someone or some people were indeed killed at the banquet, matching the treacherous banquet associated with Nefertiti in Section 13.5 and Agamemnon's death in Section 13.6.

- At the banquet Balkis was accompanied by four female slaves, 'one singing, another harping, a third dancing, and a fourth pouring out wine for the king'. It would appear that Nefertiti was fond of music and took her female musicians with her everywhere she went, as suggested by the female lyrist on the Megiddo Ivory. Although these women may have been present during the attack on the guests, the killing must certainly have been done by the soldiers who were hidden from sight.

- There was a revolt against the tyrant, not only by civilians, but also by parts of his army ('those who were officers in the army agitated amongst their soldiers'). This revolt agrees with the revolt by Egyptians against Amenhotep and the Amun priesthood, following the failed sacrifice of the firstborn.

- Balkis became queen of Sheba following the death of her husband, matching Nefertiti who became queen after the death of Akhenaten.

- She commanded an army which was 'generalled' by 12,000 officers, which suggests it was a formidable force. The only force of such size at that time must certainly have been the Egyptian army.

- Of crucial importance is the description of a large group of her ambassadors travelling to Solomon, possibly on two occasions. This supports the argument presented earlier that the Megiddo Ivory scene depicts a famous and very public visit by a foreign queen and her entourage to Canaan.

- She was escorted by the military on her journey to Canaan, as is also depicted on the Megiddo Ivory.

- Specific mention is made of the queen offering the Canaanite king wreaths of flowers. This legend is very likely based on the devotional gesture of Nefertiti offering the Canaanite king lotus flowers on the Megiddo Ivory.

- Apart from worshipping the sun ('she too is a worshipper of the sun'), she is described as being 'robed in splendour'. Although most queens of that era probably wore robes of one kind or another, Nefertiti's was specifically striking in that it was almost completely transparent. Her revealing outfit must have been known in all the countries which dealt with Egypt at that time, and one can speculate with reasonable certainty that the entire episode of Balkis' hairy legs was a twisted fable based on Solomon's ill-disguised desire to see her legs! Perhaps she chose not to wear her fabled robe and all the sorely disappointed Solomon got to see were her feet.

- It is very likely that the female Hittite musicians (see Figure 13.5) who constantly accompanied Nefertiti became her confidants, and that it was on their encouragement that Nefertiti wrote to the Hittite king after Akhenaten's death (see Section 13.4).

- Whoever wrote this version of her history obviously knew about Solomon's Ethiopian wife (see Section 13.7), but mistakenly attributed the 'Queen of Sheba' status to this wife of Solomon, whose son became the 'ancestor of the kings of Abyssinia' (Ethiopia).

To conclude, the above 'history' of the Queen of Sheba unwittingly verifies many of the hypotheses presented in this chapter and should be considered conclusive evidence that Nefertiti and the Queen of Sheba were one and the same person.

14

The conquest of Canaan

Following their departure from Egypt, the Israelites entered the Sinai desert where God gave them his Ten Commandments and promised them the land of Canaan. The Israelites were reluctant to invade this country and rebelled against God, upon which He condemned that entire generation, including Moses, to wander in the desert for 40 years[1]. Moses was succeeded by Joshua, who led the Israelites on a victorious campaign into Canaan[2]. God instructed Joshua to mercilessly slaughter all the inhabitants of the conquered cities and carry off only their wealth. Probably the most famous of all the cities that fell to the Israelites was Jericho, an ancient city that had been occupied since 9000 BCE[3]. Having used the magical powers of the Ark to stop the river Jordan from flowing, the Israelites passed through on dry ground and encamped opposite Jericho[4]. Jericho purportedly fell after Joshua's army marched around it for seven days, being led by seven priests blowing their trumpets. On the last day the people gave a loud shout and Jericho's formerly impenetrable walls collapsed. Jericho was afterwards burned to the ground.

If the conquest of Canaan happened exactly as described in the Bible, one might expect to find archaeological evidence pointing not only to the destruction of these ancient cities, but also for evidence of a mass settlement in Canaan. The Exodus must have occurred during or immediately following the reign of Akhenaten, let us assume *ca.* 1340 BCE. Having dwelled in the desert for 40 years (if that did in fact happen), the Israelites would have invaded Canaan *ca.* 1300 BCE or later, early in the thirteenth century BCE. There is, however, no archaeological evidence around this date or any other to be found that would undisputedly prove that a conquest of the nature of Joshua's ever occurred. Joshua reportedly burned and totally destroyed three cities, Jericho, Ai and Hazor. Kenyon dated the destruction of Jericho to *ca.* 1550 BCE[5], a date apparently confirmed by radiocarbon dating. The average uncalibrated carbon date of charcoal found at the site is 3370 BP (Before Present, which is before 1950 CE), which translates to 1420 BCE. The corresponding calibrated date falls within the range 1601-1566 BCE. Short-lived cereals also found at the site were also dated to 3306 ±7 years BP uncalibrated (*ca.* 1356 BCE), and 1561-1524 BCE calibrated (Bruins and Van der Plicht, 1995)[6]. Since the Exodus occurred during the Amarna period, there would have been no walled city for Joshua to conquer as also concluded by Kenyon[7], who presumably assumed that the Exodus had occurred later than 1550 BCE. Archaeological evidence found at Hazor, Galilee, suggests that the city was violently destroyed some time during the thirteenth century BCE[8], while others have claimed it to have been destroyed around 1550 BCE[9], corresponding to Kenyon's date of destruction for Jericho. The biblical city Ai appears to have been unoccupied from 2200-1200 BCE[10], in other words, there was no Ai for Joshua to 'conquer'. The story of the destruction of Ai may be a distant memory of the Hyksos who had captured the city long before they resettled in Egypt during the Second Intermediate Period.

The most recent radiocarbon dating of the Thera eruption is *ca.* 1613 ± 13 BCE (calibrated) averaged around 3320 BP (uncalibrated)[11], which more or less matches the Jericho short-lived cereal date derived by Bruins and Van der Plicht. If so, can the fall of Jericho be attributed to the eruption of Thera? For the following reasons this is quite likely:

- The walls of Jericho supposedly collapsed when the Israeli soldiers gave a loud shout. This shout would have represented the sonic boom of the eruption of Thera, preserved in folklore as a shout by people.
- The walls of Jericho would never have tumbled because of either trumpets blowing or people shouting. The massive

earthquake associated with the eruption of Thera, however, would more than likely have unsettled the brickwork of these walls.

- Jericho was destroyed by fire, as was the city of Ugarit. In the biblical plagues fire rained down from heaven, nowadays interpreted as lightning striking the earth (see Sections 15.7 and 17.2). It is possible that once the walls of the city had collapsed, neighbouring city states attacked and set Jericho alight. Lava bombs from Thera as cause of the fire is implausible.

It should be noted that the uncalibrated radiocarbon date of 3306 ±7 BP translates to the period 1363-1349 BCE, while 3320 BP uncalibrated represents 1370 BCE. The uncalibrated radiocarbon date therefore agrees with the conventional dating of the reign of Amenhotep III. In addition scarabs of Amenhotep III found in tombs in the ruins of Jericho[12] confirm that this city must have suffered a major natural catastrophe during or sometime after his reign. No evidence of later pharaohs was found at Jericho, and the fall of the city must have occurred later during the reign of Amenhotep III as he had by that time been known in Egypt's vassal states. These facts leave us with the following three possibilities:

- The calibration curves for radiocarbon dating are invalid and should not be applied. This is highly unlikely.
- The conventional chronology of the Eighteenth Dynasty should be moved back in time by about 250 years (Amenhotep III to 1613 BCE). This is equally unlikely.
- A second eruption of Thera occurred more or less 250 years after 1613 BCE, in other words around 1363 BCE. As discussed in Section 19.1, the conventional Egyptian chronology has to be moved back in time not by 250 years, but by roughly only 80 years (between 50 and 150 years), to coincide with a second eruption of Thera *ca.* 1450 BCE.

It is widely acknowledged that the central hill country surrounding Jerusalem experienced an influx of people some time during the Late Bronze Age or beginning of the Early Iron Age[13], but it is unlikely that this influx represented the Israelites of the Exodus. A victory stele by Merneptah (*ca.* 1213-1203 BCE) claimed that Israel lay wasted and that 'his seed was no more'[14]. This implies that Israel had already been established when Merneptah ascended the throne, making it unlikely that the influx of the Exodus refugees could have occurred at that time. Given that the conventional chronology of Egypt has to be moved back in time by between 50 and 150 years as established by radiocarbon dating (see Section 19.1), and that the second Exodus most likely occurred towards the end of the Amarna period ca. 1330 BCE, one should look for an influx of people into Canaan ca. 1480 – 1380 BCE. It has been suggested that Israel emerged during the Middle Bronze Age (2000-1550 BCE)[15,16], which corresponds to the rise of the Hyksos in Canaan. Urban stability and military strength in Canaan had reached its peak during the Middle Bronze Age[17]. However, it has been shown that many new small settlements arose in Canaan during the fourteenth century BCE[18]. These new settlements can most likely be attributed to the Hyksos slaves returning to Canaan following the second Exodus from Egypt. The influx of the Israelites into Canaan would not have been a violent conquest of enemy territory, but rather a reunification of a people divided 200 to 250 years earlier.

The plagues of Egypt as described in ancient sources

The general lack of undisputed historical and archaeological evidence of the Exodus and in fact the entire early history of Israel has caused many scholars to doubt whether it ever occurred[1]. It has been argued that many of the textual accounts were inventions by their authors to serve specific political goals rather than being true accounts of actual events:

> According to these scholars [the minimalists], the continuing power of the biblical narratives is testimony to the literary skill of the authors, who stitched together old myths, folktales, imaginary records, legendary narratives, and a few memories of historical facts (about the ninth to early sixth centuries BCE) into a single saga of apostasy and redemption. ... According to this premise, biblical 'history' was not only historically baseless, but powerful, focussed propaganda that delivered an essentially made-up story of the Patriarchs, Exodus, Conquest, and the glorious golden age of David and Solomon to a credulous public.[2]

Possibly the clearest documentary evidence to be found supporting the existence of a Hebrew nation is the account of the biblical plagues of Egypt that led to the eventual departure of the Israelites from Egypt under the leadership of Moses. Several researchers including popular writers such as Ian Wilson in 1985[3], Graham Phillips in 1998[4] and others[5] have concluded that the plagues of the Exodus must have been caused by an eruption of a volcano, specifically the cataclysmic eruption of Thera. In 2005 Igino Trevisanato gave a highly detailed and scientific analysis of the plagues of Egypt in terms of the Bronze Age eruption of Thera[6]. Both Wilson and Trevisanato argue that the tenth plague must have been based on human sacrifice to the Egyptian gods, in order to bring an end to the devastating plague in Egypt. Another recent book to appear was Barbara Sivertsen's *The Parting of the Sea* in 2009[7]. Trevisanato and Sivertsen both argue that there were two volcanic eruptions that influenced the Exodus of the Israelites from Egypt, as discussed in Chapter 18. In his book *The Lords of Avaris* David Rohl places the biblical Exodus before the arrival of the Hyksos in Egypt, but also argues for more than one eruption of Thera[8]. The first occurred during the reign of Ahmose and resulted in the departure of the Hyksos from Avaris, while the second occurred during the reign of Hatshepshut. The final, cataclysmic eruption of Thera occurred during the reign of Tuthmosis III. He bases the dating of the final eruption on a Greenland ice core which has been dated to 1090 BCE ± 20 years, falling within the rule of Tuthmosis according to his revised chronology, and Deucalion's flood, which occurred during the reign of Misphragmuthosis (Tuthmosis III, see Chapter 11 and Section 17.1). Whether or not one agrees with Rohl's revised chronology and his conclusions, both *A Test of Time* and *The Lords of Avaris* are well worth reading for obtaining background on various issues regarding the dating of Egyptian chronology.

For the sake of completeness many of the modern interpretations of the plagues will be repeated here, but I will emphasise aspects of those plagues that, in my opinion, have previously not been dealt with in sufficient detail, namely the floods that struck Egypt in ancient times, and the sacrifice of the firstborn.

Our most detailed source of the plagues of the Exodus is the Bible[9], followed by Josephus' similar version in his *Antiquities of the Jews*[10] and finally snippets from Jewish and Arabic texts and legends. The Bible relates that Moses confronted Pharaoh with these signs in order to convince him to allow the Israelites to leave Egypt. In each instance leading up to the tenth plague Pharaoh initially agreed to let them go, but the Lord 'hardened his heart' and he subsequently refused them permission to go. The plagues as described in the Bible and other sources will be listed so that the reader can form a mental picture of how the ancient scribes remembered these events. This will be followed by a realistic interpretation of likely events that gave rise to the biblical legends.

15.1 The plague of blood

In *Exodus* we read:

> The Lord said to Moses, 'Tell Aaron, 'Take your staff and stretch out your hand over the waters of Egypt – over the streams and canals, over the ponds and all the reservoirs' – and they will turn to blood. Blood will be everywhere in Egypt, even in the wooden buckets and stone jars.' ... He (Aaron) raised his staff in the presence of Pharaoh and his officials and struck the water of the Nile, and all the water was changed into blood. The fish in the Nile died, and the river smelled so bad that the Egyptians could not drink its water. Blood was everywhere in Egypt. But the Egyptian magicians did the same things by their secret arts, and Pharaoh's heart became hard; ... And all the Egyptians dug along the Nile to get drinking water, because they could not drink the water of the Nile.[11]

Josephus' version reads:

> For the Egyptian river ran with bloody water at the command of God, insomuch that it could not be drunk, and they had no other spring of water, for the water was not only the color of blood, but it brought upon those who ventured to drink of it, great pains and bitter torment.[12]

In the *Legends of the Jews*, a collection of Jewish legends by Louis Ginzberg, we find this legendary account:

To produce the plague, Aaron took his rod, and stretched out his hand over the waters of Egypt. Moses had no part in performing the miracle, for God had said to him, 'The water that watched over thy safety when thou wast exposed in the Nile, shall not suffer harm through thee.' Aaron had scarcely executed the Divine bidding, when all the water of Egypt became blood, even such as was kept in vessels of wood and in vessels of stone. The very spittle of an Egyptian turned into blood no sooner had he ejected it from his mouth, and blood dripped also from the idols of the Egyptians. The transformation of the waters into blood was intended mainly as a punishment for the oppressors, but it was at the same time a source of profit for the oppressed. It gave the Israelites the opportunity of amassing great wealth. The Egyptians paid them large sums for their water, for if an Egyptian and an Israelite drew water from the same trough, the portion carried off by the Egyptian was bound to be useless, it turned into blood. To be sure, nothing helped the Egyptians in their distress, for though they drank water from the same cup as an Israelite, it became blood in their mouth.[13]

15.2 The plague of frogs

In *Exodus* God's instruction to Moses reads:

Go to Pharaoh and say to him, 'This is what the Lord says: Let my people go, so that they may worship me. If you refuse to let them go, I will plague your whole country with frogs. The Nile will teem with frogs. They will come up into your palace and your bedroom and onto your bed, and into the houses of your officials and your people, and into your ovens and kneading troughs. The frogs will go up on you and your people and all your officials.' ... 'Tell Aaron, 'Stretch out your hand with your staff over the streams and canals and ponds, and make frogs come up to the land of Egypt.'' So Aaron stretched out his hand over the waters of Egypt, and the frogs came up and covered the land of Egypt.

But the magicians did the same things by their secret arts …[14]

Josephus tells us:

> An innumerable multitude of frogs consumed the fruit of the ground; the river was also full of them, insomuch that those who drew water had it plundered by the blood of these animals, as they died in, and were destroyed by, the water; and the country was full of filthy slime, as they were born, and as they died: they also plundered their vessels in their houses which they used, and were found among what they ate and what they drank, and came in great numbers upon their beds. There was also an awful smell, and a stink arose from them, as they were born, and as they died therein.[15]

The plague as recounted in the *Legends of the Jews* includes speaking frogs:

> He stretched forth his hand with his rod over the rivers, and caused frogs to come up upon the land of Egypt. Moses, whose life had been preserved by the water, was kept from poisoning his savior with the reptiles. At first only a single frog appeared, but he began to croak, summoning so many companions that the whole land of Egypt swarmed with them. Wherever an Egyptian took up his stand, frogs appeared, and in some mysterious way they were able to pierce the hardest of metals, and even the marble palaces of the Egyptian nobles afforded no protection against them. If a frog came close to them, the walls split asunder immediately. 'Make way,' the frogs would call out to the stone, 'that I may do the will of my Creator,' and at once the marble showed a rift, through which the frogs entered, and then they attacked the Egyptians bodily, and mutilated and overwhelmed them. In their ardor to fulfill the behest of God, the frogs cast themselves into the red-hot flames of the bake-ovens and

devoured the bread. Centuries later, the three holy children, Hananiah, Mishael, and Azariah, were ordered by Nebuchadnezzar to pay worship to his idols on penalty of death in the burning furnace, and they said, 'If the frogs, which were under no obligation to glorify the Name of God, nevertheless threw themselves into the fire in order to execute the Divine will concerning the punishment of the Egyptians, how much more should we be ready to expose our lives to the fire for the greater glory of His Name!' And the zealous frogs were not permitted to go unrewarded. While the others were destroyed from Pharaoh and the Egyptian houses at the moment appointed as the last of the plague, God saved those in the bake-ovens alive, the fire had no power to do them the least harm. ... all the frogs perished, and their destruction was too swift for them to retire to the water. Consequently the whole land was filled with the stench from the decaying frogs, for they had been so numerous that every man of the Egyptians gathered together four heaps of them.[16]

15.3 The plague of gnats

According to *Exodus*:

Then the Lord said to Moses, 'Tell Aaron, 'Stretch out your staff and strike the dust on the ground,' and throughout the land of Egypt the dust will become gnats.' They did this, and when Aaron stretched out his hand with the staff and struck the dust of the ground, gnats came upon men and animals. All the dust throughout the land of Egypt became gnats. But when the magicians tried to produce gnats by their secret arts, they could not.[17]

Josephus's account reads:

... for there arose out of the bodies of the Egyptians an innumerable quantity of lice, by which, wicked as they were, they miserably perished, as not able to destroy this sort of vermin either with washes or with ointments.[18]

In the *Legends of the Jews* the third plague is also listed as lice[19].

15.4 The plague of flies

This plague is described in *Exodus* as:

> Then the Lord said to Moses, '... and say to him (Pharaoh), ' ... Let my people go, ... If you do not let my people go, I will send swarms of flies on you and your officials, on your people and into your houses. The houses of the Egyptians will be full of flies, and even the ground where they are." ... Dense swarms of flies poured into Pharaoh's palace and into the houses of his officials, and throughout Egypt the land was ruined by flies.[20]

Josephus' account reads:

> God punished the Egyptians for the sake of the Hebrews, for he filled that country full of various sorts of pestilential creatures, with various properties ... by whose means the men perished themselves, and the land was destitute of farmers for its cultivation; but if anything escaped destruction from them, it was killed by a sickness the men underwent also.[21]

The fourth plague in the *Legends of the Jews* is something completely different and apparently entirely fabulous, but which may refer to freed wild animals that used to be kept as pets by the wealthy:

> God sent the fourth plague upon Egypt, a mixed horde of wild animals, lions, bears, wolves, and panthers, and so many birds of prey of different kinds that the light of the sun and the moon was darkened as they circled through the air. These beasts came upon the Egyptians as a punishment for desiring to force the seed of

Abraham to amalgamate with the other nations. God retaliated by bringing a mixture upon them that cost them their life.[22]

15.5 The plague on livestock

In *Exodus* we read:

> The Lord said to Moses, 'Go to Pharaoh and say to him, '... Let my people go ... If you refuse to let them go ... the hand of the Lord will bring a terrible plague on your livestock in the field – on your horses and donkeys and camels and your cattle and sheep and goats. ...'' And the next day the Lord did it: All the livestock of the Egyptians died, but not one animal belonging to the Israelites died.[23]

Josephus does not mention this plague specifically, but the *Legend of the Jews* renders a similar account:

> The fifth plague inflicted by God upon the Egyptians was a grievous pestilence, which mowed down the cattle and beasts chiefly, yet it did not spare men altogether. This pestilence was a distinct plague, but it also accompanied all the other plagues, and the death of many Egyptians was due to it.[24]

15.6 The plague of boils

This plague, the deadliest of all as it affected all living beings in Egypt, is described in *Exodus* as:

> Then the Lord said to Moses and Aaron, 'Take handfuls of soot from a furnace and have Moses toss it in the air in the presence of Pharaoh. It will become fine dust over the whole land of Egypt, and festering boils will break out on the men and animals throughout the land.' ... and festering boils broke out on men and animals.[25]

Josephus' description reads:

> ... for their bodies had terrible boils, breaking forth with blains, while they were already inwardly consumed; and a great part of the Egyptians perished in this manner.[26]

In the *Legends of the Jews* the plague is recorded as:

> The sixth plague, the plague of boils, was produced by Moses and Aaron together in a miraculous way. Each took a handful of ashes of the furnace, then Moses held the contents of the two heaps in the hollow of one of his hands, and sprinkled the ashes tip toward the heaven, and it flew so high that it reached the Divine throne. Returning earthward, it scattered over the whole land of Egypt, a space equal to four hundred square parasangs. The small dusts of the ashes produced leprosy upon the skin of the Egyptians, and blains of a peculiar kind, soft within and dry on top.[27]

15.7 The plague of hail

In *Exodus* this plague is described as:

> Then the Lord said to Moses, '... confront Pharaoh and say to him, 'This is what the Lord , the God of the Hebrews, says: 'Let my people go ... or this time I will send the full force of my plagues against you and your officials and your people ... at this time tomorrow I will send the worst hailstorm that has ever fallen on Egypt from the day it was founded until now. Give an order now to bring your livestock and everything you have in the field to a place of shelter, because the hail will fall on every man and animal that has not been brought in and is still out in the field, and they will die.'' ... the Lord sent thunder and hail and lightning flashed down to the ground. So the Lord rained hail on the land of Egypt; hail fell and lightning flashed back and forth.

It was the worst storm in all the land of Egypt since it had become a nation. Throughout Egypt hail struck everything in the fields – both men and animals; it beat down everything growing in the fields and stripped every tree. The only place it did not hail was the land of Goshen, where the Israelites were.[28]

Josephus' version reads:

… hail was sent down from heaven … This hail broke down their boughs laden with fruit.[29]

From the *Legends of the Jews* we learn:

As a rule, fire and water are elements at war with each other, but in the hailstones that smote the land of Egypt they were reconciled. **A fire rested in the hailstones as the burning wick swims in the oil of a lamp; the surrounding fluid cannot extinguish the flame. The Egyptians were smitten either by the hail or by the fire.** In the one case as the other their flesh was seared, and the bodies of the many that were slain by the hail were consumed by the fire. The hailstones heaped themselves up like a wall, so that the carcasses of the slain beasts could not be removed, and if the people succeeded in dividing the dead animals and carrying their flesh off, the birds of prey would attack them on their way home, and snatch their prize away. But the vegetation in the field suffered even more than man and beast, for the hail came down like an axe upon the trees and broke them. That the wheat and the spelt were not crushed was a miracle.[30]

15.8 The plague of locusts

In *Exodus* we read:

Then the Lord said to Moses, 'Go to Pharaoh, for I have hardened his heart and the hearts of his officials so that I may perform these

miraculous signs of mine among them that you may tell your
children and grandchildren how I dealt harshly with the
Egyptians ...' So Moses and Aaron went to Pharaoh and said to
him, 'This is what the Lord, the God of the Hebrews, says: 'How
long will you refuse to humble yourself before me? ... I will bring
locusts into your country tomorrow. They will cover the face of
the ground so that it cannot be seen. They will devour what little
you have left after the hail ... They will fill your houses ...'' By
morning the wind had brought the locusts; they invaded all
Egypt and settled down in every area of the country in great
numbers. ... They covered the ground until it was black. ...
Nothing green remained on tree or plant in all the land of
Egypt.[31]

Josephus relates:

After this a tribe of locusts consumed the seed which was not
hurt by the hail; so that to the Egyptians all hopes of future fruits
of the ground were entirely lost.[32]

According to the *Legends of the Jews*, the Egyptians regarded the
locusts as a source of food:

Moses lost no time in announcing the eighth plague to him, the
plague of the locusts. ... Then God sent the plague of the locusts
announced by Moses before. They ate every herb of the land, and
all the fruit of the trees that the hail had left, and there remained
not any green thing. And again Pharaoh sent for Moses and
Aaron, to ask their forgiveness, both for his sin against the Lord
God, in not having hearkened unto His word, and for his sin
against them, in having chased them forth and intended to curse
them. Moses, as before, prayed to God in Pharaoh's behalf, and
his petition was granted, the plague was taken away, and in a
rather surprising manner. When the swarms of locusts began to

darken the land, the Egyptians caught them and preserved them in brine as a dainty to be eaten. Now the Lord turned an exceeding strong west wind, which took up the locusts, and drove them into the Red Sea. Even those they were keeping in their pots flew up and away, and they had none of the expected profit.[33]

15.9 The plague of darkness

According to *Exodus*:

Then the Lord said to Moses, 'Stretch out your hand toward the sky so that darkness will spread over Egypt – **darkness that can be felt.'** ... **and total darkness covered all Egypt for three days. No one could see anyone else or leave his placed for three days.**[34]

Josephus presents a similar description:

... a thick darkness, without the least light, spread itself over the Egyptians, whereby **their sight being obscured, and their breathing hindered by the thickness of the air**, they died miserably, and under a terror lest they should be swallowed up by the dark cloud. Besides this, when the darkness, **after three days and as many nights**, was dissipated ...[35]

In the *Legends of the Jews* we find the following detailed description:

The last plague but one, like those which had preceded it, **endured seven days**. All the time the land was enveloped in darkness, only it was not always of the same degree of density. During the first three days, it was not so thick but that the Egyptians could change their posture when they desired to do so. If they were sitting down, they could rise up, and if they were standing, they could sit down. On the fourth, fifth, and sixth days, **the darkness was so dense that they could not stir from their place**. They either sat the whole time, or stood; as they were at the beginning, so they remained until the end. The last day of darkness overtook the Egyptians, not in their own land, but at the Red Sea, on their pursuit of Israel. **The darkness was not of the ordinary, earthly kind; it came from hell, and it could be felt. It was as thick as a dinar**, and all the time it prevailed a celestial light brightened the dwellings of the children of Israel, whereby they could see what the Egyptians were doing under cover of the darkness. This was of great advantage to them, for when they were about to go forth from the land, **and they asked their neighbors to lend them raiment, and jewels of gold and jewels of silver, for the journey,** the Egyptians tried to deny having any in their possession. But the children of Israel, having spied out all their treasures during the days of darkness, could describe the objects they needed with accuracy, and designate their hiding-places. The Egyptians reasoned that the words of the Israelites could be taken implicitly as they spoke them, for if they had had any idea of deceiving them, asking for a loan when they intended to keep what they laid hands on, they might have taken unobserved during the days of darkness whatever they desired. **Hence the Egyptians felt no hesitation in lending the children of Israel all the treasures they asked for.**

The darkness was of such a nature that it could not be dispelled by artificial means. **The light of the fire kindled for household uses was either extinguished by the violence of the storm, or else it was made invisible and swallowed up in the density of the darkness. Sight, that most indispensable of all the external senses, though unimpaired, was deprived of its office, for nothing could be discerned**, and all the other senses were overthrown like subjects whose leader has fallen. **None was able to speak or to hear,** nor could anyone venture to take food, but they lay themselves down in quiet and hunger, their outward senses in a trance. Thus they remained, overwhelmed by the affliction, until Moses had compassion on them again, and besought God in their behalf, who granted him the power of restoring fine weather, light instead of darkness and day instead of night.[36]

15.10 The plague on the firstborn

This plague may be considered as the most important of all, since it was only after the death of the firstborn that the Pharaoh gave the Israelites permission to leave Egypt. In *Exodus* we read:

> Now the Lord said to Moses, 'I will bring one more plague on Pharaoh and on Egypt. ... Tell the people that **men and women alike are to ask their neighbors for articles of silver and gold.'** (The Lord made the Egyptians favorably disposed toward the people, and Moses himself was highly regarded in Egypt by Pharaoh's officials and by the people.) ... 'About midnight I will go throughout Egypt. **Every firstborn son in Egypt will die, from the firstborn son of Pharaoh, who sits on the throne, to the firstborn son of the slave girl, who is at her hand mill, and all the firstborn of the cattle as well.** There will be loud wailing throughout Egypt – worse than there has ever been or ever will be again.' ... At midnight the Lord struck down all the firstborn in Egypt, from the firstborn of Pharaoh, who sat on the throne, to the firstborn of the prisoner, who was in the dungeon, and the firstborn of all the livestock as well. Pharaoh and all his officials and all the Egyptians got up during the night, and there was loud wailing in Egypt, **for there was not a house without someone dead.**[37]

Josephus' description is less detailed, but still worth listing:

> ... on that day God passed us over, and sent the plague upon the Egyptians; for the destruction of the firstborn came upon the Egyptians that night, so that many of the Egyptians who lived

near the king's palace persuaded Pharaoh to let the Hebrews go. ... They also honored the Hebrews with gifts, some in order to get them to depart quickly, and others on account of their being neighbors, and the friendship they had with them.[38]

Despite the embellished accounts of the preceding plagues, the slaying of the firstborn as recorded in the *Legends of the Jews* appears to paint a realistic picture of the event:

When Moses announced the slaying of the firstborn, **the designated victims all repaired to their fathers**, and said: 'Whatever Moses hath foretold has been fulfilled. Let the Hebrews go, else we shall all die.' But the fathers replied, 'It is better for one of every ten of us to die, than the Hebrews should execute their purpose.' **Then the firstborn repaired to Pharaoh, to induce him to dismiss the children of Israel. So far from granting their wish, he ordered his servants to fall upon the firstborn and beat them, to punish them for their presumptuous demand. Seeing that they could not accomplish their end by gentle means, they attempted to bring it about by force.** Pharaoh and all that opposed the wishes of the firstborn were of the opinion that the loss of so inconsiderable a percentage of the population was a matter of small moment. They were mistaken in their calculation, for the Divine decree included **not only the firstborn sons, but also the firstborn daughters, and not only the firstborn of the marriages then existing, but also the firstborn issuing from previous alliances of the fathers and the mothers, and as the Egyptians led dissolute lives, it happened not rarely that each of the ten children of one woman was the firstborn of its father.** Finally, God decreed that **death should smite the oldest member of every household,** whether or not he was the firstborn of his parents. What God resolves is executed. **At the exact instant marking the middle of the night,** so precise that only God Himself could determine and discern it, He appeared in Egypt, attended by nine thousand myriads of the Angels of Destruction who are fashioned some of hail and some of flames, and whose glances drive terror and trembling to the heart of the beholder. These angels were about to precipitate themselves into the work of annihilation, but God restrained them, saying, 'My wrath will not be appeased until I Myself execute vengeance upon the enemies of Israel.'

Those among the Egyptians who gave credence to Moses' words, and **tried to shield their firstborn children from death**, sent them to their Hebrew neighbors, to spend the fateful night with them, in the hope that God would exempt the houses of the children of Israel from the plague. But in the morning, when the Israelites arose from their sleep, they found the corpses of the Egyptian fugitives next to them. That was the night in which the Israelites prayed before lying down to sleep: 'Cause us, O Lord our God, to lie down in peace, remove Satan from before us and from behind us, and guard our going out and our coming in unto life and unto peace,' for it was Satan that had caused frightful bloodshed among the Egyptians. **Among the slain there were, beside the Egyptian firstborn, also the firstborn of other nationalities residing in Egypt, as well as the Egyptian firstborn dwelling outside of their own land**. Even the long dead of the firstborn were not spared. The dogs dragged their corpses out of their graves in the houses, for it was the Egyptian custom to inter the dead at home. At the appalling sight the Egyptians mourned as though the bereavement had befallen them but recently. The very monuments and statues erected to the memory of the firstborn dead were changed into dust, which was scattered and flew out of sight. Moreover, their slaves had to share the fate of the Egyptians, and no less the firstborn of the captive that was in the dungeon, **for none was so low but he hated the Hebrews, and rejoiced when the Egyptians decreed their persecution**.

The female slaves that ground corn between mill-stones were in the habit of saying, 'We do not regret our servitude, if only the

Israelites are gagged, too.' **In dealing out punishment to these aliens in the land of Egypt,** God showed that He was at once the Master of the land and the Lord over all the gods of the nations, for if the slaves and the captives of war had not been smitten, they would have said, 'Mighty is our god, who helped us in this plague.'[39]

15.11 Other miracles that can be linked to a volcanic eruption

Although not directly associated with the plagues, two other miracles related to the Exodus warrant mentioning in the context of a volcanic eruption. While the Israelites were on their way to the Red Sea, they were guided by God himself:

> By day the Lord went ahead of them in a pillar of cloud to guide them on their way, and by night in a pillar of fire to give them light, so that they could travel by day or by night. Neither the pillar of cloud by day nor the pillar of fire by night left its place in front of the people.[40]

Probably the most famous of all the miracles performed by Moses is the parting of the sea. When the Israelites reached the Red Sea, they were trapped between the sea and the pursuing Egyptian army. God then instructed Moses to part the sea and lead the Israelites to safety:

> Then the Lord said to Moses, 'Why are you crying out to me? Tell the Israelites to move on. Raise your staff and stretch out your hand over the sea to divide the water so that the Israelites can go through the sea on dry ground. I will harden the hearts of the Egyptians so that they will go in after them. And I will gain glory through Pharaoh and all his army, through his chariots and horsemen.'
>
> **Then the angel of God, who had been travelling in front of Israel's army, withdrew and went behind them. The pillar of**

cloud also moved from in front and stood behind them, coming between the armies of Egypt and Israel. Throughout the night the cloud brought darkness to one side and light to the other side, so neither went near the other all night long.

Then Moses stretched out his hand over the sea, and all the night the Lord drove the sea back with a strong east wind and turned it into dry land. **The waters were divided, and the Israelites went through the sea on dry ground, with a wall of water on their right and on their left.**

The Egyptians pursued them, and all Pharaoh's horses and chariots and horsemen followed them into the sea. During the last watch of the night the Lord looked down from the pillar of fire and cloud at the Egyptian army and threw it into confusion. He made the wheels of their chariots come off so that they had difficulty driving...

Then the Lord said to Moses, 'Stretch out your hand over the sea so that the waters may flow back over the Egyptians and their chariots and horsemen.' Moses stretched out his hand over the sea, and at daybreak the sea went back to its place. The Egyptians were fleeing toward it, and the Lord swept them into the sea. The water flowed back and covered the chariots and horsemen – the entire army of Pharaoh that had followed the Israelites into the sea. Not one of them survived.[41]

Josephus' account of this episode gives additional details:

As soon, therefore, as ever the whole Egyptian army was within it, the sea flowed to its own place, and came down with a torrent raised by storms of wind, and encompassed the Egyptians. **Showers of rain also came down from the sky, and dreadful thunders and lightning, with flashes of fire. Thunderbolts also were darted upon them.** Nor was there anything which used to be sent by God upon men, as indications of his wrath, which did not happen at this time, **for a dark and dismal night oppressed**

them. And thus did all these men perish, so that there was not one man left to be a messenger of this calamity to the rest of the Egyptians.[42]

In *Psalms*, a book of psalms and prayers in the Bible, the psalmist also remembers the storm:

> The waters saw you, O God, **the waters saw you and writhed; the very depths were convulsed**. The clouds poured down water, **the skies resounded with thunder; your arrows flashed back and forth**. Your thunder was heard in the whirlwind, your lightning lit up the world; **the earth trembled and quaked.** Your path led through the sea, your way through the mighty waters, though your footprints were not seen. You led your people like a flock by the hand of Moses and Aaron.[43]

15.12 The plagues in the Koran

The Koran presents relatively little information about the plagues of Egypt, but most notably mentions a flood:

> We sent them the flood and the locusts and the vermin and the frogs and the blood ... therefore we drowned them in the sea: because they denied Our revelations and were heedless of them.[44]
>
> (Remember also) Qarun, Pharaoh and Haman: there came to them Moses with clear signs, but they behaved with insolence on the earth; yet they could not overreach (Us). Each one of them we seized for his crime: of them, against some **we sent a violent tornado (with showers of stones); some we caught by a (mighty) blast**; some we caused the earth to swallow up; and **some we drowned (in the waters)**: it was not Allah who injured (and oppressed) them: they injured (and oppressed) their own souls.[45]

16

Could an eruption of Thera have affected Egypt?

The reader can appreciate that practically all of the plagues sent by God may have natural explanations. Some of the plagues could only have been caused by the eruption of a volcano. These include the wall of water that collapsed onto the Egyptians (a tsunami), the darkness that covered Egypt (the volcanic ash cloud descending upon Egypt), the thunder and lightning (these often accompany the fallout of ash), the water turning into blood (the rivers and all water sources being contaminated by volcanic ash containing iron oxide particles), the frogs (population explosion resulting from the death of most of the fish in the rivers), pestilences such as flies and gnats (breeding in the rotting corpses of animals in the field), the boils and blisters on people (a known effect of volcanic ash on human beings), the trembling earth (the earthquakes that followed the eruption), the pillars of cloud and fire (the eruption column of the volcano as seen by day and by night) and the shower of stones (ejecta from the volcano).

The only volcanic eruption of a scale large enough to cover Egypt in total darkness for a couple of days would have been the cataclysmic eruption of Thera. The question is, could an eruption of Thera have affected Egypt at all? Egypt is more than 800 km from Thera, which at first glance may seem to be too far to have affected Egypt in the manner described above.

16.1 Tsunami

There can be no doubt that any major eruption of Thera would have caused a massive tsunami in the Mediterranean Sea. The height of the tsunami of Thera's cataclysmic eruption has been estimated to have been between 40m and 90m at the origin, diminishing to 7m at

Tel Aviv[1]. An almost incredible 150m for the original wave height has even been suggested[2]. From the map in Figure 16.1 it is clear that the path to Egypt is both shorter and not obstructed by any islands compared to the path to Tel Aviv. Therefore, one may expect the height of the tsunami that hit Egypt to have been substantially higher. The tsunami would most certainly have swept away human life and objects in the Nile Delta and probably inland along the Nile itself. Various ancient accounts of floods in the Mediterranean Sea are discussed in Section 17.1.

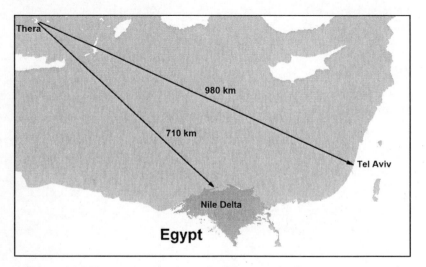

Figure 16.1 Tsunami paths from the Thera to the Egyptian coast and Tel Aviv

16.2 Ash cloud

The magnitude of a volcanic eruption is expressed in terms of its Volcanic Explosivity Index (VEI)[3]. This index is based on the estimated volume of ejecta, the height of the eruption cloud and also the destructive effect of the eruption. The scale is logarithmic and a step from one index point to the next represents a tenfold increase in the magnitude of the eruption. VEI values run from 0 for non-explosive eruptions to a maximum of 8. Table 16.1 shows some VEIs and their associated ejecta volumes.

VEI	Ejecta volume in cubic kilometres (km^3)
8	Greater than 1000
7	Greater than 100 but smaller than 1000
6	Greater than 10 but smaller than 100
5	Greater than 1 but smaller than 10
4	Greater than 0.1 but smaller than 1

Table 16.1 VEI classifications with associated volumes
of ejecta.[4]

The eruption of the Chaitén volcano in Chile in May 2008 was classified as VEI-4, with an estimated column height of 30km[5,6]. Its ash cloud drifted more than 700km across the South American continent (see Figure 16.2).

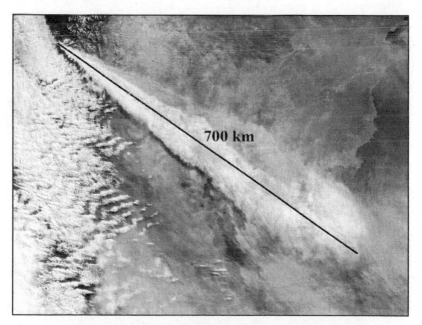

Figure 16.2. Ash cloud of the Chaitén volcano in Chile[7]

The eruption of Mount St Helens in the state of Washington in the

United States of America in 1980 was classified as VEI-5 with an estimated ejecta volume of about 3 cubic kilometres[8]. Its ash cloud rose 24km into the sky and eventually reached Edmonton in Canada, approximately 1,100km away. In the USA the ash cloud spread over a sector of radius approximately 1,800km, with some ash deposits having fallen as far as Oklahoma, 2,400km from Mount St Helens (see Figure 16.3).

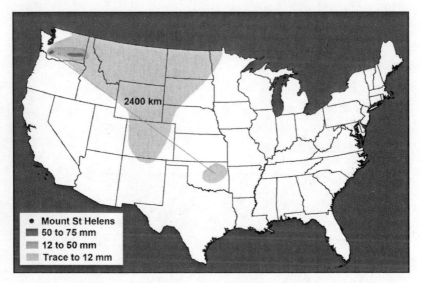

Figure 16.3. Ash fallout distribution of the 1980 eruption of Mount St Helens[9]

An even more powerful volcanic eruption occurred in 1991 when Mount Pinatubo in the Philippines erupted[10], covering an area of 125,000 square kilometres over distances as far as 2,360km from the eruption (see Figure 16.4). This eruption was rated VEI-6 and released between 6 and 16 cubic kilometres of ash into the atmosphere.

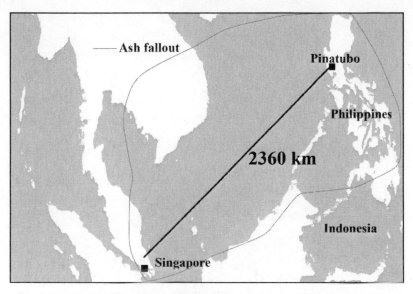

Figure 16.4. Ash fallout area of the 1991 eruption of Mount Pinatubo, Philippines[11]

An 1875 volcanic eruption in Iceland spread its ashes over Scandinavia in 48 hours, approximately 1,900km to the east (see Figure 16.5).

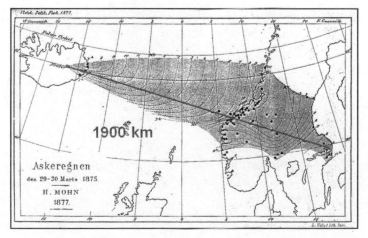

Figure 16.5. Ash fallout over Scandinavia of the Icelandic eruption of 1875[12]

The 1883 eruption of Krakatoa has a VEI of 6, with an estimated ejecta volume of 21 cubic kilometres[13]. By comparison, the estimated volume of ejecta for the Thera eruption, VEI 6 or 7[14], is between about 30 cubic kilometres[15] and 100 cubic kilometres[16], with an estimated column height of 36km[17]. There can therefore be no doubt that given the right wind direction, the ash cloud of Thera could have reached Egypt, as projected by Wilson in Figure 16.6, based on sea-bed samples.

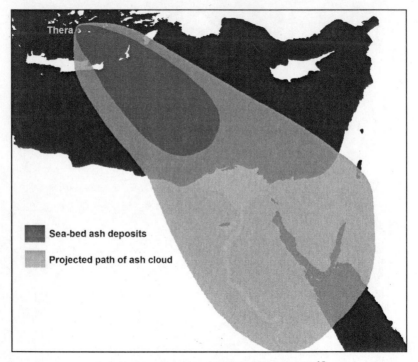

Figure 16.6. Projected Thera fallout path[18]

16.3 Volcanic bombs, earthquakes and sonic booms

The mention of 'showers of stone' in the Koran, the 'fire within hailstones' in Jewish legend and hail mixed with fire in *Exodus* suggest that rocks or lumps of lava, generally referred to as volcanic bombs, may have reached Egypt. In the simplest equation for the parabolic trajectory of an object launched into space on a flat plain, air resistance is ignored and the distance covered depends only on two variables, the launch angle and the launch velocity. The optimum launch angle is 45° and for an object to travel 800km to Egypt it would under these ideal conditions have to be launched at a velocity of 2,800m/s. (Note: the muzzle velocity of an AK-47 rifle is only about 710m/s[19] by comparison, and the speed of a jet aircraft travelling at Mach 2 is approximately 686m/s). The launched object would reach a height of 200km (well into the thermosphere!) and take just over 400 seconds to reach Egypt. The explosive energy required to launch physical (real) objects to a target more than 800km away is immense and it does not seem possible for volcanic bombs or lava fragments from Thera to have reached Egypt. Ballistic blocks ejected from volcanoes typically do not travel farther than a couple of kilometres[20]. The 'fire' mentioned in the ancient records therefore must refer to the lightning that often accompanies volcanic eruptions[21] and possibly fires ignited by lightning striking the earth.

While it would have taken some time for Thera's ash cloud to reach Egypt, the sonic boom as recorded in the Koran would have been heard after about 45 minutes. Krakatoa's sonic boom was heard 4,800km from the volcano. The tsunami would have reached Egypt's

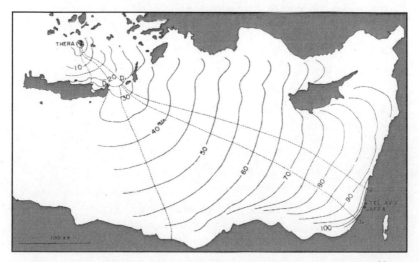

Figure 16.7. Tsunami refraction diagram with time progression[22]

shores in just over an hour as depicted in Figure 16.7, where the contours represent the position of the tsunami in 5 minute intervals.

It is instructive to compare the explosive power of volcanoes in terms of modern parameters, namely the equivalent of tons of the explosive Trinitrotoluene (TNT)[23]. The atomic bomb that was dropped on Hiroshima during the Second World War exploded with the equivalent of 15 kilotons of TNT. By comparison, the eruption of Mount St Helens had a blast equivalent to about 1,600 times the size of the Hiroshima explosion, or 24 megatons of TNT[24]. The biggest nuclear explosion in history was that of the Tsar Bomb[25], which exploded with a force of 50 megatons of TNT (some sources quote 58 megatons[26]). The force of this explosion was only a quarter of the estimated total 200 megaton eruption of Krakatoa (there were three eruptions, the final one releasing 150 megatons of energy)[27]. The eruption of Thera was possibly up to four times more powerful than the eruption of Krakatoa and therefore equivalent to between 600 and 800 megatons of TNT[28].

The earthquake unleashed by the eruption of Thera would have been felt all around the Mediterranean Sea, as much weaker eruptions of Thera during later times were felt in Egypt[29]. Furthermore, *Psalm 77* (see Section 15.11) confirms that an earthquake was felt during the time of the Exodus. In biblical times all natural disasters, including volcanic eruptions, appear to have been attributed to God. For example in *Psalm 104* we see how the psalmist recorded the phenomenon of a volcanic eruption in the limited vocabulary and insight of those times as[30]:

He who looks at the earth, and it trembles, who touches the mountains, and they smoke.[31]

16.4 Visibility on the western horizon

Evidently not knowing its true origin, the Israelites recorded that God directed them by a 'pillar of cloud' by day and a 'pillar of fire' by night. There can be little doubt that this description fits the natural phenomenon known as the eruption column (ash cloud) of a volcanic eruption. A valid question is, however, whether the eruption column of Thera would have been visible from Egypt, more than 800km away. Due to the curvature of the earth, which has a radius of nominally 6,378km, our visible horizon is severely limited as shown in Figure 16.8. For an object O moving a distance s from our vantage point H, it has to have a height h to be just visible from H. For s=800km, h = 50km (nominally). In other words, the eruption column of Thera would have had to be higher than 50km to have been at all visible from Egypt, and probably several kilometres more for clear visibility.

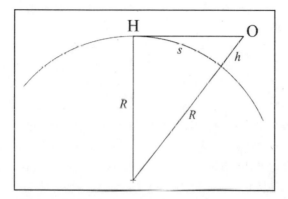

Figure 16.8. Required height h of Thera eruption column to be visible from Egypt

The maximum column height of a volcano is thought to be about 55km[32], which for the Thera eruption would have been visible just above the horizon in Egypt. Thera's theoretical column height of 36km may have been significantly higher. By comparison, the Mount St Helens eruption column was 24km high, with an estimated volume of 3 cubic kilometres. The height of an eruption column is related to the fourth root of the mass eruption rate[33] as shown in the following equation:

Column height = k (mass eruption rate) $^{1/4}$

where k is assumed to be constant for comparison purposes. That means that if the mass eruption rate of one volcano is 16 times greater than that of another, assuming all other factors to be the same, its column height would only be double that of the other. Thera's volume of ejecta was between 30 cubic kilometres and 100 cubic kilometres, which means its column height theoretically would have been between 43km and 58km using Mount St Helens as a reference. The column height of the Tsar Bomb was 64km[34] and since the Thera eruption is estimated to have been at least 12 times as powerful as the Tsar Bomb, the simplified formula would predict a column height of 119km above sea level. The circumstances were, however, vastly different and all one can really conclude is that it seems possible for an ash cloud to extend deep into the mesosphere, and that Thera's most likely did. In other words, on a clear day the Israelites and the Egyptians should have been able to see a 'pillar of cloud' on the horizon and the 'pillar of fire' by night.

It should also be noted that as the ash cloud drifted towards Egypt, it would have become progressively more visible. As a result of the volume of steam produced by the magma exposed directly to the sea after the eruption, it is probable that the glow of the magma, being refracted by the column of water vapour, would also have been visible from Egypt for quite some time after the eruption.

17

The plagues and miracles put into perspective

As discussed in the preceding section, there can be no question whether an eruption of Thera could have affected Egypt. The sonic boom would have been heard, the rumbling of the earth would have been felt, a tsunami would have hit the shores of Egypt and, given the right wind direction and speed, Egypt would have been showered by ash. In this section the plagues of Egypt are analysed in terms of the after-effects of an eruption of Thera.

17.1 Plague 0 – The flood

Although only the Koran mentions a flood by name, the legend of the wall of water that collapsed onto the Egyptian army must certainly be based on the tsunami that swept away most of low-lying Egypt. The reason why a single tsunami wave became two walls of water with a pathway through the sea is discussed in Chapter 18.

Confirmation of not one but at least two great floods that hit various Mediterranean countries is readily to be found in ancient records and legends. The identification of when these floods occurred is extremely important, as both events played a major role in the history of the Israelites.

Plato records that the Egyptians often ridiculed the Greeks for their apparent lack of history:

Thereupon one of the priests, who was of a very great age, said: O Solon, Solon, **you Hellenes are never anything but children**, and there is not an old man among you. Solon in return asked him what he meant. I mean to say, he replied, that in mind you are all young; there is no old opinion handed down among you by ancient tradition, nor any science which is hoary with age.

And I will tell you why. **There have been, and will be again, many destructions of mankind arising out of many causes; the greatest have been brought about by the agencies of fire and water**, and other lesser ones by innumerable other causes.[1]

The Egyptians evidently shared their knowledge with the Greeks in 600 BCE because the Greeks had lost their records during recurrent catastrophes and they (the Greeks) needed these records so that they could 'recover their memories'[2]. In other words, the Greeks essentially had to rebuild their records of their ancient past after each catastrophe.

Josephus also attests to this loss of knowledge by the Greeks:

But as for the place where the Grecians inhabit, ten thousand destructions have overtaken it, and blotted out the memory of former actions, so that they were ever beginning a new way of living, and supposed that every one of them was the origin of their new state.[3]

There can be no question then that the Greeks were known to have suffered numerous natural disasters throughout their existence, and specifically floods. The cause of these floods would no doubt have been eruptions of the Thera volcano.

The Floods of Ogygus and Deucalion

The flood of Ogyges and the flood of Deucalion are two floods that in particular stand out in Greek tradition. Both these floods are contemporaneous with the Exodus of the Hebrews from Egypt. In *The City of God* of St Augustine (died 430 CE) we find Varro's account of a flood:

And yet there is no consensus among historians about the date of **Ogygus himself, in whose time there also occurred a great deluge**. It was not the greatest of all floods, unknown to pagan history whether Greek or Roman, from which no human beings escaped, except those who were privileged to be in the ark. **But it was a greater deluge than the flood which occurred afterwards, in the time of Deucalion.** For Varro begins his book, which I mentioned earlier, with the reign of Ogygus, and he gives himself no earlier point from which to arrive at the history of Rome than the flood of Ogygus, I mean the flood that happened during his reign. But our Christian writers of chronicles, first Eusebius, and afterwards Jerome, record that the flood of Ogygus occurred more than 300 years later, when Phoroneus, the second king of Argos, was already on the throne; and we may be sure that they based their belief on some previous historians.

...

Then Neptune was furious, and **devastated the Athenian territory by floods of sea-water – for it is quite easy for demons to spread waters about on any scale at their pleasure**. ... The city ... being in greater fear of Neptune's waters than Minerva's arms.

...

In these times, writes Varro, when Cranaus, successor to Cecrops, was on the Athenian throne (or, according to our Christian authorities, Eusebius and Jerome, **while Cecrops was still king) there occurred a deluge which is known as 'Deucalion's flood'**, because Deucalion ruled in those parts of the world which suffered most. This deluge, however, certainly did not reach Egypt and its adjacent lands.

Moses led God's people out of Egypt at the very end of the reign of Cecrops, king of Athens, when Ascatades was on the Assyrian throne, Marathus was king of Sicyon, and Triopas king of Argos.[4]

It is curious that St Augustine makes no mention of the names of the Egyptian kings at the time of the flood and therefore of the Exodus. According to Manetho (as quoted by Syncellus):

The sixth, Misphragmuthosis, for 26 years; in his reign the flood of Deucalion's time occurred. Total, according to Africanus, down to the reign of **Amôsis, also called Misphragmuthosis**, ...[5]

The identity of the pharaoh called Misphragmuthosis is not obvious. In Syncellus' version of Manetho's king list, the kings of the Eighteenth Dynasty listed in order were 1) Amos, 2) Chebros, 3) Amenophthis, 4) Queen Amensis, 5) Misaphris, 6) **Misphragmuthosis** and 7) **Tuthmosis**.

In his version of Manetho's king list, Josephus records that a king by the name of Alisphragmuthosis overpowered the Hyksos kings of Lower Egypt and forced them to retreat to their city Avaris, and that his son, Thummosis, eventually succeeded in driving them from Egypt altogether[6]. He then lists the kings from **Alisphragmuthosis** onwards as 1) his son **Tethmosis (Thummosis, Thethoosis)**, 2) Chebron, 3) Amenophis, 4) Queen Amesses, 5) Mephres, 6) **Mephramuthosis** and 7) his son **Tethmosis** and after him another Amenophis[7].

The queen referred to as Amensis or Amesses must have been Hatshepsut, and we need to determine whether Misphragmuthosis lived before or after her time. From conventional Egyptology we know that the king who drove the Hyksos back to Avaris was Kamose and that his brother (not his son) Ahmose eventually drove them from Egypt. It therefore appears that Syncellus, when he associated the flood of Deucalion with the sixth king Misphragmuthosis (Tuthmosis III), mistook the latter for either Alisphragmuthosis or his son Thummosis. This is confirmed by his statement that Misphragmuthosis was also known as Amosis (Amose). In Josephus' list Alisphragmuthosis and Mephramuthosis are two different people. Mephramuthosis had a son called Thummosis and it seems that Syncellus associated the flood with this father/son combination, instead of the Alisphramuthosis/ Thummosis combination as recorded by Josephus. Syncellus' flood should therefore be associated with the era of King Kamose and his brother Ahmose.

Digressing momentarily, the probable reason why a flood may have been placed during the reign of Misphragmuthosis (Tuthmosis III) and not during the reign of Amenhotep III, as discussed below, is once again the confusion that existed regarding the identity the legendary King Sesostris. The name Misphragmuthosis can be translated as 'The fence that saves us from being slain by the hated' (see Chapter 11), which links Misphragmuthosis to Sesostris. As discussed in Section 6.2, exploits of Sesostris (Tuthmosis III) were often confused with those of Amenhotep III. One can understand how in legend all the great events which occurred in Egypt, good or bad, became associated with its greatest king, Sesostris.

That a flood occurred during the reign of King Ahmose is unequivocally confirmed by his lamentation in the so-called *Tempest Stele of Ahmose*:

... the gods expressed their discontent ... The gods (made?) the sky come with a tempest of (rain?); **it caused darkness in the Western region**; the sky was unleashed, without ... ... **more than the roar of the crowd**; ... was powerful... on the mountains more than the turbulence of the cataract which is at Elephantine. Each house, ... each shelter (or each covered place) that they reached... **were floating in the water like the barks of papyrus** (on the outside?) of the royal residence for ... day(s), **with no one able to light the torch anywhere**. ... His Majesty set about to strengthen the two lands, **to cause the water to evacuate** without (the aid of) his (men?), to provide them with silver, with gold, with copper, with oil, with clothing, with all the products they desired; after which His Majesty rested in the palace – life, health, strength. It was then that His Majesty was informed that the funerary concessions **had been invaded (by the water), that the sepulchral chambers had been damaged, that the structures of funerary enclosures had been undermined, that the pyramids had collapsed? all that existed had been annihilated**. His

Majesty then ordered the repair of the chapels which had fallen in ruins in all the country, restoration of the monuments of the gods, ...[8]

The 'darkness in the Western region' must certainly refer to the ash cloud of Thera and the associated flood could only have been caused by the tsunami launched by the eruption. The ash cloud which reached Egypt must have been so dense that fires could not be lit ('no one able to light the torch anywhere'), as confirmed by Jewish Legends (see Section 15.9, 'The light of the fire ... was either extinguished by the violence of the storm, or else it was made invisible and swallowed up in the density of the darkness').

Returning to the flood of Ogygus, in one of the few remaining fragments of his work, Africanus records the following:

From Ogygus, who was believed by them to be indigenous, **and in whose time the great first flood in Attica occurred**, when Phoroneus was king of Argos, according to the historical record of Acusilaus, up to the first Olympiad, from which time the Greeks believed they were accurate in their chronology, there are altogether 1,020 years. ... We assert, therefore, on the authority of this work, **that Ogygus**, who, having been saved when many perished, has given his name to the first flood, **lived at the time of the Exodus of the people with Moses from Egypt**. This is the method of my calculation: 1,020 years will be demonstrated from Ogygus up to the aforementioned first Olympiad. From the first Olympiad up to the first year of the 55th Olympiad (that is, to the first year of the reign of Cyrus, which was the year marking the end of the captivity), there are 215 years.[9]

Syncellus, a later historian and one of the main witnesses to Africanus' work, writes:

In the time of Joshua, the son of Nun, a man of the tribe Japhet, named Ogygus, an original inhabitant of the country, reigned over the land of Attica for 32 years. **In his reign a great flood occurred** and Ogygus and all that land were destroyed, as was every soul living in that land of Attica, but only there. **From that time the land remained barren and uninhabited for 206 years**, as is related in the writings of Africanus.[10]

Regarding Ogygus, Eusebius, who died in 339 CE, relates that:

Ogygus is said to have been the first [king] of the Athenians. The Greeks relate that their great ancient flood took place during his reign. Phoroneus the son of Inachus, king of the Argives, is considered to have lived at this time. Plato mentions this in the *Timaeus*, as follows: 'When he wished to acquaint them with ancient history, so they could discuss the antiquity of this city, he began his account with the old stories about Phoroneus and Niobe, and then what happened after the flood.' Ogygus lived in the time of Messapus, the ninth king of Sicyon, and Belochus, the eighth king of the Assyrians.

After Ogygus and until the time of Cecrops, it is said that there was no king in Attica for 190 years, because of the great destruction caused by the flood. The number of years is calculated from the kings of the Argives, who reigned before Ogygus. From the end of the reign of Phoroneus, king of the Argives, in whose time Ogygus' flood is said to have occurred, until Phorbas, in whose time Cecrops became king of Attica, **190 years elapsed**. From Cecrops until the first Olympiad, seventeen kings, and twelve archons for life are listed; **in this period too, the amazing fables of the Greeks are said to have unfolded**.[11]

However, unlike Africanus, Eusebius places Moses not in the time of Ogygus but in the time of Cecrops, during whose reign the flood of Deucalion occurred:

The Kings of the Athenians. **Cecrops** Diphyes, 50 years. **In his reign** Prometheus, Epimetheus and Atlas lived. He began ruling the Athenians in the time of Triopas, the seventh king of the Argives, and Marathonius, the thirteenth king of Sicyon. **At this time, Moses had become recognized amongst the Hebrews**, as we will show in due course. **Also at this time, the flood of Deucalion is said to have occurred in Thessaly**, and fire devastated the land of Ethiopia in the time of Phaethon.[12]

Syncellus, while discussing Africanus[13], states that the first flood at the time of Ogygus in Attica was followed by another flood **248 years later**, during the time of Deucalion in Thessaly. It is notable that Eusebius records a similar period between the two great floods:

> Thus it is fitting that the history of Hebrew antiquities follows our exposition of Chaldean history. The story they relate about the flood is quite different from the Greek legendary tale which places the flood during the time of Deucalion, [an event which occurred] long before Ogyges and the great flood which the Greeks say occurred in his time. The flood [recounted in Genesis] took place some 1,200 years before **Ogyges' flood, which in turn preceded Deucalion's flood by 250 years.**[14]

It is clear that even the early historians did not know exactly how to interpret the two floods. Syncellus, referring to the work of Africanus, offers valuable information about the dates of the floods of Ogygus and Deucalion relative to the chronology of the rulers of Egypt:

> Let us, then following Eusebius' calculation, ascribe 25 years to Amos' reign and 26 years to Misphragmuthosis'. Following both Africanus and Eusebius, there will thus be 120 years from the beginning of Amos' rule to the end of Misphragmuthosis'; this we are assured was the length of Moses' life. Now how can it be that

from the beginning of Moses' rule – that is, from the Exodus out of Egypt, **if we grant Africanus' opinion that he left during the reign of Amos**, or from his youth (this is also a dilemma for Africanus) – up to the death of this same Moses, **there occurred two famous floods among the Greeks?**

I mean, of course, the first flood at the time of Ogygus in Attica and the one during the time of Deucalion in Thessaly, 248 years later – this later flood unquestionably occurring during the reign of the indigenous Cranaus, the second king of Athens. Let us grant that Moses was born at the time of Amos, which is roughly contemporary with the time of Inachus, and died at the time of Misphragmuthosis; then the lapsed period turns out to be more than double [his age at death].

This Africanus himself has attested in his third book: From the time of Ogygus, because of the great destruction wrought by the flood, what is now Attica remained without a king for 189 years. Then Cecrops the Double-Natured, 50 years. After Cecrops, indigenous Cranaus, 9 years.

Altogether from the flood at the time of Ogygus up to Cecrops the first king of Athens and Cranaus the second king after him, there are 248 years. This same interval is also from the Exodus of Moses and Israel from Egypt up to the flood of Thessaly at the time of Deucalion.

It is recorded by this same Africanus that **the flood at the time of Ogygus occurred during the reign of Phoroneus and the Exodus of the people from Egypt**. And Deucalion's flood, he says, occurred during the reign of Cranaus, the second king of Athens, as he has been shown from his own writings. **Therefore, he is not correct in saying that Deucalion's flood occurred during the reign of Misphragmuthosis.**

For after Amosis, who according to both Africanus and Eusebius was the first king of the 18th dynasty, Misphragmuthosis ended his rule scarcely 85 years later. **The logical remaining conclusion, then, that we reach from this is**

that it was rather Ogygus' flood that occurred during the reign of Misphragmuthosis; and in our opinion and that of other more accurate historians, it was during his reign that Moses left Egypt with his people. ...

... **we have demonstrated that Moses was leader of his people during the reign of Misphragmuthosis, also known as Amosis, and that it was during his reign that Ogygus' flood occurred.**[15]

Assuming therefore that a period of between 200 to 250 years elapsed between the floods of Ogyges and Deucalion, and taking into Manetho's chronology into account, we arrive at the following sequence of events:

- The first flood, the one of Ogygus, occurred during the reign of Ahmose, whose reign is generally assumed to have been 1550-1525 BCE (see Table 11.1).
- The flood of Deucalion occurred 200 to 250 years later, in the timeframe 1350-1275 BCE, i.e. from the reign of Akhenaten to that of Ramesses II (see Table 11.1).
- Allowing for some inaccuracy in the ancient records, the two floods therefore match the timeframes of Ahmose and Amenhotep III, during whose reign Thera had erupted.
- It is probably more than just coincidence that it has been estimated that volcanic eruptions as large as that of Thera occur on average once every 200 to 300 years[16]. This matches the time interval between the floods of Ogygus and Deucalion. The possibility of a third eruption, which occurred about 250 years before the eruption that caused the flood of Ogygus, is discussed below.

From the Ogygus and Deucalion flood accounts it is clear that the ancient historians associated the Exodus with both floods, even though they occurred between 200 and 250 years apart. The correct interpretation of these accounts is that two Exodus events occurred, both involving the Hyksos. A detailed discussion of the two Exodus events is presented in Chapter 18.

It should be noted that some records date the flood of Ogyges back to *ca.* 1796 BCE. Africanus records it as occurring 1020 years before the first Olympiad in 776 BCE[17], namely 1796 BCE. The *Parian Chronicle*[18], as interpreted by Robertson, gives 1529 BCE for Deucalion's flood, and therefore 1779 - 1729 BCE for the flood of Ogygus. A flood in 1796 BCE would more or less correspond to the beginning of the Second Intermediate Period, when the Hyksos invaded and occupied Lower Egypt (see discussion in Section 5.1). If this earlier flood, pre-dating those of Ogyges and Deucalion, actually happened, it would explain the ease with which the Hyksos managed to invade Lower Egypt. The Egyptian forces would have been washed away by the tsunami, which was what happened to the chariot forces of Amenhotep III when Thera erupted a third time approximately 500 years later. It would seem that both Africanus and the author of the *Parian Chronicle* were aware of a flood that had occurred *ca.* 1796 BCE, but mistakenly assumed it to have been the flood of Ogygus. If so, the course of the history of the Israelites would have been determined not by two, but by three major eruptions of Thera's volcano.

That an eruption of Thera occurred *ca.* 1800 BCE is confirmed by the testimony of a sage called Neferti.

The Prophecy of Neferti

According to Manetho, a 'blast of God' struck Egypt during the reign of a king called Tutimaeus (Timaus in Josephus' version) and the Hyksos subsequently overpowered Egypt without striking a blow[19]. This 'blast' may have been a merely figure of speech, but may equally well have referred to an actual blast, namely a volcanic eruption. Further evidence for a volcanic eruption long pre-dating those associated with the floods of Ogygus and Deucalion is presented in an ancient Egyptian document generally known as *The*

Prophecy of Neferti (see Appendix G). The text describes a natural catastrophe that could only have been caused by the eruption of a volcano. In this document a king called Snefru (Sneferu, Snofru) requests a sage called Neferti (also translated Nefer-rohu), to tell him about Egypt's future. Neferti then envisions Egypt in a state of physical and social chaos, overrun by Asiatics. In particular, he refers to the land as 'completely perished', the sun 'covered over' to the extent that people cannot see, and the sun looking like the moon. This could be the result of either a thick ash cloud from a volcanic eruption descending upon Egypt, or a severe sand storm. Egyptians would, however, have been accustomed to sand storms, so one would not expect the sage to make any specific mention of a sand storm, no matter how severe. The prophecy predicts that Asiatics would invade Egypt and settle in the Nile Delta ('A foreign bird will be born in the marshes of the Northland. It has made a nest beside men, and people have let it approach through want of it.'). Neferti concluded that a king called Ameny (Ameni) would rise and expel the Asiatics from Egypt, and would build the 'Wall of the Ruler' to protect Egypt from invasions by the Asiatics.

As discussed in Section 6.1, the prophecy is generally assumed to refer to Amenemhat I, but there are two significant problems with this association:

- Snefru was a king who belonged to the Fourth Dynasty and ruled *ca*. 2613-2589 BCE[20], and was in fact the predecessor of Khufu, who is generally believed to have built the Great Pyramid[21]. Amenemhat I (1985-1955 BCE) was the first king of the Twelfth Dynasty (2055-1985 BCE), which belonged to the era generally referred to as the Middle Kingdom. Keeping in mind that all prophecies were most likely written either *post facto* or during the time of its protagonists, the two rulers are strictly speaking too far apart in time for the document to have referred to both (modern translators suggest that the scene 'was set in the court of Snefru', whatever that may mean). This discrepancy possibly suggests a different timeframe for the document.

- The only period during which Asiatics settled in the Nile Delta and took charge of Egypt was during the Second Intermediate Period, when Egypt was ruled by the Hyksos. There is no evidence that Asiatic infiltration was a problem during the First Intermediate Period[22], which preceded the Middle Kingdom, and Egypt was under domestic rule during the latter. The document therefore appears to have been written sometime during the Second Intermediate Period. The mention of Asiatics who let their beasts drink effectively identifies these Asiatics as Maneto's shepherds or Hyksos.

As discussed by Velikovsky[23], some researchers have recognised that the document could very well be describing the invasion of Egypt by the Hyksos, while others have argued that the style of document dates it back to the Middle Kingdom at the latest, if not earlier. Velikovsky, however, points out that these two arguments can be reconciled if the document was written shortly after the Hyksos invasion, before the style of the Middle Kingdom would have been lost. He makes a strong argument for the future King Ameny being Amenhotep I, the successor of Ahmose, as the prophecy of a potter serving under Amenhotep I predicted that the waterless Nile would be filled again, echoing the empty rivers of Egypt mentioned by Neferti.

A potential problem with this identification of Ameny is that Ahmose had succeeded in expelling the Hyksos from Egypt, so unless Neferti's prophecy was written early during the reign of Ahmose, would Neferti have dared to suggest that the king might not succeed, but that his son would? This is highly doubtful, as suggested by the timeframes of the lives of these two individuals[24]. Ahmose was approximately 10 years old when he acceded to the throne, and he died at the age of about 35. His conquest of Avaris occurred no later than regnal year 15, when he was 25. He died when his son Amenhotep was still young enough for his mother having to act as regent for an undetermined period. Depending on when a king was considered old enough to rule by himself, Amenhotep may even have been born after Ahmose's successful expulsion of the Hyksos. Irrespective of when he was born, there is no reason why Neferti's prophecy should have survived up to and beyond the death of Ahmose. The Hyksos were no longer around for Amenhotep to expel. Neferti's prophecy also makes no sense in the context of Ahmose and Amenhotep I being Snefru and Ameny, respectively, as there is no link of any kind between the names Ahmose and Snefru. Any link between these two kings further than one generation apart must be considered unlikely, keeping in mind that nobody can see into the future.

With the identity of Ameny as either Amenemhat I or Amenhotep I being questionable, is it possible to identify another person that could have been known by that name? We do indeed find a future king named Ameny during the Second Intermediate Period, the reign of the Hyksos. The Seventeenth Dynasty pharaoh Rahotep had a son called Ameny, as was the son of Inyotef VII, the fifth king of that dynasty[25]. Both ruled Upper Egypt when the Hyksos controlled Lower Egypt. It makes sense that a sage would attempt to lift the spirits of a despondent old king by prophesying that his son would drive the enemy from Egypt. For some reason, however, this son in the end did not become king of Egypt. As scholars like Kuhrt[26] are prepared to date the *Prophecy of Neferti* to a period much later than that of Snefru (to the reign of Amenemhat I), either of these two Amenys would be a much better match to the circumstances described in the document than to those of Amenemhat I. The Neferti text implies that the Hyksos invasion was a fairly recent event, which was indeed the case during the reign of Rahotep and also of Inyotef. Nothing is known about the family roots of Rahotep, and it is certainly possible that his father may either have had the name Snefru or was somehow associated with this name.

Incidentally, King Snefru of the Fourth Dynasty had a son called

Rahotep[27] and it is therefore possible that whoever wrote or copied this document attempted to sketch the background of the story and mistakenly identified the king in question as Snefru instead of Rahotep.

The remark that the 'Wall(s) of the Ruler' were to be built does not exclude the possibility of this document having been written in the Seventeenth Dynasty. As mentioned in Section 6.1, the Hyksos may very well have demolished these walls when they entered Egypt, and Ameny may merely have been identified as the one who would rebuild them.

The curious statement that the river of Egypt (the Nile) had dried up may suggest that an enormous quantity of sea sand and silt had been pushed up the Nile Delta by a tsunami resulting from an eruption of Thera, effectively blocking or diverting the flow of the river for some time. The darkness that descended upon Egypt must have been caused by the ash cloud of Thera's eruption, but this would have happened before the Hyksos invasion, as is portrayed in the *Prophecy of Neferti*.

The sage tells of 'the Asiatics who are throughout the land'. This must certainly refer to the invasion of Lower Egypt by the Hyksos. Manetho, as quoted by Josephus, states that:

> There was a king of ours whose name was Timaus. Under him it came to pass, I know not how, that God was averse to us, and there came, after a surprising manner, **men of ignoble birth out of the eastern parts**, and had the boldness to make an expedition into our country, **and with ease subdued it by force, yet without hazarding a battle with them**.[28]

If Thera had indeed erupted, the ensuing tsunami would have washed away all defence structures and also all troops stationed in the low lying areas. The Hyksos would then have been able to 'invade' the now desolate Lower Egypt encountering very little resistance, if any.

The Flood of Pheros

According to Herodotus, Sesostris was succeeded by his son Pheros, who 'waged no wars' and in whose time the Nile came down in a flood that was 27 feet (8m) high[29]. Whether it would have been possible for the Nile to come down in this manner is questionable. With Pheros earlier having been identified as Amenhotep III, Herodotus' remark can only refer to the tsunami that washed over the Nile Delta after the eruption of Thera. This event is confirmed by Artapanus' statement that Moses 'smote the Nile with the rod, and the river became flooded and deluged the whole of Egypt'[30]. The ancients would not have known what causes a tsunami and would have associated the 8m high flood that struck Egypt with just a particularly high annual flooding of the Nile.

Danaus and Greece's sterility

The Greeks believed that Danaus, the king of Egypt, founded the city of Argos. In Section 10.5 it was shown that Danaus and the Egyptian pharaoh Ay were one and the same person. He most likely fled to Argos when Amenhotep III and the Egyptian army (Amenhotep may already have died by that time) returned to Egypt from Ethiopia. St Augustine refers to the arrival of Danaus in Greece as an invasion:

> During this period, that is **from the departure of Israel** down to the death of Joshua...
>
> ...
>
> ... music festivals were instituted in honour of Delphic Apollo, to appease his anger, because they imagined that **the regions of Greece had been punished with sterility** by him in his wrath because they had not defended his temple when it was set on fire by King Danaus during **his invasion** of those parts.[31]

The sterility of the soil can only refer to the after-effects of Thera. The fallout would have covered and poisoned the soil for decades. The Ogygian flood was recorded by Africanus to have laid waste the territory (Attica) for close to 200 years, which links the eruption of Thera directly to the sterile soil. When Danaus (Ay) arrived on Greece's shores probably about two decades after Thera's eruption, he most likely found the coastal cities of Greece both demolished and abandoned and started rebuilding Argos, thereby becoming its 'founder'.

The Two Floods of the Heliadae

Documentary evidence by Diodorus suggests that two cataclysmic floods had hit island of Rhodes:

> The island which is called Rhodes was first inhabited by the people who were known as Telchines; these were children of Thalatta [the Sea] ... they were also the discoverers of certain arts and that they introduced other things which are useful for the life of mankind. They were also the first, men say, to fashion statues of gods, and some of the ancient images of gods have been named after them ...
>
> At a later time, the myth continues, the Telchines, **perceiving in advance the Flood that was going to come**, forsook the island and were scattered. Of their number Lycus went to Lycia and dedicated there beside the Xanthus river a temple of Apollo Lycius. And when the flood came the rest of the inhabitants perished – and since the waters, because of the abundant rains, overflowed the island, its level parts were turned into stagnant pools – but a few fled for refuge to the upper regions of the island and were saved, the sons of Zeus being among their number. Helius, the myth tells us, becoming enamoured of Rhodos, named the island after her and caused the water which had overflowed it to disappear ... And there came into being the Heliadae who were named after him [regarded by J.L. Myers to have been the early Minoan inhabitants of Rhodes] ... In consequence of these events the island was considered to be sacred to Helius.

The Heliadae, besides having shown themselves to be superior to all other men, likewise surpassed them in learning and specially in astrology; and they introduced many new practices of seamanship and established the division of the day into hours ...

Of their number Macar came to Lesbos, and Candalus to Cos and Eetis, **sailing off to Egypt, founded there the city men call Heliopolis, naming it after his father; and it was from him that the Egyptians learned the laws of astrology**. But when **at a later time there came to be a flood among the Greeks** and the majority of mankind perished by reason of the abundance of rain, it came to pass that **all written monuments were also destroyed in the same manner as mankind**; and this is the reason why the Egyptians, seizing the favourable occasion, appropriated to themselves the knowledge of astrology, and why, since the Greeks, because of their ignorance, no longer laid any claim to writing, the belief prevailed that the Egyptians were the first men to effect the discovery of the stars. Likewise the Athenians, although they were the founders of the city in Egypt men call Sais, suffered the same ignorance because of the flood.[32,33]

Two distinct floods are mentioned by Diodorus. The first no doubt refers to the Great Flood of the biblical Noah. Like Noah[34], the inhabitants received warning of the impending flood, which would not have been possible at that time for an eruption of Thera. The second refers to a much later flood that destroyed Greece, but not Egypt. This flood most certainly was caused by an eruption of Thera. The Great Flood of biblical times must have occurred thousands of years before the New Kingdom era, and it is therefore possible the first flood was mistakenly assumed to have been the Great Flood instead of the flood of Ogugus.

To conclude, the floods of Ogyges and Deucalion and their dating suggest that Thera had erupted up to three times. The eruptions occurred just before the invasion of the Hyksos in *ca.* 1650 BCE (perhaps 1750 BCE or earlier), then again during the reign of Ahmose in 1550 BCE (the Ogygian flood) and finally during the reign of Amenhotep III around 1360 BCE (the flood of Deucalion). The flood of Ogyges would have weakened the Hyksos defences sufficiently to allow Ahmose to overpower them, something his predecessor and brother Kamose was unable to do. The same happened to the Egyptians when the flood of Deucalion occurred about 200 years later, sweeping away their chariot divisions in the low lying areas of northern Egypt.

The Exodus had been associated with both floods (that of Ogyges and of Deucalion), which would make sense only if the Hyksos were indeed the Hebrews as claimed by Manetho. Under Ahmose a large group of the Hyksos managed to escape to Canaan, but those captured as slaves were to wait for more than 200 years before an eruption of Thera would lead to their freedom.

17.2 Plagues 1 to 9 – After-effects of the eruption of Thera

As mentioned earlier, several researchers have linked the first nine plagues of Egypt to the after-effects of an eruption of Thera.

Plague 1 – The plague of blood
Of crucial importance in the interpretation of this plague is that according to *Exodus*, not only the Nile turned into 'blood', but so did all the ponds and water reservoirs. Only an ash cloud covering Egypt like a blanket would have been able to poison all these water sources as recorded. The red colour of the water can be attributed to high levels of iron oxide being present in the ash. Even minor activity of Thera often results in iron oxide being released into the ocean, colouring the sea red and killing fish miles around[35].

Plague 2 – The plague of frogs
Without fish in the rivers to feed on the tadpoles, frogs would have been able to breed in vast numbers. This was exactly what happened after the Mount St Helens eruption:

...after Mount St Helens the predatory fish were decimated. The tiny would-be frogs, on the other hand, were kept safe inside their spawn. By the time they emerged, the hazardous chemicals had washed away down river, but the fish had not yet returned. The result was a plague of frogs throughout much of Washington State. In their thousands they littered the countryside – there were so many squashed on the roads that they made driving conditions hazardous: they clogged waterways, covered gardens and infested houses.[36]

Plagues 3 and 4 – The plagues of gnats and flies
The rotting of the dead fish, amphibians and land animals and probably even the corpses of people would have caused the proliferation of flies and other insects.

Plague 5 – The plague on livestock
Volcanic ash can asphyxiate animals and destroy vegetation, leading to the death of animals in affected areas, but a more probable cause would have been the poisoned water and food of the animals. Many animals died following the eruptions of Tambora, Krakatoa, Mount Peleé and Mount St Helens[37].

Plague 6 – The plague of boils
Whatever the fallout from Thera contained, it caused a deadly plague among human beings everywhere it rained down. The only time that Egypt faced a plague of the proportions described in *Exodus* appears to have been during the reigns of Amenhotep III and his son Akhenaten. Following Thera's eruption, the water and soil in Egypt must have been poisoned to such an extent that both people and animals could hardly survive. Egypt must have remained in this affected state for many years, possibly several decades. There is a distinct possibility that the 40-years-in-the-desert narrative in the Bible (the Israelites supposedly spent 40 years in the desert after departing from Egypt, as punishment for their disobedience to

God[38]) is no more than a recollection of the entire period of affliction. It would have started when Amenhotep, on the advice of his oracle, began to expel the slaves from Egypt by driving them into the desert[39] shortly after the outbreak of the plague. There they would have had to find a means of survival. If the eruption of Thera had occurred round about 1360 BCE, 40 years later brings us to the year 1320 BCE, right at the beginning of the reign of Horemheb. It was Horemheb, probably more than any other pharaoh, who attempted to erase every trace of the Amarna interlude. By that time the Egyptian army would long have returned from Ethiopia and the Israelites most likely would still have been in the desert before slowly migrating into Canaan.

The plague in Egypt was so deadly that when it spread to the north, it led to the demise of the Hittite nation. In response, Mursilis II, who ruled from approximately 1321-1295 BCE[40], wrote the poignant *Plague Prayers* (see Appendix H). Mursilis humbles himself before the Hittite Storm-god in order to bring an end to the plague. He relates that the plague had been in the Land of Hatti for 20 years, having come to his land when his father attacked the Egyptian-controlled country of Amka. Captured Egyptian soldiers were brought to his land, the Hittites unaware that they were carrying a deadly plague. This may in fact have been a deliberate and masterful ploy by the Egyptians to defeat one of their most hated enemies, the Hittites from the land of Hatti. Like the Egyptians themselves, the Hittites would have had no defence against the plague. Murislis II actually prays to his gods to send the plague into the countries of his enemies for this very purpose! As a matter of interest, it appears to have been a general belief across many nations of that time, that the gods would punish sons for the sins of their fathers ('It is only too true, however, that the father's sin falls upon the son. So, my father's sin has fallen upon me'), echoing Jehovah's promise do the same[41].

That a plague could have been so devastating was demonstrated by the Great Plague of London and the bubonic plague known as the

Black Death. The Great Plague of London, which occurred from 1665 to 1666 CE, killed more than 75,000 of the estimated 460,000 inhabitants of London[42]. The Black Death, which peaked in Europe between 1348 and 1350 CE, killed between 30% and 60% of Europe's population. In terms of numbers between 75 million and 100 million people died of the plague[43]. The disease was most likely spread by fleas on rats and close contact with an infected person. Apion claims that the Israelites escaping from Egypt were suffering from bubonic infections[44]. The epidemic affected Canaan as well, killing 70,000 of King David's people (even more of only the men already totalled 70,000) towards the end of his reign[45].

A further indication of the virulence of the plague is given in the instructions of Moses regarding 'unclean persons'. When a person died in a tent, anyone who entered the tent or anyone who had been in it before would be deemed unclean for seven days, and every open container without a lid fastened on it would be deemed unclean. Anyone out in the open who touched someone who had been killed with a sword or someone who had died a natural death or anyone who had touched a human bone or a grave would be deemed unclean for seven days. The ostracism of those affected is also alluded to:

> ...if a person who is unclean does not purify himself, he must be cut off from the community. ... anything that an unclean person touches becomes unclean, and anyone who touches it becomes unclean till evening.[46]

The symptoms of the plague must have become clearly visible within seven days after infection. According to the scribe who wrote *Numbers*, God sent fire to consume those who had sinned against him[47]. This almost certainly implies that infected people were killed and their bodies burned.

Plague 7 – The plague of hail

The description of hailstones raining down on Egypt given in *Exodus* closely matches the Koranic description of a 'shower of stones' (not necessarily hailstones) accompanied by a 'mighty blast', and the presence of 'fire' raining down from heaven also suggests a volcanic eruption. As discussed earlier, it would not appear possible for volcanic bombs from Thera to have reached Egypt, and in modern translations 'fire' is translated as 'lightning'. Volcanic ash clouds are often accompanied by lightning as discussed in Section 16.3.

According to Jewish tradition the father of the Israeli nation was Abraham, through his sons Isaac and Jacob. Joseph, the son of Jacob, became a high ranking official in Egypt. As is discussed earlier, Joseph can be linked to the Egyptian official Yuya, the father-in-law of Amenhotep III and grandfather of Prince Tuthmosis, the biblical Moses. The era of Abraham can therefore be dated back to only a couple of generations before that of Moses. That an eruption of a volcano occurred in Abraham's time may be attested to by a peculiar remark about the young Abraham in the apocryphal *Apocalypse of Abraham*:

> And it came to pass while I thus spake to my father Terah, in the court of my house, the voice of a Mighty One from Heaven came from a **fiery cloud** saying and calling: 'Abraham, Abraham.' I answered: 'Here am I.' And he said: 'The God of Gods, the Creator, you are seeking in your heart; I am he. Go out from your father Terah, get you out of his house, lest you also be killed in the sins of the house of your father.' And I went forth. And it came to pass as I went out, having hardly reached the door of the court, **there was a voice of great thunder, and he was burned, and his house, and all that was in it,** even to the earth of forty ells.[48]

Another translation reads:

I went forth. I had not reached the gate of the courtyard, when **there was a great peal of thunder and fire fell from heaven and this burnt him (the father) up, his house and everything in it** for a range of forty ells.[49]

Abraham was instrumental in the demise of the evil cities Sodom and Gomorrah. They were destroyed when Jehovah rained down upon them 'brimstone and fire out of heaven'[50]. These references seem to suggest that a volcanic eruption of some kind must have occurred somewhere near these two cities, most likely caused by the earthquake set in motion by the eruption of Thera in the Aegean Sea. The sonic boom (the peal of thunder) in the *Apocalypse of Abraham* could have originated from either Thera's eruption or the eruption of a nearby volcano, even though there are no active volcanoes in Canaan. The Dead Sea in Canaan is located on the Dead Sea fault, so it is possible that the earthquake caused by the eruption of Thera caused movement between the two tectonic plates that meet at the Dead Sea fault line, resulting in volcano-like eruptions of lava.

Regarding the destruction of Sodom and Gomorrah, Josephus raises another possibility:

...It was of old a most happy land, both for the fruits it bore and the riches of its cities, although it be now all burnt up. It is related how for the impiety of its inhabitants, it was burned by lightning; in consequence of which there are still the remainders of that **divine fire**; and the traces [or shadows] of the five cities are still to be seen, **as well as the ashes growing in their fruits**, which fruits have a color as if they were fit to be eaten: but if you pluck them with your hands, they will dissolve into smoke and ashes.[51]

The mention of lightning and ash may suggest that, like the ash cloud of the eruption of Thera during the reign of Amenhotep III, the ash cloud of this earlier eruption drifted towards Canaan and caused death and destruction in those cities. That eruption would have been the one which occurred during the reign of Ahmose as discussed earlier.

Returning to the plague of hailstones, Midrashic and Taludic sources relate that the stones which fell on Egypt were hot[52]. In the Talmud the following is recorded:

> ...Hailstones [abne elgabish]. What are **abne elgabish**? A Tanna taught: **Stones [abanim] which remained suspended** for the sake of a man [al gab ish] and came down for the sake of a man. 'They remained suspended for the sake of a man': this was Moses, of whom it is written, Now the man Moses was very meek, and it is also written, And the soldiers and hail ceased, and the rain poured not upon the earth. 'They came down for the sake of a man': this was Joshua, of whom it is written, Take thee Joshua the son of Nun, a man in whom there is spirit, and it is written, And it came to pass as they fled from before Israel, while they were at the descent of Beth-Horon, **that the Lord cast down great stones.**[53]

The curious description *abne elgabish* is most likely formed by the Hebrew words *'âb*[54] (darkness, a cloud), *nîy*[55] (lamentation, wailing), *'al*[56] (above, over, upon), *gâbahh*[57] (to soar, be lofty) and *'îysh*[58] (man, men), rendering 'The darkness of wailing that soars over men', or in other words, Thera's approaching ash cloud which struck terror in the hearts of the Egyptians and their slaves alike (see the plague of darkness). Therefore we again find a shower of stones associated with the ash cloud of the Thera eruption. Could there be an element of truth in these records?

Plague 8 – The plague of locusts
This is the only natural plague that cannot be directly linked to the eruption of a volcano. As has been pointed out by a Wikipedia contributor, the other plagues that descended upon Egypt must have destroyed most of its crops. The otherwise thinly spread

locusts that could usually be found in Egypt would have descended on whatever edible crops remained, creating the impression that Egypt had been struck by an epidemic of locusts[59].

Plague 9 – The plague of darkness

According to the Bible, total darkness covered Egypt for three days. The darkening of the sky is a familiar phenomenon associated with volcanic eruptions. The photograph in Figure 17.1 shows the frightening ash cloud of Mount St Helens over the airfield of Ephrata, 238km north-east of the volcano. This eruption led to the sun being obscured for hours at a distance of up to 500km from the volcano. The eruption of Krakatoa led to complete darkness 800km away for several days[60]. The plague of darkness probably more than any of the others links the events in Egypt directly to a volcanic eruption. The darkness associated with sandstorms typically lasts no longer than a couple of hours, whereas only the ash clouds of volcanoes can cause darkness for days on end. It should be noted that both Jewish Legends (see Section 15.9) and Egyptian records (*The Prophecy of*

Figure 17.1. The Mount St Helens ash cloud over the airfield of Ephrata, 238 km NE of the volcano[61]

Neferti, 'and no one knows the result which will come about, which is hidden from speech, sight, or hearing. The face is deaf, for silence confronts') relate that the darkness was so dense that one could neither speak to nor hear another, and that fires could not be lit (see Section 17.1).

17.3 Plague 10 – The death of the firstborn

Of the 10 plagues of Egypt, the death of the firstborn is the only plague that has no natural explanation. In other words, the death of the firstborn must have been due to human activity in one way or another. As stated earlier, several researchers have concluded that the tenth plague must have been human sacrifice of the firstborn in order to appease the perceived wrath of the gods. Other explanations, such as that grain (food) in Egypt had become contaminated and that the firstborn were always the first to be fed and therefore died (first)[62], simply do not hold water.

The sacrifice of children in the Bible

Although no evidence appears to exist that human sacrifice was practised in Egypt, sacrificing a firstborn child must have been commonplace in ancient Canaan and other Asiatic countries. For example, a Canaanite text found at Ugarit reads:

A firstborn, Baal, we shall sacrifice, a child we shall fulfil, …[63]

Also, beginning with Abraham's attempted sacrifice of Isaac[64], numerous texts in the Bible imply that the Israelites themselves turned to human sacrifice as a last resort:

Do not give any of your children to be sacrificed to Molech, for you must not profane the name of your God.[65]

The people of Judah have done evil in my eyes, declares the Lord. They have built the high places of Topheth, which is in the valley of Ben Hinnom **to burn their sons, and their daughters in** the fire – something I did not command, nor did it enter my mind.[66]

They have built the high places of Baal **to burn their sons in the fire as offerings to Baal** – something I did not command or mention, nor did it enter my mind.[67]

They built high places for Baal in the Valley of Ben Hinnon **to sacrifice their sons and daughters to Molech,** though I never commanded, nor did it enter my mind, that they should do such a detestable thing and so make Judah sin.[68]

When the king of Moab saw that the battle had gone against him, ... he **took his firstborn son ... and offered him as a sacrifice on the city wall.**[69]

He (Josiah) desecrated Topheth ..., so no one could use **it to sacrifice his son or daughter in the fire** of Molech.[70]

Topheth has long been prepared; it has been made ready for the king (of Assyria). **Its fire pit has been made deep and wide, with an abundance of fire and wood; the breath of the Lord, like a stream of burning sulfur, sets it ablaze** (NIV comment: Topheth was a place outside Jerusalem).[71]

Will the Lord be pleased with thousands of rams, with ten thousand rivers of oil? **Shall I offer my firstborn for my transgression, the fruit of my body for the sin of my soul?**[72]

An obscure law given to the Israelites by Moses consecrates the firstborn son to Jehovah, presumably for service and not to be sacrificed, and signifies the importance of this firstborn child:

Do not hold back offerings from your granaries or vats. **You must give me the firstborn of your sons.** Do the same with your cattle and your sheep. Let them stay with their mothers for seven days, but give them to me on the eighth day.[73]

To summarise, the practice of sacrificing one's children to the gods was widely known and practised in biblical times, and the method of sacrifice almost invariably appears to have been fire. The highest sacrifice any human being could make to the gods was to surrender that which he or she held dearest, and in ancient times that was the firstborn son. Solomon is infamously credited for having brought the pagan god Molech (Moloch) and by association his fire sacrifice into Canaan[74]. However, it may have been practised in Canaan long before his time. Solomon was a contemporary of the Amarna kings (see Chapter 12) and Egyptians would have been fully aware of the habits, practices and beliefs of their northern neighbours.

The tenth plague and the sacrifice of the firstborn in Egypt
Although *Exodus* states that only the firstborn sons died during that fateful night, Jewish legends suggests that the extent of the slaughter was far greater (see full quotation in Section 15.10), and that it was met with resistance from the Egyptians. The biblical account creates the impression that it was only the Pharaoh who was involved in the decision making and that the Egyptian people were essentially oblivious of the disaster that was about to strike them. In fact, although God instructed Moses to threaten the Pharaoh with the death of his firstborn[75], Moses evidently did not do so. The Pharaoh was not warned about the threat of the Lord to kill the firstborn of Egypt, as Moses after the ninth plague promised the Pharaoh never to appear before him again[76,77]. If the Bible is to be believed, the Egyptians woke up one terrible morning to find that all their firstborn had mysteriously died during the night. This contradicts Jewish legend, which makes it clear that the Egyptians knew only too well what was awaiting them. The firstborn who were destined to die pleaded first with their fathers and then with the Pharaoh to let the Israelites go so that they could be saved, and many of Egyptian families attempted to hide their firstborn. In the end, those Egyptians who refused to comply were violently forced to do so, most likely by the priesthood of Amun and the Egyptian army. The fact that all the firstborn of people and animals and of every household died in one night precludes any explanation for the death

of the firstborn other than that it was a sacrifice of the firstborn enforced upon the people of Egypt.

There can thus be no doubt that the order for the execution of the sacrifice was made by Amenhotep III on the advice of his trusted oracle also called Amenhotep. The very first person in line to be sacrificed would have been his own firstborn son, Prince Tuthmosis, but of particular importance is that the Israelites were not exempted from this sacrifice. Specific instruction was given that the firstborn child of even the slave girl should die[78], which would have included the Israelites, the largest group of slaves in Egypt at that time. They would of course have attempted to avoid doing so and may have tried to deceive the Egyptians by burning animals instead, giving rise to the Hebrew tradition of the Passover. It is very likely that the Israelites were forced by the Egyptians to sacrifice their firstborn, a tragedy that came to be commemorated by the Passover.

Human sacrifice in legends pertaining to the Exodus
Even though human sacrifice as a rule may not have been practised in ancient Egypt, this ultimate form of sacrifice must have been the last resort open to Amenhotep III in his struggle to appease the gods of Egypt and bring to an end the plague in Egypt. Having erected hundreds of statues to Sekhmet, Egypt's goddess of destruction, to no avail, his oracle must have advised him to follow the most dreadful sacrifice possible, the burning of all the firstborn offspring in Egypt. Records in this regard must once have existed, but Horemheb's initial expunging of all evidence relating to the Amarna era and the later destruction of the library of Alexandria have left us with nothing but a few vague references in legend. Most of these have already been discussed earlier under different topics, but are summarised next to present a picture as complete as possible:

- **Amenophis and Phritiphantes** – as discussed in Section 7.4, the most likely interpretation of this nickname of Amenhotep's oracle is 'Burn Phantes', Phantes being the name of the son of Aegyptus (Amenhotep III).

- **Busiris and Phrasius** – Busiris, the Egyptian tyrant-king who can be identified as Amenhotep III, was advised by his seer Phrasius to sacrifice a stranger every year in order to bring an end to a drought in Egypt (see Sections 3.12, 7.1). One of these strangers was Hercules, who escaped his bonds and killed Busiris. The sacrifice of the firstborn of visitors to Egypt is attested to in Jewish legend as quoted above. According to Apollodorus[79], Hercules killed not only Busiris (Amenhotep III who fled to Ethiopia) but also his son Amphidamas (Prince Tuthmosis who was first in line to be sacrificed in the fire). There can be no doubt that Prince Tuthmosis was saved in the nick of time, which may not have been widely known, especially abroad.

- **Bocchoris and Hercules** – another name for Amenophis according to Lysimachas (see Sections 3.3, 7.1, 7.4). As in the legend of Hercules and Busiris, Bocchoris was killed (burned alive).

- **Agamemnon and Achilles** – As argued in Section 13.6, the legend of the fall of Troy was based on the Amarna events and Agamemnon can be identified as Amenhotep III. Achilles, the 15-year-old commander of Agamemnon's forces, must have been his son, whom he rescued from a fiery death at the hands of Thetis. Achilles would therefore have been Crown Prince Tuthmosis, who was rescued in the nick of time from being sacrificed by burning.

  Agamemnon had to sacrifice his beautiful daughter Iphigenia to the gods before the weather changed and he could set off for Troy[80]. As derived in Section 13.6, her name appears to mean '(Brought) upon the people (of Egypt)', hinting on something (a curse, an edict) that was enforced upon the nation (see Aganippe below).

- **Aegyptus who sacrificed his daughter Aganippe** – Some legends about Aegyptus (identified as Amenhotep III in

Section 7.1) relate that following the instructions of the oracle at Delphi, he sacrificed his daughter Aganippe to save Egypt from a drought[81]. Her name was most likely derived from the Greek words *agō*[82] (to lead, bring) and any of the words *nēphōs*[83] (a cloud), *nēpiōs*[84] (not speaking, meaning an infant, child) or *nēphō*[85] (abstain, be sober). The latter two words are both derived from an obsolete particle *nē-*, implying negation, followed by *ēpōs*[86] (to say) and *piō / poō*[87] (to imbibe, drink), respectively. In this context the latter part of the name 'aganippe' may mean 'the bad saying', suggesting that her name should be translated as 'The bad (terrible) edict leader' or '(He who) brought the terrible edict'. In other words, Amenhotep III who issued the decree that all Egyptian firstborn should be sacrificed in the fire.

- **Chenephres and Chanethothes** – In Eusebius' quotation of the works of Artapanus, the Pharaoh of the Exodus is called Chenephres, meaning 'The grace of the ashes of the fire' (see Section 7.1), referring to the reprieve that the burning of the firstborn was supposed to have brought. The priest was called Chanethothes, meaning '(He who had to) pitch a tent after the miracle of the fire' (see Section 7.4), suggesting that the second mightiest man in Egypt (after the pharaoh himself) was banished to the wilderness when the sacrifice of the firstborn failed to cure Egypt of the plague.

- **Sesostris' treacherous banquet** – As related in Section 13.5, Sesostris (Amenhotep III) was nearly killed when his (half)-brother (Ay) supposedly set fire to the building in which they were attending a banquet. Sesostris had to lay two of his sons on the burning wood in order for him and the rest of his family to escape. This episode must certainly be just another version of the by now familiar theme of the sacrifice of the firstborn in Egypt. As referred to earlier, Ginzberg implies in his *Legends of the Jews* that the firstborn sons and daughters of every man and woman would have had to be sacrificed. In other words, the firstborn son Amenhotep had by each of his numerous wives and concubines would have had to die in the fire (see Danaus below). Some sons were therefore sacrificed, but others (those who were not the eldest in the family) were spared, as suggested by the banquet narrative.

- **Danaus and the sacrifice of his 50 sons** – Josephus, in recounting Manetho's version of the Exodus, made Danaus the brother of Aegyptus. This pair can be identified as Ay and Amenhotep III, respectively. Amenhotep had numerous wives and concubines and therefore would have had numerous firstborn sons. Legend has it that Aegyptus wanted his 50 sons to marry the 50 daughters of Danaus, but Danaus objected and fled with his daughters to Argos. They were followed to Argos by the sons of Aegyptus, upon which Danaus had no choice but to agree to the marriages. However, he instructed his daughters to kill their husbands on their wedding night, which all but one did[88].

  In the context of Aegyptus being Amenhotep III and Ay being Danaus who was expelled from Egypt by his brother, the 49 murdered sons can only refer to the sacrifice of all the firstborn sons of Amenhotep. The one who survived would have been his heir to the throne, Prince Tuthmosis, who narrowly escaped being sacrificed in fire.

Jehovah's appearance in the burning bush
In biblical tradition Moses had to flee Egypt after he had killed an Egyptian and the ruling pharaoh sought his life. God then revealed himself to Moses in a bush that kept on burning without it being consumed by the flames, instructing Moses to return to the Pharaoh and lead the Israelites from Egypt[89].

Against the background of the sacrifice by fire of the firstborn of Egypt, there can be only one interpretation of this event – the burning bush Moses faced was the fire prepared for his sacrifice. That fateful night in Egypt there were fires everywhere, and they kept on burning until all the firstborn had been killed. As grandson of Yuya (Joseph), Moses would have been torn between his loyalty towards Egypt and his compassion towards the enslaved Israelites. It is very likely that when he learned that he was to be sacrificed in a fire, or even having faced the fire, he made a pact with a god he must have believed existed, the God of the Israelites, whoever He might have been. Moses promised that should he be spared, he would dedicate his life to freeing the Israelites from the Egyptians. When he was whisked away from this fiery death in the nick of time, he honoured that undertaking.

There was of course no conversation between God and Moses as portrayed in the Bible, as the biblical God only came to life in oral tradition. The Israelites would have known exactly who Moses was and we will never exactly know how he managed to convince them to accept and trust him as their leader.

As stated before, when the sacrifice of the firstborn failed to bring relief to Egypt, a large portion of the Egyptian population rejected Amun and his priesthood, and many of them, including parts of the army, joined Moses and his Israelites who had rebelled against Amenhotep III when he attempted to have them all killed.

18

The parting of the sea and the route of the Exodus

In *Exodus* we read that when the Israelites finally left Egypt, the Pharaoh again changed his mind and pursued them:

> And when Pharao had sent out the people, the Lord led them not by the way of the land of the Philistines, which is near; thinking lest perhaps they would repent, if they should see wars arise against them, and would return into Egypt. But he led them about by the way of the desert, which is by the Red Sea: **and the children of Israel went up armed out of the land of Egypt. And Moses took Joseph's bones with him**: because he had adjured the children of Israel, saying: God shall visit you, carry out my bones from hence with you. And marching from **Socoth**, they encamped in **Etham**, in the utmost coasts of the wilderness. And the Lord went before them to show the way, by day in a pillar of a cloud, and by night in a pillar of fire; that he might be the guide of their journey at both times. There never failed the pillar of the cloud by day, nor the pillar of fire by night, before the people.
>
> And the Lord spoke to Moses, saying: Speak to the children of Israel: Let them turn and encamp over against **Phihahiroth, which is between Magdal and the sea over against Beelsephon**: you shall encamp before it upon the sea. And Pharao will say of the children of Israel: They are straitened in the land, the desert has shut them in. And I shall harden his heart and he will pursue you: and I shall be glorified in Pharao, and in all his army: and the Egyptians shall know that I am the Lord. ...
>
> And he [Pharaoh] took six hundred chosen chariots, and all the chariots that were in Egypt: and the captains of the whole army. ...And when the Egyptians followed the steps of them who

had gone before, they found them encamped at the sea side: all Pharao's horses and chariots and the whole army were in Phihahiroth, before Beelsephon. And when Pharao drew near, the children of Israel lifting up their eyes, saw the Egyptians behind them: and they feared exceedingly, and cried to the Lord. ... And the Lord said to Moses: ...**But lift up your rod, and stretch forth your hand over the sea, and divide it: that the children of Israel may go through the midst of the sea on dry ground**. ... And when Moses had stretched forth his hand over the sea, **the Lord took it away by a strong and burning wind blowing all the night, and turned it into dry ground: and the water was divided**. And the children of Israel went in through the midst of the sea dried up; **for the water was as a wall on their right hand and on their left**. And the Egyptians pursuing went in after them, and all Pharao's horses, his chariots and horsemen, through the midst of the sea. And now the morning watch had come, and behold the Lord looking upon the Egyptian army through the pillar of fire and of the cloud, slew their host. And overthrew the wheels of the chariots, and they were carried into the deep. ... And the Lord said to Moses: Stretch forth your hand over the sea, that the waters may come again upon the Egyptians, upon their chariots and horsemen. And when Moses had stretched forth his hand towards the sea, it returned at the first break of day to the former place: and as the Egyptians were fleeing away, the waters came upon them, **and the Lord shut them up in the middle of the waves. And the waters returned, and covered the chariots and the horsemen of all the army of Pharao, who had come into the sea after them, neither did there so much as one of them remain. But the children of Israel marched through the midst of the sea upon dry land, and the waters were to them as a wall on the right hand and on the left**: And the Lord delivered Israel in that day out of the hands of the Egyptians. And they saw the Egyptians dead upon the sea shore ...[1]

The supposed route of the Exodus is still debated, as the places named in the Exodus narrative are yet to be identified with certainty. Several routes of the Exodus have nevertheless been proposed based on the account that the Israelites had traversed the Red Sea, as shown in Figure 18.1. Route A is the route commonly associated with the Exodus narratives, while route B has been proposed by some scholars as an alternative. However, the absence of a 'Red Sea' to cross in the proposed northern route makes this route less acceptable in the orthodox interpretation of the Exodus narratives.

It has long been recognised that the Hebrew words translated as 'Red Sea' should have been translated as 'sea of reeds'[2], from the Hebrew yam[3] (a sea or large body of water) and suwph[4] (a reed, especially the papyrus). This description would fit only the Nile

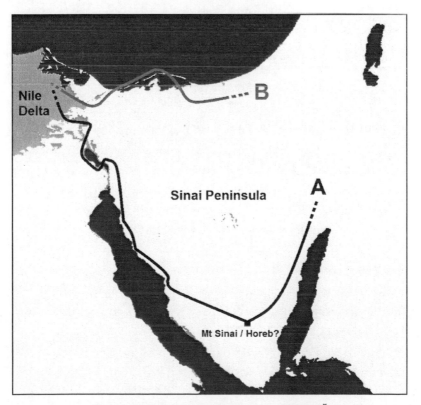

Figure 18.1. Possible routes of the Exodus[5]

Delta, as the papyrus reed is a freshwater plant and only the papyrus swamps of the Delta would qualify as a 'sea'. In other words, there was no crossing of the Red Sea.

Several researchers, including Wilson, Phillips, Trevisanato and Sivertsen, who accept that the Exodus narrative must have been based on real events, agree that the walls of water referred to in *Exodus* must be a muddled recollection of a tsunami that swept away the Egyptian forces in the low lying areas of the Nile Delta. That would explain the 'walls of water', but from where would the legend of a path through the sea have originated? In order to establish this, one has to take a closer look at the biblical narrative as well as the historical setting outlined in this treatise.

As argued earlier, there were two Exodus events of Israelites (Hyksos) from Egypt, the first when Ahmose drove a large portion of the Hyksos from Egypt, and the second when those he had captured departed from Egypt during the Amarna era. It should be noted that other authors have in various ways also recognised that there must have been two Exodus events. In his book *The Moses Legacy*, Graham Phillips argues that the Moses in the Old Testament must have been two distinct individuals living approximately 100 years apart, namely Kamose, the chief steward or foreign minister of Tuthmosis III, and Prince Tuthmosis, the firstborn son of Amenhotep III[6]. Kamose discovered God and inspired the Israelites with a new religion, but it was Prince Tuthmosis who led them out of slavery. Kamose had been tutored by a princess called Termut, meaning 'Daughter of the [goddess] Mut', whom Phillips identifies as Josephus' Thermuthis. This identification is made purely on the basis of the phonetic similarity between the names Termut and Thermuthis, but becomes untenable given the interpretation of the name Thermuthis in Section 7.2.

Roland de Vaux argues for two distinct presentations of the Exodus story[7], namely an Exodus-flight, the 'older story', and an Exodus-expulsion, the 'younger story'. Barbara Sivertsen expands his theory in her *The Parting of the Sea*. The 'older story' includes

Moses and is linked to the first nine plagues. Moses in the 'younger story' is argued to be a later insertion by scribes, as the negotiation with the Pharaoh was done not by him, but by Israelite elders. She identifies the Israelites of the 'older story' as a group of western Semites who settled south of the Hyksos in the Wadi Tumilat, and those of the 'younger story' as Sashu slaves captured by Tuthmosis III, the Pharaoh of the second exodus. When Thera erupted around 1628 BCE, the Nile Delta and specifically the Wadi Tumilat area experienced the after-effects of Thera's tsunami and ash fallout and its inhabitants fled eastward towards the Sinai Peninsula. Much later, during the reign of Tuthmosis III, an outbreak of food poisoning in Egypt resulted in the deaths of many young Egyptian children, excluding those who were being breastfed (not the 'firstborn'). Because of their isolation and different foods, the Israelites were not affected, prompting Tuthmosis III to expel them from Egypt. However, he changed his mind shortly afterwards and pursued them, but was drowned by the tsunami of a second volcanic eruption from a volcanic vent off the Aegean island of Yali. Siversten argues that his body was probably never recovered and that the mummy said to be his is more than likely that of his son. The two exodus events became conflated resulting in the Exodus-expulsion story[8].

As argued in Section 17.1, the ancient world remembered two distinct floods in the Aegean, the flood of Ogygus, which occurred during the reign of Ahmose, and the flood of Deucalion, which occurred about 200 to 250 years later. These floods must certainly have been caused by eruptions of Thera, with its accompanying ash clouds and ash fallouts. The first weakened the Hyksos enough for the Egyptians to be able to overthrow them, while the second washed away the Egyptian forces in Lower Egypt and caused the biblical plagues of the Exodus.

18.1 The First Exodus – Ahmose and the escape of the Hyksos

Of the expulsion of the Hyksos by Ahmose we have little information. Josephus offers perhaps the most detailed account, quoting from Manetho:

> He says further, 'That under a king, whose name was Alisphragmuthosis, the shepherds were subdued by him, and were indeed driven out of other parts of Egypt, but were shut up in a place that contained ten thousand acres; this place was named Avaris.' Manetho says, 'That the shepherds built a wall round all this place, which was a large and a strong wall, and this in order to keep all their possessions and their spoils within a place of strength, but that Thummosis the son of Alisphragmuthosis made an attempt to take them by force and by siege, with four hundred and eighty thousand men to lie round about them, but that, upon his despair of taking the place by that siege, they came to a composition with them, that they should leave Egypt, and go, without any harm to be done to them, wherever they would; and that, after this composition was made, they went away with their whole families and effects, not fewer in number than two hundred and forty thousand, and took their journey from Egypt, through the wilderness, for Syria; but that as they were in fear of the Assyrians, who had then the dominion over Asia, they built a city in that country which is now called Judea, and that large enough to contain this great number of men, and called it Jerusalem.' Now Manetho, in another book of his, says, 'That this nation, thus called shepherds, were also called captives, in their sacred books.' And this account of his is the truth; for feeding of sheep was the employment of our forefathers in the most ancient ages; and as they led such a wandering life in feeding sheep, they were called shepherds.[9]

The king called Alisphragmuthosis and his son Thummosis are

readily identified as Kamose and his brother Ahmose. Manetho most likely made Thummosis the son of Alisphragmuthosis since Ahmose succeeded Kamose as a son would normally succeed his father. Kamose's campaigns against the Hyksos were limited to Upper Egypt and he entered neither the Nile Delta nor Lower Egypt proper[10]. Apart from Josephus' version, the manner in which Ahmose overpowered the Hyksos is described only in a couple of brief diary entries written on the back of the *Rhind Mathematical Papyrus*, which is summarised by Redford as:

> The 'southern prince' (i.e. Ahmose) moves relatively quickly, entering Heliopolis in early July, and then bypassing Avaris to capture Sile, the frontier fort on the edge of the Sinai, in mid-October. Dimly we glimpse a superior strategy designed to cut off support from Asia and then to blockade the capital. The archaeological record confirms that Ahmose pursued the same policy as his brother in committing enemy enclaves to a fiery destruction; and when Avaris finally capitulated, it too was burned and abandoned.[11]

In addition, Redford states that few of the Hyksos would have been captured as slaves since there was a 50-year absence of a 'servile community of aliens' in Egypt following the fall of Avaris. He appears to have based this argument on the small number of Asiatic captives taken by the victorious Egyptians. According to Manetho there was no forcible capture of Avaris, which is supported by archaeological evidence that there was no widespread destruction at the end of the Hyksos period[12]. Between Kamose and Ahmose a large portion of the Hyksos population outside Avaris could have been captured, as is evident from their presence in Egypt during the reign of Amenhotep III (they must have come from somewhere). Phillips recognises the fact that there was only one period in Egyptian history when Asiatics or Semites were present in Egypt on the scale purported in the Bible, namely the Hyksos era[13]. He also argues that it was during the overthrow of the Hyksos and the campaigns of Tuthmosis III that the Israelites were enslaved[14]. Bearing in mind Tuthmosis' practice of enslaving entire peoples to become slaves in Egypt as discussed in Section 6.1, Tuthmosis III would certainly have enslaved some of the Hyksos who had escaped from Ahmose.

However, Tuthmosis' captives alone could not have represented the biblical enslavement of the Israelites. If so, it would imply a time gap of about 100 years of freedom between their initial settlement in Egypt and their escape from Ahmose (the duration of the first phase of their sojourn in Egypt), to their later enslavement by Tuthmosis III (the beginning of the second phase). Like several other scholars he believes the Hebrews to have been a sub-group of the Hyksos known as the Habiru (Hapiru)[15]. A more likely scenario is that the Hyksos and the Israelites were indeed one and the same people, but that David and his mercenaries belonged to a splinter group known as the Habiru. This group may have comprised the tribes of Judah and Benjamin, the only two tribes of Israel loyal to David when he became king. They were possibly a small group of the Hyksos who decided to stay behind in Canaan and did not settle in Egypt to begin the Second Intermediate Period.

Incidentally, one of the notes on the back of the *Rhind Mathematical Papyrus* refers to the 'Voice of Seth', which was followed by a 'precipitation of the sky' on 'the next day of Isis', which may be interpreted as references to a volcanic event[16, 17].

From Manetho's account and the *Rhind Mathematical Papyrus* diary entries we have to try to piece together what had actually happened when Ahmose attacked the Hyksos. The Egyptians harboured an intense hatred of the Asiatics and, given an opportunity, they would not have hesitated to completely destroy their arch rivals. Manetho's account in which the Egyptians amicably agreed to let them depart from Egypt is therefore rather dubious. There appears to be no evidence to support Manetho's version, and the few Egyptian records that survived suggest the opposite, that the

Egyptians sought to destroy Avaris and presumably also its inhabitants. Instead of preventing the Hyksos from being aided by the Asiatics in Canaan, Ahmose seems to have attempted to block their escape to Canaan. Reading between the lines of Manetho's account, it appears that they did manage to escape.

Of key importance in their escape is the path through the sea, which supposedly appeared at Moses' command. What could have prompted such a curious legend? The most plausible explanation is to be found in a number of 'paths through the sea' that exist along the northern Egyptian coastline. These narrow ridges of dry land, most prominently located on the northern boundaries of Lake Manzala (Manzaleh) and Lake Sarbonis (also known as Lake Bardawil) must certainly have been the origin of the legend as there simply is no other logical explanation for a path through the sea. While the Lake Manzala ridge is no longer continuous, in about 1350 BCE the sea level was about two metres lower than its present level[18] (in this 1978 article the authors appear not to have implemented radiocarbon correction through calibration, which had not yet been introduced, but even with calibration, if applicable to marine samples, the value seems to be close to 2m). The ridge must then have been either fully exposed or shallow enough to be crossed on foot. The ridge is on average probably around 250m wide at present and would have been wider in 1350 BCE. Phillips makes the keen observation[19] that the escape route of the Israelites was initially directed towards the pillar of cloud and fire (Thera's ash cloud), which at one point moved from in front of them to behind them[20]. The marshland of Lake Manzala would certainly have qualified as the 'Sea of Reeds', and the escape route proposed by Phillips (see Figure 18.2) matches the about-turn described in the Bible. Possible routes Ahmose's forces may have taken to cut off a Hyksos escape are also shown in Figure 18.2.

Phillips' route makes sense from a strategic point of view. The inhabitants of Avaris must soon have realised their impending fate and learning of Ahmose's plans to prevent their escape to Canaan, they swiftly departed on the route proposed by Phillips. They would have left few tracks in the marshland, and once on the land ridge, they would essentially have vanished from sight. They may have continued along this route along the Lake Sarbonis ridge, until they reached Canaan. If Manetho is to be believed, they either founded or settled in the ancient city of Jerusalem.

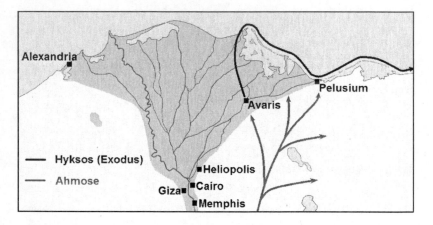

Figure 18.2. The Exodus escape route via the Lake Manzala ridge after Phillips[21], and possibly along the Lake Sarbonis ridge

18.2 The Second Exodus – Moses and the Hyksos slaves

As discussed in Chapter 8, the Israelite slaves along with a large part of the Egyptian people rebelled against Amenhotep following the failed sacrifice of their firstborn. The Israelites (the freed Hyksos slaves) appear to have held sway over Egypt for more than a decade, plundering the Egyptian temples and destroying their gods (see Chapter 10). When the impending return of the Egyptian army from Egypt became evident, the Israelites along with the rebel Egyptians left Egypt and temporarily withdrew into the Sinai desert. As mentioned earlier, the 40 years the Israelites spent in the desert[22] may refer to the period from the time that the Hyksos slaves were first expelled into the desert by Amenhotep III on the advice of his oracle, to the time they left the Sinai desert for Canaan. In Canaan they most likely met with pockets of resistance, but they appear to have been powerful enough to continue with their advance. It is in fact very likely that only the Israelites returned to Canaan, while the Egyptians who had initially joined them remained in Sinai as they would not have been welcome in Canaan.

18.3 How the two Exoduses became one

One can easily imagine how the two Exoduses of the Hyksos from Egypt could have become one as a result of the long history of oral transmission of the Exodus events:

- The two tsunamis that struck Egypt and the existence of the land ridge along the northern shores of Egypt combined to become the parting of the sea by Moses.
- The drowning of the Egyptians in the Nile Delta by the tsunami resulting from the second eruption of Thera became the drowning of the Egyptian army in the sea.
- The after-effects of the eruptions of Thera became the plagues of Egypt.

Both Sivertsen and Trevisanato argue for two volcanic eruptions having taken place in the Exodus context. Sivertsen places the first event *ca.* 1628 BCE and presumably because of a lack of evidence that Thera had erupted once more later in time, argues for an eruption from an underwater volcanic vent off the Aegean island of Yali (see Figure 1.1 for location) 178 years later[23]. Trevisanato dates the two eruptions, both from Thera, to 1602 BCE and 1600 BCE respectively[24]. Based on records of the floods of Ogygus and Deucalion, the two eruptions appear to have occurred approximately 180 years apart during the reigns of Ahmose (*ca.* 1540 BCE?) and Amenhotep III (*ca.* 1360 BCE?). This time separation is close to the period of 200 to 250 years that elapsed between the floods of Ogygus and Deacalion as recorded by several ancient historians.

This brings us to the final, crucial part of the theory, namely the much debated scientific dating of the eruptions of Thera. Without scientific verification of these dates, the link between Thera and the Exodus events cannot be established with absolute certainty.

Dating the eruptions of Thera

The dating of the cataclysmic eruption of Thera can be done by several means, including historical records concerning the event, archaeology, dendrochronology, ice core sample analysis and radiocarbon dating. Historical records of the eruption are virtually nonexistent and also nonspecific, as many of the after-effects of the eruption would be described in terms familiar to the people of that time and may therefore not be readily recognisable as such. Although archaeology is a much more scientific process than using historical records repeated over long periods of time, there often remains a degree of uncertainty in the absolute dates of archaeological finds. Of all the dating techniques, radiocarbon dating is the most accurate. An excellent overview of the problems associated with pinpointing the chronology of the New Kingdom dynasties and also the radiocarbon dating specifically of Thera's eruption is given by Sturt Manning in his 1999 book *A Test of Time*[1]. After reviewing evidence from a variety of sources and scientific disciplines, Manning concludes that the most likely date for the eruption is 1628 BCE, and rejects the possibility of an eruption date between 1560-1479 BCE[2]. His conclusion was vindicated by Friedrich and Heinemeier in 2006, who discovered and radiocarbon dated an olive tree that was buried alive on the island of Santorini by the pumice of the eruption[3]. Their dating of the eruption to 1613 ± 13 BCE must be regarded as the most accurate to date.

19.1 The time gap between C14 dating and conventional chronology

If the eruption of Thera can be reliably dated to *ca.* 1613 ±13 BCE, there is only one nearby chronological period in Egyptian history that can be associated with the eruption of a volcano. This is the rule of Ahmose as attested to by his *Tempest Stele* and also by records of a flood during his time. The conventional dating of the reign of Ahmose is 1550 – 1525 BCE. If the flood occurred around 1540 BCE, it would leave us with a discrepancy of between 60 and 86 years. A general discrepancy between radiocarbon dating and conventional Egyptian chronology has been acknowledged by, among others, Manning (50 to 70 years 'at face value', but reduced to about 25 years based on the high and low dates of the accession of Tuthmosis III)[4]. The radiocarbon based study of Egyptian chronology performed by Ramsey et al. confirms a difference of about 25 years for the Eighteenth Dynasty period[5]. However, Bruins and his associates identify a time gap of 100 to 150 years[6,7] between radiocarbon dating and the conventional chronology based on their observation that radiocarbon and archaeo-historical dating evidence points to two Minoan eruptions that must have occurred 100-150 years apart.

If only one Minoan eruption actually occurred and the evidence relates to the same event, as they are evidently assuming, their assessment would be correct in that such a time gap must exist. If the Egyptian chronological year of 1540 BCE should be pushed back in time by about 80 years, the radiocarbon dated eruption of Thera would coincide perfectly with the flood in the time of Ahmose. The same shift in time should then apply to a volcanic eruption during the reign of Amenhotep III. He ruled between *ca.* 1390 and 1352 BCE according to conventional Egyptian chronology, and if a second eruption of Thera had occurred *ca.* 1360 BCE (the conventional date), 80 years back in time takes us to 1440 BCE. The year 1450 BCE has long been argued by various archaeologists to be the date of the eruption of Thera, based on the destruction of eastern Crete at that time[8]. It would appear that most scholars at present reject any link between the destruction of Crete around 1450 BCE and an eruption of Thera, based on the most recent dating of the eruption of Thera to ±1613 BCE. However, if Thera erupted a second time approximately 150 to 180 years later, as is evident from ancient historical records, an eruption of Thera can indeed be linked to the destruction of Crete.

If the evidence discussed by Bruins points to two eruptions of Thera instead of just one, there would appear to be no need to move the conventional Egyptian chronology back in time by more than 25 years or so. That would then still leave the problem of aligning the flood of Ogygus, which occurred during the reign of Ahmose, with the 1613 BCE eruption of Thera. This flood, which could only have been caused by a major volcanic eruption, is the clearest indication that the Egyptian chronology should be moved back in time by about 80 years, if the 1613 BCE date is correct. If Thera had continuously been releasing carbon gasses before its first eruption, the carbon mixture (reservoir) on and near the island would probably have been different from the carbon reservoir in Egypt 800 km away, which could result in an erroneous calculation of the eruption date.

Possibly the clearest confirmation that a second eruption occurred during the reign of Amenhotep III is the scarab bearing his name that was found in a tomb at the Knossos palace on Crete. The presence of this scarab at Crete has been a topic of much debate as discussed in detail (and rejected as evidence of a volcanic eruption at that time) by Manning[9], but certainly suggests that an eruption of Thera could have occurred during Amenhotep's reign or soon afterwards. A dating error of 80 years on 1,550 + 1,950 = 3,500 years amounts to an error of only 2.3%. Given that we do not know exactly what the environmental conditions were 3,500 years ago, a time gap of this magnitude certainly seems feasible. It is also possible that the radiocarbon calibration data need to be refined, specifically regarding the eruption date of 1613 BCE. Could a revised date be 1540 BCE? Whatever be the case, it is clear that more work needs to be done to align the dating of Egyptian chronology to match an eruption of Thera during the reign of Ahmose.

The next question is whether any evidence can be found that would suggest a second major eruption of Thera, following the first *ca.* 1613 BCE.

19.2 Evidence for two major eruptions of Thera

Through studies of the ash deposit layers in the caldera cliffs of the islands that form the Santorini archipelago (see Figure 1.3), archaeologists have concluded that Thera had erupted violently as many as 12 times in the past[10]. It is believed that the final catastrophic eruption *ca.* 1613 BCE was not a single, massive explosion, but proceeded in four distinct phases[11,12]. This is evident from the ash layers found on the island, a part of which is shown in Figure 19.1 The ash layer of the precursory phase is only a couple of centimetres thick and is not distinguishable in Figure 19.1. The olive tree dated to 1613 BCE was found in the Phase 1 layer. Following a presentation on the Minoan deposits at the *Third International Congress on Thera and the Aegean World* [13], Prof. Colin Renfrew commented that Phase 4 represented a new sub-phase of hot activity, and that there may have been a considerable lapse of time, perhaps a decade or two, between Phase 3 and Phase 4. Prof. Steve Sparks acknowledged that the transition between the cold deposits belonging to Phase 3 and the hot deposits of Phase 4 is indeed very sharp. However, he was not totally convinced that a significant time gap would have occurred between the two phases.

To be consistent with two major eruptions, one *ca.* 1613 BCE and the other *ca.* 1450 BCE, the interval between them would have to be around 160 years. One would expect that over a period of 150 to 200 years there would be a significant number of biologically and environmentally induced changes visible in the upper part of Phase 3, which there apparently is not. However, it may be possible that the lateral force of the second eruption had sheared off the upper part of the Phase 3 deposit layer, onto which the tephra of Phase 4 was then deposited. The block visible above the two individuals on the photograph penetrated through the Phase 3 layer into the Phase 2 layer, but left no trace through the Phase 4 layer. Friedrich and Sigalas speculate that the block may have been torn from the side wall of the vent of the volcano in the second phase of the eruption and thrown out. Could it point to a second eruption about 200 years later, matching the period between the floods of Ogygus and Deucalion?

Figure 19.1. Ash layers of Thera's eruptions, the first dated
to 1613 BCE[14]

That two eruptions of Thera may have occurred is suggested by the
distribution of ash fallout over Egypt and Anatolia as shown in
Figure 19.2. In an attempt to explain the bi-directional distribution
of Thera's ash fallout, it has been suggested (see Sivertsen[15]) that the
ash of Phase 1 was carried in a south-easterly direction to Egypt, and
the ash from a later phase to Anatolia. Alternatively, it has been
suggested, different wind directions at lower and higher altitudes

may account for the bi-directional spread of ash, or the direction of the wind may have curved from Egypt towards Anatolia (see also Trevisanato[16]). The most likely explanation is that two distinct eruptions must have taken place, either during the closely spaced phases of the 1613 BCE eruption (allowing enough time between the eruptions for the direction of the wind to have changed), or possibly two eruptions separated much further in time, which would be during the reigns of Ahmose and Amenhotep III, respectively. The thick darkness recorded in the *Tempest Stele of Ahmose* ('no one able to light the torch anywhere') and later again in the *El Arish Shrine*

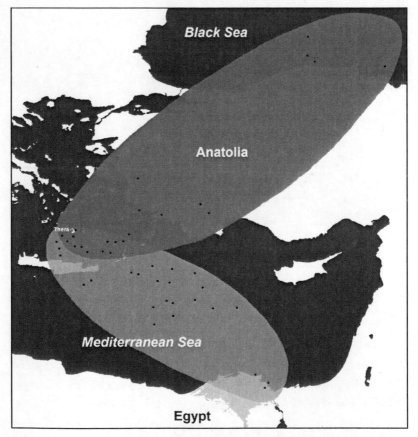

Figure 19.2. Ash fallout of Thera spread in two directions, Egypt and Anatolia[17]

Text (no one 'could see the face of his fellow'), which has been shown to be a record of the exploits of Amenhotep III and his son Prince Tuthmosis, suggests that ash from two eruptions separated by about 200 years had reached Egypt. The similar descriptions given in Jewish legend (see Section 15.9) could apply to any of these two eruptions, or possibly both.

Another hint at two distinct eruptions widely separated in time is given by the tsunami deposits found at Palaikastro in Crete. On the geological dating of these deposits, Bruins et al. state the following:

Volcanic ash appears at Palaikastro as distinct intraclasts in chaotic geoarchaeological tsunami deposits in field section 2 ... along the Promontory ... and as discrete layers more inland within and near Buildings 6 and 7 ... . These deposits are geologically dated to the Minoan Santorini eruption, because the embedded volcanic ash is proven to have the geochemical fingerprint of this eruption ... **The volcanic ash was evidently reworked by the tsunami and redeposited with the other multimodal components of the non-sorted sediment** ... Considering the eruption sequence at Santorini ... and the presence of reworked volcanic ash in the tsunami deposits at Palaikastro, **it can be concluded that airborne volcanic ash deposition over eastern Crete preceded the tsunami**. The volcanic ash was most likely deposited at Palaikastro during the 1st eruption phase (Plinian) with winds blowing from Santorini to the southeast ... The tsunami was apparently generated during the 3rd or 4th eruption phase, according to stratigraphic evidence of tsunami deposits at Thera....

Findings of discrete volcanic ash in eastern Crete are rare. Excavations at the archaeological sites ... of Mochlos ... and Palaikastro ... revealed volcanic ash in archaeological stratigraphic context. The spatial extent and thickness of the Minoan Santorini volcanic ash layer in Mediterranean deep-sea sediments indicate that eastern Crete was covered by an estimated 5 cm of volcanic tephra ... Volcanic ash particles originating from the Minoan Santorini eruption have been found in soils of eastern Crete in a dispersed state and not as a discrete layer.... It is obvious that the tsunami at Palaikastro could not have caused redeposition of discrete volcanic ash layers or discrete intraclasts from dispersed volcanic particles in soils. **Therefore, in terms of environmental geological dating, the tsunami came after the deposition over eastern Crete of airborne volcanic ash, but before the ash layer became dispersed by erosion and soil-biological mixing.** A tsunami generated in the 3rd or 4th (last) eruption phase, as found on Thera, meets the above requirement and fits the presence of discrete volcanic ash in the tsunami deposits at Palaikastro...[18]

Figure 19.3. Tsunami deposits at Palaikastro, Crete, with solidified volcanic Santorini ash[19]

From the rock-like appearance of the Santorini ash (dated to the 1613 BCE eruption) in the tsunami deposits at Palaikastro, Crete (see Figure 19.3), it is not only clear that the ash fall must have preceded a later eruption of the volcano (hence the tsunami), but also that enough time must have lapsed between the two eruptions for the ash from the first to have solidified. Had these eruptions occurred only a couple of days apart, the layers of ash could certainly not have solidified to this extent. On the other hand, once the layer of ash had solidified, it would have remained in that condition probably indefinitely, and it is therefore possible that an eruption *ca.* 1450 BCE and its ensuing tsunami could have broken up the original layer of solidified ash.

The presence of ash from Thera in Egypt is hard to detect as little must have remained after so many years. It seems to be widely recognised that the initial layers of ash could easily have dispersed over time for a variety of reasons. For instance, Stanley and Sheng (1986) state:

Sparks and others, for example, show that a discrete ash layer must be at least 0.62 cm thick to survive bioturbation and not be dispersed through the surrounding sediment. That volcanic shards from Santorini have not been recovered in North African and Levant deserts and archaeological sites is likely due to the subsequent reworking of thin ash layers by wind and dissemination of the glass particles.[20]

Sivertsen likewise quotes examples of thick layers of ash which over time have virtually disappeared, for instance the thickness of ash layer from the volcano Huaynaputina which has been reduced from 1m to 10cm in only 400 years[21]. Therefore one can expect that it would be difficult to find traces of Thera's ash in Egypt, which is a sandy and wind-blown country. Ash that fell in the Nile Delta may simply have disappeared because of thousands of years of cultivation. Traces of volcanic ash were eventually found in sediment cores from Lake Manzala (see Stanley and Sheng). The ash in the form of glass shards was concentrated at a depth of 5m to 7m in four of the five cores. Shards found at a depth of 5m were dated to 2810 BP and those found at a depth of 7m to 4380 BP. From these two dates Stanley and Sheng derived an interpolated date of 3595 BP at a depth of 6m, without detailing how the dating of the 5m and 7m layers was performed. Their method of dating (taking the average value of the two dates) is, however, questionable as one would rather have expected the two dates to represent two different layers of ash. The corresponding calibrated radiocarbon dates are approximately 860 BCE (5m) and 2430 BCE (7m), respectively, as calculated from the INTCAL09 calibration curves[22]. If the shards all came from the same eruption of Thera, as is assumed by Stanley and Sheng, these dates are 1570 years apart, which makes the accuracy of their dating technique somewhat suspect. A calibrated eruption date of 1450 BCE, the most likely date for a second eruption of Thera, corresponds to a radiocarbon date of *ca.* 3400 BP, while 1613 BCE corresponds to more or less 3560 BP. This date is close to the interpolated year of 3595 BP (CAL), but the latter must be regarded as a mathematical coincidence.

It has been observed that the size of the shards found in the Lake Manzala cores is smaller than those of the 1613 BCE eruption of Thera, and also that it has a different chemical composition compared to shards from the 1613 BCE eruption[23]. While these differences are generally interpreted to imply that the shards originated from two different volcanoes, the possibility remains that these shards found in Egypt came from a much later eruption of Thera. As far as I could establish no alternative volcanic source of the traces of ash found at Lake Manzala has been suggested.

It must be noted that some researchers have concluded that an eruption of a volcano on the Agean island Yali seem to have occurred sometime during the fifteenth century BCE, probably around 1460 BCE[24]. Sivertsen quotes additional evidence that suggests the volcanic eruption which caused the flood of Deucalion was that of Yali and not of Thera[25], and she links this eruption to the second Exodus event in Egypt. Yali may be a viable alternative if no evidence of a second eruption of Thera can be found, but whether an eruption of Yali may have been powerful enough to cause Exodus-like effects in Egypt probably still has to be established.

In conclusion, there are three additional pieces of evidence that seem to suggest a major natural cataclysm must have occurred during the reign of Amenhotep III:

- An Amarna letter in which Abi-Milku reported the destruction of Ugarit reads:

  Fire destroyed the palace at Ugarit; (rather), it destroyed half of it and so hal(f) of it has disappeared.[26]

  The odd remark that half of the palace has disappeared was interpreted by Phillips as half the city having been washed into the sea[27]. Depending on the height of the tsunami when it reached Ugarit, he may very well be correct. The palace of Ugarit was located about 1,000m from the sea on a tel 18 metres high[28]. An inrushing tsunami of sufficient height may have been able to surge up against the slope of the tel and wash away some of the walls and other structures.

- Scarabs of Amenhotep III were found in the ruins of Jericho, a city that was also destroyed by fire. The narrative of the shout of the soldiers that brought the walls tumbling down must have been based on the sonic boom of a volcanic eruption, followed by a tremendous earthquake that caused the walls to collapse.

- A scarab of Amenhotep III was found in the ruins of the palace at Knossos, Crete. Like Jericho and Ugarit, Knossos was also destroyed by fire[29]. All these events are reminiscent of the plague of lightning and fire. As inconceivable as it seems to be, archaeologists may have vastly underestimated the magnitude of the eruption of Thera and there may just be truth in the Jewish records of fire falling from the sky.

Although evidence for a second eruption of Thera *ca.* 1450 BCE is scarce, the people of ancient Egypt and the Israelites remembered these events and preserved them in traditions and various texts and inscriptions. Specifically, the drowning of the Egyptian army in the flood (during the 'parting of the sea' event) must refer to a second eruption, as Lower Egypt was ruled by the Hyksos during the reign of Ahmose *ca.* 1613 BCE, and the Egyptian army would have been confined to Upper Egypt at that time.

I have to state clearly that I have no background in volcanology and some of my technical discussions and conclusions may be based on a misunderstanding of the mechanisms of a volcanic eruption. To delve any deeper into this field of science is simply not possible and I trust that my observations, even if faulty, will at least prompt further investigation along these lines by experts in the field.

20

Abraham, father of the Hyksos

According to biblical tradition the progenitors of the Israelites were Abraham, his son Isaac and the latter's son Jacob. Abraham was a native of the Chaldean city Ur, generally assumed to be located in present-day southern Iraq. God called upon Abraham to leave his native land with the promise that God would make the descendants of Abraham a great nation. Abraham travelled to Egypt with his beautiful wife Sarai, whom he declared to be his sister when he arrived in the country for fear of being killed for his wife. She was taken into the palace of the king, but God sent plagues to Egypt, which the pharaoh interpreted to be his punishment for taking Sarai from Abraham, and he returned her to him. Despite God's promise, the couple could not produce any offspring. Sarai then offered her handmaid Hagar to Abraham to be his wife. Hagar fell pregnant, but she had to flee from Sarai and later gave birth to a son called Ishmael. Sarai, whose name was changed to Sarah, eventually gave birth to a son called Isaac. God tested Abraham by instructing him to sacrifice Isaac, but intervened just as Abraham was about to kill his son.

Isaac had two sons, the twins Jacob and Esau. Esau offered his birthright to Jacob in exchange for a pot of stew, and Jacob deceived his by then blind father Isaac to receive his blessing, normally bestowed upon the firstborn. While sleeping along a journey, Jacob had a dream about a ladder or staircase that reached all the way into heaven. From the top of this ladder God blessed Jacob, promising that Jacob's descendants would multiply across the world[1]. On the return journey Jacob encountered and wrestled with an angel of God. When the angel could not overpower Jacob, he (Jacob) demanded a blessing from the mysterious being, who pronounced that henceforth Jacob would be known as Israel. Jacob had 12 sons[2] who became the leaders of the 12 tribes of Israel. One of these sons was Joseph who served in the court of the Pharaoh of the Oppression.

The biblical origins of the Israelites as summarised above become questionable when the Israelites are equated with the Hyksos. The Hyksos were already numerous when they settled in Egypt *ca.* 1650 BCE and the Exodus occurred around 300 years later. There is no doubt that Joseph was a real person, but the same cannot be said of the three patriarchs Abraham, Isaac and Jacob. However, one of the early Hyksos rulers was named Yakubher (Ya'cob-Har)[3,4], suggesting that the name Jacob was common among the Hyksos.

Tacitus states that (see Section 3.10):

Some say they [the Hebrews] were a people that were very numerous in Egypt, under the reign of Isis; and that the Egyptians got free from that burden, by sending them into the adjacent countries...

This would suggest that the Hebrews date back to the era following the creation of the earth (in Egyptian mythology), when the gods supposedly ruled Egypt[5].

The original form of the name Abraham is *'Abrâm*[6], which is usually believed to mean 'High Father' from *'âb*[7] (father) and *rûwm*[8] (to be high, up, exalt). This name was later changed to **'Abrâhâm*[9]** by God, as Abraham would be 'the father of a multitude of nations' [10]. This version of his name can, however, be split as *'âb*, either *râ'âh*[11] (to see), *ra'*[12] (bad, evil) or *râ'âh*[13] (feed, shepherd), and *'am*[14] (people, nation). The most likely interpretation is **'Father of the shepherd people'**, or in other words, **'Father of the Hyksos'.** If this nation had for some reason been vilified by other nations, it is possible that Abraham may have been known as 'Father of the evil people', but this is unlikely. The interpretation 'Father of the shepherd people' does not appear to link Abraham to the era of Isis, but Isis was closely associated with Ra, one of the chief deities of ancient Egypt, whose name is also pronounced Re. It is very likely that the name Ab-ra-ham could have been remembered as **'Father Ra of the People'**. In other words, Abraham and the Egyptian god Ra may have been one and the same person or entity.

The Hebrew word *râ'âh* (to see) has derivatives *râ'eh*[15] (seeing) and *rô'eh*[16] (a seer, a vision), which may explain the two forms of the name of this god, Ra and Re. As such, the name Abraham may be interpreted as **'Father of the Seeing People'**. Although this may sound illogical at first, the Bible mentions a group of angels called the Watchers[17]. In the *Book of Enoch*[18] the Watchers are identified as the fallen angels who 'committed iniquity with the daughters of men'. In the *Book of Jubilees*, as in the *Book of Enoch*, the Watchers are recorded as having 'defiled themselves with the daughters of men', which was one of the reasons why God chose to destroy the earth by means of the Flood:

> For owing to these three things came the flood upon the earth, namely owing to the fornication wherein the Watchers against the law of their ordinances went a whoring after the daughters of men, and took themselves wives of all which they chose: and they made the beginning of uncleanness...[19]

The Watchers are also associated with the biblical Nephilim, the god-like creatures who mated with the daughters of men before God eventually sent the Flood to punish humankind for its wickedness:

> When men began to increase in number on the earth and daughters were born to them, the sons of God saw that the daughters of men were beautiful, and they married any of them they chose. ... The Nephilim were on the earth in those days – and also afterward – when the sons of God went to the daughters of men and had children by them. They were the heroes of old, men of renown.[20]

A more detailed description of the Nephilim is given in the *Book of*

Enoch, where they are referred to as angels:

> And it came to pass when the children of men had multiplied that in those days were born unto them beautiful and comely daughters. **And the angels, the children of the heaven, saw and lusted after them, and said to one another: 'Come, let us choose us wives from among the children of men and beget us children.'** And Semjâzâ, who was their leader, said unto them: 'I fear ye will not indeed agree to do this deed, and I alone shall have to pay the penalty of a great sin.' And they all answered him and said: 'Let us all swear an oath, and all bind ourselves by mutual imprecations not to abandon this plan but to do this thing.' **Then sware they all together and bound themselves by mutual imprecations upon it. And they were in all two hundred;** who descended in the days of Jared on the summit of Mount Hermon, and they called it Mount Hermon, because they had sworn and bound themselves by mutual imprecations upon it ... **And all the others together with them took unto themselves wives, and each chose for himself one, and they began to go in unto them and to defile themselves with them,** and they taught them charms and enchantments, and the cutting of roots, and made them acquainted with plants. **And they became pregnant, and they bare great giants, whose height was three thousand ells**: Who consumed all the acquisitions of men. And when men could no longer sustain them, the giants turned against them and devoured mankind.[21]

The name Nephilim can be interpreted as 'The Giants' from the plural form of $n^ephîl$[22] (a bully or tyrant, giant) or 'The Fallen Ones' from n^ephal [23] (fall down) or *nephel* [24] (something fallen, therefore an abortion, untimely birth). It is therefore clear that the 'sons of God' who married the daughters of men were also known as the Fallen Ones, the Watchers, the Nephilim and the Giants.

Genesis begins with the story of God's creation of the earth, which was completed by the creation of Adam and Eve. Their offspring multiplied greatly, but became so wicked that God decided to wipe mankind off the face of the earth by sending a great flood to drown them all except Noah, who had found favour in the eyes of the Lord. He instructed Noah to build an ark into which he was to bring his family along with a male and female of every living creature on the earth. This Noah did, the Flood came and only Noah and all those in the ark survived. From his descendants Abraham would later be born. In the *Genesis Apocryphon* **Noah is claimed to be a descendant of the Giants**[25], and according to Eusebius, Pseudo-Eupolemus states:

> Eupolemus in his book *Concerning the Jews of Assyria* says that the city Babylon was first founded by those who escaped from the Deluge; and that they were giants, and built the tower renowned in history. But when this had been overthrown by the act of God, the giants were dispersed over the whole earth.[26]
>
> In certain anonymous works, however, we found that **Abraham traced back his origin to the giants**, and that [those] dwelling in Babylonia were destroyed by the gods for their impiety; but that one of them, named Belus, escaped death and settled in Babylon, and lived in a tower which he had built, and which was called Belus from the Belus who built it: and that Abraham having been instructed in the science of astrology came first into Phoenicia, and taught astrology to the Phoenicians, and afterwards passed on into Egypt.[27]

Eusebius also states:

> Most authors agree that in the time of Isis certain giants of great size, arrayed in monstrous fashion, stirred up war against the gods Zeus and Osiris.[28]

It would seem, therefore, that Abraham can be linked to the time when Isis and Ra ruled Egypt, or at least, to the time of ancient mythology. According to Tacitus' sources the Israelites were expelled from Egypt and must therefore have settled in Canaan if not somewhere in Anatolia, where they became the people known as the Hyksos. A detailed examination of the possible link between the ancient Israelites and Egyptian mythology falls beyond the scope of this treatise, but if Tacitus' sources are correct, it would be fair to conclude that the Israelites are at least as old, if not older, than the Egyptians themselves.

The Israelites were also known as the Ermiuth (see Section 3.6), which can be interpreted as 'The Watchers who came from the ruins', from '*Êr* (watchful)[29], *m^e'îy* (a pile of rubbish, a ruin)[30] and '*ûwth* (to come)[31], or '(Those-who) came from the ruined city', from *m^e'îy,'ûwth* and '*îyr* (a city guarded by a watch)[32]. There is an ancient story that tells of the survivors of a city that was destroyed, the fabled city of Atlantis[33]. The Atlanteans had reportedly conquered Egypt before their island and its city had sunk into the ocean, and the ancestors of the Israelites therefore appear to be linked to whatever the origins of the Atlantis story might be. As discussed in Section 9.3, Jehovah (*Yâ'âh- hôvâh*) may mean 'Ruined and swept aside' (by the Flood?), which appears to confirm the Atlantis connection. All one can really conclude is that the origins of the ancestors of the Israelites appear to date back to the darkest mists of ancient mythology.

Appendix A

The Gebel Barkal Stela of Tuthmosis III

Mark-Jan Nederhof, transliteration and translation for *The Gebel Barkal stela of Tuthmosis III*, following the transcription of De Buck (1948), pp. 56-63. The transliteration throughout follows Hannig (1995). For published translations, see Cumming (1982), number 365 (pp. 1-7); Helck (1984), number 365 (pp. 5-12); Reisner (1933). Created on 2006-11-04 by Mark-Jan Nederhof. Last modified 2009-06-08. Reprinted with kind permission by Mark-Jan Nederhof.

Bibliography

J.W.B. Barns. Some readings and interpretations in sundry Egyptian texts. The Journal of Egyptian Archaeology, 58:159-166, 1972.

A. De Buck. Egyptian Reading Book. Ares Publishers, Chicago, Illinois, 1948.

B. Cumming. Egyptian Historical Records of the Later Eighteenth Dynasty – Fascicle I. Aris and Phillips, Warminster, 1982.

R. Hannig. Grosses Handwörterbuch Ägyptisch-Deutsch: die Sprache der Pharaonen (2800-950 v.Chr.). Verlag Philipp von Zabern, 1995.

W. Helck. Urkunden der 18. Dynastie – Übersetzung zu den Heften 17-22. Akademie-Verlag, Berlin, 1984.

G.A. Reisner and M.B. Reisner. Zeitschrift für ägyptische Sprache und Altertumskunde, 69:24-39, 1933.

Year 47, third month of the Season of Inundation, day 10, under the majesty of Horus: Mighty bull appearing in Thebes; Two Ladies: Enduring of kingship like Re in heaven; Gold Horus: Sacred of appearance, mighty of strength; The king of Upper and Lower Egypt: Menkheperre; Son of Re, of his body, his beloved, lord of every foreign land: Tuthmosis, beautiful of form. He created it as his monument for his father Amun-Re, lord of the Thrones of the Two Lands, in the fortress 'Slayer of the foreigners', making for him a resting place of eternity because he made the victories of My Majesty greater than those of any king who had been. I seized the southerners under the command of his spirit, and the northerners in accordance with his guidance. He created the son of Re, Tuthmosis, ruler of Thebes, given life like Re forever, the good god who seizes with his arm, who strikes the southerners and beheads the northerners, who smashes the heads of the evil-minded, who carries out a massacre of the Bedouin tribes of Asia, who overthrows the rebels among the Bedouin, who subjugates the lands at the ends of the world, who smites the nomads of Nubia, who attained the boundaries of the foreign lands of those who attacked him, who confronts the battlefield furiously. All foreign lands were united, standing prepared to fight as one. There were no deserters, relying on the numerous troops, with limitless people and horses. They advanced, their hearts being bold, without fear in their hearts. But the one mighty of strength overthrew them, the one with powerful arm, who tramples his enemies. He is a king who fights alone, without crowds behind him. He is more effective than a million of numerous soldiers. No equal to him has been found: warrior, hero on the battlefield, in whose vicinity there is no resistance, who immediately overpowers all foreign lands, as commander of his army, while he rushes between the barbarians as a star that crosses the sky, who enters the turmoil of battle, while his glowing breath [attacks] them with fire, who eradicates them, while they lie in their blood. It is his serpent-diadem that overthrows them for him, his flame that drives away his enemies. The numerous army of Metjen was overthrown within an hour, as perished as those who have never been, [...] in the manner of a consuming flame, as what the arms of the good god did, who is great of strength in battle, who carries out a massacre of everyone, his only leader, the king of Upper and Lower Egypt Menkheperre (may he live forever!). He is Horus, with a powerful arm, an excellent fortress to his army, a refuge to the subjects, who

attacks every land with infighting, who rescues Egypt on the battlefield, a protector who does not fear the rapacious. He is a brave bull
**whose southern borders reach to the crest of the world, to the ends
of this world, and the northern to the ends of Asia, to the supports
of heaven**. They come to him with bowed heads seeking his breath
of life. He is a king valiant like Montu, who robs but from whom one
cannot rob, who tramples all rebellious foreign lands without there
being anyone to protect them in that land of Naharina, which its
lord had abandoned in fear. I damaged his towns and his people and
I set fire to them. My Majesty turned them into ruins, so that they
could not be reconstructed. I captured all their people, who were
brought as prisoners, their cattle without limit, and their possessions as well. I took the crops away from them, tore out their barley,
and felled all their trees and all their fruit trees. Their districts were
massacred. My Majesty devastated them so that they became [...] [...]
on which there were no trees. **Now My Majesty travelled to the
ends of Asia.** I let many ships be constructed of cedar, on the hills of
the God's Land, in the presence of the mistress of Byblos, and they
were put on carts pulled by oxen. They went before My Majesty to
cross that great river that flows between this foreign land and
Naharina, a king who is lauded for his arms in battle. **He crossed the
Euphrates after him who had attacked him, as chief of his army,
chasing that vile enemy** [...] foreign lands of Metjen. But he fled
from His Majesty to another land, a distant place, in fear. **Then My
Majesty erected my stela on that mountain of Naharina, carved out
of the mountain on the western side of the Euphrates.** There is no
enemy of mine in the southern lands, and the northerners come
bowing to my might. It is Re who commanded it for me, for I have
grasped all that his Eye revolves around. He gave me the land in its
length and its breadth. **I tied up the Nine Bows, the islands in the
middle of the ocean, the inhabitants of the Aegean Sea and the
rebellious lands.** I returned southward to Egypt and subjugated
Naharina, greatly feared in the mouths of the Bedouin, their gates
being closed because of it, and they couldn't go out for fear of the

bull. He is a brave king, an excellent fortress to his army, a castle of iron. He attacks every land with his strength, without millions of men behind him. A sure marksman every time he takes aim, whose arrows cannot miss. Now another victory that Re commanded for me: He again did for me a very brave act, at the lake of Nija. **He made me round up herds of elephants. My Majesty hunted them, a herd of 120.** Never had anything similar been done by a king since the god of those who had received the white crown. I have said this without boasting and without lie. I did this according to what [...] ordered to me [...], **who guides My Majesty on the good road, through his excellent plans.** He united for me the black land and the red land, what the sun revolves around is in my grasp. Now I'll speak again to you, so hear, people! He conferred on me the foreign lands of Retjenu during the first expedition, as they came to engage My Majesty, being millions of men, hundreds of thousands of the finest of all foreign lands, standing on their chariots, 330 princes, each one thereof with his army. They were in the valley of Qina, and a successful act took place against them caused by me. **My Majesty attacked them and they fled immediately, falling in heaps.** They entered Megiddo and my Majesty besieged them for seven months, until they came out beseeching My Majesty, saying: 'Give us your breath, our lord! The foreigners of Retjenu will not rebel again.' **Then that enemy and the princes who were with them had sent to My Majesty all their children, with many tributes of gold and silver, all their horses that were with them, their large chariots of gold and silver and those that were undecorated, all their coats of mail, their bows, their arrows, and all their weapons.** This is what they had come with to fight and conspire against My Majesty, and now they brought them as gifts to My Majesty. They stood on their walls giving praise to My Majesty in order to be given the breath of life. Then My Majesty ordered that they be made to swear an oath: 'We will not again do evil against Menkheperre (may he live forever!), our lord, in our lifetime, for we have seen his might. He has given us breath as he wishes. His father has done it [...] It is not an act of people.' Then My Majesty ordered that they be granted passage to their towns. They all went on donkeys, since I had taken their horses. **I captured their inhabitants for Egypt and their properties as well.** My father gave them to me, [...] the excellent god, who is successful, whose plans do not fail, who sent My Majesty to seize the lands and all foreigners together. I overthrew them as he ordered, in the way that he used to do. He let me smite all foreigners and there was none who dared approach me. My mace overthrew the Asiatics, and my ...-mace smited the Nine Bows. My Majesty subjugated every land. Retjenu is under my feet, the Bedouin of Asia are subject to My Majesty. They are subservient to me as one, charged with tributes of millions of many things from the crest of the world, and much gold from Wawat, its quantity without limit. One constructs there for the palace, each and every year, 'eight'-ships and many ships for the crew of sailors in addition to **the tributes the Bedouin of Asia in ivory and ebony.** Precious wood comes for me from Kush, consisting in branches of doum palm and furniture without limit of southern acacia. My army hewed them in Kush, which was there by the millions. [...] many ships of doum palm, **which My Majesty had carried off in victory.** [...] constructed [...] Djahi each and every year from real cedar from Lebanon, which is brought to the palace. Precious wood comes for me to Egypt, brought south, [...] real [...] from Negau, the pick of the God's Land, which were assigned, [...-wood] **like alabaster for supply to the residence,** without expiration of the coming of the appropriate season of a single year. My army, which is in Ullaza as occupying force, comes [...] which is from cedar from conquests of My Majesty, by the plans of my father [...] who conferred on me all foreigners. I didn't give of it to the Asiatics, since it is wood that he likes. He subjugated, and they acknowledge my lord, and the misery from them has been pacified. [...] My [...] So hear, people of the southern land that is at the sacred mountain, which was called the Thrones of the Two Lands among the people when it wasn't known yet. May you know the wonder of [...] before the people [...] to come to meet in the night, to carry out the regular watch; there were two observers. **A star fell, falling to their south. The like had not happened before. It struck them opposite to him. None could stand there [...] [...] in heaps. But [...] after them with fire in their faces. None of them offered resistance, and none looked back. They no longer had horses, which had bolted in [...] [...] to let all foreigners see the might of My Majesty.** I returned southward, my heart being glad, after I had triumphed for my lord, [...] the one who had ordered this victory, and caused the fright [...] [...] in my time. He placed the fear of me among all foreigners, and they fled far away from me. All that the sun shines upon is bound together under my feet. My Majesty myself says: [...] **strength, because I am very skilled in strength and victory, which my noble father Amun, lord of the Thrones of the Two Lands, has given to me. He has made me lord of the five portions, ruler of what the sun revolves around.** [...] strong [...] fright of My Majesty to the southern boundary marker. There is no road to me, since he has sealed the entire land for me. **There is no limit to what became mine in victory.** He placed my might in Upper Retjenu. [...] They [...] me their produce to the place where My Majesty is, at every season. The foreign land extracts for me everything good that is in it, which it had hidden from other kings. It spread them out **[...] all kinds of precious stones, all kinds of sweet-smelling herbs that grow in Punt, and everything good from the southern land.** Everything that comes before My Majesty through trade is his. I fill his house and repay him for his protection [...] [...] on the battlefield. I will also give offerings, precious goods from all foreign lands as [...] which his strong arm had attacked. He ordered it to me against all foreigners. These courtiers [...] '[...] the Thrones of the Two Lands, the great god of the primordial time, the primeval god who created your beauty. He has given you every land. Lead it for him who knows that you have come forth from him. It is he who guides Your Majesty on the [...] road.' [...] **fear of me in the ends of Asia,** My army cut down the flagpoles on the Cedar-terraces [...] [...] for the monuments of my forefathers, all the gods of Upper and

Lower Egypt. in the harbour [of] Lebanon in the fortress [...] **All the princes of Lebanon [...] the royal ships, to travel south therein, to fetch all kinds of precious goods [...] the southern land, to the palace.** The princes of [...] **The princes of Retjenu dragged these flagpoles with oxen to the harbour, and they came with their tributes to the place where His Majesty was, to the residence in [...] with all good products that were brought as precious goods from the south, [...] charged as tributes of the annual requirements, as all subjects of My Majesty.** What the people said: '[...] [...] the foreigners [...] your might. **Your fame has pervaded the crest of the world.** Your esteem has shaken the hearts of those who attack [...] the people [...] [...] every [...] **who will disrespect your plans.** It is your father who [...] His Majesty was in [...].'

The El Arish Shrine Text

Francis Llewellyn Griffith and Édouard Naville, *The Mound of the Jew and the City of Onias,* London: Kegan Paul, Trentch, Trubner & Co., 1887, pp. 71-73.

Pl. xxiv.1. The majesty of Shu was as a good king of heaven, earth and the underworld, of water and winds, of the primeval waters, of the hills and of the sea, [giving] all regulations upon the throne of his father Ra Harmakhis as triumphant. **Now behold the majesty of Shu was in [his] palace in Memphis: his majesty said** to the great cycle of the nine gods which followed him, 'Come now, **let us proceed to the Eastern [horizon], to my palace in At Nebes, and see our father Ra-Harmakhis in the Eastern horizon**: let us pass? [thither] by the canal (??), let us employ ourselves? in ordering our palace in At Nebes.' Then they did according to all that his majesty decreed: The majesty of Shu [proceeded] to his palace in the House of the Aart. Then were built all the apartments ? of Hat Nebes [like] heaven upon its four supports: then was built the house of Sepd anew for? the majesty of Shu, it is the temple that he loves; [account of] all its arrangements as to the points to which it faced, whether towards the south the north the west or the east: the temples were erected [in] all the [pla]ces where they had been; eight chapels were made on the left, eight on the right, eight in the court? of the Eastern Horizon: This [temple belongeth] to Shu in his name of Sepd lord of the East: the face of each of these chapels was toward its fellow: [they were] the apartments? [of the] great cycle of nine gods, and of the lesser cycle, of the gods who attended on Ra and the gods who attended on Shu: moreover there were built enclosures for Shu in [Hat Nebe]s? surrounding his temple: (now) the face of this temple was toward the east, the sun's rising; and those (deities) who dwelt [in the places of] the temples of each nome dwelt in it, in case? the nome should fall into confusion, let one explain? this arrangement: [the enclosure of Hat?] Nebes reached to Hat Nebes on its North, and its face was toward the South: the temples were on [its] sides and their faces [were] towards the East: a pool was on its South side, a pool on its North side; a great storehouse? of [....] was in front of the temple reaching to Per Art. Now Per Art was of the time of? Ra: the majesty of Shu placed his staff upon the At [... and it became] a sacred locality in At Nebes, its southern face was towards the Per art: gods, goddesses, men, and all flesh (animal creation?) had not entered it [to] see the secrets in the horizon: it (the privilege) was granted in the time of Ra, who made a great wall standing around it of [....] cubits on its four sides, 20 cubits high, 15 cubits thick. As **to the sacred lake in At Nebes** it was [....] cubits [....] of At Nebes: **Shu himself digged it in the time of the majesty of Ra**: its arrangement was not seen nor sealed ? to the [gods – goddesses?] men and flesh: **A circuit was set up on every side of it, of 190 cubits (in length), 110? cubits in breadth** [.... Cubits]in height, 15 cubits in thickness: separating all temples from? it by mysterious and secret work? in [....] Then came the majesty of Shu and raised up At Nebes even as the sky is fixed, and all its temples even as the horizon. **Now it happened that [he] departed [to be enthroned] as king of the gods in At Nebes**, at the time that he ascended? the throne of Harmakhia. **Then the children of the dragon Apep, the evil-doers [of Usheru?] and of the red country came upon the road of At Nebes, invading Egypt at nightfall** .... now these evil-doers came from the Eastern hills [upon] all the roads of At Nebes: then the majesty Shu, the gods who attended Ra and the gods who attended Shu caused [to be fortified?] all the places around At Nebes: these places were since the time of Ra when the majesty of Ra was in At Nebes .... At Nebes they are the mighty walls of Egypt repelling the evil-doers when Apep penetrates? to Egypt: the gods who are in them are the defences of this land, they are the supports of heaven that watch? the .... of the eternal horizon: they are the throne? of Shu in Hat Nebes: those who dwell in the places in At Nebes they raise the land .... Per Sepd: they are the spirits of the East to .... Ra Harmachis they elevate Ra to heaven in the morning upon? the pillars of heaven: they are the possessors of the Eastern Hills: they are the rescuer of Ra from Apep. Account of all the [places] around Hat Nebes together with the gods who are in them: **the Place of the Whirlpool? in At Nebes is a pool upon the East of Hat Nebes in which the majesty of Ra proceeded**. (Another pool is mentioned on the East of Hat Nebes.)

Pl. xxvi. 1,2. The fragments of the inscription show that the list of localities was continued on the left side.

Pl. xxv. (back). '**Now it came to pass that the majesty of Shu obtained the whole land,** none could stand before him, no other god was in the mouth of his soldiers [but sickness came upon him?] .... **confusion seized the eyes?: he made his chapel .... evil fell upon this land, a great disturbance in the palace, disturbed .... those who were of the household of Shu. Then Seb saw [Tefnut] and loved her greatly,** his heart desired her: he wandered over? the earth in search of her great affliction. **The majesty of Shu departed to heaven with his attendants. Tefnut was in the place of her enthronement in Memphis.** Now she proceeded to the royal house of Shu in the time of mid-day: the great cycle of nine gods were upon the path of eternity, the road of his father Ra Harmakhis. **Then the majesty of [Seb met her] he found her in this ? place which is called Pekharti?: he seized her by force: [the palace was in great affliction]. Shu had departed to heaven**: there was no exit from the palace by the space of nine days. **Now these [nine] days were in violence and tempest: none whether god or man could see the face of his fellow. The majesty of Seb came forth appearing? on the throne of his father Shu**: every royal dwelling? did him homage. Then after 75 days **Seb proceeded to the North country**: Shu had flown up to heaven, the great chief of the plain at the head of his city ?? the prince of the hills ... came? **he went not to Heliopolis:** moreover? **certain Asiatics carried his scepter, called Degai,** who live on what the gods abominate; behold he went to the East of

Usher: He entered the house of the Aar the Eastern gate? of At Nebes: he discussed the history of this city with the gods who attended him [and they told him] all that happened when the majesty of Ra was in At Nebes, **the conflicts of king Tum** in this locality, the valour of his majesty Shu in this city, the deeds of Shu in .... the [wonders] of the goddess Ankhet done to Ra when he was with her: the victories of the majesty of Shu, smiting the evil ones, when he placed her (the serpent) upon his brow. Then said the majesty of Seb I also [will place] her upon my head even as my father Shu did. Seb entered Per Aart together with the gods who were with him: **then he stretched forth his hand to take the case in which [Ankhet] was: the snake came forth and breathed its vapour upon the majesty of Seb, confounding him greatly: those who followed him fell dead: his majesty? burned with this venom?** his majesty proceeded to the north of at Nebes with this burning of the uraeus Hert Tep, then his majesty reached the fields of *henna* but [his majesty] was not healed ? then he said to the gods who followed him, 'Come! Let this Aar (cap? or wig?) of Ra be brought here.' [They said to him: 'Nay] let thy majesty go to see its mystery: it will heal his majesty [of that which is?] ... upon thee': behold the majesty of Seb had the Aart placed upon his head in ? the Per Aart and had **made for it a box of real hard stone (or metal), it was hidden in [this?] place**, namely, the Per Aart near the sacred Aart of the majesty of Ra: then was healed this heat in the limbs of the majesty of Seb. **Now years passed after this**, then this Aart of the majesty of Seb was taken [back] to the Per Aart in? the At Nebes: it was carried to the great lake of Per Aart: (the place of the whirlpool ? is its name) to wash it: behold the Aart became a crocodile: when it reached the water it became Sebek in At Nebes.

Now when the majesty of Ra-Harmachis [fought] with the evil-doers in this pool, the Place of the Whirlpool, the evil-doers prevailed not over his majesty. His majesty leapt into the so-called Place of the Whirlpool ? his legs became those of a crocodile, **his head** that of a hawk **with bull's horns upon it: he smote the evil-**

doers in the Place of the Whirlpool ? in the Place of the Sycamore: the Aart of Seb also in its turn did after this sort.

Now the majesty of Seb appeared in the seat of the crocodile gods, of Sebek-Ra, of Shu, of Seb, and of Osiris-Ra, upon the throne of his father Shu as king of the gods of men and all flesh, in heaven, earth and the underworld, water, hills, winds, the ocean and the rocks: his majesty was in his castle of Ruling the Two Lands in the Land of Henna? **his majesty had sent messengers to summon to him the foreigners and Asiatics from their land**. Now the majesty of Seb said to the great circle of nine gods that accompanied him, 'What did my father Shu when first he appeared on the throne of his father Atum, when the majesty of Shu was in his castle in At Nebes.' This cycle of nine gods said to the majesty of Seb: 'When thy father Shu appeared upon the throne of his father Atum, he smote all those who injured his father Atum: he slew the children of Apep: he made all the enemies of his father Ra to shrink. Now after he had given refreshing shade? to the two lands, the gods and the mortals who followed Atem, lord of the Northern? Anu, he brought water to the cities, he ordered the nomes, he raised up the walls of Egypt, he built the temples in the South country and the North': the majesty of Seb said to these gods, 'Tell me the places which were made in the time of the majesty of Ra which he set up over the land: also tell me the nomes which the majesty of Shu formed (lit. built) in his time: I will proclaim ? the places of the time of the majesty of Ra in all the nomes formed by the majesty of [Shu]. For I shall form them anew, I desire to make them in my reign.' They read before the majesty of Shu, out of the hieroglyphs .... myriads of ?? localities proclaimed by the majesty of Ra in all the nomes which the majesty of Shu formed and registered in writing in the time of the majesty of Atum when he was [on earth?] and at the time that Shu ascended to the throne of his father Ra, and at the time that Seb ascended to the throne of his father Shu. Names of? the places themselves ? the nomes according to their names, excepting the nomes formed by the majesty of Ra in his own time. Abu (Elephantine), Nekheb (Eileithyiapolis), Southern

Behud (Apollinopolis Magna), Neshent, Northern? Uas (Diopolis in the Delta), Anu (Helipolis), Ab? Khenit (Silsilis) Makhenu, Per Merit, ... Hef, Anit (Latopolis) Southern An (Hermonthis), Abdu (Abydos), Hat Sekhem (Diospolis parva), Neehit, Per Benu, Hat Desher, Eastern Behud, Met (Aphroditopolis), Ap (Panopolis), Unnu (Hermopolis Magna), ... urt Reqrert (Lycopolis), Aner Tehen, Per Desher, At Red, Khai, Henesuten (Herackleopolis Magna), Ta She (in the Fayoum), Hat Shedi (Crocodilopolis), Bend, Ta Desher?, She ...

Appendix C

Hymn to Ra (Amenhotep III)

Alexandre Moret, *The Nile and the Egyptian Civilization*, Kegan Paul, Trentch, Trubner & Co., 1927, pp. 318-9.

Adoration to Amon, when he rises as Harakhti, from Seth and Horus, Directors of the Works of Amon. They say:

Hail to thee, fair Ra of every day, who dost rise in the morning without ceasing, Khepri, who never tirest of thy labours! Thy rays are on (our) heads, one knows not how. Gold does not shine like thy rays. Thou art Phtah, (for) thou dost model thy own flesh; thou art thy own creator, not having been created. Unique in kind, he ranges over Eternity, on the ways, with the millions (of men) whom he leads. Thy brightness is as the brightness of the sky; thy colour shines more than its colour. When thou sailest in the sky, all faces watch thee; when thou walkest in the mysterious region (*iment*), the faces pray to thee. ... When thou givest thyself (to men) in the morning, they prosper; when thou sailest in all thy majesty, the day passes quickly; (and yet) thou dost go thy road, millions, hundreds of thousands of *itru* long. The measure of thy day depends on thee. ... Thou dost accomplish the hours of the night in the same way; they hasten for thee, and thou dost not halt in thy labours. All eyes look at thee; but thy labours do not cease when thou dost rest (at night). Thou wakest to rise, in the morning, and thy brightness opens the eyes of the beasts. When thou dost rest in Manu (the Mountain of the West), then they sleep as if they were dead. Hail to thee, Disk (Aten) of the Day, who dost create mortals and make them live, great Falcon with the feathers of many colours ... who creates himself, and is not begotten, Horus the Elder (dwelling) in the heart of Nut (the Sky), to whom acclamations are made alike when he rises and when he sets; who models the creatures of the soil, Khnum and Amon of men; who conquers the Two Lands, from the great to the small, august mother of gods and men, craftsman great-souled and unwearying in endless creation; valiant shepherd who pastures his flock, who is their fold and makes them live. ... He is heat when he wills and coolness when he wills; he wearies bodies, and he embraces them (to revive them). Every land prays when he rises every day, to adore him.

Appendix D

The Great Hymn to the Aten

Pritchard, James B. (ed.); *The Ancient Near East.* © 1958 Princeton University Press, 1986 renewed PUP; pp. 227-230. Reprinted by permission of Princeton University Press.

Praise of Re Har-akhti, Rejoicing on the Horizon, in His Name as Shu Who Is in the Aton-disc, living forever and ever; the living great Aton who is in jubilee, lord of all that the Aton encircles, lord of heaven, lord of earth, lord of the House of Aton in Akhet-Aton; (and praise of) the King of Upper and Lower Egypt, who lives on truth, the Lord of the Two Lands: Nefer-kheperu-Re Wa-en-Re; the Son of Re, who lives on truth, the Lord of Diadems: Akh-en-Aton, long in his lifetime; (and praise of) the Chief Wife of the King, his beloved, the Lady of the Two Lands: Nefer-neferu-Aton Nefert-iti, living, healthy, and youthful forever and ever; (by) the Fan-Bearer on the Right Hand of the King ... Eye.

He says: **Thou appearest beautifully on the horizon of heaven,**
Thou living Aton, the beginning of life!
When thou art risen on the eastern horizon,
Thou hast filled every land with thy beauty.
Thou art gracious, great, glistening, and high over every land;
Thy rays encompass the lands to the limit of all that thou hast made:
As thou art Re, thou reachest to the end of them;
(Thou) subduest them (for) thy beloved son.
Though thou art far away, **thy rays are on earth;**
Though thou art in their faces, no one knows thy going.

When thou settest in the western horizon,
The land is in darkness, in the manner of death.
They sleep in a room, with heads wrapped up,
Nor sees one eye the other.
All their goods which are under their heads might be stolen,
(But) they would not perceive (it).
Every lion is come forth from his den;
All creeping things, they sting.
Darkness is a shroud, and the earth is in stillness,
For he who made them rests in his horizon.

At daybreak, when thou arisest on the horizon,
When thou shinest as the Aton by day,
Thou drivest away the darkness and givest thy rays.
The Two Lands are in festivity every day,
Awake and standing upon (their) feet,
For thou hast raised them up.
Washing their bodies, taking (their) clothing,
Their arms are (raised) in praise at thy appearance.
All the world, they do their work.

All beasts are content with their pasturage;
Trees and plants are flourishing.
The birds which fly from their nests,
Their wings are (stretched out) in praise to thy ka.
All beasts spring upon (their) feet.
Whatever flies and alights,
They live when thou hast risen (for) them.
The ships are sailing north and south as well,
For every way is open at thy appearance.
The fish in the river dart before thy face;
Thy rays are in the midst of the great green sea.
Creator of seed in women,
Thou who makest fluid into man,

Who maintainest the son in the womb of his mother,
Who soothest him with that which stills his weeping,
Thou nurse (even) in the womb,
Who givest breath to sustain all that he has made!
When he descends from the womb to breathe
On the day when he is born,
Thou openest his mouth completely,
Thou suppliest his necessities.
When the chick in the egg speaks within the shell,
Thou givest him breath within it to maintain him.
When thou hast made him his fulfillment within the egg, to break it,
He comes forth from the egg to speak at his completed (time);
He walks upon his legs when he comes forth from it.

How manifold it is, what thou hast made!
They are hidden from the face (of man).
O sole god, like whom there is no other!
Thou didst create the world according to thy desire,
Whilst thou wert alone: **All men, cattle, and wild beasts,**
Whatever is on earth, going upon (its) feet,
And what is on high, flying with its wings.

The countries of Syria and Nubia, the land of Egypt,
Thou settest every man in his place,
Thou suppliest their necessities:
Everyone has his food, and his time of life is reckoned.
Their tongues are separate in speech,
And their natures as well;
Their skins are distinguished,
As thou distinguishest the foreign peoples.
Thou makest a Nile in the underworld,
Thou bringest forth as thou desirest
To maintain the people (of Egypt)

According as thou madest them for thyself,
The lord of all of them, wearying (himself) with them,
The lord of every land, rising for them,
The Aton of the day, great of majesty.

All distant foreign countries, thou makest their life (also),
For thou hast set a Nile in heaven,
That it may descend for them and make waves upon the
mountains,
Like the great green sea,
To water their fields in their towns.
How effective they are, thy plans, O lord of eternity!
The Nile in heaven, it is for the foreign peoples
And **for the beasts of every desert** that go upon (their) feet;
(While the true) Nile comes from the underworld for Egypt.

Thy rays suckle every meadow.
When thou risest, they live, they grow for thee.
Thou makest the seasons in order to rear all that thou hast made,
The winter to cool them,
And the heat that they may taste thee.
Thou hast made the distant sky in order to rise therein,
In order to see all that thou dost make.
Whilst thou wert alone,
Rising in thy form as the living Aton,
Appearing, shining, withdrawing or approaching,
Thou madest millions of forms of thyself alone.
Cities, towns, fields, road, and river –
Every eye beholds thee over against them,
For thou art the Aton of the day over the earth....

Thou are in my heart,
And there is no other that knows thee
Save thy son Nefer-kheperu-Re Wa-en-Re,

For thou hast made him well-versed in thy plans and in thy
strength.

The world came into being by thy hand,
According as thou hast made them.
When thou hast risen they live,
When thou settest they die.
Thou art lifetime thy own self,
For one lives (only) through thee.
Eyes are (fixed) on beauty until thou settest.
All work is laid aside when thou settest in the west.
(But) when (thou) risest (again),
[Everything is] made to flourish for the king, ...
Since thou didst found the earth
And raise them up for thy son,
Who came forth from thy body: the King of Upper and Lower
Egypt, ... Ak-en-Aton, ... and the Chief Wife of the King ... Nefert-
iti, living and youthful forever and ever.

Appendix E

The Admonitions of Ipuwer

Pritchard, James B.; *Ancient Near Eastern Texts Relating to the Old Testament.* © 1950 Princeton University Press, 1978 renewed, 2nd Edition 1955, 1983 renewed PUP; 1969, pp. 441-444. Reprinted by permission of Princeton University Press.

(i I) ... Door[keepers] say: 'Let us go and plunder.

'...The laundryman refuses to carry his load... **Bird[catchers] have marshaled the battle array... [Men of] the Delta marshes carry shields**. ... (5) ... A man regards his son as his enemy.

... A man of character goes in mourning because of what has happened in the land. ... **Foreigners have become people everywhere**...

(ii 2)... 'Why really, the [face] is pale. The bowman is ready. **Robbery is everywhere**. There is no man of yesterday. ...

Why really, the Nile is in flood, (but) no one plows for himself, (because) every man says: 'We do not know what may happen throughout the land!'

Why really, women are dried up, and none can conceive. Khnum cannot fashion (mortals) because of the state of the land.

Why really, **poor men have become the possessors of treasures. He who could not make himself a pair of sandals is (now) the possessor of riches**. ...

Why really, many dead are buried in the river. The stream is a tomb, and the embalming-place has really become the stream.

Why really, **nobles are in lamentation, while poor men have joy**. Every town says: 'Let us banish many from us.

'Why really,... dirt is throughout the land. There are really none (whose) clothes are white in these times.

Why really, the land spins around as a potter's wheel does. The robber is (now) the possessor of riches...

(10) Why really, **the River is blood. If one drinks of it, one rejects (it) as human and thirsts for water**.

Why really, **doors, columns, and floor planks are burned up, (but) the flooring of the palace – life, prosperity, health! – (still) remains firm**. ...

Why really, crocodiles [sink] down because of what they have carried off, (for) men go to them of their own accord. ...

(iii 1) [Why] really, the desert is (spread) throughout the land. **The nomes are destroyed. Barbarians from outside have come to Egypt. ... There are really no people anywhere**. ... (5) ...

Why really, **they who built [pyramids, have become] farmers. They who were in the ship of the god are charged with forced [labor]**. No one really sails north to [Byb]los today. What shall we do for cedar for our mummies? Priests were buried with their produce and [nobles] were embalmed with the oil thereof as far away as Keftiu. (But) they come no (longer). Gold is lacking. ... How important it (now) seems when the oasis-people come carrying their festival provisions: reed-mats, ... fresh redmet-plants, (10)... of birds, and...

Why really, Elephantine, the Thinite nome, and the [shrine] of Upper Egypt **do not pay taxes because of [civil] war**... What is a treasury without its revenues for? The heart of the king (must) indeed be glad when truth comes to him!' But really, every foreign country [comes]! Such is our welfare! What can we do about it? Going to ruin!

Why really, laughter had disappeared, and is [no longer] made. It is wailing that pervades the land, mixed with lamentation...

(iv 1)... Why really, **the children of nobles are dashed against the walls**. The (once) prayed-for children are (now) laid out on the high ground... (5) ...

Why really, the entire Delta marshland will no (longer) be hidden: the confidence of the Northland is (now) a beaten path. What is it that one could do?

Behold, it is in the hands of those who did not know it, as well as those who knew it; **foreigners are (now) skilled in the work of the Delta**... (10) ...

Why really, all maid-servants make free with their tongues. When their mistresses speak, it is burdensome to the servants. ...

(v 10)... Why really, the ways [are not] guarded roads. Men sit in the bushes until the benighted (traveler) comes, to take away his burden and steal what is on him. He is presented with the blows of a stick and slain wrongfully. ... Ah, would that it were the end of men, no conception, no (vi 1) birth! Then the earth would cease from noise, without wrangling!...

Why really, **grain has perished on every side**... Everybody says: 'There is nothing!' The **storchouse is stripped bare; its keeper is stretched out on the ground**. ...(5) ... Ah, would that I had raised my voice at that time - it might save me from the suffering in which I am!

Why really, the writings of the augurs enclosure are read. **The place of secrets which was (so formerly) is (now) laid bare.**

Why really, magic is exposed. Go-spells and enfold-spells are made ineffectual because they are repeated by (ordinary) people.

Why really, (public) offices are open, and their reports are read. **Serfs have become the owners of serfs**...

Why really, **the writings of the scribes of the mat have been removed**. The grain-sustenance of Egypt is (now) a come-and-get-it.

Why really, the laws (10) of the enclosure are put out of doors. Men actually walk on them in the highways. Poor men tear them up in the streets. ...

Why really, the children of nobles are abandoned in the streets. He who knows says: 'Yes, (it is so)!' The fool says: 'No, (it is not)!' It is fair in the sight of him who knows it not. ...

(vii 1). Behold now, the fire has mounted up on high. Its flame goes forth against the enemies of the land.

Behold now, **something has been done which never happened for a long time: the king has been taken away by poor men.**

Behold, he who was buried as a falcon (now lies) on a (mere) bier. What the pyramid hid has become empty.

Behold now, **it has come to a point where the land is despoiled of the kingship by a few irresponsible men.**

Behold now, **it has come to a point where (men) rebel against the uraeus**, the ... of Re, which makes the Two Lands peaceful.

Behold, the secret of the land, whose limits are unknown(able), is laid bare. **The Residence (may) be razed within an hour.** ... (5) ...

Behold, the (guardian-) serpent is taken from her hole. The secrets of the Kings of Upper- and Lower Egypt are laid bare. ... (10) ...

Behold, **nobles' ladies are (now) gleaners, and nobles are in the workhouse. (But) he who never (even) slept on a plank is (now) the owner of a bed.** ...

Behold, **the owners of robes are (now) in rags. (But) he who never wove for himself is (now) the owner of fine linen.** ...

Behold, he who knew not the lyre is (now) the owner of a harp. He who never sang for himself (now) praises the goddess of music. ... (viii 1) ...

Behold, the bald-headed man who had no oil has become the owner of jars of sweet myrrh.

(5) Behold, **she who had not (even) a box is (now) the owner of a trunk. She who looked at her face in the water is (now) the owner of a mirror**.... (10) ...

Behold, the king's men trash around among the cattle of destitute. ...

Behold, the king's men trash around among geese, which are presented (10) the gods instead of oxen.

... (ix 1) ...

Behold, **nobles' ladies are growing hungry, (but) the king's men are sated with what they have done.**

Behold, not an office is in its (proper) place, like a stampeded herd which has no herdsman.

Behold, cattle are (left) free-wandering, (for) there is no one to take care of them. Every man takes for himself and brands (them) with his name...

Behold, he who had no grain is (now) the owner of granaries. (5) He who had to get a loan for himself (now) issues it. ... (x 1)...

So Lower-Egypt weeps. The storehouse of the king is a (mere) come-and-get-it for everybody, and the entire palace is without its taxes. To it (should belong) barley, emmer, birds, and fish. To it (should belong) white cloth, fine linen, metal, and (5) ointment. To it (should belong) rug, mat, [flowers], palanquin, and every good revenue. ...

Remember (xi 1)... how fumigation is made with incense, how water is offered from a jar in the early morning.

Remember fattened ro-geese, terep-geese, and sat-geese, how the divine offerings are made to the gods.

Remember how natron is chewed and how white bread is prepared by a man on the day of moistening the head.

Remember how flagstaffs are set up and a stela is carved, while a priest purifies the temples and the house of god is whitewashed like milk; how the fragrance of the horizon is made sweet, and how offering-bread is established.

Remember how (ritual) regulations are adhered to, how (religious) dates are distributed, how (5) one who has been inducted into priestly service may be removed for personal weakness – that is, it was carried out wrongfully. ...

... It shall come that he brings coolness upon the heart.

(xii 1) Men shall say: 'He is the herdsman of all men. Evil is not in his heart. Though his herds may be small, still he has spent the day caring for them.'...

Would that he might perceive their character from the (very first generation! Then he would smite down evil; he would stretch forth the arm against it; he would destroy the seed thereof and their inheritance. ...(5)... (But) there is no pilot in their hour. Where is he today? Is he then sleeping? Behold, the glory thereof cannot be seen. ..(10)...

... Authority, Perception, and Justice are with thee, (but) it is confusion which thou wouldst set throughout the land, together with the noise of contention. Behold, one thrusts against another. Men conform to that which thou hast commanded. If three men go along a road, they are found to be two men; it is the greater number that kills the lesser. Does then the herdsman love death? So then thou will command that

(xiii 1) a reply be made: 'It is because one man loves and another hates. That is, their forms are few everywhere.' This really means that thou hast acted to bring such (a situation) into being, and thou hast spoken lies. ...

All these years are civil strife. A man may be slain on his (own) roof, while he is on the watch in his boundary house. Is he brave and saves himself? – that means that he will live. ...(5)...

Would that thou mightest taste of some of the oppressions thereof! Then thou wouldst say:...

...(10)... But it is still good when the hands of men construct pyramids, when canals are dug, and when groves of trees are made for the gods.

But it is still good when men are drunken, when they drink miyet and their hearts are happy.

But it is still good when shouting is in the mouths (of men), when the notables of the districts are standing and watching the shouting

(xiv 1) from their houses, clothed in a cloak, purified already and firm bellied... (10)...

'...None can be found who will stand in their places.

...Every man fights for his sister, and he protects his own person. Is (it) the Nubians? Then we shall make our (own) protection. Fighting police will hold off the barbarians. Is it the Libyans? Then we shall turn away. The Madjoi fortunately are with Egypt. How is it that every man kills his brother? **The military classes (xv 1) which we marshal for ourselves have become barbarians, beginning to destroy that from which they took their being and to show the Asiatics the state of land. And yet all the foreigners are afraid of them.** ...(10)...'

That which Ipuwer said, when he answered the majesty of the All-Lord: '...To be ignorant of it is something pleasant to the heart. Thou hast done what is good in their hearts, for) thou hast kept people alive thereby. (But still) they cover up (xvi 1) their faces for fear of the morrow.'

'Once upon a time there was a man who was old and in the presence of his salvation, while his son was (still) a child, without understanding...'

Appendix F. Manetho King Lists

Josephus AA	Theophilus A	Theophilus B	Syncellus (Africanus)	Syncellus (Eusebius)
Tethmosis 25	Tethmosis 25	Amasis 25	Amos	Amosis 25
Chebron 13	Chebron 13	Chebron 13	Chebros 13	Chebron 13
Amenophis 21	Amenophis 21	Amenophis 21	Amenophthis 24	Ammenophis 21
Amessis 22	Amesse 21	Amessa 21	Amensis 22	
Mephres 13	Mephres 13	Mephres 13	Misaphris 13	Miphres 12
Mephramuthosis 26	Mephrammuthosis 21	Methramuthosis 21	Misphragmuthosis 26	Misphragmuthosis 26
Thummosis 10	Tuthmoses 10	Tythmoses 10	Tuthmosis 9	Tuthmosis 9
Amenophis 31	Amenophis 31	Damphenophis 19	Amenophis 31	Amenophis 31
Orus 36	Orus 36	Orus 35	Orus 37	Orus 36
Acencheres 12	Acencheres 12	Orus' daughter 10	Acherres 32	Achencherses 12
Rathotis 9	Rathotis 9	Mercheres 12	Rathos 6	
Acencheres 12	Acencheres 12		Chebres 12	Acherres 8
Acencheres 12	Acencheres 12		Acherres 12	Cherres 15
Harmais 4	Harmais 4	Armais 30	Armais 5	Armais 5
Ramesses 1	Ramesses 1	Messes son of Miammus 6	Ramesses 1	Ramesses (Aegyptus) 68
Harmesses Miamun 66	Ramesses Miamun 66	Rameses 1		
Amenophis 19	Amenophis 19	Amenophis 19	Amenophath 19	Ammenophis 40
Sethos (Ramesses) 59	Sethos (Ramesses) 10	Thoessus & Rameses 10		

Note: Months rounded off to nearest year.

Josephus: Against Apion; Theophilus A: *Manetho with an English Translation*, W.G. Waddell, Harvard University Press, 1964, pp. 109-111;

Theophilus B: *Theophilus to Autolycus*, Book III, Chapter XX [Alexander Roberts and James Donaldson, *The Writings of Tatian and Theophilus and the Clementine Recognitions: Ante Nicene Christian Library Translations of the Fathers Down to AD 325*. Part Three, 1867, Kessinger Publishing's Rare Reprints, p. 123];

Syncellus (Africanus): Syncellus quoting Africanus, *Manetho with an English Translation*, Waddell, p. 111-113;

Syncellus (Eusebius) : Syncellus quoting Eusebius, *Manetho with an English Translation*, Waddell, p. 115-116.

Appendix G

The Prophecy of Neferti

Pritchard, James B.; *Ancient Near Eastern Texts Relating to the Old Testament.* © 1950 Princeton University Press, 1978 renewed, 2nd Edition 1955, 1983 renewed PUP; 1969, pp. 444-446. Reprinted by permission of Princeton University Press.

Now IT HAPPENED THAT the majesty of the King of Upper and Lower Egypt: Snefru, the triumphant, was the beneficent king in this entire land. On one of these days it happened that the official council of the Residence City entered into the Great House-life, [prosperity], health! – to offer greeting. Then they went out, that they might offer greetings (elsewhere), according to their daily procedure. Then his majesty – life, prosperity, health! – said to the seal-bearer who was at his side: 'Go and bring me (back) the official council of the Residence City, which has gone forth hence to offer greetings on this [day].' (Thereupon they) were ushered in to him immediately. Then they were on their bellies in the presence of his majesty a second time.

Then his majesty – life, prosperity, health! – said to them: '(My) people, behold, I have caused you to be called to have you seek out for me a son of yours who is wise, or a brother of yours who is competent, or a friend of yours who has performed a good deed, one who may say to me a few fine words or choice speeches, at the hearing of which my [majesty] may be entertained.'

Then they put (themselves) upon their bellies in the presence of his majesty – life, prosperity, health! – once more. THEN THEY SAID BEFORE his majesty- life, prosperity, health!: 'A great lector-priest of Baster,' O Sovereign, our lord, whose name is Nefer-rohu – he is a commoner valiant [with] his arm, a scribe competent with his fingers; he is a man of rank, who has more property than any peer of his. Would that he [might be permitted] to see his majesty!' Then his majesty – life, prosperity, health! – said: 'Go and [bring] him to me!'

Then he was ushered in to him immediately. Then he was on his belly in the presence of his majesty – life, prosperity, health! Then his majesty – life, prosperity, health! – said: 'Come, pray, Nefer-rohu, my friend, that thou mayest say to me a few fine words or choice speeches, at the hearing of which my majesty may be entertained!' Then the lector-priest Nefer-rohu said: 'Of what has (already) happened or of what is going to happen, O Sovereign – life, prosperity, health! – [my] lord?' Then his majesty – life, prosperity, health! – said: 'Rather of what is going to happen. If it has taken place by today, pass it [by].' Then he stretched forth his hand for the box of writing equipment; then he drew forth a scroll of papyrus and a palette; thereupon he put (it) into writing.

What the lector-[priest] Nefer-rohu said, that wise man of the east, he who belonged to Bastet at her appearances, that child of the Heliopolitan nome. AS HE BROODED over what (was to) happen in the land, as he called to mind the state of the east, **when the Asiatics would move about with their strong arms**, would disturb the hearts [of] those who are at the harvest, and would take away the spans of cattle at the plowing. He said:

Bestir thyself, O my heart; as thou bewailest this land in which thou didst begin! To be silent is repression. Behold, there is something about which men speak as terrifying, for, behold, the great man is a thing passed away (in the land) where thou didst begin. BE NOT LAX; BEHOLD, IT is before thy face! Mayest thou rise up against what is before thee, for, behold, although great men are concerned with the land, what has been done is as what is not done. Re must begin the foundation (of the earth over again). **The land is completely perished**, (so that) no remainder exists, (so that) not (even) the black of the nail survives from what was fated.

THIS LAND IS (SO) DAMAGED (that) there is no one who is concerned with it, no one who speaks, no one who weeps. How is this land? **The sun disc is covered over. It will not shine (so that) people may see. No one can live when clouds cover over (the sun). Then everybody is deaf for lack of it.**

I shall speak of what is before my face; I cannot foretell what has not (yet) come.

THE RIVERS of Egypt are empty, (so that) the water is crossed on foot. Men seek for water for the ships to sail on it. Its course is [become] a sandbank. The sandbank is against the flood; the place of water is against the [flood] – (both) the place of water and the sandbank. The south wind will oppose the north wind; the skies are no (longer) in a single wind. **A foreign bird will be born in the marshes of the Northland. It has made a nest beside men, and people have let it approach through want of it.'** DAMAGED INDEED ARE THOSE good things, those fish-ponds, (where there were) those who clean fish, overflowing with fish and fowl. Everything good is disappeared, **and the land is prostrate because of woes from that food, the Asiatics who are throughout the land.**

Foes have arisen in the east, and Asiatics have come down into Egypt .... No protector will listen .... Men will enter into the fortresses. Sleep will be banished from my eyes, as I spend the night wakeful. THE WILD BEASTS OF THE DESERT WILL drink at the rivers of Egypt and be at their ease on their banks for lack of someone to scare them away.

This land is helter-skelter, and no one knows the result which will come about, which is hidden from speech, sight, or hearing. The face is deaf, for silence confronts. I show thee the land topsy-turvy. That which never happened has happened. Men will take up weapons of warfare, (so that) the land lives in confusion. MEN WILL MAKE ARROWS of metal, beg for the bread of blood, and laugh with the laughter of sickness. There is no one who weeps because of death; there is no one who spends the night fasting because of death; (but) a man's heart pursues himself (alone). (Dishevelled) mourning is no (longer) carried out today, (for) the heart is completely separated from it. A man will sit still while crooking his back while one man kills another. I show thee the son as a foe, the brother as an enemy, and a man killing his (own) father.

EVERY MOUTH IS FULL OF 'LOVE ME!', AND everything GOOD has disappeared. The land is perished, (as though) laws were destined for it: the damaging of what had been done, the emptiness of what had been found, and the doing of what had not been done. Men take a man's property away from him, **and it is given to him who is from outside**. I show thee the possessor in need and the outsider satisfied. He who never filled for himself (now) empties. Men will give something (simply) out of hate, in order to silence the mouth that speaks. If a statement is answered, an arm goes out with a stick, and men speak with: 'Kill him!' THE UTTERANCE OF SPEECH IN THE HEART is like a fire. Men cannot suffer what issues from a man's mouth.

The land is diminished, (but) **its administrators are many; bare, (but) its taxes are great**; little in grain, (but) the measure is large, and it is measured to over-flowing.

Re separates himself (from) mankind. If he shines forth, then the hour exists. **No one knows when midday falls, for his shadow cannot be distinguished**. There is no one bright of face when seeing [him]; the eyes are not moist with water, **when he is in the sky like the moon**. His prescribed time does not fail. His rays are indeed in (men's) faces in his former way.

I SHOW THEE THE LAND TOPSY-TURVY. The weak of arm is (now) the possessor of an arm. Men salute (respectfully) him who (formerly) saluted. I show thee the undermost on top, turned about in proportion to the turning about of my belly. Men live in the necropolis. The poor man will make wealth …. It is the paupers that will be eating bread, while the servants jubilate. The Heliopolitan nome, the birthplace of every god, will no (longer) be on earth.

(THEN) IT IS THAT A KING WILL COME, BELONGING TO THE SOUTH, Ameni, the triumphant, his name. He is the son of a woman of the land of Nubia; he is born in Upper Egypt. He will take the [White] Crown; he will wear the Red Crown; he will unite the

Two Mighty Ones; he will satisfy the Two Lords' with what they desire. The encircler-of-the-fields (will be) in his grasp, the oar ...

REJOICE, ye people of his time! The son of a man will make his name forever and ever. They who incline toward evil and who plot rebellion have subdued their speech for fear of him. **The Asiatics will fall to his sword, and the Libyans will fall to his flame**. The rebels belong to his wrath, and the treacherous of heart to the awe of him. The uraeus-serpent which is on his brow stills for him the treacherous of heart.

THERE WILL BE BUILT the Wall of the Ruler – life, prosperity, health! – and the Asiatics will not be permitted to come down into Egypt that they might beg for water in the customary manner, in order to let their beasts drink. And justice will come into its place, while wrongdoing is driven out. Rejoice, he who may behold (this) and who may be in the service of the king!

The learned man will pour out water for me,' when he sees what I have spoken come to pass. IT HAS COME (TO ITS END) in [success], by the Scribe ...

Appendix H

The Plague Prayers of Mursilis

Pritchard, James B.; *Ancient Near Eastern Texts Relating to the Old Testament*. © 1950 Princeton University Press, 1978 renewed, 2nd Edition 1955, 1983 renewed PUP; 1969, pp. 394-396. Reprinted by permission of Princeton University Press.

1. Hattian Storm-god, my lord, and ye, Hattian gods, my lords! Mursilis, the great king, your servant, has sent me (with the order:) Go! To the Hattian Storm-god, my lord, and to the gods, my lords, speak as follows:

What is this that ye have done? A plague ye have let into the land. The Hatti land has been cruelly afflicted by the plague. For twenty years now men have been dying in my father's days, in my brother's days, and in mine own since I have become the priest of the gods. When men are dying in the Hatti land like this, the plague is in no wise over. As for me, the agony of my heart and the anguish of my soul I cannot endure any more,

2. When I celebrated festivals, I worshiped all the gods, I never preferred one temple to another. The matter of the plague I have laid in prayer before all the gods making vows to them (and saying) : **'Hearken to me, ye gods, my lords! Drive ye forth the plague from the Hatti land! The reason for which people are dying in the Hatti land – either let it be established by an omen, or let me see it in a dream, or let a prophet declare it!' But the gods did not hearken to me and the plague got no better in the Hatti land. The Hatti land was cruelly afflicted.**

3. **The few people who were left to give sacrificial loaves and libations were dying too.** Matters again got too much for me. So I made the anger of the gods the subject of an oracle. I learnt of two ancient tablets. The first tablet dealt with the offerings to the river

Mala. The old kings had regularly presented offerings to the river Mala. But now a plague has been rampant in the Hatti land since the days of my father, and we have never performed the offerings to the river Mala.

4. The second tablet concerned Kurustama. When the Hattian Storm-god had brought people of Kurustama to the country of Egypt and had made an agreement concerning them with the Hattians so that they were under oath to the Hattian Storm-god – although the Hattians as well as the Egyptians were under oath to the Hattian Storm-god, the Hattians ignored their obligations; the Hattians promptly broke the oath of the gods. **My father sent foot soldiers and charioteers who attacked the country of Amka, Egyptian territory**. Again he sent troops, and again they attacked it. When the Egyptians became frightened, **they asked outright for one of his sons to (take over) the kingship. But when my father gave them one of his sons, they killed him as they led him there**. My father let his anger run away with him, he went to war against Egypt and attacked Egypt. He smote the foot soldiers and the charioteers of the country of Egypt. The Hattian Storm-god, my lord, by his decision even then let my father prevail; he vanquished and smote the foot soldiers and the charioteers of the country of Egypt. **But when they brought back to the Hatti land the prisoners which they had taken a plague broke out among the prisoners and they began to die.**

5. **When they moved the prisoners to the Hatti land, these prisoners carried the plague into the Hatti land. From that day on people have been dying in the Hatti land**. Now, when I found that tablet dealing with the country of Egypt, I made the matter the subject of an oracle of the god (and asked): 'Those arrangements which were made by the Hattian Storm-god – namely that the Egyptians and the Hattians as well were put under oath by the Hattian Storm-god, that the Damnassaras deities were present in the temple of the Hattian Storm-god, and that the Hattians promptly broke their word – has this perhaps become the cause of the anger of the Hattian Storm-god, my lord?' And (so) it was established.

6. Because of the plague, I made the offerings to the river Mala the subject of an oracle also. And in that matter too it was established that I should have to account for myself before the Hattian Storm-god. See now! I have admitted my guilt before the Storm-god (and said): 'It is so. We have done it.' I know for certain that the offence was not committed in my days, that it was committed in the days of my father .... But, since the Hattian Storm-god is angry for that reason and people are dying in the Hatti land, I am (nevertheless) making the offerings to the Hattian Storm-god, my lord, on that account.

7. **Because I humble myself and cry for mercy**, hearken to me, Hattian Storm-god, my lord! Let the plague stop in the Hatti land!

8. The reasons for the plague that were established when I made the matter the subject of a series of oracles, these have I removed. I have made [ample] restitution. The matter of the (broken) oath which was established (as a cause) in connection with the plague, offerings for those oaths I have made to the Hattian Storm-god, my lord. I have also made (offerings) [to the other gods]. The offerings have been presented to thee, Hattian Storm-god, my lord; the offerings have been presented to them too. (As for) the offerings to the river Mala that were established (as a cause) in connection with the plague – since I am now on my way to the river Mala, acquit me of that offering to the river Mala, O Hattian Storm-god my lord, and ye gods, my lords! The offering to the river Mala I promise to make, I promise to complete it properly. The reason for which I make it – namely the plague – O gods, my lords, take pity on me and let that plague abate in the Hatti land!

9. Hattian Storm-god, my lord, (and) ye gods, my lords! It is only too true that man is sinful. My father sinned and transgressed against the word of the Hattian Storm-god, my lord. But I have not sinned in any respect. **It is only too true, however, that the father's sin falls upon the son. So, my father's sin has fallen upon me.** Now, I have confessed before the Hattian Storm-god, my lord, and before the gods, my lords (admitting): 'It is true, we have done it.'

And because I have confessed my father's sin, let the soul of the Hattian Storm-god, my lord, and (those) of the gods, my lords, be again pacified! Take pity on me and drive the plague out of the Hatti land! Suffer not to die the few who are still left to offer sacrificial loaves and libations!

10. See! I lay the matter of the plague before the Hattian Storm-god, my lord. Hearken to me, Hattian Storm-god, and save my life! This is of what I [have to remind] thee: The bird takes refuge in (its) nest, and the nest saves its life. Again: if anything becomes too much for a servant, he appeals to his lord. His lord hears him and takes pity on him. Whatever had become too much for him, he sets right for him. Again: if the servant has incurred a guilt, but confesses his guilt to his lord, his lord may do with him whatever he pleases. But, because (the servant) has confessed his guilt to his lord, his lord's soul is pacified, and his lord will not punish that servant. I have now confessed my father's sin. It is only too true, I have done it. If there is to be restitution, it seems clear that with all the gifts that have already been given because of this plague, with all the prisoners that have been brought home, in short with all the restitution that Hattusa has made because of the plague, it has already made restitution twentyfold. And yet the soul of the Hattian Storm-god, my lord, and of the (other) gods, my lords, is not pacified. But, if ye demand from me additional restitution, tell me of it in a dream and I will give it to you.

11. See! I am praying to thee, Hattian Storm-god, my lord. So save my life! If indeed it is for those reasons which I have mentioned that people are dying, – as soon as I set them right, let those that are still able to give sacrificial loaves and libations die no longer! If, on the other hand, people are dying for some other reason, either let me see it in a dream, or let it be found out by an oracle, or let a prophet declare it, or let all the priests find out by incubation whatever I suggest to them. Hattian Storm-god, my lord, save my life! Let the gods, my lords, prove their divine power! Let someone see it in a dream! For whatever reason people are dying, let that be found out!

... Hattian Storm-god, my lord, save my life! Let this plague abate again in the Hatti land!

Additional text as translated by O.R. Gurney,

What is this, O gods, that ye have done? **A plague ye have let into the land. The Hatti land, all of it, is dying; so no one prepares sacrificial loaves and libations for you. The plowmen who used to work the fields of the god are dead**; so no one works or reaps the fields of the god at all. **The grinding women who used to make the sacrificial loaves for the gods are dead**; so they do not make the sacrificial loaves any longer. From whatever corral (or) sheepfold they used to select the sacrifices of sheep and cattle, **the cowherds and the shepherds are dead** and the corral [and the sheepfold are empty]. So it comes to pass that the sacrificial loaves (and) libations, and the offerings of animals have stopped. And ye, O gods, come on this day and hold us responsible. Man has lost his wits, and there is nothing that we do aright. O gods, whatever sin you behold, either let a prophet rise and declare it, or let the sibyls or the priests learn about it by incubation, or let man see it in a dream! ... O gods, take ye pity again on the Hatti land! On the one hand it is afflicted with a plague, on the other hand it is afflicted with hostility. The protectorates beyond the frontier, (namely) the Mitanni land (and) the Arzawa land, each one has rebelled; they do not acknowledge the gods and have broken the oaths of the gods. They persist in acting maliciously against the Hatti land, and the temples (?) of the gods they seek to despoil. Let the gods take an interest therein again! **Send ye the plague, hostility, famine (and) evil fever into the Mitanni land and the Arzawa land!** Rested are the rebellious countries, but the Hatti land is a weary lane. Unhitch the weary, but the rested harness!

Moreover, those countries which belong to the Ham land, (namely) the Kashkean country (they are swine-herds and weavers of linen), also the country Arawanna, the country of Kalasma, the

Lukka country, the country of Pitassa – these lands have also renounced the Sun-goddess of Arinna. They cast off their tributes and began to attack the Hatti land in their turn. In olden days the Hatti land with the help of the Sun-goddess of Arinna used to take on the surrounding countries like a lion. Moreover, cities like Halba (and) Babylon that it would destroy – from all such countries they took goods, silver (and) gold, and their gods placed them before the Sun-goddess of Arinna.

But now all the surrounding countries have begun attack the Hatti land. Let it again become a matter of concern to the Sun-goddess of Arinna! O god, bring not thy name into disrepute!

Whatever rage (or) anger the gods may fed, whosoever may not have been reverent toward the gods, – let not the good perish with the wicked! If it is one town, or one [house], or one man, O gods, let that one perish alone! Look ye upon the Hatti land with favorable eyes, **but the evil plague give to [those other] countries!**

Appendix I

The History of the Queen of Sheba

S. Baring-Gould, *Legends of Old Testament Characters, from Talmud and Other Sources*, London and New York: Macmillan and Co., 1871, pp. 343-349.

He [Solomon] called to the eagle, and bade it go through the roll-call of the birds, and ascertain which was absent. The eagle obeyed, and found that the peewit was missing. ... Soar aloft! exclaimed Solomon to the eagle, and seek me this runaway... Then the eagle brought the culprit before the king ... the bird exclaimed ... I bring thee news of a land and a queen of which thou hast not even heard the name – the land of Sheba, and the queen, Balkis ... **who commands an army generalled by twelve thousand officers**. ...

Sheba, said the peewit, is the name of the king who founded the kingdom; it is also the name of the capital. **Sheba was a worshipper of the sun**, Eblis having drawn him from the true God, who sends rain from heaven, and covers the earth with plenty, and who reads the thoughts of men's hearts. A succession of kings followed Sheba: **the last of the dynasty was Scharabel, a tyrant of such dissolute habits that every husband and father feared him**. He had a vizir of **such singular beauty** that the daughters of the Jinns took pleasure in contemplating him, and frequently transformed themselves into gazelles that they might trot alongside of him as he walked, and gaze with admiration on his exquisite beauty. One of these Jinn damsels, Umeira by name, conceived for the vizir a violent passion, and forgetting the great distance which separates the race of the Jinns from that of mortals, she appeared to him one day as he was hunting, and offered him her hand, on condition that he should fly with her into her own land, and that he should never ask her origin. **The vizir, dazzled by the marvellous beauty of Umeira**, gladly

379

yielded, and she transported him to an island in the midst of the ocean, where she married him. At the end of nine months she gave birth to a daughter, whom she named Balkis. The vizir, all this while, was ignorant of the nature of his bride, and one day forgot himself so far as to ask her to what race she belonged. No sooner had he asked the fatal question, than, with a wail of sorrow, **she vanished for ever from his sight.**

The vizir now left the island, and, regaining his native country, retired with his babe to a valley far from the capital, and there lived in seclusion. **As Balkis grew up, her beauty became more striking, and was of such a superhuman nature, that her father became uneasy lest the fame of it should reach the dissolute monster then seated on the throne of Sheba, and lest his daughter should be ravished from his arms. He therefore redoubled his precautions to guard Balkis, keeping her much at home, and only allowing her to appear veiled in public.** But these precautions were vain. Scharabel was in the habit of travelling about his empire in disguise, and making himself, by this means, personally acquainted with the condition of his estates.

On one of these expeditions he appeared, dressed in rags, as a mendicant, at the door of the ex-vizir, and obtained a glimpse of Balkis, then thirteen years old, lovely as a houri ; she stepped out to give the beggar alms. At the same moment, the father hurried out towards his daughter. **The eyes of the two men met; a mutual recognition ensued. The vizir fell at the feet of his king, and entreated pardon, telling him all that had happened; and Scharabel, who had fallen in love at first glance with Balkis, readily pardoned him, restored him to his place as grand vizir, and lodged him in a magnificent palace near Sheba.**

Installed there, the vizir was full of disquiet. His daughter observing this, inquired the cause, and received from her father the answer that he dreaded lest the tyrant should carry her off to his harem; and, said the unhappy man, I had rather see thee dead, Balkis, than in the power of this licentious monster.

Do not fear for me, my father, replied Balkis; what thou dreadest shall not take place. Appear cheerful before the king. If he wishes to marry me, then ask him to give me a splendid wedding.

A few days after, Scharabel sent to ask the hand of Balkis. The virgin replied that it should be his if he would solemnize the marriage with great pomp. To this the king agreed, **and a magnificent banquet was prepared**. After dinner, the vizir and all the company retired, leaving Balkis alone with the king. There were, however, four female slaves present, one singing, another harping, a third dancing, and a fourth pouring out wine for the king. **Balkis took the goblet, and plied her royal bridegroom well, till he fell drunk upon the floor, and then, with a dagger, she stabbed him to the heart.**

She at once communicated with her father, and bade him send orders throughout the town that all the citizens were to bring their daughters before the king, **that he might add the comely ones to his already extensive list of wives and concubines**. He obeyed her, and the commotion in the town was prodigious. Parents gathered their friends, those who were officers in the army agitated amongst their soldiers, **and the whole town rose up in revolt**, and rushed furiously to the palace, determined on the death of the tyrant. '

Then Balkis cut off the head of the king, and showed it to the excited multitude from a window. A cry of joy rang through Sheba. **The palace gates were thrown open, and Balkis was unanimously elected queen in the room of the murdered tyrant.**

From that hour she has governed Sheba with prudence, and has made the country prosperous. She sits to hear suits, and gives judgment on a throne of gold, **robed in splendour**. All prospers under her wise administration: but, alas! like her predecessors, **she too is a worshipper of the sun**.

When Solomon heard the story of the peewit, he wrote a letter and sealed it with his ring, gave it to the bird, and bade him carry it immediately to the Queen of Sheba. The peewit flew like an arrow, and on the morrow appeared before Balkis, and gave her the missive. The queen broke the seal and read:

'Solomon, son of David, and servant of the Most High God, to Balkis, queen of Sheba, sendeth greeting. In the name of the merciful and gracious God, peace be to those who walk in His ways. Do what I bid thee: submit immediately to my sceptre.'

The queen, startled at the abrupt and peremptory command, read the letter to her council, and asked their advice. They urged her to follow her own devices, and promised to agree to whatever she thought fit. She then said: You know what disasters follow on war. The letter of Solomon is threatening; **I will send him a messenger,** and propitiate him with gifts. If he accepts them, he is not above other kings; if he rejects them, he is a prophet, and we must yield to his sway. She then dressed five hundred boys as girls, and five hundred girls she equipped in boys' clothes. She collected, for presents, a thousand carpets of gold and silver tissue, a crown adorned with pearls and diamonds, and a great quantity of perfumes. She also placed a pearl, a diamond cut through in zigzags, and a crystal goblet, in a box, **and gave it to her chief ambassador.**

Finally, she wrote a letter to Solomon, telling him that, if he was a prophet, he would be able to distinguish boys from girls **in the train of the ambassadors,** that he would be able to guess the contents of the box, pierce the pearl, thread the diamond, and fill the goblet with water which came neither from earth nor heaven. The chief nobles of Sheba were sent to bear the letter. Before they left, she said to them:

'If Solomon receives you with arrogance, fear nothing; pride is a sure token of weakness. If he receives you graciously, be careful he is a prophet.' The peewit, who had watched all these proceedings, and listened to the message and advice, now flew to Solomon and told him all.

The great king immediately ordered his Jinns to spread his carpet seven leagues long, leading from his throne towards Sheba. He then surrounded himself with gold and gems, and gathered all his courtiers and officers together, and prepared for the audience.

When the ambassadors of Sheba set their feet on the carpet the end of which was beyond the range of vision they were full of astonishment. This astonishment increased, and became terror, when they passed between ranks of demons, and Jinns, and nobles, and princes, and soldiers, extending for many miles. **When the leaders of the embassy reached the foot of the throne,** Solomon received them with a gracious smile. Then they presented the letter of the queen. Solomon, without opening it, told them its contents, for it had been read by the peewit. They offered the box, and he said that in it were a pearl, a diamond, and a goblet. He next ordered his servants to bring silver ewers before the train of the ambassadors, that they might wash their hands after their journey. Solomon watched intently, and he picked out the boys from the girls at once; for the boys dipped their hands only in the water, whilst the girls tucked up their sleeves to their shoulders and washed arms as well as hands. Then the box was opened and the pearl produced. Solomon unclasped his pouch and drew forth Schamir, applied it to the pearl, and a hole was drilled through it immediately. Next he took the diamond. The hole pierced in it wound about, and a thread inserted in one end would not pass through to the other end. Solomon took a piece of silk, called to him a worm, put one end of the thread in its mouth and inserted it in the diamond. The worm crawled down the winding passage, and appeared at the other opening with the silk. In gratitude to the little creature, Solomon gave it for its food forever the mulberry-tree. Then he took the crystal goblet. He summoned to him a huge negro slave, bade him mount a wild horse and gallop it about the plain till it streamed with sweat. Then, with ease, the monarch filled the chalice with water that came neither from earth nor heaven. Solomon, having accomplished these tasks, said to the ambassadors:

Take back your presents, I do not want them. Tell the queen what you have seen, and bid her submit to my rule.

When Balkis had heard the report of her servants, she saw that it was in vain for her to resist. Solomon, said she, is a great prophet, and I must myself do him homage. She accordingly hasted to prepare for her journey, **and marched to King Solomon at the head of her twelve thousand generals, and all the armies they commanded**. When she was a league from Solomon, the king hit upon a scheme. He called to him a demon, and bade him transport immediately from Sheba the throne of the queen and set it beside his own. The Jinn replied that he would bring it before noon, but the king could not wait, for the queen would soon be there; then Asaph, his vizir, said,

Raise thine eyes, sire, to heaven, and before thou canst lower them the throne of Balkis will be here.

Asaph knew the ineffable name of God, and therefore was able to do what he said. Solomon looked up, and before he looked down Asaph had brought the throne. As soon as Balkis appeared, Solomon asked her if she recognized the seat. She replied,

It is mine, if it is that which it was. A reply which, we are told, charmed Solomon.

Now the Jinns were envious of Balkis, and they sought to turn away the heart of Solomon from her ; so they told him that she had hairy legs.

Solomon, accordingly, was particularly curious to inspect her legs. He therefore directed the Jinns to lay down in front of the throne a pavement of crystal one hundred cubits square. Upon this pavement he ordered them to pour water, so that it might appear to be water.

In order to approach Solomon, Queen Balkis raised her petticoats, lest they should be wet in passing through what she supposed to be water of considerable depth. The first step, however, convinced her that the bottom was nearer the surface than she anticipated, and so she dropped her petticoats, but not before the great king had seen that the Jinns had maligned her, and that the only blemish to her legs was three goat's hairs; and these he was enabled to remove by a composition of arsenic and lime, which was the first depilatory preparation ever employed. This was one of the five arts introduced by Solomon into the world. The others were the art of taking warm baths, the art of piercing pearls, the art of diving, and the art of melting copper.

The queen stepped gracefully towards the king, and bowing, **offered him two wreaths of flowers**, whereof one was natural, the other artificial, asking him which he preferred. The sagacious Solomon seemed perplexed; he who had written treatises on the herbs, 'from the cedar to the hyssop,' was nearly outwitted. A swarm of bees was fluttering outside a window. Solomon ordered the window to be opened, and the insects flew in, and settled immediately on the wreath of natural flowers, not one approaching the artificial wreath. I will have the wreath the bees have chosen, said the king, triumphantly.

Solomon took Balkis to be his wife, and she worshipped the true God. She gave him all her realm, but he returned it to her ; and when she went into her own land, **she bore with her the fruit of her union with Solomon, and in the course of time bore a son, who is the ancestor of the kings of Abyssinia.**

References

Notes to References

1. Unless otherwise specified, all quotations from the Bible are from the NIV translation (see Bibliography).

2. Shortened book titles are regularly used in the references, followed by the author's name. See Bibliography for complete book titles.

3. SH# denotes the list number of the Hebrew word in *The New Strong's Expanded Dictionary of Bible Words* (see Bibliography).

4. SG# denotes the list number of the Greek word in *The New Strong's Expanded Dictionary of Bible Words*.

5. 'Antiquities', 'Against Apion' and 'The Jewish War' references are from *The New Complete Works of Josephus* (Whiston).

6. Rabbinic literature is quoted from *Judaic Classics* (Kantrowitz).

Chapter 1 Introduction

1. Exodus, the second book of the Bible (*NIV Study Bible*, Barker).

2. *World Religions in America* (Neusner), p. 126.

3. *The Hebrew Pharaohs of Egypt* (Osman).

4. *Act of God* (Phillips), Chapter 11.

5. *The Moses Legacy* (Phillips), Chapter 5.

6. *A Test of Time* (Rohl), Chapters 9, 10.

7. *Manetho* (Waddell), Introduction.

8. *The Oxford History of Ancient Egypt* (Shaw), Chapter 8.

9. Ibid., Chapter 9.

10. Exodus 3:1-21.

11. *The Oxford History of Ancient Egypt* (Shaw), Chapter 10.

12. *NIV Study Bible* (Barker), Introductions to Judges and I Samuel.

13. 'Trojan war.' *The Dictionary of Mythology* (Coleman).

14. Mladjov, Ian. 'Ian Mjadlov's Resources.' Department of History, University of Michigan. 23 September 2011 http://sitemaker. umich.edu / mladjov / files/ane1350.jpg.

15. *The New Complete Works of Josephus* (Whiston).
16. *Ancient Nubia: Egypt's Rival in Africa* (O'Connor), p.3.
17. *New Kingdom Egypt* (Healy), p.4.
18. Dahl, Jeff. 'Map of Ancient Egypt, showing the Nile up to the fifth cataract, and major cities and sites of the Dynastic period (c. 3150 BC to 30 BC)'. 23 September 2011 http://en.wik ipedia.org /wiki/ File: Ancient_Egypt_map-en.svg.
19. Aston, M.A. and Hardy, P.G. 'The Pre-Minoan Landscape of Thera: a Preliminary Statement.' Figure 2 after Heiken and McCoy 1984. *Thera and the Aegean World III, Vol. II* (Hardy), pp. 348-361.
20. McCoy, Floyd W. 'The eruption within the debate about the date.' *Time's Up!* (Warburton), p.78.
21. Friedrich, Walter L. and Sigalas, Nikolaos. 'The effects of the Minoan eruption.' ibid. p.91.

Chapter 2 The Exodus as described in religious sources

1. Genesis Chapters 11-50.
2. Exodus, Chapter 1.
3. 'Jewish Antiquities' and 'Against Apion.' *The New Complete Works of Josephus* (Whiston).
4. Exodus 6:20.
5. Exodus 1:10; 13:17.
6. Exodus 1:16,22.
7. Exodus 2:1-6,10.
8. Exodus 2:11-15.
9. Exodus Chapters 4-12.
10. Exodus 12:29.
11. Exodus 12:37-38.
12. Exodus 13:9.
13. Exodus 12:35-36.
14. Exodus 14:9.
15. Exodus 14:28.
16. Exodus 12:40.

17. 'Jewish Antiquities, Book II.' *The New Complete Works of Josephus* (Whiston).
18. Antiquities 2.9.5 (224).
19. Antiquities 2.9.7 (233).
20. Antiquities 2.9.7 (234-236).
21. Antiquities 2.9.7 (237).
22. Antiquities 2.10.2 (247-243).
23. Antiquities 2.11.1 (254,255).
24. Antiquities 2.11.1 (256-257).
25. Antiquities 2.14.6 (314).
26 Antiquities 2.15.1 (315).
27. Antiquities 2.15.1 (317).
28. Antiquities 2.16.2 (338).
29. Antiquities 2.16.3 (343-344).
30 Antiquities 2.16.6 (349).
31. *Recommendation whether to confiscate, destroy, and burn all Jewish books* (Reuchlin).
32. Jacobs, Joseph, et al. 'Moses.' *Jewish Encyclopedia*. 23 September 2011 http:// www. jewishencyclopedia.com/view.jsp? artid=830 &letter=M.
33. *The Holy Quran* (Ali).
34. *The Meaning of the Glorious Koran* (Pickthall).
35. *The Koran: Commonly Called the Alcoran of Mohammed* (Sale).
36. The Koran, Surah 12.56.
37. The Koran, Surah 7.127.
38. The Koran, Surah 7.133.
39. The Koran, Surah 29:40.
40. The Koran, Surah 7.137.
41. The Koran, Surah 20.10-11.
42. The Koran, Surah 28.6,8; 28:76,79; 29:39; 40:24,36.
43. The Koran, Surah 66:11.

Chapter 3 The Exodus in the words of the historians

1.   'Against Apion, Books I & II.' *The New Complete Works of Josephus*

(Whiston).

2. *Manetho* (Waddell), Introduction.

3. Against Apion 1.14 (75-78).

4. Against Apion 1.14 (82-84, 91-92).

5. Against Apion 1.14 (86-89); 1.15 (94); 1.26 (241).

6. Against Apion 1.14 (90).

7. Against Apion 1.26 (229).

8. Against Apion 1.26 (230-238).

9. Against Apion 1.26 (238-242, 250).

10. Against Apion 1.32 (296).

11. Against Apion 1.26 (243-247).

12. Against Apion 1.26 (248-249); 1.28 (262).

13. Against Apion 1.29 (270,275).

14. Against Apion 1.26 (247); 1.27 (251); 1.28 (266); 1.29 (276).

15. Against Apion 1.15 (94-98,100-102); 1.26 (231).

16 Against Apion 1.15 (98-102).

17 Against Apion 1.26 (231).

18. Against Apion 1.26 (245).

19. Against Apion 1.33 (300).

20. *Chaeremon* (Van der Horst), p. ix.

21. Against Apion 1.32 (288).

22. Against Apion 1.32 (289-290).

23. Against Apion 1.32 (290-291).

24. Against Apion 1.32 (297).

25. Against Apion 1.32 (292, 300).

26. Against Apion 1.32 (299).

27. Against Apion 1.34 (301).

28. Hata, Gohei. 'The Story of Moses Interpreted within the Context of Anti-Semitism'. *Josephus, Judaism and Christianity* (Feldman), pp. 180-197.

29. Against Apion 1.34 (305).

30. Against Apion 1.34 (306-307).

31. Against Apion I.34 (308-311, 318).

32. Kohler, Kaufmann. 'Apion'. *Jewish Encyclopedia*. 23 September

2011 http://www.jewishencyclopedia. com/view.jsp?artid=1641 &letter=A.

33. Against Apion 2.1 (2); 2.2 (10).

34. Against Apion 2.2 (15).

35. *Iulius Africanus Chronographiae* (Wallraff), pp. xiii-xiv.

36. Ibid., p. xv.

37. Ibid., Fragment 34, pp. 79-81.

38. *Jews in the Mediterranean diaspora* (Barclay), p.127.

39. *Eusebius – Praeparatio Evangelica* (Gifford), 9.18, 21, 27.

40. 'Herodotus'. *The New Oxford American Dictionary* (McKean).

41. *Histories – Herodotus* (Rawlinson), 2.102-119.

42. *Diodorus, Library of History* (Oldfather), Introduction

43. Ibid., 1.53-59.

44. Syme, Ronald. 'The Date of Justin and the Discovery of Trogus.' *Historia: Zeitschrift für Alte Geschichte.* Vol. 37 1988, pp. 358-371.

45. *Marcus Junianus Justinus – Epitome of the Philippic History of Pompeius Trogus* (Watson), 36.2.

46. *Tacitus – The Histories* (Wellesley), Introduction.

47. Ibid., 5.2-5.

48. *The New Complete Works of Josephus* (Whiston), Dissertation 3, p. 1006.

49. 'Strabo.' *Encyclopædia Britannica*, www. britannica.com.

50. *Strabo Geography* (Jones), 15.1.6; 16.4.4; 17.1.5,25,30-31.

51. *Apollodorus – The Library* (Frazer), 2.1.5; 2.5.11.

52. 'Busiris'. *Isocrates* (Van Hook), 11.31, p. 121.

53. *St Augustine – City of God* (Bettenson), 18.12.

Chapter 4 Interpretation of various accounts of the Exodus

1. *Akhenaten, Egypt's False Prophet* (Reeves), p. 56.

2. Against Apion 1.26 (228-231)

Chapter 5 From the arrival of the Israelites in Egypt to Joseph

1. *The Library of Alexandria* (MacLeod), pp. xi, 9, 10.

2. *The Sumerians* (Kramer), pp. 28, 298.

3. Genesis 37-50.
4. Genesis 15:13.
5. Exodus 12:40-41.
6. Against Apion 1.14 (84).
7. Midrash Rabbah – Genesis LVII:4, XCI:2, *Judaic Classics* (Kantrowitz).
8. Midrash Rabbah – Exodus XVIII:1, ibid.
9. Midrash Rabbah – The Song of Songs II: 21, 28, 47, ibid.
10. Talmud – Mas. Baba Bathra 120a, ibid.
11. Midrash Rabbah – Numbers XIII:20, ibid.
12. Talmud – Mas. Nedarim 32a, ibid.
13. Against Apion 1.25 (224).
14. *Egypt – Gods* (Gahlin), p. 90.
15. *The Ancient Near East* (Kuhrt), p. 173.
16. *The Moses Legacy* (Phillips), p. 74.
17. *The Bible Unearthed* (Finkelstein), p. 55.
18. D. Franke. 'The Career of Khnumhotep III of Beni Hasan and the so-called Decline of the Normarchs.' *Middle Kingdom Studies* (Quirke), pp. 51-67.
19. Kurohito, 23 September 2011 http://nl.wikipedia.org /wiki/ Bestand: Beni-Hassan-Asiatiques1.jpg, Creative Commons License.
20. *Egypt – Gods* (Gahlin), p. 90.
21. Genesis 37-50.
22. Genesis 41:40-44.
23. Genesis 45:8.
24. Genesis 41:45.
25. Genesis 45:17-20.
26. Ibid. ('New Advent Multilingual Bible.' *Catholic Encyclopedia*).
27. Genesis 45:23.
28. Genesis 46:32-34; 47:1.
29. Genesis 47:20.
30. Genesis 50:26.
31. Exodus 1:8-14.

32. 'Israelites.'*Catholic Encyclopedia*.

33. *The Hebrew Pharaohs of Egypt* (Osman), Introduction.

34. Ibid., pp. 127-128.

35. Ibid., Note 1, p. 82.

36. Ibid., p. 5.

37. *Amenhotep III – Perspectives on his Reign* (O'Connor), p. 5.

38. *The Hyksos period in Egypt* (Booth), p. 36.

39. Genesis 47:6.

40. *Hebrew Pharaohs* (Osman), p. 121.

41. Ibid., p. 52.

42. Ibid., p. 15.

43. Genesis 41:40.

44. *Histories – Herodotus* (Rawlinson), 2.36.

45. *Tomb of Yuaa and Thuiu* (Quibell), Plates LVII and LVIII.

46. Sweeney, Deborah. 'Review: Osman, 'Stranger in the Valley of the Kings'.' *The Jewish Quarterly Review*, New Series, Vol. 82, No. ¾ (Jan.-Apr. 1992), pp. 575-579.

47. *Hebrew Pharaohs* (Osman), p. 122.

48. Cook, David. trans. 'Joseph and Aseneth'. *The Apocryphal Old Testament* (Sparks), pp. 473-503, XXIX.

49. *Hebrew Pharaohs* (Osman), pp. 126-8.

50. Deuteronomy 34:5,6.

51. Justin, *Epitome of the Philippic History* (Watson), 36.2.

52. Against Apion 1.32 (290-291).

53. Against Apion 1.28 (261, 265).

54. *Hebrew Pharaohs* (Osman), p.14.

55. *Amenhotep III – Perspectives on his Reign* (O'Connor), p. 5.

56. Against Apion 1.33 (299).

57. SH#3084.

58. SH#3130.

59. SH#614.

60. SH#625.

61. SH#3050.

62. SH#3068.

63. SH#3115.
64. SH#3257.
65. SH#2969.
66. SH#3261.
67. *Eusebius – Praeparatio Evangelica* (Gifford), 9.23.
68. *Chronicle of the Queens of Egypt* (Tyldesley), p. 116.
69. *Hebrew Pharaohs* (Osman), p. 155.
70. Cook, David. trans. 'Joseph and Aseneth'. *The Apocryphal Old Testament* (Sparks), I.
71. Ibid., XXIX.
72. Against Apion 1.15 (98); 1.26 (245); 1.32 (288); 1.33 (300).
73. SH#636.
74. SH#5572.
75. SH#854.
76. SH#855
77. *Eusebius – Praeparatio Evangelica* (Gifford), 9.27.
78. SH#6213.
79. SH#4999.
80. SH#2089.
81. SH#3922.
82. SH#8377.
83. SH#3050.
84. Genesis 41:45.
85. SH#2197.
86. SH#5421.
87. SH#6284.
88. SH#4998.
89. SH#4999.
90. Genesis 39
91. Midrash Rabbah – Genesis LXXXVI:3, *Judaic Classics* (Kantrowitz).
92. Talmud – Mas. Sotah 13b, *Judaic Classics* (Kantrowitz).
93. SH#6596.
94. SH#6336.

95. SH#6547.

96. Against Apion 1.32 (290).

97. SH#6601.

98. SH#6612.

99. SH#6613.

100. SH#6621.

101. SH#5586.

102. SH#5588.

103. SH#6435

104. SH#2953.

105. SH#784.

106. *Apollodorus – The Library* (Frazer), 2.5.11.

107. *Ages in Chaos* (Velikovsky), p. 268.

108. Deuteronomy 4:43.

109. I Kings 22:3.

110. SH#3372.

111. SH#4191.

112. Thematic guide to world mythology (Stookey), p.4

113. *Mummies, Tombs, and Treasure* (Perl), p. 55.

114. *A History of Ancient Egypt* (Van De Mieroop), p. 205.

115. Genesis 45:20.

116. *An Introduction to DNA Analysis* (Rudin).

117. Hawass, Zahi, Gad, Yehia Z., Ismail, Somaia et al. 'Ancestry and Pathology in King Tutankhamun's Family'. *Journal of the American Medical Association (JAMA)*. 2010; 303(7):638-647.

Chapter 6 The identity of King Sesostris

1. *Histories – Herodotus* (Rawlinson), 2.102-111.

2. *Diodorus, Library of History* (Oldfather), 1.53-59.

3. *Strabo Geography* (Jones), 15.1.6; 15.4.4,7; 17.1.5,25.

4. *Dicaearchus of Messana* (Fortenbaugh), p. 69.

5. Bedrosian, Robert. 'Eusebius' Chronicle' (The Egyptian Chronicle, 48). 23 September 2011 http:// rbedrosian.com /euseb.html.

6. Against Apion 1.15 (98), 1.26 (231).

7. *Histories – Herodotus* (Rawlinson), 2.107.

8. *Diodorus, Library of History* (Oldfather), 1.57.6.

9. *Black Athena* (Bernal), pp. 187-273.

10. *Egypt's Golden Empire* (Tyldesley), pp. 44-45.

11. *Ancient Times – A History of the Early World* (Breasted), p.85.

12. *Egypt's Golden Empire* (Tyldesley), p. 86.

13. Nederhof, Mark-Jan. 'The Gebel Barkal Stela of Tuthmosis III'. 23 September 2011 http:// www.cs.st-andrews.ac.uk/~mjn/ egyptian/texts/corpus/pdf/GebelBarkalTuthmosisIII.pdf.

14. SG#4571.

15. SG#4674.

16. SG#5151.

17. SG#4675.

18. SG#3745.

19. SG#4862.

20. SG#5522.

21. *Thutmose III, A New Biography* (Cline), pp. 103-104.

22. *Histories – Herodotus* (Rawlinson), 2.103.

23. *Diodorus, Library of History* (Oldfather), 1.53, 55.

24. *Histories – Herodotus* (Rawlinson), 2.108.

25. *Diodorus, Library of History* (Oldfather), 1.56.2.

26. Ibid., 1.56.1.

27. *Egypt's Golden Empire* (Tyldesley), p. 87.

28. *Histories – Herodotus* (Rawlinson), 2.103, 106.

29. *Diodorus, Library of History* (Oldfather), 1.55.7.

30. *Egypt's Golden Empire* (Tyldesley), p. 86.

31. *Encyclopædia of the Pharaohs* (Baker), p. 465.

32. *Diodorus, Library of History* (Oldfather), 1.53.6.

33. *Ancient Egyptian Literature* (Lichtheim), pp. 35-39.

34. *Hatshepsut* (Caldecott), pp. 136, 242.

35. *Diodorus, Library of History* (Oldfather), 1.53.6.

36. *Histories – Herodotus* (Rawlinson), 2.108.

37. *Diodorus, Library of History* (Oldfather), 1.57.2.

38. *Strabo Geography* (Jones), 17.1.25.

39. *Ancient Records of Egypt* (Breasted), p. 260, §650.

40. *Diodorus, Library of History* (Oldfather), 1.53.5.

41. Ibid., 1.54.1.

42. Ibid., 1.54.6; 1.55.12.

43. *The Search For Ancient Egypt* (Vercoutter), p.65.

44. *Ancient Records of Egypt* (Breasted), pp. 227-234, §574-592.

45. *Histories – Herodotus* (Rawlinson), 2.102.

46. *Diodorus, Library of History* (Oldfather), 1.55.2.

47. *Egypt's Golden Empire* (Tyldesley), pp. 85-6.

48. *Histories – Herodotus* (Rawlinson), 4.42.

49. *Strabo Geography* (Jones), 15.1.4.

50. *Diodorus, Library of History* (Oldfather), 1.55.4.

51. Nederhof, Mark-Jan. 'Poetical Stela of Tuthmosis III'. 23 September 2011 http://www.cs.st-andrews .ac.uk/~mjn /egyptian/texts/corpus /pdf/PoeticalTuthmosisIII.pdf

52. *Histories – Herodotus* (Rawlinson), 2.111.4.

53. Jon Bodsworth, 23 September 2011 http://en.wikipedia.org/ wiki/File: ThutmosesIII-RaisingObelisks-Karnak.png, Wikimedia Commons Free License.

54. *Histories – Herodotus* (Rawlinson), 2.110.1.

55. *Diodorus, Library of History* (Oldfather), 1.57.5.

56. *Egypt (Fletcher)*, pp. 215-216.

57. *Diodorus, Library of History* (Oldfather), 1.55.1, 10.

58. Ibid., 1.53.4; 1.54.4.

59. Ibid., 1.53.8.

60. SG#1.

61. SG#2339.

62. SG#5100.

63. *Antiquities* 2.9.5 (224).

64. *Diodorus, Library of History* (Oldfather), 1.57.4.

65. 'The Prophecy of Neferti.' *Ancient Near Eastern Texts* (Pritchard), pp. 444-446.

66. *The Encyclopædia of the Pharaohs* (Baker), p.21.

67. *The Oxford History of Ancient Egypt* (Shaw), p, 158.

68. *The Tale of Sinuhe* (Parkinson), p. 21.

69. *Diodorus, Library of History* (Oldfather), 1.58.3.

70. *The Encyclopædia of the Pharaohs* (Baker), pp. 105, 472.

71. Against Apion 1.26 (231).

72. *Amenhotep III – Perspectives on his Reign* (O'Connor), p. 1.

73. *Histories – Herodotus* (Rawlinson), 2.107-108.

74. *Diodorus, Library of History* (Oldfather), 1.57.6-7.

75. Against Apion 1.15 (98-102).

76. Against Apion 1.26 (231).

77. *The Encyclopædia of the Pharaohs* (Baker), p. 64.

78. *Tutankhamen* (El Mahdy), p. 311.

79. *Dicaearchus of Messana* (Fortenbaugh), p. 69.

80. *Histories – Herodotus* (Rawlinson), 2.106.

81. Ibid., 2.110.1.

82. *Diodorus, Library of History* (Oldfather), 1.57.5.

83. *Tell el Amarna and the Bible* (Pfeiffer), p. 33.

Chapter 7 Amenhotep III and his scribe Amenhotep, Son of Hapu

1. Against Apion 1.26 (232, 243).

2. *Ancient Times – A History of the Early World* (Breasted), p. 378, §924.

3. SH#215.

4. SH#217.

5. SH#5785.

6. SH#5789.

7. SG#3735.

8. SG#3736.

9. 'Aurum.' *Cassell's Latin-English Dictionary* (Simpson).

10. 'Aureus.' ibid.

11. SH#950.

12. SH#7389.

13. SG#995.

14. SG#5565.

15. 'Boo.' *Cassell's Latin-English Dictionary* (Simpson).
16. 'Chorus.' ibid.
17. *Manetho* (Waddell), pp. 165-9.
18. *Egypt – Gods* (Gahlin), p. 91.
19. *Histories – Herodotus* (Rawlinson), 2.137-141.
20. Against Apion 1.15 (98,100-102), 1.26 (231).
21. Against Apion 1.26 (245-247).
22. *Tacitus – The History* (Wellesley), 5.3.
23. *St Augustine – City of God* (Bettenson), 18.12.
24. *Apollodorus – The Library* (Frazer), 2.5.11.
25. 'Busiris'. *Isocrates* (Van Hook), 11.31, p. 121.
26. *Diodorus, Library of History* (Oldfather 1935), 4.27.2-3.
27. SG#1016.
28. SG#2463.
29. 'Bos.' *Cassell's Latin-English Dictionary* (Simpson).
30. SH#6381.
31. SH#4479.
32. SH#226.
33. SH#784.
34. SH#6466.
35. SH#4521.
36. SH#2580.
37. SH#665.
38. *Eusebius – Praeparatio Evangelica* (Gifford), 9.27.
39. *Amarna Sunset* (Dodson), pp. 4, 15.
40. SG#5342.
41. SG#5411.
42. SG#4253.
43. SG#2316.
44. Antiquities 2.9.5 (224).
45. *Eusebius – Praeparatio Evangelica* (Gifford), 9.27.
46. The Koran, Surah 28:9, 66:11.
47. The Koran (Ali), Note 5549 to Surah 66:11.
48. SG#2339.

49. SG#3454.

50. SH#4806.

51. SH#376.

52. SH#4805.

53. SH#8491.

54. SH#8493.

55. SH#8494.

56. *Apollodorus – The Library* (Frazer), 2.1.4.

57. SG#956.

58. *Histories – Herodotus* (Rawlinson), 2.111.

59. SG#302.

60. SG#5494.

61. SG#3539.

62. Genesis 40

63. Exodus 6:20.

64. SH#5972.

65. SH#7213.

66. SH#3068.

67. SH#3515.

68. SH#2244.

69. SH#5707.

70. *Prophets in the Quran* (Wheeler), p. 176.

71. *Amenhotep III – Perspectives on his Reign* (O'Connor), p. 12.

72. *Apollodorus - The Library* (Frazer), 2.5.11.

73. SG#297.

74. SG#1150.

75. *Apollodorus – The Library* (Frazer), Note 1, p.226.

76. SG#2462.

77. SG#1714.

78. SG#3839.

79. SG#3843.

80. *Apollodorus – The Library* (Frazer), 2.1.5.

81. SH #539.

82. SH#2583.

83. SH#6256.

84. SH#226.

85. SH#784.

86. Redford, Donald B. 'The Identity of the High-Priest of Amun at the Beginning of Akhenaten's Reign'. *Journal of the American Oriental Society*, Vol. 83, No. 2, 1963, pp. 240-241.

87. Against Apion 1.26 (236).

88. 'Phrasis.' *Cassell's Latin-English Dictionary* (Simpson).

89. SG#5420.

90. SG#5433.

91. *Amenhotep III – Perspectives on his Reign* (O'Connor), pp. 9-10.

92. *The Encyclopædia of the Pharaohs* (Baker), p. 46.

93. *Amenhotep III – Perspectives on his Reign* (O'Connor), pp. 261-270.

94. 'Merymose.' Encyclopedia of Ancient Egypt (Bunson).

95. *Amenhotep III – Perspectives on his Reign* (O'Connor), p. 270.

96. *Histories – Herodotus* (Rawlinson), 2.110.

97. *The Oxford Encyclopedia of Ancient Egypt* (Redford), Vol. 2, p. 553.

98. *Egypt – Gods* (Gahlin), p. 90.

99. *The Encyclopædia of the Pharaohs* (Baker), p. 392.

100. *Amenhotep III – Perspectives on his Reign* (O'Connor), pp. 11-12.

101. *A History of Ancient Egypt* (Grimal), pp. 223-225.

102. Fairman, H.W. 'The Inscriptions'. *The City of Akhetaton* (Pendlebury), pp. 155-56.

103. *Diodorus, Library of History* (Oldfather, 1935), 4.27.2-3.

104. *Akhenaten, Egypt's False Prophet* (Reeves), p. 61.

105. *Amenhotep III – Perspectives on his Reign* (O'Connor), pp. 20-21.

106. *Akhenaten, Egypt's False Prophet* (Reeves), p. 61.

107. *Apollodorus – The Library* (Frazer), 2.1.4

Chapter 8 Prince Tuthmosis, the prince who disappeared

1. *Act of God* (Phillips), p. 285-287.

2. *The Moses Legacy* (Phillips), pp. 102-130.

3. Exodus 2.

4. *Folk-lore in the Old Testament Studies* (Frazer), Volume II, p. 450.

5. *Prophets in the Quran* (Wheeler), p. 177.

6. Exodus 4:14-16.

7. Jacobs, Joseph, et al. 'Moses, Wishes to Avoid Death.' *Jewish Encyclopedia*. 23 September 2011 http:// www. jewishencyclopedia. com/view.jsp? artid=830&letter =M>.

8. Against Apion 1.27 (251).

9. Against Apion 1.29 (274).

10. Against Apion 1.32 (292).

11. Against Apion 1.26 (241).

12. Dodson, Aidan. 'Crown Prince Djhutmose and the Royal Sons of the Eighteenth Dynasty'. *Journal of Egyptian Archaeology*, Vol. 76, 1990, pp. 87-97.

13. *Amarna Sunset* (Dodson), p. 15.

14. Against Apion 1.26 (238, 250).

15. SH#5789.

16. SH#6145.

17. SH#5486.

18. Against Apion 1.32 (290).

19. SH#2907.

20. SH#8351.

21. SH#371.

22. *Ages in Chaos* (Velikovsky), p. 58.

23. *Velikovsky Reconsidered* (Pensée), Note following Contents.

24. 'Editorial Statement'. *Kronos: A Journal of Interdisciplinary Synthesis*. Vol.1 No. 1, 1975.

25. *Amenhotep III – Perspectives on his Reign* (O'Connor), p. 15.

26. *Ancient Records of Egypt* (Breasted), p. 241, §606.

27. 'at.' *Egyptian Hieroglyphic Dictionary* (Budge), p. 96.

28. 'h-at.' ibid., p. 457.

29. Mewhinney, Sean. 'El-Arish Revisited'. *Kronos* XI:2, 1986.

30. 'a.' *Egyptian Hieroglyphic Dictionary* (Budge), p. 105.

31. *Thebes in Egypt* (Strudwick), pp. 196-197.

32. *Amenhotep III – Perspectives on his Reign* (O'Connor), pp. 13-14.

33. *Thebes in Egypt* (Strudwick), p.53.

34. 'Cubit'. *The Encyclopedia of Ancient Egyptian Architecture* (Arnold).

35. *Egypt – Gods* (Gahlin), p. 90.

36. Against Apion 1.14 (86).

37. Against Apion 1.34 (306-308).

38. *Histories – Herodotus* (Rawlinson), 2.111.

39. *Ages in Chaos* (Velikovsky), p. 62.

40. Exodus 14:9.

41. Against Apion 1.15 (100).

42. The Koran (Sale), LXVI Note 4, p. 458.

43. Against Apion 1.14 (75).

44. *Ages in Chaos* (Velikovsky), p. 63.

45. Exodus 4:1-5.

46. *Dictionary of Egyptology*, p. 231.

47. *Egypt – Gods* (Gahlin), p. 47.

48. *Wörterbuch der ägyptischen Sprache* (Erman), 1.268.18.

49. *Histories – Herodotus* (Rawlinson), 2.155.

50. Ibid., 2.111.

51. Corbis Images, Image IH019958, 'Stele of Amenhotep III' http://www.corbisimages.com

52. Exodus 25:9-22.

53. II Samuel 6:2-7.

54. 'per.' *Egyptian Hieroglyphic Dictionary* (Budge), p. 237.

55. 'art.' Ibid., p. 73.

56. *The Great Goddesses of Egypt* (Lesko), p. 137.

57. Against Apion 1.26 (251), 1.32 (292).

58. Antiquities 2.16.6 (349).

59. SH#1710.

60. SH#1770.

61. SH#5856.

62. Exodus 7:14-24.

63. Exodus 20:2-17.

64. Deuteronomy 5:6-21.

65. Exodus 34:29,35.

66. SH#7160.
67. Jeff Dahl, 23 September 2011 http://en.wikipedia.org/ wiki/ File:Horus_standing.svg, Creative Commons Free License.
68. Jeff Dahl, 23 September 2011 http://en.wikipedia.org /wiki/ File:Hathor.svg, Creative Commons Free License.
69. *Pilgrimage* (Davidson), p. 421.
70. Researches in Sinai (Petrie), Chapter 5.
71. Exodus 24:18.
72. *Oxford Essential Guide* (Redford), pp. 3, 335.
73. *The Nile and Egyptian Civilization* (Moret), pp. 318-319.
74. *Oxford Essential Guide* (Redford), pp. 23-24.
75. *Amenhotep III – Perspectives on his Reign* (O'Connor), p. 28.
76. *Gods of Ancient Egypt*, (Watterson), p. 33.
77. *Egypt – Gods* (Gahlin), p. 91.
78. *The Ancient Near East - Anthology* (Pritchard), pp. 227-230.
79. *Oxford Essential Guide* (Redford), p. 325.
80. *Egyptian Myth and Legend* (Mackenzie), p. 332.
81. *Akhenaten, Egypt's False Prophet* (Reeves), p. 166.
82. *The Oxford History of Ancient Egypt* (Shaw), p. 274.

Chapter 9 Akhenaten and his religious revolution

1. *Akhenaten, the Heretic King* (Redford).
2. 'Akhenaten.' *The Encyclopædia of the Pharaohs* (Baker).
3. *A History of Ancient Egypt* (Van De Mieroop), pp. 209-210.
4. *The Rise and Fall of Ancient Egypt* (Wilkinson), p. 279.
5. Ibid., p. 283.
6. Ibid., p. 284.
7. *The Encyclopædia of the Pharaohs* (Baker), p. 15.
8. *Thutmose III, A New Biography* (Cline), p. 13.
9. Shorter, Alan W. 'Historical Scarabs of Tuthmosis IV and Amenophis III'. *The Journal of Egyptian Archaeology*, Vol. 17, No ½ , 1931, pp. 23-25.
10. *The Encyclopædia of the Pharaohs* (Baker), p. 15.
11. *Conceptions of God in Ancient Egypt* (Hornung), p. 248.

12. *Moses and Monotheism* (Freud), pp. 30, 47 (Note 1).
13. *Moses and Akhenaten* (Osman), p. 3.
14. Exodus 2:23.
15. Antiquities 2.13.2 (277).
16. Against Apion 1.32 (289).
17. *The Moses Legacy* (Phillips), p. 120.
18. *Oxford Essential Guide* (Redford), pp. 18-20.
19. Against Apion 2.2 (10).
20. *The Ancient Near East* (Kuhrt), p. 12.
21. *Myths of Babylon and Assyria* (MacKenzie), p. 222.
22. Sailko, 23 September 2011 http://en.wikipedia.org/wiki/File: Codice_di_hammurabi_03.JPG, Creative Commons Free License.
23. *Archaeology and the Old Testament* (Hoerth), p. 171.
24. Exodus 21:15 (English Standard Version Bible).
25. *Archaeology and the Old Testament* (Hoerth), p. 171.
26. Exodus 21:16 (English Standard Version Bible).
27. *The Book of the Dead* (Budge), p. 6.
28. Ibid., pp. 572-584.
29. Exodus 20:1-17.
30. Deuteronomy 5:6-21.
31. Against Apion 2.2 (21).
32. Leviticus 18:22.
33. Job 31:1, 7.
34. *The Moses Legacy* (Phillips), p. 115.
35. *Tutankhamun - Exodus Conspiracy* (Collins), pp. 150,151.
36. Psalm 104 (NIV).
37. *The Moses Legacy* (Phillips), p. 119.
38. Martin, Geoffrey, T. Review of 'Découverte à Saqqarah: le vizir oublié' by Alain Zivie. *The Journal of Egyptian Archaeology*, Vol. 80, 1994, pp. 251-253.
39. SH#410.
40. Hoffmeier, James K. 'The Evangelical Contribution to Understanding the (Early) History of Ancient Israel in Recent

Scholarship'. *Bulletin for Biblical Research*, Vol. 7, 1997, pp. 77-90 (Note 24).

41. SH#5650.
42. SH#666.
43. 'aper.' *Egyptian Hieroglyphic Dictionary* (Budge), p.118.
44. Ibid., p.119.
45. *Tutankhamun - Exodus Conspiracy* (Collins), pp. 292-294.
46. *Moses and Monotheism* (Freud), p. 40, Note 2 (Weigall).
47. *The Book of the Dead* (Budge), p. 118.
48. Genesis 1.
49. *Gods and Myths of Ancient Egypt* (Barnett), p. 66.
50. 'Yehovah (Yahweh).' *Catholic Encyclopedia*.
51. SH#3068.
52. SH#1961.
53. SH#136.
54. SH#113.
55. *The Nile and Egyptian Civilization* (Moret), p. 318.
56. *Moses and Monotheism* (Freud), p. 42.
57. *Moses and Akhenaten* (Osman), pp. 166-169.
58. SH#3257.
59. SH#3261.
60. SH#1933.
61. SH#1942.
62. SH#1943.
63. 'heh.' *Egyptian Hieroglyphic Dictionary* (Budge), p. 451.
64. 'ha.' ibid., p. 439.
65. 'ia.' ibid., p. 142.
66. 'ua.' ibid., p. 144.
67. Exodus 3:14.
68. *The Moses Legacy* (Phillips), p. 115.

Chapter 10 'Those fatally determined 13 years'

1. Against Apion 1.26 (247).
2. *Amenhotep III – Perspectives on his Reign* (O'Connor), p. 70, Note

43.

3. *Ancient Records of Egypt* (Breasted), p. 378, §924.

4. Against Apion 1.14 (76).

5. *Religion and Magic in Ancient Egypt* (David), pp. 241-242.

6. *Amenhotep III – Perspectives on his Reign* (O'Connor), p. 1.

7. Ibid., p. 22.

8. Hawass, Zahi, Gad, Yehia Z., Ismail, Somaia et al. 'Ancestry and Pathology in King Tutankhamun's Family.' *Journal of the American Medical Association*. Vol. 303(7), 2010, pp. 638-47.

9. *The Oxford History of Ancient Egypt* (Shaw), p. 260.

10. *Chronicle of a Pharaoh – Amenhotep III* (Fletcher), p. 161.

11. *Akhenaten, Egypt's False Prophet* (Reeves), p. 174.

12. *Egypt – Gods* (Gahlin), p. 90.

13. *Akhenaten, Egypt's False Prophet* (Reeves), pp. 174-177.

14. Against Apion 1.15 (100).

15. *Akhenaten, Egypt's False Prophet* (Reeves), p. 110-111.

16. Ibid., pp. 182-183.

17. *The Nile and Egyptian Civilization* (Moret), p. 323.

18. *Texts from the Amarna Period in Egypt* (Murnane), pp. 101-103.

19. *Africa and Africans* (Hansberry), p. 10.

20. *L'Égyptologie en 1979*, p. 308.

21. *The French Foreign Legion* (Lepage), Introduction.

22. Cáceres, Marco. 'The Crucifixions – Those Uppity Nubians.' 23 September 2001 http:// crucifixions.wordpress. com / the-uppity-nubians/

23. 'ia.' *Egyptian Hieroglyphic Dictionary* (Budge), p. 142.

24. 'Kheta.' Ibid., p. 1028.

25. *Hittite Warrior* (Bryce), p. 20.

26. *The Trojan War – A New History* (Strauss), p. 141.

27. *Ancient Near Eastern Texts* (Pritchard), pp. 441-444.

28. Ibid., Note 3 p. 441.

29. Against Apion 1.14.76.

30. *The Hebrew Pharaohs of Egypt* (Osman), p. 66.

31. *Ancient Near Eastern Texts* (Pritchard), p. 233.

32. Ibid.

33. Against Apion 1.32 (292).

34. *Amenhotep III – Perspectives on his Reign* (O'Connor), p. 23.

35. SG#3404.

36. 'mess.' *Egyptian Hieroglyphic Dictionary* (Budge), p.321.

37. 'en.' Ibid., p. 200.

38. 'u.' Ibid., p. 144.

39. 'mess.' Ibid., p. 323.

40. Exodus 32:1-6.

41. 'Mesen.' *Egyptian Hieroglyphic Dictionary* (Budge), p. 325.

42. *The Nile and Egyptian Civilization* (Moret), p. 329.

43. *Nefertiti* (Tyldesley), p. 83.

44. *Akhenaten – King of Egypt* (Aldred), p. 286.

45. SH#4551.

46. SH#369.

47. SH#4938.

48. *Tutankhamen* (El Mahdy), p. 108.

49. Jacobs, Joseph, et al. 'Moses.' *Jewish Encyclopedia*. 23 September 2011 http:// www. jewishencyclopedia.com/view.jsp? artid =830&letter=M.

50. Ibid., 'King in Ethiopia'.

51. Egyptian Museum, Berlin. Inv. No. 15000, photo by Andreas Praefcke, 23 September 2011 http:// en.wikipedia.org/wiki/File: Spaziergang_im_Garten_Amarna_Berlin.jpg

52. Deuteronomy 34:7.

53. *Chronicle of the Queens of Egypt* (Tyldesley), p. 115.

54. Dodson, Aidan. 'Crown Prince Djhutmose and the Royal Sons of the Eighteenth Dynasty'. *Journal of Egyptian Archaeology*, Vol. 76, 1990, pp. 87-97.

55. *Amarna Sunset* (Dodson), p. 4.

Chapter 11 Manetho's New Kingdom king list

1. *Egypt – Gods* (Gahlin), p. 90.

2. *The Oxford History of Ancient Egypt* (Shaw), p. 481.

3. Against Apion 1.15 (85 - 102).

4. Against Apion 1.15 (94).

5. Against Apion 1.26 (241).

6. Against Apion 1.34 (305).

7. Against Apion 1.26 (232).

8. Against Apion 1.15 (102).

9. Against Apion 1.26 (231).

10. Against Apion 1.15 (98).

11. Against Apion 1.15 (102).

12. Against Apion 1.26 (231).

13. Against Apion 1.15 (98).

14. Against Apion 1.26 (231).

15. *The New Complete Works of Josephus* (Whiston), 'Sethosis' in Maier's Index.

16. Against Apion 1.26 (231).

17. *Amenhotep III – Perspectives on his Reign* (O'Connor), p. 9.

18. *A History of Ancient Egypt* (Grimal), p. 242.

19. SG#3404.

20. SG#5418.

21. SG#2380.

22. SG#4982.

23. SG#3165.

24. SG#1692.

25. SG#213.

26. *Tutankhamun - Exodus Conspiracy* (Collins), p. 168.

27. *The Head of God* (Laidler), p. 35.

28. *Kingdom of the Ark* (Evans), p. 27.

29. *Jesus – Last of the Pharaohs* (Ellis), pp. 36-37,65.

30. *A History of Ancient Egypt* (Van De Mieroop), p. 334.

31. *Manetho – Egyptian Chronology* (Greenberg), p. 89.

32. Ibid, p. 81.

33. 'aakh.' *Egyptian Hieroglyphic Dictionary* (Budge), p. cxv.

34. 'Ba-en-Shu.' Ibid., p. 200.

35. 'kheres.' Ibid., p. 562.

36. SH#252.

37. SH#371.

38. SH#2791.

39. Exodus 7.

40. SH#2580.

41. *The Encyclopædia of the Pharaohs* (Baker), p. 480.

42. 'tut.' *Egyptian Hieroglyphic Dictionary* (Budge), p. 826.

43. 'aankh.' Ibid., p. 112.

44. 'Ra-neb-Kheperu.' Ibid., pp. 933, 1265.

45. 'neb.' Ibid., p. 357.

46. 'kheperu.' Ibid., p. 542.

47. *The Encyclopædia of the Pharaohs* (Baker), p. 480.

48. 'thut.' *Egyptian Hieroglyphic Dictionary* (Budge), p. 853.

49. 'is.' Ibid., p. 143.

50. 'us.' Ibid., p. 181.

51. *In the Name of Heaven* (Engh), p. 13.

52. SG#1155.

53. SG#1156.

54. 'δάνος.' *A Greek-English Lexicon* (Liddle and Scott).

55. 'er.' *Egyptian Hieroglyphic Dictionary* (Budge), p. 414.

56. 'ma, mai.' Ibid., p. 269.

57. 'mai.' Ibid., p. 280.

58. *Akhenaten, Egypt's False Prophet* (Reeves), pp.179-189.

59. Abydos King List, 23 September 2011 http://en.wikipedia
    .org/wiki /Abydos_king_list.

60. Saqqara Tablet, 23 September 2011 http://en.wikipedia.org/
    wiki/ Saqqara_Tablet

61. *Manetho* (Waddell), pp. 107-109.

62. Ibid., p. 111.

63. Ibid., p. 115.

64. *The Complete Royal Families* (Dodson), p. 162.

65. *The Encyclopædia of the Pharaohs* (Baker), p. 412.

66. Ibid., p. 411.

67. Exodus 12:36.

Chapter 12 Saul, David and Solomon – Amarna contemporaries

1. *Israel's Golden Age* (Fleming).
2. I Samuel, II Samuel.
3. *David and Solomon* (Finkelstein), p. 17.
4. I Samuel 18:1.
5. I Samuel 24, 26.
6. II Samuel 1:27.
7. *The Sins of King David* (Greenberg), cf. comment by Dr. David Noel Freedman, inside cover flap.
8. II Samuel 16:7-8.
9. II Samuel 11.
10. *The Quest for the Historical Israel* (Finkelstein), p. 117.
11. Ibid., pp. 57-65, 120-125.
12. I Kings 6:1.
13. I Kings 14: 25-26; II Chronicles 12:2-9.
14. *The Complete Bible Handbook* (Bowker), p. 135.
15. *Egypt – Gods* (Gahlin), p. 91.
16. *The Bible Unearthed* (Finkelstein), p. 161.
17. *The Quest for the Historical Israel* (Finkelstein), pp. 120, 123-125.
18. SH#7895.
19. SH#8337.
20. SH#8341.
21. SH#8154.
22. SH#251.
23. *Empire of Thebes* (Sweeney), p. 110.
24. *A Test of Time* (Rohl).
25. *The Mysterious Numbers of the Hebrew Kings* (Thiele), pp. 35, 80.
26. *A Test of Time* (Rohl), Chapters 9, 10.
27. *The Amarna Letters* (Moran), Introduction.
28. Psalm 57:4.
29. SH#3833.
30. *A Test of Time* (Rohl), p. 239, 242.
31. Ibid., pp. 252-253.
32. I Samuel 20:30-31 (The New Jerusalem Bible, Standard Edition).

33. *A Test of Time* (Rohl), p. 266.

34. Ibid., p. 267.

35. Ibid., p. 270.

36. II Samual 24:1-16.

37. *A Test of Time* (Rohl), pp. 215-6.

38. I Kings 11:19.

39. SH#2945.

40. SH#5211.

41. 'Danaus.' *The Dictionary of Mythology* (Coleman).

42. Exodus 1:11.

43. *Ramesses* (Tyldesley), Chapter 4.

44. Ibid., p. 82.

45. *A Test of Time* (Rohl), p. 176.

46. Ibid., p. 279.

47. Ibid., p. 280.

48. Ibid., p. 283.

49. Ibid., pp. 288-297.

50. *Historical Dictionary of Ancient Egypt* (Bierbrier), p. 259.

51. *Egypt – Gods* (Gahlin), p. 90.

Chapter 13 Nefertiti, the Queen of Sheba and Helen of Troy

1. Egyptian Museum, Berlin, Inv. No. 21300, photo by Philip Pikart, 23 September 2011 http:// en.wikipedia.org/ wiki/File: Nofretete_Neues_Museum.jpg, Creative Commons License

2. *Nefertiti* (Tyldesley), pp. 40-48.

3. I Kings 10:1-13; II Chronicles 9:1-13.

4. Matthew 12:42, Luke 11:31.

5. Antiquities 8.6.2 (157-159); 8.6.5 (165-175).

6. The Koran, Surah 27.20-24 (Pickthall).

7. The Koran (Ali) Note 3264 to Surah 27.23.

8. Jacobs, Joseph and Blau, Ludwig. 'Sheba, Queen of:.' *Jewish Encyclopedia*, 23 September 2011 http://www.jewishencyclopedia. com/view.jsp?artid=566&letter=S.

9. *The Kebra Nagast* (Budge), 1932.

10. II Samuel 11-12.

11. SH#1339.

12. SH#1323.

13. SH#7651

14. SH#7650

15. I Chronicles 3:5.

16. II Samuel 23:34.

17. SH#5971.

18. SH#410.

19. II Samuel 20.

20. *The Quest for the Ark of the Covenant* (Munro-Hay), p. 20.

21. II Samual 12:7-9.

22. I Samuel 18:19-21, 25:44; II Samuel 3:13-16.

23. 'The Family of David.' *The Legends of the Jews, Vol. 4* (Ginzberg).

24. II Samuel 6:14-23.

25. Talmud Mas. Sanhedrin 19b, *Judaic Classics* (Kantrowitz).

26. SH#6406.

27. SH #6403.

28. I Samuel 25.

29. II Samuel 15:16.

30. II Samuel 16:22.

31. II Samuel 20:3.

32. *The Sins of King David* (Greenberg), p. 6.

33. Erich Lessing Photo Archive, < http:// www. lessing-photo.com >, image no. 08-05-05/21.

34. Megiddo Ivory line drawing, The Israel Museum, Jerusalem.

35. *In Search of God* (Mettinger), p. 128.

36. *The Lost Testament* (Rohl), pp. 373-374.

37. *Empire of Thebes* (Sweeney), pp. 152-153.

38. II Samuel 5:11; I Kings 5:1.

39. I Kings 10:18-19.

40. Fragmentary relief showing two pairs of horses, Limestone, Egypt, Amarna, Collection of The Israel Museum, Jerusalem, photo by Meidad Suchowolski.

41. National Museum of Beirut, photo by Elie plus, 23 September 2011 http://en.wikipedia.org/wiki/ File:Ahiram.jpg.

42. *The Rock Tombs of El Amarna* (Davies), p. 20.

43. *The Complete Royal Families* (Dodson), p. 155.

44. *Akhenaten, Egypt's False Prophet* (Reeves), p. 148.

45. *Eternal Egypt – Masterworks* (Russmann), '60', p. 144.

46. Altes Museum, Berlin, photo by Schengili-Roberts, 23 September 2011 http://en.wikipedia.org /wiki/File: Unfinished Stele-NefertitiPouringWineIntoAkhenatens Cup.png.

47. Egyptian Museum, Berlin, Inv. No. 21263, photo by Praefcke, 23 September 2011 http:// en.wikipedia.org/ wiki/ File:Nefertiti_ Standing-striding_ Berlin.jpg.

48. The British Museum, image no. 00496547001, Limestone stela with a seated figure of Akhenaten.

49. *Tutankhamen* (El Mahdy), pp. 103 107.

50. Richard Seaman, http:// www. richard-seaman.com.

51. *The Complete Tutankhamen* (Reeves), p. 184.

52. *Tutankhamen* (El Mahdy), p.134.

53. GlowImages, http:// www. glowimages.com/, Heritage Imagestate RM image 0390001304.

54. Photo by Rama, 23 September 2011 http:// commons. wikimedia. org/wiki /File: Akhenathon_ and _ Nefertiti _ E15593 _ mp3h8770.jpg

55. 'beard.' *British Museum Dictionary of Ancient Egypt* (Shaw).

56. *Tutankhamun's Armies* (Darnell), p. 68.

57. Surah LXVI (Sale, Note 4, p. 458).

58. Allen, J.P., 'The Amarna Succession.' *Causing His Name to Live* (Brand).

59. *Egypt – Gods* (Gahlin), p. 90.

60. *Nefertiti* (Tyldesley), Chapter 6.

61. 's-menkh.' *Egyptian Hieroglyphic Dictionary* (Budge), p.602.

62. 'ka.' Ibid., pp. 782, 783.

63. Güterbock, H.G., 'The Deeds of Suppiluliuma as told by his son, Mursili II.' *Journal of Cuneiform Studies*, 10 (1956), p. 41-68, 75-98,

107-130.

64. *Akhenaten – King of Egypt* (Aldred), p. 298.

65. *Akhenaten, Egypt's False Prophet* (Reeves), p. 176.

66. Bryce, Trevor R. 'The Death of Niphururiya and Its Aftermath.' *The Journal of Egyptian Archaeology*, Vol. 76, 1990, pp. 97-105.

67. *Akhenaten, Egypt's False Prophet* (Reeves), p. 177.

68. Antiquities 8.6.2 (158-159).

69. *Histories – Herodotus* (Rawlinson), 2.100.

70. *Manetho* (Waddell), pp. 53-55.

71. 'Nitiqret.' *Who's Who in Ancient Egypt* (Rice).

72. SG#3506.

73. SG#5520.

74. SG#5521.

75. *The Eskeles Genealogy* (Eshkolot), p.3; 23 September 2011 http://www.loebtree.com/kings.html

76. I Kings 3:1; 9:16.

77. SG#5017.

78. SG#3512.

79. SG#3588.

80. SG#2920.

81. SG#3558.

82. SG#5557.

83. 'Punt.' *British Museum Dictionary of Ancient Egypt* (Shaw).

84. *Hatchepsut* (Tyldesley), p. 145.

85. I Kings 9:28.

86. Peters, Carl. 'Ophir and Punt in South Africa'. *Oxford Journal of African Affairs*, Vol. 1, Issue II, 1902, pp. 174-183.

87. *Ancient Egypt* (Atiya), p. 272.

88. Erich Lessing Photo Archive, http:// www. lessing-photo.com, image no. 08-01-04/12.

89. *Histories – Herodotus* (Rawlinson), 2.100.

90. Ibid., 2.107-8.

91. The Koran, Surah 66.11.

92. *In Search of the Trojan War* (Wood).

93. *Histories – Herodotus* (Rawlinson), 2.112-115, 118-120.

94. *The Odyssey* (Homer), Book IV.

95. Photo by Than Ball, 23 September 2011 http://en.wikipedia
.org/wiki /File:Colossi_of_Memnon.jpg.

96. Pausanius's Description of Greece (Frazer), 1.42.3, p. 64; 4.31.5,
p. 226; *10.31.7*, p. 546.

97. SG#3419.

98. SG#71.

99. SG#3420.

100. SG#2992.

101. SG#4092.

102. SG#2386.

103. SG#3844.

104. SG#2447.

105. *Troy – The World Deceived* (Lascelles), pp. 170-171.

106. *Diodorus, Library of History* (Oldfather), 1.56.4.

107. *Strabo Geography* (Jones), 17.1.34.

108. *Ancient Records of Egypt* (Breasted), p. 315, §800; p. 352, §875.

109. 'Priam.' *Dictionary of Ancient Deities* (Turner).

110. Antiquities 2.16. 3.

111. *Quintus Smyrnaeus, Fall of Troy* (Way), 2.133, 680-730.

112. *Apollodorus – Epitome* (Frazer), 3.18-3.19.

113. Ibid., 3.21.

114. *In Search of the Trojan War* (Wood), pp. 280-1.

115. SG#1909.

116. SG#1074.

117. SG# 383.

118. SG#303.

119. SG#3579.

120. *St Augustine – City of God* (Bettenson), 18.12.

121. *Histories – Herodotus* (Rawlinson), 2.119.

122. SG# 2564.

123. 'chaos.' *Pocket Oxford Classical Greek Dictionary* (Morwood).

124. SG#5475.

125. *Homer – The Odyssey* (Butler), Book IV.

126. SG#2808.

127. SG#5037.

128. SG#3423.

129. *In Search of the Trojan War* (Wood), Preface.

130. *Caeser's Calendar* (Feeney), p. 142.

131. *Apollodorus – Epitome* (Frazer), 3.16.

132. *The Argonautica – Apollonius* (Seaton) 4.757-776, 865-884.

133. *The Quest for the Ark of the Covenant* (Munro-Hay), p. 133.

134. Against Apion 2.2 (17-19).

135. 'Dido.' *Dictionary of Ancient Deities* (Turner).

136. 'Aeneas.' Ibid.

137. *Apollodorus – The Library* (Frazer), Note 1, p. 224.

138. *The Trojans and their Neighbours* (Bryce), p. 2.

139. SG#2462.

140. SG#4215.

141. NIV, Introduction to Song of Songs.

142. *The Song of Songs* (Thrupp), pp. 29-30.

143. Song of Songs 1:9.

144. Ibid., 1:5.

145. NIV Note to Song of Songs 1:5.

146. Antiquities 2.10.2 (252-253).

147. Numbers 12:1.

148. *Legends of OT Characters* (Baring-Gould), pp. 343-349.

Chapter 14 The conquest of Canaan

1. Numbers 14:33-34.

2. Joshua 1:1-9.

3. 'Jerico.' *Encyclopædia Britannica*, www. britannica.com.

4. Joshua 3:1-17.

5. *Archaeology and the Old Testament* (Hoerth), p. 209.

6. Bruins, Hendrik J. and Van Der Plicht, Johannes. 'Tell Es-Sultan (Jericho): Radiocarbon Results of Short-Lived Cereal and Multilayer Charcoal Samples from the End of the Middle Bronze

Age.' *RADIOCARBON*, Vol. 37, No.2, 1995, pp. 213-220.

7.   *Archaeology and the Old Testament* (Hoerth), p. 209.

8.   *The New Lion Handbook to the Bible* (Alexander), p. 229.

9.   'Hazor.' *Eerdmans Dictionary of the Bible* (Freedman), p561.

10. *Archaeology and the Old Testament* (Hoerth), p. 211.

11. Heinemeier, Jan, Friedrich, Walter L, Kromer, Bernd and Ramsey, Christopher Bronk. 'The Minoan eruption of Santorini radiocarbon dated by an olive tree buried by the eruption.' *Time's Up!* (Warburton), pp. 285-293.

12. *The Bible Is History* (Wilson), p. 73.

13. *The Ancient Near East* (Kuhrt), p. 432.

14. *Ancient Egyptian Literature* (Lichtheim), pp. 73-78.

15. *The Bible Unearthed* (Finkelstein), p. 36.

16. *No Other Gods* (Gnuse), p. 39.

17. *Amenhotep III – Perspectives on his Reign* (O'Connor), p. 224.

18. Ibid., Note 4, p. 224.

Chapter 15. The plagues of Egypt as described in ancient sources

1.   *The Quest for the Historical Israel* (Finkelstein), pp. 9-20.

2.   Ibid., pp. 12-13.

3.   *The Exodus Enigma* (Wilson).

4.   *Act of God* (Phillips), reprinted as *Atlantis and the Ten Plagues of Egypt* (Phillips, 2003).

5.   *Black Athena* (Bernal), pp. 291-293.

6.   *The plagues of Egypt* (Trevisanato).

7.   *The Parting of the Sea* (Sivertsen).

8.   *The Lords of Avaris* (Rohl), pp. 30, 64-66, 249-257.

9.   Exodus 7-12.

10. Antiquities 2.14.

11. Exodus 7:19-24.

12. Antiquities 2.14.1 (294).

13. 'The Plagues Brought Through Aaron.' *The Legends of the Jews*, Vol. 2 (Ginzberg).

14. Exodus 8:1-6.

15. Antiquities 2.14.2 (296-297).

16. 'The Plagues Brought Through Aaron.' *The Legends of the Jews, Vol. 2* (Ginzberg).

17. Exodus 8:16-18.

18. Antiquities 2.14.3 (300).

19. 'The Plagues Brought Through Aaron.' *The Legends of the Jews, Vol. 2* (Ginzberg).

20. Exodus 8:20-24.

21. Antiquities 2.14.3 (302-303).

22. 'The Plagues Brought Through Moses.' *The Legends of the Jews, Vol. 2* (Ginzberg).

23. Exodus 9:1-6.

24. 'The Plagues Brought Through Moses.' *The Legends of the Jews, Vol. 2* (Ginzberg).

25. Exodus 9:8-10.

26. Antiquities 2.14.4 (304).

27. 'The Plagues Brought Through Moses.' *The Legends of the Jews, Vol. 2* (Ginzberg).

28. Exodus 9:13-26.

29. Antiquities 2.14.4 (305).

30. 'The Plagues Brought Through Moses.' *The Legends of the Jews, Vol. 2* (Ginzberg).

31. Exodus 10:1:15.

32. Antiquities 2.14.4 (306).

33. 'The Plagues Brought Through Moses.' *The Legends of the Jews, Vol. 2* (Ginzberg).

34. Exodus 10:21-23.

35. Antiquities 2.14.5 (308-309).

36. 'The Plagues Brought Through Moses.' *The Legends of the Jews, Vol. 2* (Ginzberg).

37. Exodus 11:1-6; 12:29-30.

38. Antiquities 2.14.6 (313-314).

39. 'The Smiting of the Firstborn.' *The Legends of the Jews, Vol. 2* (Ginzberg).

40. Exodus 13:21-22.
41. Exodus 14:15-28.
42. Antiquities 2.16 (343-344).
43. Psalm 77:16-20.
44. The Koran, Surah 7.133, 136 (Pickthall).
45. The Koran, Surah 29.39–40 (Ali).

Chapter 16 Could an eruption of Thera have affected Egypt?

1. Yokoyama, I. 'The Tsunami Caused by the Prehistoric Eruption of Thera.' *Thera and the Aegean World I* (Doumas), pp. 277-283.
2. *World's Worst Historical Disasters* (McNab), p. 14.
3. Newhall, Christopher G. and Self, Stephen. 'The Volcanic Explosivity Index (VEI): An Estimate of Explosive Magnitude for Historical Volcanism,' *Journal of Geophysical Research*, Vol. 87, No. C2, pp. 1231 1238, February 20, 1982.
4. *Volcanoes Global Perspectives*, (Lockwood), p. 124.
5. 'Chaitén (volcano).' *Wikipedia*, 23 September 2011 http://en.wikipedia.org/wiki/Chaitén_(volcano)
6. 'Category: VEI-4 volcanoes' *Wikipedia*, 23 September 2011 http://en.wikipedia.org/wiki/Category:VEI-4_volcanoes.
7. Plume from eruption of Chaiten volcano, Chile, NASA MODIS image, 23 September 2011 http://en.wikipedia.org/wiki/File:Plume_from_eruption_of_Chaiten_volcano,_Chile.jpg.
8. 'Mount St. Helens.' *Wikipedia*, 23 September 2011 http://en.wikipedia.org/wiki/Mount_St._Helens.
9. Tilling, Robert L., Topinka, Lyn and Swanson, Donald A., 'Eruptions of Mount St. Helens: Past, Present, and Future' *USGS Special Interest Publication*, 1990.
10. 'Mount Pinatubo.' *Wikipedia*, 23 September 2011 http://en.wikipedia.org/wiki/Mount_Pinatubo.
11. Paladio-Melosantos et al. 'Tephra Falls of the 1991 Eruptions of Mount Pinatubo.' *USGS*, 23 September 2011 http://pubs.usgs.gov/pinatubo/paladio/, Figure 9.
12. Mohn, Hendrik, 'Volcanic ash distribution from Iceland to

Scandinavia in 1875.' *Wikipedia*, 23 September 2011 http:// en. wikipedia.org/wiki/File:Akseregnen-1875-03-mohn-1877.jpg.

13. 'Krakatoa.' *Wikipedia*, 23 September 2011 http://en. wikipedia .org/wiki/Krakatoa.

14. 'Minoan eruption.' *Wikipedia*, 23 September 2011 http://en. wikipedia.org/wiki/Minoan_eruption.

15. Pyle, D.M. 'New Estimates for the Volume of the Minoan Eruption.' *Thera and the Aegen World III, Vol. II* (Hardy), pp. 113-121.

16. Global Volcanism Program, Santorini, Eruptive history, *Smithsonian Institution*, 23 September 2011 http:// www. volcano.si.edu/index.cfm.

17. Sparks, R.S.J. and Wilson, C.J.N. 'The Minoan Deposits: a Review of their Characteristics and Interpretation.' *Thera and the Aegen World III, Vol. II* (Hardy), pp. 89-99.

18. *The Bible Is History* (Wilson), p. 47.

19. *The Britannica Guide to Inventions That Changed the Modern World* (Curley), p. 293.

20. Personal correspondence with experts in volcanology.

21. 'What's it like during an ash fall?' *USGS*, 23 September 2011 http:// volcanoes.usgs.gov/ash/ashfall.html.

22. Yokoyama, I. 'The Tsunami Caused by the Prehistoric Eruption of Thera.' *Thera and the Aegean World I* (Doumas), pp. 277-283, Figure 4.

23. 'TNT Equivalent.' *Wikipedia*, 23 September 2011 http://en. wikipedia.org/wiki/TNT_equivalent.

24. *Welcome to Planet Earth* (Hull), p. 305.

25. *The Bomb – A Life* (DeGroot), pp. 259, 370.

26. *Weapons of Mass Destruction* (Croddy), p. 163.

27. *Encyclopedia of Disaster Relief* (Penuel), Vol. 1: p. 375.

28. Bunney, Sarah. 'Thera's outburst and the decline of Crete.' *New Scientist*, 9 August 1984, p. 20.

29. *The Plagues of Egypt* (Trevisanato), p. 64.

30. Ibid., p. 45.

31. Psalm 104:32.

32. Wilson, L, Sparks, R.S.J., Huang, T.C. and Watkins, N.D. 'The Control of Volcanic Column Heights by Eruption Energetics and Dynamics.' *Journal of Geophysical Research*, Vol. 83, No. B4, April 10, 1978, pp. 1829-1836.

33. Wilson, L. 'Energetics of the Minoan Eruption.' *Thera and the Aegean World I* (Doumas), pp. 221-228.

34. *A Geography of Russia and Its Neighbors* (Blinnikov), p. 57.

Chapter 17 The plagues and miracles put into perspective

1. *The Dialogues of Plato* (Jowett), Timaeus 22, p. 443.

2. *Catastrophobia* (Clow), p. 100.

3. Against Apion 1.1 (10).

4. *St Augustine – City of God* (Bettenson), 18.8-11.

5. *Manetho* (Waddell), p. 113.

6. Against Apion 1.15 (86-89).

7. Against Apion 1.15 (94-96).

8. Davis, E.N. 'A Storm in Egypt during the reign of Ahmose.' *Thera and the Aegean World III, Vol. III*, pp. 232-235.

9. *Iulius Africanus Chronographiae*, (Wallraff), F34, p. 75.

10. Ibid., T54C, p. 161.

11. Bedrosian, Robert. *Eusebius' Chronicle*, 1.64, 23 September 2011 http://www.tertullian.org/fathers /eusebius_chronicon_02_text .htm..

12. Ibid., 1.66.

13. *Iulius Africanus Chronographiae*, (Wallraff), T55, p. 165.

14. Bedrosian, Robert. *Eusebius' Chronicle*, 1.22, 23 September 2011 http://www.tertullian.org/fathers /eusebius_chronicon_02_text .htm..

15. *Iulius Africanus Chronographiae*, (Wallraff), T55, pp. 165,167.

16. Decker, R.W. 'How often does a Minoan Eruption Occur?' *Thera and the Aegean world III, Vol.II* (Hardy), pp. 444-452.

17. *Iulius Africanus Chronographiae*, (Wallraff), Material from Book 3, p. 75.

18. *The Parian Chronicle* (Robertson), p. 24.

19. *Manetho* (Waddell), Fr. 42, p. 79.

20. *Egypt – Gods* (Gahlin), p. 90.

21. 'Khufu.' *British Museum Dictionary of Ancient Egypt* (Shaw).

22. *The Oxford History of Ancient Egypt* (Shaw), p. 139.

23. *Ages in Chaos* (Velikovsky), pp. 64-68.

24. *Encyclopædia of the Pharaohs* (Baker), Ahmose, pp. 9-11; Amenhotep I, pp. 37-39.

25. *The Complete Royal Families* (Dodson), pp. 116-117.

26. *The Ancient Near East* (Kuhrt), p. 163.

27. *The Complete Royal Families* (Dodson), p. 61.

28. Against Apion 1.14 (75).

29. *Histories – Herodotus* (Rawlinson), 2.111.

30. *Eusebius – Praeparatio Evangelica* (Gifford), 9.27.

31. *St Augustine – City of God* (Bettenson), 18.12.

32. *Diodorus, Library of History* (Oldfather), 5.55-56.

33. *Before the Flood* (Wilson), p. 321.

34. Genesis 6.

35. *The Bible Is History* (Wilson), p. 46.

36. *Act of God* (Phillips), p. 247.

37. *The Exodus Enigma* (Wilson), p. 121.

38. Numbers 14:31-35.

39. Against Apion 1.32 (289-290); 34 (306-308).

40. *The Kingdom of the Hittites* (Bryce), p. xv.

41. Exodus 20:5; Leviticus 26:39-40; Numbers 14:18; Deuteronomy 5:9; Jeremiah 32:18.

42. 'The Great Plague of London.' *Encyclopædia Britannica*, www.britannica.com.

43. *A Pest in the Land* (Alchon), p. 21.

44. Against Apion 2.2.21.

45. II Samuel 24:15; I Chronicles 21:14.

46. Numbers 19:20-22.

47. Numbers 11:1-3, 16:31-35.

48. Anderson, E.H., Haag, R.T. and Bonwetsch, G. Nathaniel, 'The

Book of the Revelation of Abraham, *Improvement Era*, Vol. I, No. 10, August 1898, p. 712.

49. *According to the Evidence* (von Däniken), p. 199.

50. Genesis 19:24 (King James Version).

51. The Jewish War 4.8.4 (483-484).

52. *Worlds in Collision* (Velikovsky), p. 69.

53. Talmud – Mas. Berachoth 54b.

54. SH#5645.

55. SH# 5204.

56. SH#5921.

57. SH#1361.

58. SH#376.

59. 'Plagues of Egypt.' Wikipedia, 23 September 2011 http://en. wikipedia.org/wiki/Plagues_of_Egypt.

60. *Act of God* (Phillips), pp. 241-242.

61. Photograph by Mike Cash, Associated Press image no. 800519043.

62. *The Miracles of Exodus* (Humphreys), pp. 140-142.

63. *The Bible Is History* (Wilson), p. 49.

64. Genesis 22.

65. Leviticus 18:21.

66. Jeremiah 7:30-31.

67. Jeremiah 19:5.

68. Jeremiah 32:35.

69. II Kings 3:26-27.

70. II Kings 23:10.

71. Isaiah 30:33.

72. Micah 6:7.

73. Exodus 22:29-30.

74. I Kings 11:7.

75. Exodus 4:22-23.

76. Exodus 10:28-29.

77. Antiquities 2.14.5 (310).

78. Exodus 11:5.

79. *Apollodorus – The Library* (Frazer), 2.5.11.

80. 'Iphigenia.' *The Dictionary of Mythology* (Coleman).

81. 'Danaus.' *Dictionary of Ancient Deities* (Turner).

82. SG#71.

83. SG#3509.

84. SG#3516.

85. SG#3525.

86. SG#2031.

87. SG#4095.

88. 'Danaus.' *Dictionary of Ancient Deities* (Turner).

89. Exodus 3:1-10.

Chapter 18 The parting of the sea and the route of the Exodus

1. Exodus 13:17-14:31 (*Catholic Encyclopedia*).

2. *On the Reliability of the Old Testament* (Kitchen), pp. 261-263.

3. SH#3220.

4. SH#5488.

5. *The Times Concise Atlas of the Bible* (Pritchard), pp. 34-35.

6. *The Moses Legacy* (Phillips), Chapter 5.

7. *The Early History of Israel* (de Vaux), p. 370.

8. *The Parting of the Sea* (Sivertsen), pp. 37, 42-43, 118-119, 128, 136-139.

9. Against Apion 1.14 (86-91).

10. *The Political Situation in Egypt* (Ryholt), pp. 172-175.

11. *Egypt, Canaan and Israel in Ancient Times* (Redford), pp. 128-129.

12. *The Parting of the Sea* (Sivertsen), p. 89.

13. *The Moses Legacy* (Phillips), pp. 77, 81, 86.

14. Ibid., pp. 74-77.

15. Ibid., pp. 78-80.

16. *Black Athena* (Bernal), Note 80, p. 593.

17. *The Lords of Avaris* (Rohl), p. 251.

18. Rapp, G. and Kraft, J.C. 'Aegean Sea Level Changes in the Bronze Age.' *Thera and the Aegean World I* (Doumas), pp. 181-194, Figure 4.

19. *Act of God* (Phillips), p. 254.

20. Exodus 14:19.

21. *Act of God* (Phillips), p. 255.

22. Numbers 32:13.

23. *The Parting of the Sea* (Sivertsen), pp. 134-135, 140-142, 148, 150.

24. *The plagues of Egypt* (Trevisanato), pp. 169-170, 188.

Chapter 19 Dating the eruptions of Thera

1. *A Test of Time* (Manning), Introduction.

2. Ibid., pp. 335-336.

3. Heinemeier, Jan, Friedrich, Walter L., Kromer, Bernd and Ramsey, Christopher Bronk, 'The Minoan eruption of Santorini radiocarbon dated by an olive tree buried by the eruption.' *Time's Up!* (Warburton), pp. 285-293.

4. *A Test of Time* (Manning), pp. 333, 338.

5. Christopher Bronk Ramsey, Michael W. Dee, Joanne M. Rowland, Thomas F. G. Higham, Stephen A. Harris, Fiona Brock, Anita Quiles, Eva M. Wild, Ezra S. Marcus and Andrew J. Shortland. 'Radiocarbon-Based Chronology for Dynastic Egypt' *Science*, Vol. 328 no. 5985 pp. 1554-1557, June 2010.

6. Bruins, Hendrik J., Van der Plicht, Johannes and MacGilivray, J. Alexander 'The Minoan Santorini Eruption and Tsunami Deposits in Palaikastro (Crete): Dating by Geology, Archaeology, ^{14}C, and Egyptian Chronology.' *Radiocarbon*, Vol. 51, Nr 2, 2009, pp. 397-411.

7. Bruins, Hendrik J. 'Dating Pharaonic Egypt', *Science*, Vol. 328, 2010, June 2010, pp. 1489-1498.

8. Page, D. 'On the Relationship between the Thera Eruption and the Desolation of Eastern Crete c. 1450 B.C.' *Thera and the Aegean World I* (Doumas), pp. 691-698.

9. *A Test of Time* (Manning), pp. 220-229.

10. *Santorini Volcano* (Druitt), Chapter 3.

11. Sparks, R.S.J. and Wilson, C.J.N. 'The Minoan Deposits: a Review of their Characteristics and Interpretation.' *Thera and the*

Aegean World III, Vol. II (Hardy), pp. 89-99

12. Friedrich, Walter L. and Sigalas, Nikolaos. 'The effects of the Minoan eruption.' *Time's Up!* (Warburton), pp. 91-100.

13. *Thera and the Aegean World III, Vol. II* (Hardy), p. 99.

14. *Time's Up!* (Warburton), p. 93.

15. *The Parting of the Sea* (Sivertsen), pp. 27-29.

16. *The plagues of Egypt* (Trevisanato), pp. 65-67,72.

17. *The Parting of the Sea* (Sivertsen), p. 29.

18. Bruins, Hendrik J., Van der Plicht, Johannes and MacGilivray, J. Alexander 'The Minoan Santorini Eruption and Tsunami Deposits in Palaikastro (Crete): Dating by Geology, Archaeology, ^{14}C, and Egyptian Chronology.' *Radiocarbon*, Vol. 51, Nr 2, 2009, pp. 397-411.

19. Ibid., Figures 4 and 5.

20. Stanley, Daniel Jean and Sheng, Harrison 'Volcanic shards from Santorini (Upper Minoan ash) in the Nile Delta, Egypt.' *Nature*, Vol. 320, 24 April 1986.

21. *The Parting of the Sea* (Sivertsen), pp. 28-30.

22. Intcal09 supplementary data to Reimer et al., *Radiocarbon* Vol 51 Nr 4, 2009, www.radiocarbon.org/IntCal09.htm

23. *The Parting of the Sea* (Sivertsen), Note 28 to Chapter 3, p. 168-169.

24. Liritz, I., Michael, C. and Galloway, R.B. 'A Significant Aegean Volcanic Eruption during the Second Millenium B.C. Revealed by Thermoluminescence Dating.' Geoarchaeology, Vol. 11, No. 4, 1996, pp. 361-371.

25. *The Parting of the Sea* (Sivertsen), pp. 134-135.

26. *The Amarna Letters* (Moran), EA 151, p. 238.

27. *Act of God* (Phillips), p. 278.

28. 'Ugarit and the Bible.' *Quartz Hill School of Theology*. 23 September 2011 http://www.theology.edu /ugarbib.htm.

29. *The Civilization of Ancient Crete* (Willetts), p. 136.

Chapter 20 Abraham, father of the Hyksos

1. Genesis 28:10-15.
2. Genesis 35:22-29.
3. *The Cambridge Ancient History* (Edwards), pp. 59-60.
4. *The Political Situation in Egypt* (Ryholt), p. 96.
5. *Handbook of Egyptian Mythology* (Pinch), Chapter 2.
6. SH#87.
7. SH#1.
8. SH#7311.
9. SH#85.
10. Genesis 17:5.
11. SH#7200.
12. SH#7451.
13. SH#7462.
14. SH#5971.
15. SH#7202.
16. SH#7203.
17. Daniel 4:13, 17, 23 (King James Version).
18. *The Book of Enoch* (Charles), Chapters XII-XVI.
19. *The Book of Jubilees* (Charles), VII.21.
20. Genesis 6:1-4 (NIV)
21. *The Book of Enoch* (Charles), Chapters V1-VII.
22. SH#5303.
23. SH#5308.
24. SH#5309
25. Reeves, John C. 'Utnapishtim in the Book of Giants?' *Journal of Biblical Literature*, Vol. 112, No. 1, 1993, pp. 110-115.
26. *Eusebius - Praeparatio Evangelica* (Gifford), 9.17.
27. Ibid., 9.18.
28. Ibid., 2.1.
29. SH#6147.
30. SH#4596.
31. SH#225.
32. SH#5892.

33. *The Atlantis Dialogue – Plato* (Shepard), pp. 26-28.

Bibliography

Alchon, Suzanne Austin. *A Pest in the Land – New World Epidemics in a Global Perspective*. Albuquerque, NM: University of New Mexico Press, 2003.

Aldred, Cyril. *Akhenaten – King of Egypt*. New York, NY: Thames & Hudson, 1999.

Alexander, Pat and David, eds. *The New Lion Handbook to the Bible*. Oxford: Lion Publishing plc, 1999.

Ali, Abdullah Yusuf. *The Holy Quran, text, translation and commentary*. Lahore: SH. Muhammad Ashraf, Kashmiri Bazar, 1969.

Arnold, Dieter. *The Encyclopedia of Ancient Egyptian Architecture*. London: I.B. Taurus & Co Ltd, 2003.

Atiya, Farid. *Ancient Egypt*. Giza: Farid Atiya Press, 2006.

Baker, Darrell D. *The Encyclopædia of the Pharaohs Volume I*. London: Stacey International, 2008.

Barclay, John M. G. *Jews in the Mediterranean Diaspora: from Alexander to Trajan (323 BCE – 117 BCE)*. Berkeley, Los Angeles, London: University of California Press, 1996.

Baring-Gould, S. *Legends of Old Testament Characters, from Talmud and Other Sources*. London and New York: Macmillan and Co., 1871.

Barker, Kenneth, ed. *The NIV Study Bible (New International Version)*, Grand Rapids, MI: Zondervan Publishing House, 1985.

Barnett, Mary. *Gods and Myths of Ancient Egypt*. Rochester: Grange Books, 1999.

Bernal, Martin. *Black Athena Volume II*, New Brunswick: Rutgers University Press, 2002.

Bettenson, Henry, trans. *St Augustine – City of God*. London, New York, Victoria, Toronto, New Delhi, Auckland and Johannesburg: Penguin Books, 1984.

Bierbrier, Morris L. *Historical Dictionary of Ancient Egypt, Second Edition*. Lanham, Maryland: The Scarecrow Press, Inc., 2008.

Blinnikov, Mikhail S., *A Geography of Russia and Its Neighbors*. New

York, NY: The Guilford Press, 2011.

Booth, Charlotte. *The Hyksos Period in Egypt*. Princes Risborough: Shire Publications Ltd, 2005.

Bowker, John. *The Complete Bible Handbook*. London: Dorling Kindersley, 2004.

Brand, Peter and Cooper, Louise, eds. *Causing His Name to Live: Studies in Egyptian Epigraphy and History in Memory of William J. Murnane*. Leiden: Brill Publishers, 2009.

Breasted, J.H. *Ancient Records of Egypt Volume II*. Chicago: University of Chicago Press, 1906.

Breasted, J.H. *Ancient Times – A History of the Early World*. Boston: Ginn and Company, 1914.

Bryce, Trevor. *Hittite Warrior*. Botley, Oxford and New York, NY: Osprey Publishing, 2007.

Bryce, Trevor. *The Kingdom of the Hittites*. Oxford, New York: Oxford University Press, 2010.

Bryce, Trevor. *The Trojans and their Neighbours*. Abingdon, Oxfordshire: Routeledge, 2006.

Budge, Wallis, E. A. *The Book of the Dead*. New York: Gramercy Books, 1999.

Budge, Wallis, E. A. *An Egyptian Hieroglyphic Dictionary*. London: John Murray, 1920.

Budge, Wallis, E. A. *The Kebra Nagast: The Queen of Sheba and Her Only Son Menyelek*. Chicago, IL: Research Associates School Times Publications and Frontline Distribution Int'l Inc., 2000.

Bunson, Margaret R. *Encyclopedia of Ancient Egypt, Revised Edition*, New York: Facts on File, Inc., 2002.

Butler, Samuel. *Homer – The Odyssey*. Digireads.com Publishing: www.digireads.com, 2009.

Caldecott, Moyra. *Hatshepsut: Daughter of Amun*. Bath: Mushroom eBooks, 2001.

Catholic Encyclopedia. New Advent CD-ROM Version 2.1.

Charles, R.H. *The Book of Enoch*. London: S.P.C.K., 1952.

Charles, R.H. *The Book of Jubilees or The Little Genesis*. London: Adam and Charles Black, 1902.

Cline, Eric H. and O'Connor, David, eds. *Thutmose III – A New Biography*. University of Michigan Press, 2009.

Clow, Barbara Hand, *Catastrophobia – The Truth Behind Earth Changes in the Coming Age of Light*. Rochester, VT: Bear & Company, 2001.

Coleman, J.A. *The Dictionary of Mythology*. Royston: Eagle Editions Limited, 2007.

Collins, Andrew and Ogilvie-Herald, Chris. *Tutankhamun – the Exodus Conspiracy*. London: Virgin Books, 2002.

Croddy, Eric A. and Wirtz, James J. *Weapons of Mass Destruction – An Encyclopedia of Worldwide Policy, Technology and History*. Santa Barbara, CA: ABC-CLIOO, Inc., 2005.

Curley, Robert, ed. *The Britannica Guide to Inventions That Changed the Modern World*. New York, NY: Britannica Educational Publishing, 2010.

Darnell, John Coleman and Manassa, Colleen. *Tutankhamun's Armies – Battle and Conquest During Egypt's Late 18th Dynasty*. Hoboken, NJ: John Wiley & Sons, Inc., 2007.

David, Rosalie. *Religion and Magic in Ancient Egypt*. London: Penguin Books Ltd, 2002.

Davidson, Linda Kay and Gitlitz, David Martin. *Pilgrimage: From the Ganges to Graceland: An Encyclopedia, Volume 1*. Santa Barbara, CA: ABC-CLIO, Inc., 2002.

Davies, N. de G. *The Rock Tombs of El Amarna, Part VI – Tombs of Parennefer, Tutu, and Aÿ*. London: Archaeological Survey of Egypt, Eighteenth Memoir, 1908.

de Vaux, Roland. *The Early History of Israel*. Philadelphia, PA: Westminster John Knox Press, 1978.

DeGroot, Gerhard J. *The Bomb – A Life*. London: Jonathan Cape Random House, 2004.

Dictionary of Egyptology. New Lanark: Geddes & Grosset, 1999.

Dodson, Aidan. *Amarna Sunset*. Cairo, New York: The American University in Cairo Press, 2009.

Dodson, Aidan and Hilton, Dyan. *The Complete Royal Families of*

Ancient Egypt. London: Thames & Hudson Ltd, 2004.

Doumas, C., ed. *Thera and the Aegean World I, Papers presented at the Second International Scientific Congress, Santorini, Greece*. London: Thera and the Aegean World, 1978.

Druitt, T.H., Edwards, L., Mellors, R.M., Pyle, D.M., Sparks, R.S.J., Lanphere, M., Davies, M. and Barriero, B. *Santorini Volcano*. Geological Society Memoir No. 19. London: The Geological Society, 2002.

Edwards, I.E.S., Gadd, C,J., Hammond, N.G.L and Solleberger,E., eds. *The Cambridge Ancient History. Vol. II Part 1*. Cambridge, New York, Oakleigh, Madrid, Cape Town: Cambridge University Press, 2000.

El Mahdy, Christine. *Tutankhamen – The Life and Death of a Boy King*. London: Headline Book Publishing, 2000.

Ellis, Ralph. *Jesus – Last of the Pharaohs*. Dorset: Edfu Books, 1999.

Engh, Mary Jane. *In the Name of Heaven: 3000 years of Religious Persecution*, Amherts, NY: Prometheus Books, 2007.

Erman, Adolf and Grapow, Hermann, eds. *Wörterbuch der ägyptischen Sprache*. Berlin: Akademie Verlag, 1963.

Eshkolot, Zeev. *The Eskeles Genealogy*. Haifa: Eltan Communication Ltd., 1995.

Evans, Lorraine. *Kingdom of the Ark*. London, Sydney, New York, Tokyo, Singapore, Toronto: Pocket Books, 2001.

Feeney, Denis. *Caesar's Calendar – Ancient Time and the Beginnings of History*. Berkeley and Losangeles, CA: University of California Press, 2008.

Feldman, Louis H. and Hata, Gohei, eds. *Josephus, Judaism and Christianity*. Detroit: Wayne State University Press, 1987.

Finkelstein, Israel and Mazar, Amihai. *The Quest for the Historical Israel*. Atlanta: Society of Biblical Literature, 2007.

Finkelstein, Israel and Silberman, Neil Asher. *David and Solomon*. New York, NY: Free Press, 2006.

Finkelstein, Israel and Silberman, Neil Asher. *The Bible Unearthed*. New York, London, Toronto, Sydney and Singapore: Touchstone,

2002.

Fleming, John Dick. *Israel's Golden Age; The Story of the United Kingdom*. Edinburgh: T. & T. Clarke, 1907.

Fletcher, Joann. *Chronicle of a Pharaoh – The Intimate Life of Amenhotep III*. New York, NY: Oxford University Press, Inc., 2000.

Fletcher, Joann, Humphreys, Andrew, Jenkins, Siona and Sattin, Anthony. *Egypt (Lonely Planet Country Guide)*. Lonely Country Publications, 2004.

Fletcher, Joann. *The Search for Nefertiti*. London: Hodder & Stoughton, 2004.

Fortenbaugh, William W. and Schütrumpf, Eckart, eds. *Dicaearchus of Messana: Text, Translation, and Discussion*. New Brunswick, NJ: Transaction Publishers, 2001.

Frazer, James George. *Apollodorus – The Library, Volume I, Books 1-3.9*. Loeb Classical Library No. 121. Cambridge, MA: Harvard University Press, 1921.

Frazer, James George. *Apollodorus – The Library, Volume II, Book 3.10-end. Epitome*. Loeb Classical Library No. 122. Cambridge, MA, Harvard University Press, 1921.

Frazer, James George. *Folk-lore in the Old Testament; studies in comparative religion, legend and law*. London: Macmillan and Co., Limited, 1919.

Frazer, James George. *Pausanias's Description of Greece*. London: Macmillan and Co., Limited, 1898.

Freedman, David Noel, ed. *Eerdmans Dictionary of the Bible*. Grand Rapids, MI: Wm. B. Eerdmans Publishing Co., 2000.

Freud, Sigmund and Jones, Katherine, trans. *Moses and Monotheism*. Letchworth: The Garden City Press Limited, 1939.

Gahlin, Lucia. *Egypt – Gods, Myths and Religion*. London: Lorenz Books, 2001.

Gifford, E.H. *Eusebius Pamphili of Caesarea – Praeparatio Evangelica*. Volume 3. Oxford, 1903.

Ginzberg, Louis. *The Legends of the Jews – Volume IV*. Philadelphia: The Jewish Publication Society of America, 1913.

Gnuse, Robert Karl. *No Other Gods – Emergent Monotheism in Israel.* Sheffield: Sheffield Academic Press Ltd, 1997.

Greenberg, Gary. *Manetho – A Study in Egyptian Chronology.* Warren Center, PA: Shangri-La Publications, 2003.

Greenberg, Gary. *The Sins of King David.* Naperville: Sourcebooks, Inc., 2002.

Grimal, Nicolas. *A History of Ancient Egypt.* Malden, MA: Blackwell Publishers, 2001.

Hansberry, William Leo and Harris, Joseph E. *Africa and Africans as seen by Classical Writers (African History Notebook Volume Two).* Washington, DC: Howard University Press, 1981.

Hardy, D.A., Keller, J., Galanopoulos, V.P., Flemming, N.C. and Druitt, T.H., eds. *Thera and the Aegean World III, Volume Two, Earth Sciences, Proceedings of the Third International Congress.* London: The Thera Foundation, 1990.

Hardy, D.A. and Renfrew, A.C., eds. *Thera and the Aegean World III, Volume Three, Chronology, Proceedings of the Third International Congress.* London: The Thera Foundation, 1990.

Healy, Mark and McBride, Angus. *New Kingdom Egypt.* Oxford, New York: Osprey Publishing Ltd., 2005.

Hoerth, Alfred J. *Archaeology and the Old Testament.* Grand Rapids, MI: Baker Books,1998.

Hornung, Erik and Baines, John, trans. *Conceptions of God in Ancient Egypt – the One and the Many.* Ithaca, NY: Cornell University Press, 1996.

Hull, Robert. *Welcome to Planet Earth - 2050 - Population Zero.* AuthorHouse http://www.authorhouse.com/, 2011.

Humphreys, Colin J. *The Miracles of Exodus.* London, New York: continuum, 2003.

Jones, Horace Leonard. *Strabo Geography Volume I, Books 1-2.* Loeb Classical Library No. 49. Cambrige: Harvard University Press, 1917.

Ibid., *Volume II, Books 3-5*, No. 50, 1923.

Ibid., *Volume III, Books 6-7*, No. 182, 1924.

Ibid., *Volume IV, Books 8-9*, No. 196, 1927.

Ibid., *Volume V, Books 10-12*, No. 211, 1928.

Ibid., *Volume VI, Books 13-14*, No. 223, 1929.

Ibid., *Volume VII, Books 15-16*, No. 241, 1930.

Ibid., *Volume VIII, Book 17*, No. 267, 1932.

Jowett, B. *The Dialogues of Plato, translated into English with Analyses and Introductions, Vol. III*, London: Oxford University Press, 1931.

Kantrowitz, David. *Judaic Classics*. Version 3.0.8. Davka Corporation.

Kitchen, K.A. *On the Reliability of the Old Testament*. Grand Rapids, MI: Wm. B. Eerdmans Publishing Co., 2003.

Kramer, Samuel Noah. *The Sumerians: Their History, Culture, and Character*. Chicago and London: The University of Chicago Press, 1963.

Kuhrt, Amélie. *The Ancient Near East c. 3000 – 330 BC*. London and New York: Routledge, 2002.

L'Égyptologie en 1979: axes prioritaires de recherches, Part 1. Centre national de la recherche scientifique (France), 1982.

Laidler, Keith. *The Head of God*. London: Orion Books Ltd, 1999.

Lascelles, John. *Troy – The World Deceived: Homer's Guide to Pergamum*. Victoria, BC: Trafford Publishing, 2005.

Lepage, Jean-Denis G.G., *The French Foreign Legion: An Illustrated History*. Jefferson, NC: McFarland & Company, Inc. Publishers, 2008.

Lesko, Barbara S. *The Great Goddesses of Egypt*. Norman, OK: University of Oklahoma Press, 1999.

Lichtheim, Miriam. *Ancient Egyptian Literature – Volume II: The New Kingdom*. Berkeley, Los Angeles and London: University of California, 1976.

Liddell, Henry George and Scott, Robert. *A Greek-English Lexicon*. Oxford: Clarendon Press, 1940.

Lockwood, John P. and Hazlett, Richard W., *Volcanoes – Global Perspectives*. Chichester, West Sussex: Wiley-Blackwell, 2010.

Mackenzie, Donald. *Egyptian Myth and Legend*. London: The Gresham Publishing Company Limited, 1913.

Mackenzie, Donald. *Myths of Babylon and Assyria*. The Gresham Publishing Company, 1915.

MacLeod, Roy, ed. *The Library of Alexandria: centre of learning in the ancient world*. London: I.B. Taurus & Co Ltd, 2005.

Manning, Sturt W. *A Test of Time*. Oxford and Oakville: Oxbow Books, 1999.

McKean, Erin. *The New Oxford American Dictionary (Second Edition)*. Oxford, New York et al.: Oxford University Press, 2005.

McNab, Chris. *World's Worst Historical Disasters*. New York, NY: The Rosen Publishing Group, Inc., 2009.

Mettinger, Tryggve N.D . *In Search of God – The Meaning and Message of the Everlasting Names*. Fortress Press ex libris publication, 2005.

Moran, William L. *The Amarna Letters*. Baltimore, London: The Johns Hopkins University Press, 1992.

Moret, Alexandre. *The Nile and Egyptian Civilization*. New York: Dover Publications, Inc., 2001.

Morwood, James and Taylor, John, eds. *Pocket Oxford Classical Greek Dictionary*. Oxford: Oxford University Press, 2002.

Munro-Hay, Stuart. *The Quest for the Ark of the Covenant*. London: I.B. Taurus & Co Ltd, 2005.

Murnane, William J. *Texts from the Amarna Period*. Atlanta, GA: Scholars Press,1995.

Neusner, Jacob, ed. *World Religions in America* (Fourth Edition). Westminster: John Knox Press, 2009.

O'Connor, David. *Ancient Nubia: Egypt's Rival in Africa*. Philadelphia: Publications Department, The University Museum, University of Pennsylvania, 1993.

O'Connor, David and Cline, Eric. H., eds. *Amenhotep III – Perspectives on His Reign*. University of Michigan Press, 2004.

Oldfather, C.H. *Diodorus Siculus – Library of History, Vol. I, Books 1-2.34*. Loeb Classical Library No. 279. Cambride: Harvard University Press, 1933.

Oldfather, C.H. *Diodorus Siculus – Library of History, Vol. II, Books 2.35-4.58*. Loeb Classical Library No. 303. Cambride: Harvard

University Press, 1935.

Oldfather, C.H. *Diodorus Siculus – Library of History, Vol. III, Books 4.59-8*. Loeb Classical Library No. 340. Cambride: Harvard University Press, 1939.

Osman, Ahmed. *The Hebrew Pharaohs of Egypt*. Rochester: Bear & Company, 2003. Originally published under the title *Stranger in the Valley of the Kings*. London: Souvernir Press Limited, 1987.

Osman, Ahmed. *Moses and Akhenaten: The Secret History of Egypt at the Time of the Exodus*. Rochester, VT: Bear & Company, 2002.

Parkinson, R.B. *The Tale of Sinuhe and Other Ancient Egyptian Poems 1940-1640 BC*. New York: Oxford University Press, 2009.

Pendlebury, J. S., ed. *The City of Akhetaton*, Vol. 3, EEM 44, Oxford: Egypt Exploration Society, 1951.

Pensée editors. *Velikovsky Reconsidered*. London: Sidgwick & Jackson,1976.

Penuel, K. Bradley and Statler, Matthew, eds. *Encyclopedia of Disaster Relief*. Thousand Oaks, CA, New Delhi, London, Singapore: Sage Publications Ltd., 2011.

Perl, Lila and Weihs, Erika. *Mummies, Tombs, and Treasure: Secrets of Ancient Egypt*, Volume 34. New York: Clarion Books, 1987.

Petrie, William Matthew Flinders and Currelly, Charles Trick. *Researches in Sinai*. London: John Murray, 1906.

Pfeiffer, Charles F. *Tell el Amarna and the Bible*. Grand Rapids, MI: Baker Books House, 1963.

Phillips, Graham. *Act of God: Moses, Tutankhamun and the Myth of Atlantis*. London and Basingstoke: Pan Books, 1998. Reprinted under the title *Atlantis and the Ten Plagues of Egypt: The Secret History Hidden in the Valley of the Kings*. Rochester, VT: Bear & Company, 2003.

Phillips, Graham. *The Moses Legacy*. London: Sidgwick & Jackson, 2002.

Pickthall, Mohammed Marmaduke. *The Meaning of the Glorious Koran*. New York, London, Victoria, Toronto and Auckland: Mentor.

Pinch, Geraldine. *Handbook of Egyptian Mythology*. Santa Barbara, CA: ABC-CLIO, Inc., 2002.

Pritchard, James B., ed. *Ancient Near Eastern Texts Relating to the Old Testament*. Princeton, NJ: Princeton University Press, 1969.

Pritchard, James B., ed., *The Ancient Near East – Volume 1: An Anthology of Texts and Pictures*. Princeton, New Jersey: Princeton University Press, 1958.

Pritchard, James B., ed. *The Times Concise Atlas of the Bible*. London: Times Books, 1991.

Quibell, James Edward. *Tomb of Yuaa and Thuiu*. Le Caire: Impr. de l'Institut Français d'archéologie Orientale, 1908.

Quirke, Stephen and Bourriau, Janine, eds. *Middle Kingdom Studies*. New Malden: SIA Pub., 1991.

Rawlinson, George, trans. and Griffith, Tom ed., *Histories – Herodotus*. Ware: Wordsworth Edition Limited, 1996.

Redford, Donald B. *Akhenaten, the Heretic King*. Princeton, NJ: Princeton University Press, 1987.

Redford, Donald B. *Egypt, Canaan, and Israel in Ancient Times*. Princeton, NJ: Princeton University Press, 1992.

Redford, Donald B., ed. *The Oxford Encyclopedia of Ancient Egypt*. New York: Oxford University Press, 2001.

Redford, Donald B., ed. *The Oxford Essential Guide to Egyptian Mythology*. New York: Berkley Books, 2003.

Reeves, Nicholas. *Akhenaten – Egypt's False Prophet*. London: Thames & Hudson Ltd, 2001.

Reeves, Nicholas. *The Complete Tutankhamun*. London: Thames & Hudson Ltd., 2008.

Reuchlin, Johann. *Recommendation whether to confiscate, destroy, and burn all Jewish books*. New Jersey: Paulist Press, 2000.

Rice, Michael. *Who's Who in Ancient Egypt*. London: Routledge, 1999.

Robertson, Joseph. *The Parian Chronicle, or the Chronicle of the Arundelian Marbles; with a Dissertation Concerning its Authenticity*. London: J. Walter Charing-Cross, 1788.

Rohl, David. *A Test of Time*. London: Century Press Ltd (Arrow),

1995.

Rohl, David. *The Lords of Avaris*. London: Arrow Books, 2008.

Rohl, David. *The Lost Testament. From Eden to Exile: The Five-Thousand-Year History of the People of the Bible*. London: Century, 2002.

Rudin, Norah and Inman, Keith. *An Introduction to Forensic DNA Analysis*. Boca Raton, Florida: CRC Press LLC, 2002.

Russmann, Edna R. *Eternal Egypt – Masterworks of Ancient Art from the British Museum*. Berkeley and Los Angeles, CA: University of California Press, 2001.

Ryholt, Kim S.B. *The Political Situation in Egypt during the Second Intermediate Period*. Copenhagen: Museum Tusculanum Press, 1997.

Sale, George. *The Koran: Commonly Called the Alcoran of Mohammed, translated into English immediately from the original Arabic with explanatory notes taken from the most approved commentators*. Philadelphia: J.B. Lippincott & Co., 1860.

Seaton, Robert Cooper, trans. *The Argonautica – Apollonius Rhodius*. London: Heinemann; New York, NY: G.P. Putnam's SOns, 1919.

Shaw, Ian, ed. *The Oxford History of Ancient Egypt*. Oxford: Oxford University Press, 2000.

Shaw, Ian and Nicholson, Paul. *The British Museum Dictionary of Ancient Egypt*. London: The British Museum Press, 1995.

Shepard, Aaron ed., Jowett, B. trans. *The Atlantis Dialogue – Plato*. Los Angeles, Shepard Publications, 2001.

Simpson, D.P. *Cassell's New Latin-English English-Latin Dictionary*. London: Cassell, 1975.

Sivertsen, Barbara J. *The Parting of the Sea*. Princeton and Oxford: Princeton University Press, 2009.

Sparks, H. F. D. ed. *The Apocryphal Old Testament*. Oxford: Oxford University Press, 1984.

Stookey, Lorena Laura. *Thematic Guide to World Mythology*. Westport, CT: Greenwood Press, 2004.

Strauss, Barry. *The Trojan War – A New History*. London: Hutchinson,

2007.

Strong, James. *The New Strong's Expanded Dictionary of Bible Words*. Nashville: Thomas Nelson Publishers, 2001.

Strudwick , Nigel and Helen. *Thebes in Egypt – A Guide to the Tombs and Temples of Ancient Luxor*. Ithaca, NY: Cornell University Press, 1999.

Sweeney, Emmet John. *Empire of Thebes or Ages in Chaos Revisited*. New York, NY: Algora Publishing, 2006.

Thiele, Edwin R. *The Mysterious Numbers of the Hebrew Kings (New Revised Edition)*. Grand Rapids, MI: Kregel Publications, 1983.

Thrupp, Joseph Francis. *The Song of Songs: A Revised Translation with Introduction and Commentary*. Cambridge and London: Macmillan and Co, 1862.

Trevisanato, Siro Igino. *The Plagues of Egypt – Archaeology, History, and Science Look at the Bible*. Piscataway: Euphrates, 2005.

Turner, Patricia and Coulter, Charles Russel. *Dictionary of Ancient Deities*. Oxford: Oxford University Press, 2001.

Tyldesley, Joyce. *Chronicle of the Queens of Egypt*. London: Thames & Hudson Ltd, 2006.

Tyldesley, Joyce. *Egypt's Golden Empire*. London: Headline Book Publishing, 2001.

Tyldesley, Joyce. *Hatchepsut the Female Pharaoh*. London: Penguin Books, 1998.

Tyldesley, Joyce. *Nefertiti – Unlocking the Mystery Surrounding Egypt's Most Famous and Beautiful Queen* (revised). London: Penguin Books, 2005.

Tyldesley, Joyce. *Ramesses, Egypt's Greatest Pharaoh*. London: Penguin Books, 2001.

Van De Mieroop , Marc. *A History of Ancient Egypt*. West Sussex: Wiley-Blackwell, 2011.

Van Der Horst, Pieter Willem. *Chaeremon – Egyptian Priest and Stoic Philosopher*. Leiden: E.J. Brill, 1984.

Van Hook, Larue. *Isocrates in Three Volumes with an English Translation Volume III*. Loeb Classical Library No. 373. Cambridge: Harvard

University Press; London: William Heinemann Ltd, 1945.

Velikovsky, Immanuel. *Ages in Chaos* (unchanged edition). Paradigma Ltd., 2009 (original edition New York: Doubleday & Company, Ltd., 1952).

Velikovsky, Immanuel. *Worlds in Collision.* Paradigma Ltd., 2009 (original edition New York: Doubleday & Company, Ltd., 1950).

Vercoutter, Jean. *The Search for Ancient Egypt.* New York: Abrams, 1992.

Von Däniken, Erich. *According to the Evidence.* London: Souvenir Press Ltd, 1998.

Waddell, W.G. *Manetho with an English translation,* Cambridge: Harvard University Press, London: William Heinemann Ltd, 1964.

Wallraff, Martin, ed. and Adler, William, trans. *Iulius Africanus Chronographiae – The Extant Fragments.* Berlin, New York: Walter de Gruyter, 2007.

Warburton, David A. ed. *Time's Up! Dating the Minoan eruption of Santorini, Monographs of the Danish Institute at Athens Volume 10.* Printed in Denmark: The Danish Institute at Athens, 2009.

Watson, John Selby. *Marcus Junianus Justinus – Epitome of the Philippic History of Pompeius Trogus.* London: Henry G. Bohn, 1853.

Watterson, Barbara. *Gods of Ancient Egypt.* Phoenix Mill Thrupp, Gloucestershire: Sutton Publishing Limited, 2003.

Way, A.S., trans. *Quintus Smyrnaeus – The Fall of Troy.* Loeb Classical Library No. 19. Cambrige: Harvard University Press, 1913.

Wellesley, Kenneth. *Tacitus – The Histories.* London: Penguin Books Ltd, 2009.

Wheeler, Brannon M. *Prophets in the Quran.* London: Continuum, 2002.

Whiston, William, trans. and Maier, Paul L. *The New Complete Works of Josephus.* Grand Rapids, MI: Kregel Publications, 1999.

Wilkinson, Toby. *The Rise and Fall of Ancient Egypt.* London, Berlin, New York: Bloomsbury Publishing, 2010.

Willetts, R.F. *The Civilization of Ancient Crete.* London: Phoenix Press,

2004.

Wilson, Ian. *Before the Flood*. London: Orion Books Ltd., 2001.

Wilson, Ian. *The Bible Is History*. Washington, DC: Regnery Publishing, Inc.,1999.

Wilson, Ian. *The Exodus Enigma*. London: Guild Publishing, 1985.

Wood, Michael. *In Search of the Trojan War*. London: BBC Books, 2005.

Figure and text credits and permissions

Figure 1.1 Following Ian Mladjov; 1.2 Following Jeff Dahl; 1.3 Pre-eruption coastline after Heiken and McKoy; 1.4 Pre-eruption coastlines after McCoy, Friedrich and Sigalas; 5.1 Photo by Kurohito; 5.2 Photos from Quibell; 6.2 Photo by Jon Bodsworth; 8.1 Photo © GreatStock/Corbis; 8.2 Images by Jeff Dahl; 9.1 Photo by Sailko; 10.1 Photo by Andreas Praefcke; 13.1 Photo by Philip Pikart; 13.2 Photo © Erich Lessing, line drawing © The Israel Museum, Jerusalem; 13.3 Photo © The Israel Museum, Jerusalem; 13.4 Eli plus at en.wikipedia (left), Erich Lessing (right); 13.5 Erich Lessing; 13.6 Photo by Keith Schengili-Roberts (left), Praefcke (right); 13.7 Erich Lessing; 13.8 Photo by Andreas Praefcke (left), Praefcke (right); 13.9 Photo © The Trustees of the British Museum (cropped image); 13.10 Photo © Richard Seaman; 13.11 Photo © Ann Ronan Pictures / Heritage Imagestate / Glow Images; 13.12 Photo © Cleveland Museum of Art; 13.13 Photo by Rama; 13.14 Photo © Erich Lessing; 13.5 Photo by Than Ball; 16.2 MODIS image, NASA; 16.3 Following Tilling et al.; 16.4 Following USGS: Ma. Lynn O. Paladio-Melosantos et al.; 16.5 Author Henrik Mohn; 16.6 Following Ian Wilson; 16.7 Adapted from I. Yokoyama; 17.1 Photo © Associated Press, Mike Cash; 19.1 Photo by Spyridon Marinatos I, kind permission granted by Walter Friedrich; 19.2 Following Barbara Sivertsen; 19.3 Photo © Radiocarbon (Bruins et al.)

Appedix A: Mark-Jan Nederhof; Appendix B: F.L. Griffith and E. Naville; Appendix C: Alexandre Moret; Appendix D: Princeton University Press; Appendix E: Princeton University Press; Appendix G: Princeton University Press; Appendix H: Princeton University Press; Appendix I: S. Baring-Gould

Comprehensive summary Section 5.3, Permission kindly granted by Ahmed Osman and Inner Traditions (www.InnerTraditions.com); Section 12.3 Permission kindly granted by David Rohl

Index